Evil Gods and Reckless Saviours

Evil Gods and Reckless Saviours

Adaptation and Appropriation in Late Twentieth-Century Jesus Novels

TIMO ESKOLA

◆PICKWICK *Publications* · Eugene, Oregon

EVIL GODS AND RECKLESS SAVIOURS
Adaptation and Appropriation in Late Twentieth-Century Jesus Novels

Copyright © 2011 Timo Eskola. All rights reserved. Except for brief quotations in critical publications or reviews, no part of this book may be reproduced in any manner without prior written permission from the publisher. Write: Permissions, Wipf and Stock Publishers, 199 W. 8th Ave., Suite 3, Eugene, OR 97401.

Pickwick Publications
An Imprint of Wipf and Stock Publishers
199 W. 8th Ave., Suite 3
Eugene, OR 97401

www.wipfandstock.com

ISBN 13: 978-1-61097-118-8

Cataloguing-in-Publication data:

Eskola, Timo.

    Evil gods and reckless saviours : adaptation and appropriation in late twentieth-century Jesus novels / Timo Eskola.

    x + 338 pp. ; 23 cm. Includes bibliographical references.

    ISBN 13: 978-1-61097-118-8

    1. Jesus Christ—In literature. 2. Comparative literature. 3. Literature, Modern—History and criticism. I. Title.

PR888 J4 E75 2011

Manufactured in the U.S.A.

For my father, Markku Eskola
(1931–2010)

Contents

Preface / ix

Introduction / 1

1. Source Texts and Subtexts in Contemporary Jesus-Novels / 41
2. Turning God-Incarnate into a Faustian Frivol / 80
3. Contesting the Moral Values of the Gospels / 130
4. Challenging the Biblical Role of Women / 163
5. Dissolving Sacrificial Religion / 195
6. Attacking Biblical Theism / 222
7. Reinjecting Mystery into Religion / 261
8. Iconoclastic Intertextualism / 287

Conclusion: Nietzschean Themes in Contrast-Novels / 316

Bibliography / 327

Preface

Theodore Ziolkowski opened his monograph *Fictional Transfigurations of Jesus* by speaking about points at which innovation intersects convention. He referred to T. S. Eliot's notion about a tension between "Tradition and the Individual Talent." Any Jesus-novel concentrating on Jesus' unique personality faces an intertextual relationship where the author's imagination is both directed and restrained by the canonical figure. My personal interest in recent Jesus-novels grew from the observation that, in late twentieth-century novels and some of the books from the new decade, the weight has shifted to the "Individual Talent." Even though the characters remain the same, the narratives have started to take a distance from the biblical story and also question it. As a scholar of both the New Testament and comparative literature I have had the opportunity to investigate this intertextual relationship. The present investigation suggests some explanations about the nature of the new adaptations.

I wrote the analysis when working as a New Testament teacher at the Theological Institute of Finland, and as a Privatdozent (adjunct professor) at the University of Helsinki, Faculty of Theology. During my additional studies at the Faculty of Arts, I began to prepare a dissertation on the subject. My supervisors, Professors Hannu K. Riikonen, Heta Pyrhönen, and Kai Mikkonen have accorded me unfailing support whenever I needed it. Furthermore, Professors Linda Hutcheon, Suzanne Keen, and Irene Kacandes have read parts of the manuscript. I am very grateful for their suggestions and advice.

Several people have discussed the topic with me and I am grateful for all the help that I have received even though it is not possible to thank each person individually here. Special thanks are due to Dr. Privatdozent Markku Ihonen for his support. I am also grateful for the help and advice of Dr. Francisco Peña Fernández, an expert on Saramago, who kindly shared his views and discussed the observations and conclusions presented in his own investigation.

Furthermore, I want to express my special gratitude to Dr. Sydney Palmer for a highly professional work with the language revision. She has also given me precious advice on how to express myself in English and shown remarkable understanding for the problems a Finn faces when writing in a foreign language.

I thank the Theological Institute of Finland and its general secretary, Henrik Perret, for making this investigation possible. Warm thanks go also to our secretary, Mrs. Kirsi Sell, who has constantly assisted me over the years by acquiring literature and helping in practical matters. I also thank Wipf and Stock Publishers for accepting my monograph under their distinguished Pickwick imprint, and Christian Amondson for his kind assistance.

When writing these lines, I have warm memories of my father, the late Markku Eskola, and feel grateful gratitude to my mother Raija Eskola. Their love of literature gradually drew me into the world of novels and poetry. Even during the period of my father's illness they followed the development of my investigation with great interest.

Timo Eskola
Helsinki, Finland

Introduction

The literary tradition of repeating, paraphrasing, and reinterpreting Gospel narratives is rich and colorful. Alice Birney in her bibliography *The Literary Lives of Jesus* presents over one thousand works where some kind of Jesus-character is playing a leading role. Birney's list reaches only to the end of the 1980s.[1] Since then, over the last twenty years, several new Jesus-novels have been published. The authors comprise Nobel Prize winners and other celebrities of the literary community. Over the years attitudes have changed, and many of these newer novels are no longer content with merely paraphrasing canonical ideas as many previous books were. Instead, they represent a new trend of inversive reading where simple rewriting has turned into strict revisioning and deconstructing previous structures and hierarchies in the source text.

1. POLARISATION IN RECENT JESUS-NOVELS

As fiction, Jesus-novels are unique since they are inevitably related to the canonical Gospels. They can be read as independent novels, but their *raison d'être* is in the fact that Jesus and his disciples appear in the story in their original geographical and historical surroundings. Contemporary Jesus-novels are deliberate adaptations and, therefore, want to make a statement. Their message and meaning depends on their treatment of the canonical original. Moreover, the reading of these novels is tied with the reader's knowledge of the New Testament. The dialogical process of reading is guided by Western Christian tradition where the stories of the Bible still belong to our cultural heritage.

> For a reader, spectator, or listener, adaptation *as adaptation* is unavoidably a kind of intertextuality *if the receiver is acquainted with the adapted text.* It is an ongoing dialogical process, as

---

1. See especially the Introduction in Birney, *Literary Lives*, xxiii–xxiv.

Mikhail Bakhtin would have said, in which we compare the work we already know with the one we are experiencing.[2]

The authors of recent Jesus-novels make ample use of this and rely on the fact that the reader will simultaneously read their novel in the light of the canonical text. From this one can estimate the basic intertextual relationship between these books and the original Gospels. This is also a clue for understanding different kinds of polarisations between a given novel and its Biblical source text.

Adaptive Jesus-novels in general can be classified in several ways. Firstly, there are novels where the Jesus-character has been transferred to a new context. These are stories about "a thirty-year-old man" whose life and message differ greatly from the world of the Bible.[3] Secondly, rewritten New Testaments describe events that take place at the time of the New Testament, and the main character is usually Jesus himself. Here, in particular, it is possible to consider the novel's relation to the canonical Gospels. Traditional novels explicitly build on the New Testament and describe Jesus' personality through images and art. These novels usually follow the canonical story quite faithfully. Over the last two decades, however, several critical Jesus-novels have been published. In these writings the traditional picture of Jesus has been turned inside out. The figure of the Nazarene has been described according to premises that actually contest the views of the canonical Gospels. Material for the present investigation will be selected from these inversive late twentieth-century novels.

Adaptation as such can mean rather simple paraphrasing or more intentional transforming of the original work. In certain cases, however, it turns into appropriation. It can be an interpretive act or even a hostile takeover. Contemporary Jesus-novels contain features from both of these approaches, up to direct deconstruction of biblical ideas and events.[4] The inversive trend has actually been recognised in scholarship for a number of years. In 1976 Robert Detweiler traced several principles functioning in religious fiction as follows:

> The theological trends I find functioning in recent fiction are four: the need to let language speak itself, the disappearance of

---

2. Hutcheon, *Theory of Adaptation*, 21.

3. See Ziolkowski, *Fictional Transfigurations*, 277.

4. The key methodological concepts of adaptation and appropriation will be defined in detail below in chapter 1.1.

the subject, the evocation of presence, and the shaping of alternate worlds. These are not only theological trends, of course; they are, for example, philosophically, psychologically, and linguistically determined as well.[5]

Detweiler's ideas apparently derive from European poststructuralist philosophy, which has always been closely connected with literary criticism. Jesus-novels' factual relation to poststructuralist approaches will be investigated more closely in the analysis. The novels often present alternate worlds in order to discuss or even question the original Gospel narratives. In these cases the relation between the text and canonical Gospels is clearly present, as the new stories are usually critical towards the New Testament. It is not difficult to find examples of ideological antitheses and intentional contradictions. For instance, when describing José Saramago's general outline in *The Gospel According to Jesus Christ*, David Frier pays attention to the recurring contradictory features appearing in the novel.

> Many critics have already commented on major features of the novel, some of which are clearly departures from Christian tradition: the ambiguous role of the Devil figure; more daringly, the unambiguously negative portrayal of God as an authoritarian and bloodthirsty tyrant, who is interested only in the expansion of his kingdom, regardless of the human cost involved; the conflictive relationship between Jesus and God, which displaces completely the Christian doctrine of the Holy Trinity; the non-resurrection of Lazarus; the loving relationship between Jesus and Mary Magdalene, which becomes a sexual one on their very first encounter and which endures throughout Jesus's adult life. . . .[6]

The new literary trend of questioning traditional Christian beliefs raises questions. How should the new adaptations and intertextual revisions be explained? What are the principles behind the intertextual strategy that dissolves structures and overturns traditional hierarchies? To approach such questions, I have chosen novels that give harsh critiques of traditional Christianity. The best example of these is Saramago's abovementioned novel, *O Evangelho segundo Jesus Cristo* (1991). Also Norman Mailer's *The Gospel According to the Son* (1997) falls into this

---

5. Detweiler, "Trends," 225.
6. Frier, "Outline," 370.

category, as does the popular *Da Vinci Code* (2003) by Dan Brown in a slightly different genre. There are other books that focus on questions of power and deconstruction. These novels include, for instance, Walter Jens's *Der Fall Judas* (1975), Taylor Caldwell and Jess Stearn's *I, Judas* (1977), Göran Tunström's *Ökenbrevet* (1978; *The Letter from the Wilderness*, translated only partly)[7], and C. K. Stead's *My Name Was Judas* (2006). Finally, there are feminist novels that contest Christian patriarchy, such as Luise Rinser's *Mirjam* (1983), Michèle Roberts' *Wild Girl* (1984), Regina Berlinghof's *Mirjam* (1995), Marianne Fredriksson's *According to Mary* (Swedish original, *Enligt Maria Magdalena*, 1997), and Ki Longfellow's *The Secret Magdalene* (2005).

Since an effective investigation must focus on only a few main examples selected from a more extensive group, I have chosen Saramago, Mailer, Tunström, Roberts, and Fredriksson for this purpose. Saramago's and Mailer's novels are perfect for the aims of this analysis because, as new gospels, they have a direct relationship with the New Testament. Furthermore, they are distinctively ideological and have a strict intertextual strategy. These novels openly rewrite the canonical Gospels. Roberts and Fredriksson provide another view since they have written feminist gospels and make ample use of Gnostic writings. Tunström, in turn, exploits the Dead Sea Scrolls and, in addition to using the New Testament, discusses the ideology of the Qumran sect. Through this variety, the selected novels represent different approaches to intertexual rewriting. Other Jesus-novels are then compared with these more extensive analyses and commented on during the investigation.

Jesus-novels are historical novels by definition. The investigated novels are not identical, however, since some of them pointedly propose a new gospel. There are some differences between the gospel genre proper and more general Jesus-novels. Saramago calls his work *The Gospel According to Jesus Christ*, and Mailer uses the title *The Gospel According to the Son*. They both use a tremendous amount of canonical material. Persons, events, and even many of the stories are the same as in the Bible. Saramago does expand Jesus' stay in the wilderness with the Devil, but even here the point of departure is the story of Jesus' temptation. Fredriksson's *According to Mary* begins with the biblical expression,

---

7. Martinus's translation will be used but passages that are not included there will be translated from the Swedish original, *Ökenbrevet*.

but the focus shifts onto Mary's character.[8] Other novels about Mary Magdalene are more or less Jesus-novels, and Judas-novels belong to the same category. Their focalisation is distanced from that of the canonical Gospels. The point is in expanding the source and making one of Jesus' followers the leading character. Mary Magdalene and Judas appear to be perfect candidates for this.

Furthermore, authors often comment that the original canonical Gospel from which they draw is somewhat defective. Saramago opens his book by quoting Luke (1:1–4): "Forasmuch as many have taken in hand to set forth in order a declaration of those things which are most surely believed among us, . . . it seemed good to me also, having had perfect understanding of all things from the very first, to write unto thee in order, most excellent Theophilus . . ." What follows is Saramago's version of the story, of which he has "perfect understanding" even though it may disagree somewhat with the canonical text.[9]

Corrective motivation is apparent in many Jesus-novels. Mailer, for instance, deliberately confronts the canonical writers:

> While I would not say that Mark's gospel is false, it has much exaggeration. And I would offer less for Matthew, and for Luke and John, who gave me words I never uttered and described me as gentle when I was pale with rage. Their words were written many years after I was gone and only repeat what old men told them. Very old men.[10]

The question about the narrator is essential as well. Mailer's novel is a gospel, but it is told by the risen Jesus himself. He is the narrator who wishes to give his "own account." And in doing this he naturally

---

8. As regards the titles of the novels, it is evident that Luise Rinser's *Mirjam* already departs from the gospel tradition by focusing on Mary, and Michèle Roberts's *Wild Girl* suggests a completely new interpretation of history.

9. In Saramago's *Gospel*, on the first page. "Adopting Luke's words to introduce his own narrative suggests that Saramago would like it to be considered on the same level with the Gospels, as one more version of the well-known story." Kaufman, "Evangelical Truths," 453. Later in the work Saramago plays with the idea of the omnipotent author: "[W]e know the story better than anyone. Just think how little the main characters of this gospel know about each other, Jesus does not know everything about his mother and father, Mary does not know everything about her husband and son, and Joseph, who is dead, knows nothing about anything. Whereas we know everything that has been done, spoken and thought, whether by them or by others, although we have to act as if we, too, were in the dark. . . ." Saramago, *Gospel*, 150.

10. Mailer, *Gospel*, 3–4.

hopes to "remain closer to the truth" than his apostolic collaborators.[11] This is a bold choice and makes a statement that raises several questions concerning the consistency of Mailer's narrative and the trustworthiness of the narrator's message.[12] Jesus is the narrator also in Tunström's *Letter from the Wilderness*, but here the setting is different from Mailer's. The novel is a *Bildungsroman* and, therefore, the questions the narrator deals with are rather more personal and psychological than theological.

Roberts' *Wild Girl* is Mary Magdalene's account. The story begins with an introduction: "here begins the book of the testimony of Mary Magdalene. She who writes it does so at the command of the Saviour himself and of Mary his blessed mother." Roberts emphasises that everything Mary sets down "is the truth."[13] Fredriksson follows Roberts's line. Depending on the support of other women in her community, Mary submits her own testimony. Her message contradicts the theology of the apostles. Mary meets all of the apostles during her lifetime and also after Easter, but a male religion such as Paul's does not suit her or her memories: "But she could not make Paul's vision fit in with the young man she had loved". Therefore, Fredriksson makes Mary's friend Leonidas state: "her writings will still be here when the bickering between the various Christian sects has long been forgotten."[14]

Tunström has written an apocryphal gospel that informs the reader about Jesus' early years. Jesus' education at the Qumran monastery remains superficial, however, and the novel describes his journey from one fellowship to another, pondering his role in this life. Jesus does tell his own story here, but it does not develop into a cosmic history. Instead, Tunström writes a narrative that describes Jesus' inner struggle and growth into independence.[15] In these novels, additional information

---

11. Ibid., 4. Mailer further depends on a kind of Harnackian idea about the degeneration of Christian tradition when stating that original gospel writers were just "seeking to enlarge their fold" and each writer "looked to give strength to his own church". Later, after a fiery combat, one church alone prevailed and condemned the others. This idea coincides with von Harnack's theory about the degeneration of an enthusiast's Christianity gradually into a dogmatic church. In Mailer's words, the winner's religion has always defined other views about Jesus as "shameless lies." Ibid. See Harnack, *Wesen des Christentums*, 115–30.

12. The question concerning Mailer's narrator will be dealt with in chapters 1.2. and 8.1.

13. Roberts, *Wild Girl*, 11.

14. Fredriksson, *According to Mary*, 220, 199, 169.

15. Tunström, *Ökenbrevet*, 69–70.

is available, and the reader is given an insider's perspective into the life of Jesus.

Saramago's narrator is something of a mystery. Above all, (s)he is an ominscient figure who does not essentially differ from an implied author. (S)he even discusses literary critics and their "rules of narration" and plays with these in his story. In this connection (s)he admits that the present narrator is a liar: "They also claim this is the narrative process which best serves the ever desirable effect of verisimilitude, for if the episode imagined and described is not and is never likely to become or supplant factual reality, then there must be at least some similitude. Not as in the present narrative, in which the reader's credence has clearly been put to the test . . ."[16] The narrator is above both God and the Devil, obviously, as (s)he knows everything that concerns their relationship. This may have interesting implications for the interpretation of the work, and we will return to these issues at the end of the investigation.

Moreover, in this analysis, I have chosen to speak practically and simply of the "author" and his or her "readers." Only in passages where it seems necessary will I briefly discuss the role of the implied author. In the present study, however, this does not mean that I hold the real authors personally responsible for the ideological or religious views that appear in the novels. My assessment concerns the particular novels themselves.

At this point, it is necessary to discuss the nature of historical novels briefly. Jesus-novels from the end of the twentieth century are no longer typical historiographies. Some of the earlier novels, investigated by Theodore Ziolkowski, were quite clearly traditional rewritings of the Gospels. Their purpose was, for instance, to clarify and to illuminate the content of the Bible for a modern reader. They expanded the stories and made them understandable for the modern reader. The factual knowledge of history varies from novel to novel, though. This holds true also in the more recent books. It is naturally tempting for the reader of a Jesus-novel to make his judgment merely by making a comparison with the famous source text. In this case the reader's notions about the novel are mainly reflections against the background of the world of the Bible. This has been noted for instance by the Finnish author and scholar Markku Envall.

---

16. Saramago, *Gospel*, 165–66.

> A historical novel about Jesus, as a genre, is rather problematic.... Its most important source text is well known by the readers, and it has a canonical status in the religious community. Problems culminate when Jesus' speeches are rewritten. If the speeches are simply repeated in the same form as given by the Gospel writer, one wonders why a new book should be written to accompany them. If Jesus' words are changed in order to support some special interpretation or view, the writer drifts into the area of exegesis. In this case the credentials of the novelist are not worth much.... In every case a historical novel about Jesus is an attempt to improve the original source, which, to the misfortune of the writer, in its own genre is anything but poor.[17]

As long as one thinks that the value of a historical novel should be assessed from the point of view of historical accuracy, Envall's comments are proper. There are, no doubt, several Jesus-novels that attempt to exploit detailed historical information in their presentation. Among these books are, for instance, Lewis Wallace's *Ben-Hur* (1880) and Robert Graves's *King Jesus* (1946). In Finnish literature the many novels by Tatu Vaaskivi and Mika Waltari belong to this tradition.[18] In these works the atmosphere of the New Testament is being sought in the manner Envall describes above. Ziolkowski calls such novels *fictionalizing biographies*. They may have been written in the manner of ancient apocryphal writings about Jesus' youth, or they can simply be rewritings of the canonical Gospels.[19]

There are several methodological questions here that need to be addressed. Historiography, in literature, is not merely a question of rewriting or rewording history "as it really happened." As Markku Ihonen has noted, there are two different readings of a historical novel. On the one hand, it can be read merely as a description of history. In this case

---

17. Envall, *Pitkä marssi*, 44–45. My translation.

18. Waltari, who is widely known for his *Sinuhe the Egyptian* (1945), has also written several Jesus-novels and other fictional historiographies describing New Testament times especially his *Valtakunnan salaisuus*. Vaaskivi, in turn, started a major Jesus-novel, *Pyhä kevät* (1943), but never finished it on account of his untimely death. The first part was published posthumously.

19. There are two kinds of "fictionalising biographies." Some works present an apocryphal gospel, which hopes to reveal new knowledge about Jesus' youth, about the silent years. Others, in turn, present conservative rewritings of the New Testament in the manner of Wallace's *Ben-Hur*; see Ziolkowski, *Fictional Transfigurations*, 13–17. Apocryphal rewritings and ideological renderings should probably be kept separate in the analysis.

the reader uses his own knowledge of history and sources and compares the novel with this information. On the other hand, the novel can always be read merely as fiction. In this case the reader ignores his previous knowledge about the characters or the events they are engaged in, apart from the information given in the text.[20]

The distinction is necessary because fictionality cannot merely be a matter of expressions. Certain passages can be read both as historical statements when they appear in a historical context, and as historical fiction when they are a part of a fictional story with an individual purpose and particular orientation. Fiction, even historiographical fiction, is mainly a world the author creates. The past is past also for a historian, and all explanations of history depend on construction and interpretation. But the past for an author is a fictional past and is more open to interpretation and reinterpretation than the work of a historian. Nevertheless, if an author chooses a historical subject, he must have a reason. It stands to reason that this is the case especially with the new gospels we call Jesus-novels.

These novels are usually connected with real history through historical characters in the story. This must not mislead one to think that the characters themselves were "real" people—and this caveat extends even to the Jesus-figure of the novels. The novels produce an illusion of reality precisely with the help of such characters and alleged events. One could call the characters of historical novels "fictionalisings." They are not completely fictional creations but in the context of the narrative they are creatures of the artist. They serve the aims of the fictional work functionally. "In historical study people refer directly to reality, while in fiction they refer to reality indirectly via fictionalisings."[21] There is no narrative without a rhetorical discourse. The narrative itself does not derive from history. Hence the characters in the narrative cannot simply be identified with persons known from history. We have knowledge of an event described in a historical novel merely as rhetorical discourse.

Such a distinction essentially alters the traditional definition of the nature of historical novel. In his famous book *The Forms of Historical Fiction*, Harry Shaw, a well-known Walter Scott scholar, still assumes that in a historical novel the author can accurately describe facts of his-

---

20. Ihonen, *Museovaatteista historian valepukuun*, 34.
21. Haapala, "Fiktio," 224; Kettunen, "Tehty menneisyys," 111.

tory.²² He uses terms such as "fictional probability."²³ It is true, of course, that in several historical novels one can find an intentional approach where the author aims at historical accuracy. However, historical novels usually differ from scholarly history owing either to artistic intentions or ideological presuppositions. In this sense there is a clear difference between a history book and a fictional novel. The critical discussion about the nature of historical novel has changed the general view about the historical approach in these same writings. In *Encyclopedia of Literature and Criticism* Shaw reminds us that the "otherness" of historical situations and cultural differences change the whole question concerning history. Therefore, in the study of historical novels we are dealing also with the intellectual problems of our own time.²⁴

According to some scholars, the new change is typical of postmodern literature. It has been defined as essentially self-reflexive. Postmodern literature no longer represents the external world. Instead, it tends to explore it own literary conventions. Therefore, postmodern literature suggests alternate histories. As Elisabeth Wesseling notes:

> Postmodernist novelists do not straightforwardly project inspiring alternatives for the status quo into the future. Rather, they turn to the past in order to look for unrealized possibilities that inhered in historical situations, and subsequently imagine what history would have looked like if unrealized sequences of events and courses of action had come about. This results in the invention of alternate histories which evidently have never taken place and therefore cannot lay any claim to historical truth, but which may perhaps come true at some point in the future as the return of the repressed.²⁵

Such a notion may help the assessment of recent Jesus-novels, even though one needs to remember that they cannot be defined simply as postmodern novels. What is evident, however, is that it leads to new questions.

---

22. Shaw, *Forms of Historical Fiction*, 20–22, 30–31.

23. This kind of definition has been common also elsewhere. Cuddon's *Dictionary of Literary Terms and Literary Theory* (s.v. "historical novel") speaks of a "reconstruction" of history. The *Oxford Companion to English Literature* (s.v. "historical novel") in turn states that historical novels aim at historical accuracy and trustworthiness.

24. Shaw, "Historical Novel," 541.

25. Wesseling, *Writing History*, 13.

As the contrasts between ancient texts and the modern novel have shown, both readers and scholars need to address two more issues. Firstly, one needs to investigate how the story actually differs from general history. Secondly, one needs to ask what the author's reinterpretive aim is. These are the standard questions within intertextual investigation. Therefore, the theory of intertextuality is of utmost importance in the present study. Questions concerning methodology will be discussed later in a chapter of their own.[26]

The present study's interest lies in the polarisation between the canonical Gospels and recent Jesus-novels, or between Christianity and the ideology behind the new narrative. The focus is on the process of adaptation. Hence, an element alien to simple historical accuracy is assumed to affect the descriptions of the novels from the very start. Moreover, one can state that already a generation ago the age of robust historicism was replaced by postmodern readings. Now scholars recognise that previous approaches to history have been insensitive to the biased nature of their sources. For instance, feminist readings and gender criticism have altered even the epistemology of literary criticism.

Therefore, suffice it to say that when answering the first methodological question concerning the nature of historiography one needs to distinguish between reading as history and reading as fiction. Writing a historiography means reinterpretation of previous documents and, thus, also Jesus-novels can be read as constructions rather than reconstructions. They represent fictionalising. As mentioned above, however, I will deal more with this and other methodological issues such as the nature of rewriting and the role of ideologies and ethical readings in the following chapter.

The adaptation and appropriation of Gospel narratives in contrast-novels is based on an idea of discontinuity. In polarised Jesus-novels the contradiction is obvious and even surprising. Provocative descriptions and expressions aim at shaking conventional convictions about religion. In the Western history of ideas there is one source that explains the emergence of such an approach. I will argue that these novels are related to Nietzsche's ideology and his early idea of a clash of cultures: Jewish-Christian biblical tradition colliding with the enlightened humanism of modern scientific society. This is why the present treatise will focus particularly on Nietzschean themes in the novels. The decision to choose

---

26. See below, chapter 1.1.

Nietzsche as a point of departure will be explained in detail below (in section 4) but even here it can be said that a hypothesis of Nietzschean influence covers the essential intentions of the investigated novels well.

The aim of this dissertation, therefore, is to analyse adaptation and appropriation in late twentieth-century Jesus-novels. I will investigate how these novels quote and use New Testament passages, and why they leave out others. Therefore, the focus of the investigation is, first of all, in the treatment of the original source text and its reduction to a smaller collection of passages. The Bible as a source text is so influential and deeply rooted in Western cultural history that any novel's relation to it is inevitably interesting. Secondly, what is more important still, one needs to analyse the deliberate changes these novels make in their adaptation. They select their material very carefully and place it in a new context. Furthermore, they present an intertextual change that is loaded and intentional. It is motivated by an ideological turn that, in most cases, opposes the doctrines of the canonical text. Since the Second World War different philosophical traditions have attempted to tear down and replace previous Western metanarratives, Christianity being probably the most prominent of these. This is why the themes appearing in these novels, as the present hypothesis states, have a Nietzschean tone, leading recent Jesus-novels to contest the so-called Christian slave morality and even to proclaim a death-of-God ideology. Therefore, the chapters of this study will be defined in terms of different themes in Nietzsche's atheist philosophy. Such an investigation cannot help being interdisciplinary. In addition to intertextual analysis one needs to be aware of both theological and philosophical elements that affect the writing of the corpus novels.

With this point of departure certain other books also need to be mentioned here. Albert Camus has a prominent place among fiction writers discussing Christian tradition in the spirit of Nietzsche. His essays in the book *The Rebel* will be of substantial help in this study and will be compared with the Jesus-novels in question.[27] In assessing different feminist Jesus-novels, Elisabeth Schüssler Fiorenza's monograph *In Memory of Her* plays a significant role, as does Elaine Pagel's *The Gnostic Gospels*, both of which lay the groundwork for a feminist treatment of the New Testament.[28] In addition, several monographs on death-of-God

---

27. Camus, *Rebel*; the original *L'Homme Revolte* was published in 1947.

28. Schüssler Fiorenza, *In Memory of Her*, from the year 1983; Pagels, *Gnostic Gospels*, published for the first time in 1979.

theology will be discussed during the investigation, and they will be introduced in their proper context.

What is special for the Jesus-novels treated in the present study is that the polarisation they pose in relation to the source text is very harsh. The figure of Jesus is altered almost beyond recognition. The Christian message is either changed completely or turned into another religion—or even a version of secularism. Traditional Christian views are contested through the development of the story itself. All this betrays the Nietzschean attitude towards the canonical Gospels.

2. INVESTIGATING REWRITTEN GOSPELS

The novels investigated in this study have been written during a period that actively dealt with the painful memories of the two World Wars and especially the horrors of the Nazi regime in Germany. Many of the books are reactive and attempt to cope with the inexplicable violence suffered by the previous generation. In both literature and philosophy this is a time when truth is questioned, meaning is dismantled, and metanarratives die. In theology too despair prevails and the status of the biblical God is threatened. Therefore, it is only to be expected that the intertextual rewriting of the canonical Gospels, which at least some of the Jesus-novels represent, also questions the Christian tradition and biblical truth. According to Ron Rosenbaum, Norman Mailer has claimed that Holocaust agony has been "the most fundamental idea" of his career.

> It's often forgotten that Mr. Mailer was one of the first non-theologians to speculate about the unconscious cultural impact of the Holocaust in the 50's. The first sentence of his controversial essay "The White Negro" declared: "Probably we will never be able to determine the psychic havoc of the concentration camps ... upon the unconscious mind of almost everyone alive ... in these years."[29]

The cultural *angst* of the West evidently affects the authors, at least in a general sense on the level of "the unconscious mind." This is also what separates many recent novels from earlier rewritings of the Gospels. In *Jesus through the Centuries* (1985), Jaroslav Pelikan investigates descriptions of Jesus in general literature from earlier centuries and encounters another kind of literary world.[30] The same is mostly true for

---

29. Rosenbaum, "Mailer Was the Rage."
30. Pelikan, *Jesus through the Centuries.*

the only particular monograph there is in English on Jesus-novels and the appearance of the figure of Jesus in literature, Theodore Ziolkowski's *Fictional Transfigurations of Jesus* (1972). He studies especially the period of rationalism and its later developments, and in the novels he analyses Jesus remains a positive figure. Ziolkowski focuses on different transfigurations, though. Therefore, the subjects and persons appearing in the investigated novels are usually not directly related to Jesus and his disciples. Ziolkowski is interested in Jesus-figures who have been transferred to new contexts. Historical Jesus-novels are in fact neglected in his analysis.[31]

There are also other kinds of analyses of Jesus-literature. Wesley Kort treats religious meanings present in literature in his *Narrative Elements and Religious Meanings* (1975). Kort's analysis remains on a quite general level. Northrop Frye is more detailed in his study in *The Great Code: The Bible and Literature* (1982). Frye, however, has turned the approach into its opposite and writes "a study of the Bible from the point of view of a literary critic." He comments on the biblical text with the help of later writings, not the other way round.[32] Hence, earlier analyses of Jesus-novels have little to contribute to the investigation of recent rewritings.

As regards the investigation of particular novels, the situation is different. Contrast-novels with their challenging attitude have been analysed in several distinguished articles. Helena Kaufman interprets Saramago's *Gospel* as a postmodern rewriting and Teresa Cristina Cerdeira da Silva attends to the ironic dialogue between the novel and the New Testament.[33] Ilan Stavans analyses the humanisation of the Jesus-figure, Douwe Fokkema studies the nature of such a reversal, and Harold Bloom explains this change by Saramago's intended questioning of the traditional values of writing history.[34] Ziva Ben-Porat calls this change *prototypical rewriting*, and Francisco Peña Fernández calls it

---

31. Ziolkowski, *Fictional Transfigurations*, 4–7, 13–15. Markku Envall has written a study on Jesus-novels, but it has been published only in Finnish.

32. Frye, *Great Code*, xi (introduction). In addition to Birney's bibliography mentioned earlier Georg Langenhorst has in his article "The Rediscovery of Jesus as a Literary Figure" expanded the list and presented and analysed especially German literature; see esp. 85–91. Cf. also Vettenniemi, "Jeesus-marssi jatkuu," 213–17 (in Finnish).

33. Kaufman, "Evangelical Truths," 449–58; Silva, "Saramago," 205, 240.

34. Stavans, "Fisher," 675–76; Fokkema, "Art of Rewriting," 395–402; Bloom, "One with the Beard," 155–66.

inverse intertextuality.³⁵ Saramago's aims and real object have also been discussed in detail. David Frier suggests that Saramago is not primarily attacking Christian doctrines but the history of the Catholic Church instead. Other scholars, however, like Fokkema, assume that Saramago constructs a polarisation between Christian doctrines and his own views.³⁶

Mailer in his *Gospel According to the Son* has often irritated his readers by either his ideas or the quality of his expression and poetry, but scholars are divided in their conclusions. Some sardonic critics hold that Mailer in his "Gospel of Norman" just copies New Testament ideas in order to do away with their content: "By now, though, the idea of presenting Jesus as fallible, even a sexual, human being is a little old hat, and Mailer's book will probably induce not outrage so much as mild amusement that the old man is up to his antics again."³⁷ Furthermore, Wood states that the "very melody of the book is foolish."³⁸ And finally, as Gordon remarks, we encounter the problem of bad poetry: "Most of these faults are failures of voice."³⁹

There are others, however, who present Mailer as an ideologue and assume that in his novel he has offered readers a strict critique of the Christian tradition. Ron Rosenbaum speaks of Mailer's post-holocaust theodicy, and Brian McDonald concludes that Mailer, who is interested in the problem of evil, persistently deals with this issue in this novel.⁴⁰ One can then assume that if the essentially Jewish problem of theodicy really is the most fundamental idea of Mailer's works it must be a burning issue also in his most straightforward book on God and Jesus' message.

What unites all these assessments of different novels is their focusing on the method of reversal. The investigated novels are considered

---

35. Ben-Porat, "Prototypical Rewriting," 93; Peña, *José Saramago*, 24.

36. Frier ("Outline," 369) suggests that Saramago focuses mainly on the Catholic Church. Stavans notes that even though Saramago himself never meant to dismiss "what others have written about Jesus," his novel inevitably contradicts Christian belief. Fokkema ("Art of Rewriting," 400) too holds that Saramago contradicts Christian doctrines. Several other articles treat Saramago's novel, and these views shall be taken into consideration when particular themes are discussed.

37. Allen, "Gospel of Norman," 77.

38. Wood, "He Is Finished," 30.

39. Gordon, "Superstar," 27.

40. Rosenbaum, "Mailer Was the Rage"; McDonald, "Theodicy," 81.

inversive and often hostile in their intertextual rewriting. Such a result confirms the present analysis's point of departure. Not many scholars have suggested that such a polarisation would have a larger cultural motivation, however. The present work will claim that the opposition these novels adopt is the inheritance of Nietzschean thinking. The inversive rewriting resuscitates an opposition towards the ostensible Christian slave morality and a false view of God.

Hence, recent Jesus-novels do not simply repeat and paraphrase. Instead, in their adaptation, they replace previous strategies by revising, dissolving, and even perverting the source text. Therefore, the methodological discussion must include approaches that are able to treat the processes of producing narratives and narrating history. Following Linda Hutcheon, one could state that historiographies, as descriptions of the past and interpretations of events, are ideological constructions. They are statements the coherence of which is being produced by a common system of signs that is significant in a certain cultural context. "Both history and fiction are cultural sign systems, ideological construction whose ideology includes their appearance of being autonomous and self-contained."[41]

Hutcheon, of course, is an expert on postmodern investigation, and this is the reason why she holds that postmodernity keeps reworking the past. One can extend this insight to recent Jesus-novels, saying that a key term in that line of fiction is "the presence of the past." This does not result in a resuscitation of previous historiographic approaches. The past is not present as such. Instead, its presence is represented by a second thought, a critical position, ironical dialogue, all of which produce a parody of history. This explains why irony has become so popular: "Herein lies the governing role of irony in postmodernism."[42] On these grounds Hutcheon concludes that historiography in literature is metafiction, where consciousness about history is presented as a rethinking of historical events and persons.

---

41. Hutcheon, *Poetics*, 112. For Hutcheon, there are tensions in the postmodern tradition: "postmodernism is a contradictory phenomenon, one that uses and abuses, installs and then subverts, the very concepts it challenges—be it in architecture, literature, painting, sculpture, film, video, dance, TV, music, philosophy, aesthetic theory, psychoanalysis, linguistics, or historiography." Ibid., 3.

42. Ibid., 4.

> Historiographic metafiction incorporates all three of these domains: that is, its theoretical self-awareness of history and fiction as human constructs (historio*graphic meta*fiction) is made the grounds for its rethinking and reworking of the forms and contents of the past.[43]

Jesus-novels often take this metafictional strategy one step further. Since they are stories describing ancient times, they read history backwards, in which case one can speak of "the presence of the future." The New Testament is rewritten by constructing the new narrative in a critical and sometimes ironical dialogue with the realised history of the Christian church.

Several recent Jesus-novels fall into the category of historiographic metafiction and represent a thorough reworking of the original text as well as the whole phenomenon of Christianity. Therefore, one can learn from Hutcheon's description of postmodern historiography. On the one hand, her conception of metafiction can easily be applied to the study of certain Jesus-novels which aim at a deconstruction of traditional religious hierarchies. On the other hand, Hutcheon herself has adopted an ideological stance in her approach. She maintains that this is not merely a tool for the analysis of literature but rather a matter of philosophy of science. Metafiction is a tool for the investigation of history as such.[44]

Speaking about postmodernism is no longer without risk in literary scholarship, though. The entire trend has been questioned—and usually with good reason, at least as long as philosophy is involved. Scholars joke about writers playing "post-games" and committing acts of irresponsible deconstruction. It is not, however, a matter of asking whether there is such a phenomenon as postmodernism. Instead one should pay attention to the fact that both in literature itself and in literary criticism ethical reading has become a new standard, which is represented in the *Methodenlehre* by strictly defined approaches. The basic Selden–Widdowson–Brooker's guide, for instance, introduces feminist theories, as well as poststructuralist, postmodern, postcolonial, and gay

---

43. Ibid., 5.

44. This is also how Kaufman approaches Saramago's Gospel. "It is clear that the metafictional as well as historiographic commentary, so prominent in Saramago's previous novels, plays an important role in *Evangelho*, placing it within the thematic concerns of other recent narratives inspired by the Gospels." Kaufman, "Evangelical Truths," 453.

theories without hesitation.[45] The alleged *postmodern*, if you will, is precisely what novels bearing these intentions appear to be, even though the phenomenon itself might today be better called ethical reading.

3. ETHICAL READING AND ETHICAL READINGS

There is a moralistic tone in many of the investigated Jesus-novels. The general descriptions of these books, quoted in the previous section, already prove that they challenge certain Christian beliefs and doctrines on ethical grounds. Some Jesus-novels present themselves almost as apologies for the oppressed and those discriminated against. These novels oppose the rich and the beautiful, and the patriarchal apostolic church allied with power and the leaders of society. Should one then, on these grounds, understand Jesus-novels particularly as ethical readings of Christianity? This is not only possible but probable. According to these novels, as will soon become apparent, biblical views are to be considered unhealthy for human beings. The novels often represent kind of normative readings and reworkings of the canonical text since their revision is based on new values. Their intertextual transformation is, even from the outset, quite negative. This is evident even before entering into any detailed investigation. In this particular respect these novels may be called ethical readings. But if this is true and if the readings appear to be normative according to postmodernism, should the assessment of such novels be normative, as well? There are several problems in the theory of intertextual analysis, and the question of the ethics of reading is undoubtedly one of them.

Compared with previous Jesus-novels investigated by Ziolkowski, the normative reading is what is new in these books. Recent novels adopt values that differ from those of the Christian tradition. Therefore, certain philosophical points of departure need to be discussed before deciding about the nature of ethical readings. This leads us to the philosophical discussion of the late twentieth century. Theoretical problems concerning "postmodernism" focus on poststructuralist epistemology and its conception of truth. Moving beyond its phenomenological roots, poststructuralism has questioned both the possibility to reach beyond a phenomenon and the existence of the "transcendental signified."[46] In a

---

45. Selden et al., *Contemporary Literary Theory*, 200–205, 243–44.
46. The standard justification for this view is Derrida's famous text (*Of Grammatology*)

philosophical sense, this resulted in relativism where meaning was held dependent on language games, and truth became an aspect of a particular discourse. These views were also largely used in literary criticism.[47]

The theoretical problem lies in the fact that neither Nietzsche's Christian slave morality critique nor the poststructuralist challenging of metanarratives was ever really based on relativism. Instead, already in the 1960s and 1970s previous metanarratives were rejected in the name of higher values. Postmodernism has always been a moralistic movement. In the age of the new revolution different ideologies struggled over intellectual values. There is no longer room here for the traditional class struggle. As Lyotard maintained, it was a struggle over definitions of knowledge: "To speak is to fight, in the sense of playing."[48] The detecting of such commitments in philosophy has resulted in a re-evaluation of poststructuralist premises. Furthermore, it has produced what scholars call the "ethical paradox" of the postmodern.[49] Skepticism towards metanarratives has always been based on high values. The age of ethical reading has meant a battle between ideologies. But the adoption of new values, for instance in feminist studies, gay and lesbian studies, or postcolonial studies, has been paradoxically and constantly justified by the deconstruction of the transcendental signified and the lack of any firm foundation for values.

> Postmodernism works to show that all repairs are human constructs, but that, from that very fact, they derive their value as well as their limitation. All repairs are both comforting and illusory. Postmodernist interrogations of humanist certainties live within this kind of contradiction.[50]

New readings of the canonical Gospels usually wish to understand history from the reader's perspective. But how far can this kind of ap-

---

rejecting the transcendental signified. He aimed at the "de-construction of *the greatest totality*—the concept of the *episteme*." Ibid., 49.

47. See Selden et al., *Contemporary Literary Theory*, 150; McHale, *Postmodernist Fiction*, 27–31.

48. Lyotard, *Postmodern Condition*, 10.

49. The definition was given by Bauman: "The ethical paradox of the postmodern condition is that it restores to agents the fullness of moral choice and responsibility while simultaneously depriving them of the comfort of the universal guidance that modern self-confidence once promised." Bauman, *Intimations of Postmodernity*, xxii. The issue will be discussed in detail later in chapter 8.3.

50. Hutcheon, *Poetics*, 7.

proach be stretched? What would it mean in terms of power, sexuality, or a conception of God? Could history be written anew according to the juxtaposition and polarisation that the new reading produces? The postmodern, for instance, opposes patriarchy, religious hierarchies, dogmatism, laws and regulations. These attitudes and structures are said to prevent the exercise of one's responsibility and ethical assessment in the sense the new generation understands it. Traditional Christian sexual morals are also criticised because they restrict the subject's right to self-determination. Furthermore, according to this critique of religion, theism—i.e., the monotheistic conception of a personal God—restricts the freedom of religious experience and subjective interpretation of faith.

What kind of rewriting does this ideological discussion produce? If the reading process is emphasised, we have at least two different possibilities. On the one hand, if the sources themselves are investigated as products of ancient people and ancient societies, their later interpretation becomes important. Such an interpretation may be feminist, political, or it may reflect a critique of religion, if the reader himself or herself has adopted such views. In this case the content of the source will be placed into a productive dialogue with the position of the reader. On the other hand, if ancient writings are considered merely as expressions of, e.g., patriarchal oppression, violent religious propaganda, or sexual asceticism, the documents can be dismissed as sources for even remotely reliable history. In this case, the new historiography attempts to change the history known from the extant texts. Some of these historiographies go even further. They amend and revise the very sources cited in the novels, and this revision is made according to the principles of reader-response theory. Both of these attitudes and approaches can be detected in the investigated novels. The precise result of these approaches will be investigated in the following chapters.

All of the abovementioned aspects emphasise that, concerning Jesus-novels, making a distinction between historical reading and fictional reading is essential. It seems obvious that different ways of reading begin to influence and even distort each other. If a novel is primarily being read as fiction its rhetorical discourse implies that one is not at all dealing with historiography. This means simply that previous knowledge, for instance, about biblical history or Jewish culture, cannot really help one to understand the story at hand. Instead, it may merely build a tension between general history and the story of the novel.[51]

The question about ethical reading thus raises one difficult methodological problem. As many novels prove to be ethical readings of Christianity, should their analysis also adopt this approach? What is the nature of the investigation's ethical reading? To my understanding, literary criticism should not be normative in the sense that it adopts a philosophy-of-religion approach in its analysis. It is not the task of comparative literature to assess the nature of a religion. Its objects of investigation are the novels themselves and their views, expressions, narrative structure, and intertextual strategies.

All in all, one needs to be careful when writing an ethical interpretation. In the analysis of the selected Jesus-novels it is proper to assess the novels' own ethical norms and practices, but one must remember that there is a distinction between ethical reading as a methodological tool and the ethical readings of the novels themselves. In this respect, contrast-novels are special because they themselves have adopted a high-profile moralistic stance. This raises several questions. What kinds of polarisations do they use? Are the authors able to follow their own norms in their writing? And, quite important in the present investigation, what are the implications of their views and how should one define the norms they appear to follow? Thus, in this investigation, ethical reading in a strict sense means the ethical reading that scholars present in the Jesus-novels.

4. ON THE HISTORY OF JESUS-NOVELS

There is a long history of rewritten Gospels in the Western world. There is no need for a thorough presentation of the history of Jesus-novels here, but certain interesting details need to be pointed out for the analysis. Already in the ninth century pious writers produced messiads that presented the main events of Jesus' life and passion in free prose style. These messiads became especially popular in sixteenth and seventeenth centuries. In addition to this kind of religious epic, legends of the saints centering on the person and works of Christ were written.[52]

---

51. This subject would easily lead to a renewed discussion about historiography. Such developments must be left to literary theory, though. Suffice it to say that historiography is evidently altered when the author intentionally writes against history.

52. In Finnish scholarship this tradition is referred to by Envall, *Pitkä marssi*, 27–28.

It was not until the age of rationalism, however, that a more imaginative literature on Jesus' life emerged. The Enlightenment had liberated many authors and philosophers from the guidance of ecclesiastical dogmatics. As rationalism itself was based on an epistemological conviction that mere *ratio* provides a sufficient justification for truth, the assessment of the trustworthiness of biblical texts was transferred to the reading process. Empirical evidence in the meaning of history was no longer needed. The status of the source text in the process of interpretation was changed. In such an atmosphere Gospel stories were moulded and revised according to the standards of naturalism. The supernaturalistic New Testament with its miraculous Messiah was suppressed by the criticism of rationalistic reader, and in this context the story of Jesus was given quite a new meaning. A short overview of these writings is helpful because many of these principles still work in postmodern Jesus-novels.[53]

The principles of rationalism changed primarily the picture of Jesus' ordinary life. According to the new critics, there was a natural explanation behind every miraculous story. The miracle of the feeding of the four or five thousand was explained as an opening of the hearts of men and women. Jesus' prayer meeting and teaching day on the mountain turned into a picnic when people shared their bread with those who had not been wise enough to bring any food with them. The raising of Jairus's daughter, in turn, was explained merely as a normal event. Jesus just woke the sick girl up when he entered the room at the request of her parents. There were also more ingenious revisions. When John the Baptist baptised Jesus in Jordan there was a voice from heaven. This voice had been produced by a meteorite that had happened to fly over the place at that moment. And further, the famous story about the walking on water was a result of a misinterpretation. Jesus' disciples had not seen the coastline when they saw him walking on the shore on a dark and misty night.[54]

In the spirit of the Enlightenment many writers also began to produce complete novels about the "real" life of Jesus. One of the earliest was

---

53. I have written on such hermeneutical change elsewhere. Eskola, *Uuden testamentin hermeneutiikka*, 11–13 (in Finnish). See also Ziolkowski, *Fictional Transfigurations*, 31–32

54. On the interpretations of the time of rationalism see especially Schweitzer, *Historical Jesus*, 48–59. For instance in the beginning of the nineteenth-century German scholars H. Paulus and K. Hase presented several naturalistic interpretations in their scientific writings.

K. F. Bahrdt's 1782 novel, *Popular Letters about the Bible*. It was a combination of self-assertive rationalism and religious pluralism. In Bahrdt's book, Jesus, a natural son of Mary, was raised as a good Essene. For some peculiar reason it was the Essenes who also taught him the philosophy of Plato and Socrates. In addition to this, a mysterious Persian introduced Jesus to esoteric knowledge, thanks to which he was able to perform several amazing tricks. There was nothing supernatural in all this, though. Even his walking on water was explained with the aid of a log on which Jesus was standing and thus deceiving the disciples. It is interesting that some of these rationalist revisions appear also in recent Jesus-novels.[55]

In Germany one of the most famous books in the early stage was K. H. Venturini's *Non-Supernatural History of the Great Prophet of Nazareth* (*Natürliche Geschichte des grossen Propheten von Nazareth*, 1800–1802). Venturini's Jesus was a normal healer who travelled around Galilee and helped people with his pharmaceutical knowledge. Supernatural stories were, according to Venturini, results of mistaken interpretations. For instance the wine miracle at Cana was a result of a misunderstanding. Jesus had brought the wine with him as his present for the married couple, and the jars were carried in when the feast was at its peak.[56] Furthermore, Venturini's Jesus was connected with the Essenes—a theme that appears again in the most recent Jesus-novels.[57]

The so-called *Leben Jesu* tradition became a major trend in Europe in the nineteenth century. This was primarily due to David Strauss's monograph *Das Leben Jesu* in 1835. Strauss was a straightforward rationalist who undertook a large scholarly investigation about the historicity of the Gospel tradition. Strauss's Jesus is a Jewish gentleman about whom we do not have much real information. Strauss is an important

---

55. Schweitzer, *Historical Jesus*, 38–41 Ziolkowski remarks that Bahrdt attempted to connect Jesus with some kind of secret society: "These works, which are heavily indebted to the Gothic romances of the late eighteenth century, present Jesus as a member of a secret society, not unlike the Freemansons or Rosicrucians or Illuminati, that trains him and aids him in his mission." Ziolkowski, *Fictional Transfigurations*, 32.

56. It is evident that rationalistic interpretation and revision needed to change details in the story itself. It was not merely a matter of giving new interpretations for the extant text. The six wine jars mentioned in the text were actually heavy stone jars (*hydria*) for Jewish rites of purification. They contained some 100 litres of water each, and their weight must have been around 140–150 kilograms. This would make a somewhat excessive, 900 kg (2,000 lbs) wedding present.

57. On Venturini see Schweitzer, *Historical Jesus*, 44–47. His work was imitated in Germany by several other writers; see ibid., 161–62.

figure, however, since he presents a new solution for the scientific problem of the rationalists. There must be some other kind of explanation for the emergence of supernatural stories. In his explanation, the New Testament is filled with imaginative interpretations about the mythical messiahship of Jesus. None of these stories have a reference point in history. Gospel stories, for Strauss, are theological statements invented only after Jesus' death for the purposes of the ecclesia. Such an argument is also explicit in many of the novels to be investigated here.[58]

Another early Jesus-novel with huge influence is *The Life of Jesus* (*La vie de Jésusi*, 1863) by the French Catholic and skeptic Ernst Renan. Renan writes in the *Leben Jesu* tradition and his work is filled with rationalistic humanism and simplistic optimism. The Galilean Jesus is an aesthete, and the Sermon of the Mount represents for Renan merely the eternal harmony of creation. The characters in the narrative are healthy and beautiful and seek a good life with ethical foundations. The Gospel of John is the primary source for this lyrical novel. Jesus proclaims love and presents ethical ideals for the humankind. Yet there is an even more substantial change in Jesus' life. Renan makes Jesus turn to radical eschatology. Gradually his words become harder, and contradiction with temple priests grows. This is how Renan explains Jesus' death as a martyr—which naturally would have been inconsistent had Jesus been merely a nature lover and great humanist.[59]

There is a deconstructive intention in rationalistic interpretations of the Gospels, at least in the sense that the canonical Jesus is reduced to a nineteenth-century bourgeois humanist. Biblical structures are turned inside out, even though this is not yet done so that all religious features in Jesus' life are destroyed. The early contradiction lies between the biblical, supernatural Jesus, and the affectionate philanthropist whose agenda has been dictated by natural aesthetics. Rationalism's influence did not extend as far into poetry, though. Lewis Wallace's *Ben Hur* (1880) holds to a conservative standard. In Italy as well, Giovanni Papini's romantic novel *The Life of Christ* (*Storia di Cristo*, 1921) is written along the lines of the canonical text.[60]

---

58. See Kümmel, *Investigation*, 120–25, on Strauss; cf. also Schweitzer, *Historical Jesus*, 68–71.

59. Schweitzer, *Historical Jesus*, 180–92; Renan, *Vie de Jésus*.

60. Later traditional Jesus-novels include for instance Robert Graves' *King Jesus* and L. C. Douglas' two novels, *The Robe* and *The Big Fisherman*. Recently Anne Rice has

After Nietzsche, contradictions grow ever more pronounced and rigid. D. H. Lawrence's *The Man Who Died* (1931) is, as Wood says, "a Nietzschean fantasy in which Jesus does not die on the cross but survives at the last minute. Alive, he realizes that he has never really lived, that his philosophy has been life-denying and death-obsessed."[61] This is probably the first time Nietzsche's direct influence can be seen in Jesus-literature. In its straightforward ideology it is second only to Alfred Rosenberg's *The Myth of the Twentieth Century* (*Der Mythus des zwanzigsten Jahrhunderts*), which was published just a year earlier in 1930 and could not have influenced Lawrence's work. Lawrence has been acclaimed for the moral seriousness in his novels, and this is one of the important features of Nietzschean literature. A true Nietzschean approach means a battle against the so-called Christian slave morality, and most of the recent Jesus-novels to be investigated here belong to Lawrence's tradition. A similar experiment with an imagined sexual experience can be found in *The Last Temptation* by Niko Kazantzakis (1952), where Jesus' relationship with Mary Magdalene is brought into the story. A similar idea can later be detected, for instance, in Fredriksson's *According to Mary*. Mary Madgelene is Jesus' concubine in most of the investigated novels.[62]

There have also been attempts to link Jesus with other religions, which is interesting since recent feminist novels do the same almost without exception. Levi H. Dowling's *The Aquarian Gospel of Jesus Christ* takes Jesus to India making him a disciple of Eastern wise men. Paul Park does the same by making Jesus a companion to Corax, a runaway slave travelling from Palestine to the Himalayas. These two meet Zoroastrians and Buddhists, and Jesus learns from both of them. The novel suggests and emphasises an Eastern influence on Jesus' teaching and apparently favors Buddhism over the canonical message.[63]

---

followed this tradition in her *Christ the Lord*. As Hannu Riikonen has shown, in these kind of novels, Christianity usually opposes the values of the heathen world. Riikonen, *Antike im historischen Roman*, 182–83.

61. Wood, "He Is Finished," 33.

62. Temptation is the main subject also in Jim Crace's *Quarantine* which, however, as a book remains quite faithful to the stories of the New Testament. The narrative is an interesting rewriting of Jesus' temptations in the wilderness, but Crace keeps his distance from the canonical texts. In the end of the story his Jesus dies of dehydration and is buried. Therefore he cannot be identified with the Gospel's Jesus completely. See *Quarantine*, 160–67, 224–26.

63. Dowling's esoteric gospel was ahead of its time making Jesus an avatar, a mystic

During the twentieth century, then, we find examples of the "comrade Jesus" or the "existentialist Jesus," as Ziolkowski has observed. These novels often follow rationalist principles but their basic point of departure is sympathetic to biblical ideas. They attempt to create a positive Jesus-character who still could serve as a teacher of ethical standards for a decent lifestyle.[64]

Already towards the end of the twentieth century, however, some authors proceed into contradictions. Ziolkowski notes that certain writers learn from the death-of-God ideology or theological movement, and serious treatment gives way to parody.[65] The shift into the era of recent Jesus-novels, then, means the introduction of completely new kinds of revised gospels. They move towards inversion and even perversion, and the adaptation is based on contradiction. This is no coincidence. Behind it one can detect the influence of the Nietzschean ideology that quickly found its way into post-war theology, Heideggerian existentialism, and poststructuralist deconstructionism.

5. NIETZSCHEAN TRADITION AND THE GOSPEL OF ZARATHUSTRA

In interpreting the nature of recent Jesus-novels, the new tradition of revising, dissolving, and perverting begs for an explanation. Describing certain Jesus-novels as Nietzschean is no doubt a daring point of departure but it can be defended. There are specific features both in the modern critique of religion and in Jesus-literature that derive from the writings of the father of nihilism. My thesis here is that these novels do not just playfully speculate about ideas but rather embark on an intentional Nietzschean revision. There are also solid theoretical reasons justifying such a viewpoint.

Friedrich Nietzsche's (1844–1900) role in the present discussion is ambiguous, though. On the one hand, for most readers, he represents the master morality and outright evil that led gradually to the anti-

---

and divine incarnation like Buddha and Zarathustra appearing at the turn of the aeons and playing with these millennial aeons, an approach that became popular later in the New Age movement. Park's novel is more like a thriller, making Corax rescue Jesus from jail. Together these two travel east and drift into troubles wherever they go. Park, *Gospel of Corax*, 130–33, 196f.

64. Ziolkowski, *Fictional Transfigurations*, 55–66, 182–83.

65. Ibid., 226–27.

Semitic horrors of Hitler's Third Reich. On the other hand, Nietzsche has become a hero in the postmodern movement for being the first philosopher to cast doubt on the transcendental signified. So the very same authors and philosophers who are convinced that Nazi nihilism represents demonic evil are ready to build on Nietzschean hermeneutics in their writings. This is destined to create problems and one of the aims of the present study is to investigate what kinds of difficulties it produces in the presentations of recent Jesus-novels. The connection, of course, is Nietzsche's *Thus Spoke Zarathustra* (1883–1885), which is a paradigmatic Jesus-novel for any author in this tradition. One cannot forget, however, that Nietzsche's work includes his *Anti-Christ* (1888) and, therefore, any discussion about Nietzschean influence needs to take his whole corpus and its ramifications into account. There are also certain logical inferences that lead in the same direction.

A Jesus-novel, such as that of Saramago's or Mailer's, is a book on Jesus. It cannot help being one even if the author would wish to use his story merely as a tool for speaking about the present instead to the past. The novel's primary intention, however, is that of casting doubt. The basic question the inversive contrast-novels implicitly pose is as follows: What if the historical Jesus has nothing to offer? What if he is merely a puppet of a violent God or a weak idealist who is unable to help human beings? There are two ways to interpret these questions. First, such pondering can be held as pure imagining. Second, the new revision can be seen as a complete ideological reduction of the original story.

Some scholars, such as Frier and da Silva, defend the imagining hypothesis and assume that, for instance, Saramago does not attack or deny Christian tradition as such but merely wishes to have an ironic dialogue with it. Reinterpretation and contextualisation would thus aim at a fictive rereading and critique. It plays with ideas. The focus is on the present church. Jesus himself, in this scenario, would probably be right in his teaching, but the church has been going astray—even from the very beginning.[66] Frier and da Silva's point of departure may be justified but this is not a neutral approach. According to this interpretation Jesus and his Christian religion are incapable of removing evil even from the believing community. Even in the first scenario where the historical Jesus could still be recognised as the Son of God, he is powerless to change people's lives. Christian faith and the church do not even appear

---

66. Frier, "Outline," 377; Silva, "Saramago," 241.

to oppose evil but, instead, even serve it themselves. This results in a contrast novel that drifts into an opposition with the canonical Jesus. There is no such thing as an ideologically neutral scenario that would have no implications.

It may also be that, according to the author, Jesus really has nothing to offer. In a reductionist interpretation the author wishes to show that there never was a Jesus whose message could resolve the problems the novel brings up, such as violence, arrogant authority, and patriarchy. In this "Straussian" version the novel becomes a rationalist *Entmythologisierung* of the canonical Bible. Both of these alternatives imply a negative view of Christianity. Unconsciously or not, they adopt an atheist premise: the problems of the present world are so huge and difficult that they question the relevance and even the essence of Christian faith and Jesus' message. Were this not so, the novel's story would not be consistent.[67]

Therefore, when exploring the intertextual strategy and explaining inversive reading, one is inevitably led to Nietzsche's ideology and negative rhetorics. In philosophy, Nietzsche developed the idea of a clash of cultures, culminating in the Judeo-Christian slave morality in opposition to the ill-sounding master morality.[68] Since he became famous for his atheistic gospel, he can be understood as an, at least indirect, influence on later Jesus-novels. In what follows, the Nietzschean influence will be investigated primarily as a large cultural, if not pantextual, phenomenon. The influence is real because without his writings this kind of literature would lack these similar features. And they can be called Nietzschean because they so closely resemble elements in his original works. There is no need to prove any genealogical relationship between Nietzsche and the investigated writers. Nor are we aiming at an analysis of direct quotations of Nietzsche's works in the novels under investigation. The analysis focuses on themes. A book stands in a Nietzschean tradition if it creates polarisations in the New Testament similar to those in Nietzsche's own

---

67. This view has also been supported in scholarship, and some writers suppose that authors such as Saramago really attack Christianity as a religion. Both Fokkema ("Art of Rewriting," 401) and Krysinski ("Observations," 408–9) refer to Bultmann and his demythologising program in this connection.

68. Some authors use the term "Jewish-Christian" to refer both to Judaism and Christianity but this is not a correct expression. "Jewish-Christian" denotes Christians with a Jewish background. Therefore, it is more proper to use the expression "Jewish/Christian," or refer to the "Judeo-Christian tradition."

writings. From this perspective, Nietzsche acts as a reference point for identifying the approach of several recent Jesus-novels.[69]

Recent philosophers have also been interested in Nietzsche, especially because he declared the relativity of meaning. He further offered certain premises for a critique of traditional Western ethics. For both philosophers and liberal theologians there was, however, one essential theme that supported antagonism towards Christian faith: death-of-God philosophy.

It is true that Nietzsche made statements about the vagueness of linguistic meaning and about the contextual nature of truth. Firstly, in his critique of Hegel he abandoned the idea of a synthesis (Aufhebung) as a justification for epistemological truth. Secondly, in his comments on rhetoric, Nietzsche gave a linguistic argument for the idea of discontinuity.[70]

> What is truth? A mobile army of metaphors, metonyms, anthropomorphisms, in short, a sum of human relations which were poetically and rhetorically heightened, transferred, and adorned, and after long use seem solid, canonical, and binding to a nation. Truths are illusions about which it has been forgotten that they *are* illusions, worn-out metaphors without sensory impact, coins which have lost their image and now can be used only as metal, and no longer as coins.[71]

For some writers Nietzsche was simply the father of postmodern deconstruction. The battle of discourses was based mainly on the

---

69. Nietzsche is quite popular, however, in the liberal theology tradition, namely among theologians who themselves identify their views as Nietzschean and who quote him repeatedly in their works. This kind of theological tradition is quite obviously a cultural parallel for recent Jesus-novels. See for instance Altizer, *Gospel*, 21–22; Taylor, *Erring*, 20–25.

70. Zima, *Deconstruction*, 19.

71. See Nietzsche's writings on rhetoric in Gilman et al., *Nietzsche on Rhetoric*, 250; cf. 22–25, esp. 25: "What is usually called language is actually all figuration." Strong assumes that Nietzsche's nihilism is basically dependent on his view of language. Nihilist ideology starts when people find "both that there is no truth, and that they should continue to seek it." This was already Nietzsche's conclusion in his rather early books. "As Nietzsche notes at the very end of the *Genealogy of Morals*, 'man would rather will the void, than be void of will.' Here, then, is the position the epistemology arrives at: *the present structure of human understanding forces men to continue searching for that which their understanding tells them is not to be found.* This is the epistemology of nihilism." Strong, *Politics of Transfiguration*, 77.

idea that truth is a linguistic game. If language were but a collection of illusions and tropes, it would dissolve reality behind metaphors and figures.[72] Douwe Fokkema adopts this approach in his analysis of Saramago's novel: "In the wake of Nietzsche this century has become the age of individual truth, or situation-bound truth; and the value attached to the individual interpretation of texts enhanced the tendency to rewrite them."[73]

Nietzsche's antithesis was the so-called Christian slave morality. For him, Christianity was a religion of mercy and pity. It attempted to help and to support people who were suffering and who were oppressed by society. By clinging to such vain empathy Christianity had forced humanity to remain at a low level of intellectual evolution: "they have preserved too much of what *ought to perish*." He speaks of cultural degeneration, which is really the result of church's message: "what more should they have to do to work with such conviction and a good conscience for the preservation of everything sick and suffering, that is to say, to work in deed and in truth for the *degeneration of the European race*?"[74]

Of all the influential themes affecting ideologies, theology, and literature in Western culture, the Nietzschean idea of Christian slave morality, *Sklavenmoral*, is evidently the most important one. An attack on absolute morals belongs to the *Destruktionen* of Nietzsche's philosophical program. Since the theme appears countless times in much later books on philosophy, theology, and comparative literature, it is to be considered the main argument in a Western pursuit to contest biblical moral values. It also clears a path for criticism of patriarchy and its ideology through critiques of male dominion in culture and society. However, the Nietzschean counterpart *Herrenmoral* is less popular. It went out of fashion during the Fascist regimes in Europe. There is one problem, though. The theme of slave morality is incomprehensible

---

72. This is mainly how Yale deconstructionists later assessed Nietzsche's significance for postmodern ideology. See Man, *Allegories of Reading*, 110–13.

73. Fokkema, "Art of Rewriting," 395.

74. Nietzsche, *Beyond Good and Evil*, § 62. Italics his. Fleischer notes that, in philosophy, Nietzsche's destructive program was outlined in his work *Destruktionen*, where he aimed at dissolving most of the traditional fundaments of European philosophy. He attacked logic, metaphysics, and the ideal of absolute morals. This program climaxed in Nietzsche's death-of-God theology. His criticism of religion cannot thus be separated from his philosophical aims. Fleischer, "Nietzsche," 512.

without master morality. Nietzsche bases his ideas on a polarised discontinuity. The ethics of humanist rationalism contradicts *Sklavenmoral* and questions the whole biblical view of human beings. In his philosophy—and tradition—there is no neutral civilised way to oppose slavish religion. It is always a matter "beyond good and evil," as his famous book proclaims. Nietzsche himself represents an opposing intention, a "will to power," as it is called.[75]

According to Nietzsche, slavish Christianity has only maintained "sickness and suffering" when encouraging desperate people and helping those who cannot defend themselves. The Christian church has adopted the task of breaking strong personalities, denying independence, and rooting out manful domination. This is how the human race has been driven to uncertainty and self-destruction. For Nietzsche, Christianity is the greatest problem of humanity, which he states also before *The Anti-Christ*, even in his earlier work *Beyond Good and Evil* (1886): "That is to say: Christianity has been the most disastrous form of human presumption yet."[76] When the authors of the investigated Jesus-novels confront biblical morality and present it in a negative light or replace it by its inversion, they drink from a Nietzschean well. Even a short analysis shows that this theme is extremely popular in recent literature.

One cannot mitigate the primary point of departure that, for Nietzsche, slave morality originates in Judaism. According to him it is based on the biblical concept of sin. As a liberal humanist Nietzsche had adopted the view that human beings are not evil from birth. Human conduct is not perfect, but the reason for that is not sin but mere stupidity or false education. Sin has always been but a violent tool for the priests to oppress people.[77] Because the origins of the concept of sin are rooted in the Bible it is, for Nietzsche, a "Jewish" invention. Further, all speculation about sin is based on a language of slaves.

> *Origin of sin.* —Sin, as it is now experienced wherever Christianity holds sway or has held sway, is a Jewish feeling and a Jewish invention. Regarding this background of all Christian

---

75. Nietzsche, *Beyond Good and Evil*, § 36: "The world as it is seen from the inside, the world defined and described by its 'intelligible character'—would be simply 'will to power' and that alone." Cf. § 259.

76. Ibid., § 62.

77. Nietzsche was a keen follower of the materialistic atheist Schopenhauer, whom he praised in, e.g., one of his early essays, *Unmodern Observations*, 163–66.

morality, Christianity did aim to "Judaize" the world. How far it has succeeded in Europe is brought out by the fact that Greek antiquity—a world without feelings of sin—still seems so very strange to our sensibility, although whole generations as well as many excellent individuals have expended so much good will on attempts to approach and incorporate this world. "Only if you repent will God show you grace"—that would strike a Greek as ridiculous and annoying. He would say: "Maybe slaves feels that way."[78]

Even though Nietzsche's anti-Judaic or occasionally even anti-Semitic overtones no longer find a positive reception in postmodernity, his concept of the "Judaising" of the world has had its influence.[79] Speculation about sin belongs only to slave morality. It offends the independence of an autonomous Western thinker who lives "beyond good and evil." For Nietzsche, all this is a result of a false conception of God. Christians presuppose a powerful God who enjoys revenge. God cannot be violated, he can only be insulted. "Every sin is a slight to his honor, a *crimen laesae majestatis divinae*—and nothing else."[80] The novelists' use of this theme will become evident in this analysis, especially in the sense of making Judaism look like a religion of restrictive laws and inhuman precepts. The great problem of Nietzschean nihilism is that its anti-Semitic views are embedded in the crusade against Judeo-Christian *Sklavenmoral*.[81]

78. Nietzsche, *Gay Science*, § 135. As noted also in the footnotes of Walter Kaufmann's translation, the original expression, "verjüdeln," placed in quotation marks, is a nasty word with evident anti-Semitic overtones. In *Beyond Good and Evil*, Nietzsche himself actually admits that his attitudes have been negative: "May I be forgiven that I too, during a short, hazardous stay in a very infected area, did not remain entirely spared by the disease and, like everyone, began to think about things that were none of my business." Ibid., § 251. In spite of such later hesitation, Nietzsche in the very same monograph makes several anti-Judaic statements—known also from his other books (ibid., § 195; *Gay Science*, § 135; *Anti-Christ*, § 44).

79. Diethe in her *Historical Dictionary of Nietzscheanism*, 142, says: "Suffice it to say that Nietzsche vigorously rejected anti-Semitism on numerous occasions, though this did not prevent him from attacking Judaism as a religion quite as pestilential as Christianity (which it had spawned)." This distinction is necessary and emphasises that Nietzsche's nihilism is strictly anti-Judaic.

80. Nietzsche, *Gay Science*, § 135. The Latin expression referring to offending someone's honor is usually translated into English by using a French form *lèse-majesté*. Nietzsche was really convinced that the Jews had invented the very concept of sin as inextricable from the human condition. See Fleischer, "Nietzsche," 516.

81. "The 'redemption' of the human race (from 'the masters,' that is) is going for-

Master morality is further described in the book *Beyond Good and Evil*. Based on these examples it is easy to understand why authors and even some scholars often present a reductive view of Nietzsche. For Nietzsche, the average life of average people is an abomination and an offence against the will to power. He advocates hard values and even ruthlessness. His Master of the master morality, the *Übermensch*, is able to raise himself above traditional ethics. He is a philosopher whose will dictates everything:

> Indeed, in private they admit to a *joy* in saying No and in dissecting; they admit to a certain cruel concentration that knows how to wield the knife surely and subtly, even when the heart is bleeding. They will be *harsher* (and perhaps not always only towards themselves) than humane people may wish.[82]

According to Nietzsche, one cannot influence society without extreme actions accompanied by a harsh attitude. "And whoever must be a creator in good and evil: verily, he must first be an annihilator and shatter values. Thus does the highest evil belong to the highest good: but this latter is the creative."[83] In *Zarathustra* this ideology is further expressed in a short statement: "All creators, however, are hard."[84] This creation of good and evil, for Nietzsche, is not merely a matter of new thoughts, though. Had it been such, his views would not have aroused so heated a discussion and disagreement. For Nietzsche, the journey beyond meant also the contesting of Christian pity and compassion. For some reason, and probably just because the subject concerns ethics, he sometimes writes like a hard-boiled social Darwinist.

> To see others suffer does one good, to make others suffer even more: this is a hard saying but an ancient, mighty, human, all-too-human principle to which even the apes might subscribe; for it has been said that in devising bizarre cruelties they anticipate man and are, as it were, his "prelude." Without cruelty there is no festival: thus the longest and most ancient part of human history teaches—and in punishment there is so much that is *festive!*—[85]

---

ward; everything is visibly becoming Judaized, Christianized, mob-ized (what do the words matter!)." Nietzsche, *Genealogy of Morals*, 36.

82. Nietzsche, *Beyond Good and Evil*, § 210.

83. Nietzsche, *Thus Spoke Zarathustra*, 100.

84. Ibid., 78.

85. Nietzsche, *Genealogy of Morals*, 67. One should note that Nietzsche did not accept Darwin's views in principle. The theory of evolution was about recognizing human

All this leads finally to the devastating proclamations in *The Anti-Christ*. "The weak and ill-constituted shall perish: first principle of *our* philanthropy. And one shall help them to do so." For Nietzsche, pity really is a form of sickness. This is not just a mere slogan invented by later authors. "What is more harmful than any vice?—Active sympathy for the ill-constituted and weak—Christianity..."[86] Nietzsche's nihilistic morality cannot be called just a literary invention describing an inner struggle for an independent life. He speaks of ethics and precisely because of that he ends up with views that confront traditional Christian ethics and charity. This is something that modern and postmodern readers seldom want to see in him, but inevitably these themes will come up when investigating Nietzschean threads in recent Jesus-novels. In the Western world there is an implicit antagonism between wanting to oppose both the Nietzschean master morality and Christian ethics.

One of the evident outcomes resulting from Nietzsche's ethical views and *Herrenmoral* is the questioning of Christianity as a sacrificial religion. There is nothing in human beings that would need atonement. Even mentioning redemption would mean a fall into slavish religion and being under God's control. This theme is often repeated in literature after Nietzsche.

> No image of torture. —I want to proceed as Raphael did and never paint another image of torture [*Marterbild*, i.e., picture of the Crucified One]. There are enough sublime things so that one does not have to look for the sublime where it dwells in sisterly association with cruelty; and my ambition also could never find satisfaction if I became a sublime assistant at torture.[87]

These particular themes lead finally to Nietzsche's great vision about the death of God. If the conception of a heavenly Lawgiver and Judge who will judge human beings according to their works in the end of times has died, so has God died. In the well-known passage called *The Madman* in chapter 125 of *The Gay Science* (1882), a fool circulates on a market place and preaches the death of God.

---

beings as animals while Nietzsche sought the opposite: the Superman.

86. Nietzsche, *Anti-Christ*, § 2.

87. Nietzsche, *Gay Science*, § 313. The English translation following the lexical meaning no longer attains the original nature of the German word *Marterbild*, which denotes a picture of the Crucified.

"Whither is God?" he cried; "I will tell you. *We have killed him—you and I*. All of us are his murderers. . . .

Do we not feel the breath of empty space? Has it not become colder? Is not night continually closing in on us? Do we not need to light lanterns in the morning? Do we hear nothing as yet of the noise of the gravediggers who are burying God? Do we smell nothing as yet of the divine decomposition? . . . .

How shall we comfort ourselves, the murderers of all murderers? What was holiest and mightiest of all that the world has yet owned has bled to death under our knives: who will wipe this blood off us?[88]

Nietzsche contests the Christian metanarrative by attacking the very concept of God. For Nietzsche, the death of God does not merely mean the death of "the fossilized institution of religion," as Gilman has suggested.[89] Nietzsche's criticism is rooted deeper. It is based on his attack on metaphysics and in the relativity of both language and meaning. In this scheme the Church no doubt has her role as a suppressing and enslaving community, but Nietzsche's primary target is the biblical God and even the concept of God. In such a situation a philosopher becomes an undertaker who delivers spades to all those whose eyes are open to the new reality. There is no hope for this world outside humanity. On the one hand, there is just a cold cosmos that freezes honest thinkers. On the other, humankind must take its destiny into its own hands with the help of the "master morality." The *Übermensch* is alone in this world. For Nietzsche, the concept of God is no longer convincing. Traditional definitions for a divine Being or Being itself are no longer to be accepted. The crisis of faith is simultaneously a crisis of meaning. In this respect already Nietzsche proclaims an "incredulity towards a Christian metanarrative." This can most clearly be read in *The Anti-Christ*.[90]

> The thing that sets us apart is not that we are unable to find God, either in history, or in nature, or behind nature—but that we

---

88. Ibid., § 125.

89. Gilman, *Nietzschean Parody*, 73.

90. This is an application of Lyotard's standard definition of postmodern thinking "incredulity towards metanarratives," which no doubt suits the interpretation of Nietzsche's atheist philosophy. Cf. for instance Lyotard, *Postmodern Condition*, 37. Sarles (*Nietzsche's Prophecy*, 174) speculates on Nietzschean premises: "All we need do is to seek out those directives and live our lives within their outlines. . . . But, as Nietzsche proclaimed, so many of us doubt that the deity gave us meaning, gives us meaning. In this sense of death of the idea of God we experience some crisis *of* meaning."

regard what has been honoured as God, not as "divine," but as pitiable, as absurd, as injurious; not as a mere error, but as a *crime against life*.... We deny that God is God.... If any one were to *show* us this Christian God, we'd be still less inclined to believe in him.[91]

Therefore, in Nietzsche's estimation, God cannot be trusted, even if he is alive. Later radicalised theology has wanted to take this challenge into account. For several authors, theology can be constructed only on the premises that Nietzsche has laid down.[92] This death-of-God philosophy continues its influence in some of the recent Jesus-novels. They put Nietzsche's ideas into practice by writing their opposition to the heavenly Despot into a new story.

While the questioning of Christianity's great metanarrative along with the basic postmodern antithesis building on the Nietzschean critique of slave morality have been major sources of influence for many authors who contest Christian tradition, there is another factor which has greatly influenced later Jesus-novels: namely the new picture of Jesus. Nietzsche's *Thus Spoke Zarathustra* is a paradigmatic new gospel that has provided a pattern for rewriting Biblical tradition. The picture of Jesus is altered already in Nietzsche's own works. As an alternate gospel *Thus Spoke Zarathustra* presents readers with an ideal Messiah. In this poetic novel one finds an anti-Christian Savior who, simultaneously, is a rather traditional preacher of a renewed Sermon on the Mount. Zarathustra is also introduced in the same manner as Jesus in the canonical Gospels.

Nietzsche's Jesus, it is useful to remember, is a historical reconstruction. In *The Anti-Christ* he states that canonical tradition, however, is a forgery.

> I shall go back a bit, and tell you the *authentic* history of Christianity. —The very word "Christianity" is a misunderstanding—at bottom there was only one Christian, and he died on the cross. The "Gospel" *died* on the cross. What, from that moment

---

91. Nietzsche, *Anti-Christ*, § 47. Gilman (*Nietzschean Parody*, 73) further assumes that Nietzsche's God simply died "through his sympathy with man." This quotation from Zarathustra cannot, however, completely explain Nietzsche's fiery attack on theism in other passages. Death-of-God philosophy is not merely a question of aesthetics.

92. The Nietzschean reception in the Atheist Christianity movement from Robinson to Altizer will be treated later in chapter 6.5.

onward, was called the "Gospels" was the very reverse of what *he* had lived: "bad tidings," a "*Dysangelium*."[93]

The real Jesus of history may well have existed, in Nietzsche's estimation, but the Bible does not know him. The oppressive gospel of slave morality is a *dysangelium*, an evil message. All preachers of the biblical good news are but traitors. Nietzsche's *Zarathustra* attempts to correct the situation and save the world from this historical error. Somewhat surprising, however, is that in his own mission Zarathustra is far from being a cynic or a cold nihilist. Already in the beginning of the narrative he proclaims, "I love human beings."[94]

In addition to this, in his own Sermon of the Mount—at the beginning of the gospel—Zarathustra lists a dozen objects of love. Zarathustra loves "the great despisers" because their reverence is great. He loves those who are not willing to be sacrifices, but "who sacrifice themselves to the earth," so that the earth may one day belong to the Superhuman/ *Übermensch*. He loves those who love their virtue but he loves also those who hold back "not one drop of spirit" for themselves, but live completely for other people instead. Zarathustra's love is actually rather demanding. He loves those whose soul "squanders" itself and wants no thanks. These people give without receiving any response. Zarathustra loves him whose words are "golden" and who "keeps even more than he promises."[95]

Thus, Nietzsche's revised Sermon on the Mount appears to be but a rendering of Jesus' speech in the canonical Gospel. Nietzsche has not gotten rid of Jesus even though he no doubt has done his best trying to. In Jesus' footsteps he seeks an altruistic love and perfect virtue. He demands faithfulness and a commitment of the heart. A polite life and mediocre integrity is not sufficient for Nietzsche. He wants more. In a sense, Nietzsche's Zarathustra is a reconstruction of the real historical Jesus behind the canonical *Dysangelium*, the evil Gospel. Simultaneously, however, Nietzsche's text is a Sermon of the Anti-Christ. It is a text of a writer who goes beyond good and evil. It opposes an alleged religion of oppression that produces victims. Or does it? How should one define Nietzsche's ethics ind this context?

93. Nietzsche, *Anti-Christ*, § 39. This is a word-play concerning the biblical word for "gospel," *eu/angelion* in Greek, literally "good news."

94. Nietzsche, *Zarathustra*, 10.

95. Ibid., 13–14.

One could probably say that Nietzsche the moralist is simply an enlightened German gentleman who accepts responsibility and does his best. No reconciliation or forgiveness are needed, though. One just needs to take life seriously and to keep high moral standards. Through this, the lightning of justice strikes the earth, as he says, and that lightning is called *Übermensch*.[96] In this sense the Nietzschean Overhuman/Superman is a post-Christian European who understands his moral responsibility. He is a convinced Kantian who searches for moral values that exceed those of the Bible. Actually, it is surprising how close Nietzsche comes to Kant, who in his moral philosophy predicts that a universal ethical community will finally replace Christianity and all other "historical" religions. For Kant, common knowledge of right and wrong and universal morality make humanity rational. The categorical imperative directs and even forces mankind to live ethically, and this is how a universal (non)religion—an ethical society—will be achieved.[97] A similar utopian ideal seems to inspire many authors of recent Jesus-novels. It remains to be seen how they put this pursuit into practice.

All this does not mean that Nietzsche would have identified himself as a Kantian, though. In his somewhat paradoxical presentation of moral life he actually rejects Kant's ethics.[98] He poses his own view of morality against all other traditions of moral reasoning. Nevertheless, he cannot escape his role as an ethical philosopher. As a teacher of master morality he is merely one of the moralists of his time. He is not very original or inventive, either. Zarathustra in his ethics more or less repeats the golden rule of Christian ethics. The Nietzschean gospel, in certain respects, is more of an imitation of the canonical story than its polarised counterpoint.[99]

96. In the end of the nineteenth century there were several neo-Kantian theologians in Germany who taught that the essence of Christian faith is altruistic morals. Naturalism had cleansed the Bible of its myths, and sin and reconciliation had been removed from the core of Christianity. For instance Adolf von Harnack thought that dogmatic faith should be replaced by the religion of Jesus, i.e., the high-standard ethics of the Sermon of the Mount. For Harnack, Jesus himself did not belong to the message of the gospel. He just preached a gospel about the Father. See Harnack, *Wesen des Christentums*, 86f.

97. See Kant's work *Religion within the Boundaries of Mere Reason*, 3.1.4–6. For the ideas, see Michaelson, *Kant and the Problem of God*, 100ff.

98. On Nietzsche's opposition to Kant, see *Beyond Good and Evil*, § 187, 259.

99. Kantian influence in nineteenth-century Germany is quite overwhelming. In philosophy, the *Marburger neu-Kantianer* started a tradition that affected theology, as

Introduction

Whatever one thinks of Nietzsche's rewriting of the biblical Christ, in his many books he opposes the Jesus described in the Gospels. The Jesus of the New Testament is, for Nietzsche, a legendary, invented figure whose project is directed against true humanity. Moreover, he is a Jewish Jesus. Nietzsche's anti-Judaic attitude, of which there are several examples in his works, extends to his assessment of Jesus' personality. Since the biblical Jesus preaches the wrath of God he is still a perfect representative of the religion of oppression—namely Judaism. The grace Jesus proclaimed was possible only against the dark background of the concept of a God who is a heavenly Judge. To the misfortune of humanity both of these ideas were products of the imagination. God is dead, and grace has neither content nor significance. The error of the real historical Jesus, as reconstructed by Nietzsche, is that he is not able to expose the deception of the Jews. The historical Jesus adopted their illusions and preached both wrath and pity. In this way the first Messiah was humiliated and he became just one Jew among the others.

> *Too Jewish.* —If God wished to become an object of love, he should have given up judging and justice first of all; a judge, even a merciful judge, is no object of love. The founder of Christianity was not refined enough in his feelings at this point—being a Jew.[100]

Nietzsche's anti-Judaic criticism is thus confirmed in Christology. It then actually becomes anti-Semitic since Jesus, in Nietzsche's estimation, is not merely a preacher of the oppressing religion. He is a Jew, and this explains his error. Nietzsche returns to his basic claim: it is all about *race*.[101] Such an approach has not usually been welcome, partly because the Third Reich adopted and exploited it in excess. Despite their ideological role in twentieth-century Europe's most dire conflicts, Nietzschean ideas quickly crawled into theology and literature—and a critique of this ideological assimilation will provide a hermeneutical basis for the present investigation.

---

the abovementioned example concerning Harnack shows. In the history of ideas one can state that the gradual transition from a Christian society into a secular society that started as a critique against metaphysics generated a vast discussion on ethics. Nietzsche can be seen as an extreme example of such a pursuit. See especially Michaelson, *Kant and the Problem of God*, 105–10.

100. Nietzsche, *Gay Science*, § 140.
101. Nietzsche, *Anti-Christ*, § 44.

Consistent with these observations is the hypothesis of a deconstructive tone in Nietzsche's *Zarathustra*. He is a philosopher of conflict. Nietzsche has turned biblical structures of Christian faith inside out. He has rejected the metanarrative that gave signification to the texts of the New Testament. Against all this he wrote his own gospel of the *Übermensch*. The new narrative was to become a paradigmatic example for many writers in the years to come. Nietzsche's grand idea is in contradiction and discontinuity. As Tracy Strong has noted, his idea of redemption means redemption from the past. For Nietzsche, redemption means freeing oneself for instance from Judeo-Christian tradition and recreating everything into "thus I willed it."[102]

The main chapters in the following analysis will be constructed on the basis of the abovementioned Nietzschean themes. The investigation will focus on Jesus' role, Christian ethics and moral values, women's roles in a patriarchal setting, questions of sacrificial religion, and death-of-God philosophy. Furthermore, a later Nietzschean idea about the re-enchantment of life will be investigated as a feature leading to new mysticism. Finally, the iconoclastic enthusiasm of the new readings of recent Jesus-novels will be discussed in a thematic closing chapter.

---

102. Strong, *Politics of Transfiguration*, 223. "If men are to be *redeemed* from what they are, they must be redeemed *from* their past."

1

Source Texts and Subtexts in Contemporary Jesus-Novels

THE NEW TESTAMENT IS a challenging source text. Any adaptation is obliged to define its position in relation to a text that has affected the whole course of Western history, the emergence of the civilised society, our concept of justice, and our view of humane morality. As the late twentieth-century Jesus-novels propose new gospels, they take on the immense task of contributing to a tradition that in many ways has moulded the author herself or himself. Furthermore, as the revisions appear to question the values represented by the canonical texts, there immediately arises questions both about the motivation and the purpose of adaptations and rewritings. In this chapter a general introduction to the novels' use of source texts will be given. The focus is mainly on the author's use of historical texts, not on their creation of completely new ideas.

1. ADAPTATION AND APPROPRIATION

There are three kinds of source texts in the investigated novels, and in each case the treatment of the intertextual relationship has its distinctive features. First group of source texts comprises ancient writings. The New and Old Testaments are naturally the most important of these, but the novels also treat the Dead Sea Scrolls and Gnostic writings, as well as a number of apocryphal gospels. The second source text, a text in a pantextual sense, is Christian history, particularly in the manner each author understands and interprets it. Saramago in particular applies this kind of pantextual approach by putting Christian history in a critical dialogue with Gospel stories and their theological ideas. In several novels from Roberts to Longfellow feminist ideology is made a dialogue partner with the canonical tradition. The third source text, according to the hypothesis of the present work, is Nietzschean ideology, as discussed above in the final section of the Introduction. This text is not simply a group of Nietzsche's books but an ideology in a more general sense, the spirit of his *Anti-Christ* that opposes the so-called biblical slave morality.

Since Jesus-novels' intertextual relationships involve extant manuscripts and texts, it is necessary to return to the methodology of adaptation. The act of rewriting is usually a multidimensional process of adaptation and appropriation where, as Julie Sanders says, an adaptation "signals a relationship with an informing source text or original."[1] Writing on Jesus who lives in ancient Israel, or calling a novel a gospel, strongly signals such an approach. Most Western people—at least those with a Christian background—reading these new novels automatically locate them in a particular tradition. Meanings in these novels are constructed in a relationship with the Bible, not autonomously inside the text itself.

> Adaptation and appropriation are dependent on the literary canon for the provision of a shared body of storylines, themes, characters, and ideas upon which their creative variations can be made. The spectator or reader must be able to participate in the play of similarity and difference perceived between the original, source, or inspiration to appreciate fully the reshaping or rewriting undertaken by the adaptive text.[2]

Adaptive Jesus-novels trust that readers can recognise any variation and inversion the new story proposes. This creates a situation that Linda Hutcheon describes as follows: "If we know that prior text, we always feel its presence shadowing the one we are experiencing directly."[3] Jesus-novels share most details with their canonical source. The story is similar, the characters are the same, and most events have been taken from the New Testament narrative. Several direct or slightly altered quotations emphasise the relationship. This is a good point of departure for an adaptation.

It is not too easy to define adaptation as such, though. Sanders has noted that already the terminology used in methodological discussion reveals that adaptations can possess different aims.

1. Sanders, *Adaptation and Appropriation*, 26,
2. Ibid., 45.
3. Hutcheon, *Theory of Adaptation*, 6.

As well as throwing up potent theoretical intertexts of their own, adaptation studies mobilize a wide vocabulary of active terms: version, variation, interpretation, continuation, transformation, imitation, pastiche, parody, forgery, travesty, transposition, revaluation, revision, rewriting, echo. As this list of terms suggests, adaptations and appropriations can possess starkly different, even opposing aims and intentions.[4]

Adaptation, in a general sense, means acknowledged transposition and rewriting. Its mode, however, changes from case to case. Adaptation can be mere echo of the source text or it can produce a revaluation or a forgery. Since adaptation is a form of intertextuality, it can be seen as part of a reception process. Therefore, it is not merely a matter of transposing but also a "creative and interpretive act of appropriation."[5]

The investigated Jesus-novels, as noted already in the Introduction, are not content with copying the original text. Neither do they attempt to explain the New Testament or interpret the "true" meaning of Jesus' original teaching. Instead, they belong to those novels that create a "manifestly different interpretation." Jesus-novels conduct imitation and transformation. Some of the contemporary works aim at hostile revision and appropriation. Appropriation, as Sanders says, is a "more decisive journey away from the informing source into a wholly new cultural product and domain."[6] These approaches are situated on a continuum where authors move from slight adaptation to deconstructive appropriation, and ultimately to the direct challenge of biblical views even though they keep the characters and some of the events that occur in the source text. This is why the analysis must focus on the novels' own themes.[7]

Adaptation can even aim at intentional confusion. It may well be the whole purpose of the adaptation in many cases, and this is very true for inversive Jesus-novels.[8] Audiences, however, are dependent on

---

4. Sanders, *Adaptation*, 18.

5. Hutcheon, *Theory of Adaptation*, 8. Sanders (*Adaptation*, 19) remarks that adaptation often involves a transition from one genre to another. Even though the concept is used when analysing films or drama, it is useful for investigating novels as well.

6. Sanders, *Adaptation*, 26. This is what Genette means by hypertextuality; see Allen, *Intertextuality*, 108–9.

7. First, a genuinely *literary* theme, that is, one significantly contributing to the general "meaning" of a work, must be one of the shaping forces and guiding principles of the text, not something the critic adds from outside. Wolpers, *Thematic Criticism*, 90.

8. Hutcheon, *Theory of Adaptation*, 73. Cf. Sanders who notes that in some instanc-

sources: "When giving meaning and value to an adaptation *as an adaptation,* audiences operate in a context that includes their knowledge and their own interpretation of the adapted work." They must not be left in confusion since the final effect of a rewriting depends on reader's ability to recognise the source text. Therefore, adaptations, by their very existence, "remind us there is no such thing as an autonomous text or an original genius that can transcend history, either public or private."[9] This is why adaptation and appropriation are the perfect means for producing a transformation, whatever the reason for it.

In the analysis of Jesus-novels, both adaptation and appropriation are important factors. The novels are adaptive since they constantly use the Bible, as well as some apocryphal gospels, the Dead Sea Scrolls, and Gnostic writings. Their rewriting is not traditional, however, since reinterpretation and revaluation of Christian concepts are signs of appropriation. In Jesus-novels the whole process of narration is based on a play between the well-known source text and the novel itself. These novels refer to a source text, the New Testament, even though the relation between them is complex. The novel's story stays inevitably in a reciprocal relationship with canonical Gospels.

Ideologies also affect adaptation. Sanders reminds us that "adaptations and appropriations are impacted upon by movements in, and readings produced by, the theoretical and intellectual arena as much as by their so-called sources."[10] The pantextual approach in intertextuality has always claimed that both individual expressions and larger revisions turn out to be cultural phenomena. Allen, when describing Barthes's view on intertextuality, notes that a pantextual approach has to do "with the entire cultural code."[11] According to Barthes a novel is a woven fabric with countless cultural threads. Phelan calls the source for this kind of influence a cultural narrative, whose author is "a larger collective entity,

---

es "the process of adaptation starts to move away from simple proximation towards something more culturally loaded." Sanders, *Adaptation*, 21.

9. Hutcheon, *Theory of Adaptation*, 111. "The process of adapting should make us reconsider our sense of literary critical embarrassment about intention and the more personal and aesthetic dimensions of the creative process."

10. Sanders, *Adaptation*, 13.

11. "Every text, being itself the intertext of another text, belongs to the intertextual, which must not be confused with a text's origins: to search for the 'sources of' and 'influence upon' a work is to satisfy the myth of filiation." Barthes, *Textual Strategies*, 77. Cf. Allen, *Intertextuality*, 74.

perhaps a whole society or at least some significant subgroup of society." These cultural narratives "typically become formulas that underlie specific narratives whose authors we can identify, and these narratives can vary across a spectrum from totally conforming to the formula to totally inverting it."[12] The aim of the present investigation is to ask whether Nietzschean ideology could be interpreted as such a cultural narrative, influencing the adaptive work of contemporary Jesus-novels. My investigation will also prove that the interpretation of recent Jesus-novels remains incomplete unless their critique of religion is given proper notice.

These ideas are closely related to a more general discussion in the field of intertextuality. Many theorists have attempted to find a path between a pantextual approach and a more simple intertextuality that treats particular texts. Laurent Jenny, in his mediating view, emphasises that even though no text is comprehensible without intertextuality, intertextuality is also related to source criticism. Extant sources are the basis on which the work of transformation and assimilation can be done. One essential methodological change has taken place here, though. The intertextual approach can no longer be identified with source criticism. For Jenny, it is the hypertext, or the "focal text" as he calls it, which keeps control over the meaning that is based on a reworking of the subtexts.[13] This is also what Graham Allen suggests in his summary.

> However, the two main strands which dominate theories of intertextuality have constantly reasserted themselves and proved their interconnectedness as we have moved from the term's origins to its later adaptations. Whether it be based in poststructuralist or Bakhtinian theories, or in both, intertextuality reminds us that all texts are potentially plural, reversible, open to the reader's own presuppositions, lacking in clear and defined boundaries, and always involved in the expression or repression of the dialogic "voices" which exist within society.[14]

Therefore, following the ideas of Hutcheon, Sanders, and Jenny, the present investigation will focus on adaptations, transformations, and assimilations in Jesus-novels. In addition to this, one should note that there are many other ancient writings that have also helped to shape postmodern Jesus-novels. These influences, as well as the influence of one's general knowledge of biblical times, are often mere echoes of cul-

---

12. Phelan, *Living to Tell*, 8.
13. See Jenny, "Strategy of Form," 39–40, 45.
14. So Allen, *Intertextuality*, 209.

ture. The author may not even be fully aware of all of these factors when writing his or her novel.

The question about the source text's status in the writing process is not simple, though. One is naturally inclined to think that the source text is an extant historical writing available to every reader who wishes to get acquainted with it. For modern Jesus-novels, the New Testament together with Gnostic writings and the Qumran scrolls are all such texts. This, however, is different from a subtext, and it is useful to make a distinction between a source text and a subtext. Subtext is a literary conception. It can be defined as the particular selection of passages from the original source text present in the novel. One could also say that a source text is transformed into a subtext when a selection of an ancient text is taken into a novel.[15] In this respect a subtext is a feature in the novel itself, not a real entity outside the present text. Therefore the subtext belongs not only in the sphere of historical reading but also and even more clearly in the sphere of fiction. Thus, we have three independent categories in this analysis:[16]

1. Source text: the Bible, Dead Sea Scrolls, Gnostic writings
2. Subtext: selection of source text passages in the novel
3. Hypertext: the novel

Hence, a subtext must be investigated as part of the novel itself, a feature of the hypertext, not completely independent of it. Even though the subtext is, by definition, directly derived from the source text, the essential factor is that the reduced subtext itself influences signification, that is, the process of constructing the novel's meaning. This distinction becomes especially important for recent Jesus-novels because the subtext represents only a small part of the source text. Meanings in the hypertext are not produced merely by referring to a relation to or a contrast with the original source text but also by the subtext, which can be considered an interpretation of the source text. In a literary sense the subtext is the primary source for the author (or implied author). When meanings are constructed in the novel, the information needed

---

15. Ihonen, *Museovaatteista historian valepukuun*, 36.

16. The novel itself could also be called intertext, as for instance Barthes does, even though there is no general agreement among scholars about these identifications. Some prefer calling the source text an intertext. I follow Genette who uses the term hypertext. For the discussion and Genette's views, see Allen, *Intertextuality*, 108.

for the adaptation exists primarily in the subtext. This does not mean, however, that the setting is only intratextual and that the original source should be neglected. Instead, the subtext becomes significant only in relation to its source text. There is a triad where the hypertext, the novel, uses and revises the source text, the New Testament, by interpreting the vast number of passages and themes that have *not* been taken into the subtext. One could even say that the distance between source text and hypertext can be assessed on the grounds of the subtext.

Adaptation of biblical texts is evident in Jesus-novels, but one also needs to pay attention to pantextual elements. In many novels, Christian history appears in a critical dialogue with Gospel stories. The particular features that the author considers negative or inhumane in church history are written into the novel and contested. Such an intertextual process is essential for instance in Saramago's, Roberts's, and Fredriksson's books. This is not simply a common pantextual situation, however, where the hypertext would be seen as a fabric of threads of culture. Instead, it is a matter of reading later history into a rewriting of an ancient text. Saramago, as will gradually become evident, is an expert in this technique. Feminist novels too exploit this idea in excess since it serves to write women into history.[17]

The third kind of source text, in the present analysis, is Nietzschean ideology. It differs from both of the abovementioned kinds of texts. The novels' relationship to Nietzsche's thinking is not merely a matter of using his books. According to my present hypothesis many authors have adopted a Nietzschean attitude towards Christianity. They criticise similar things in Christian faith and reject the same views and doctrines he rejected. In practice, they oppose the so-called biblical slave morality and follow the ideas of death-of-God ideology. In this respect, there is a Nietzschean cultural narrative behind the novels. The relationship has both pantextual and source text features: the ideas are general with the exception that there is one particular source behind them all, Nietzsche with his nihilist philosophy. The investigated authors use Nietzschean themes without referring to any of his books. The thesis of the present investigation is that the Nietzschean background actually explains the authors' intertextual strategy.

The notions of adaptation and appropriation cannot really be applied to this last source text. Nietzsche's ideas are not material that, ac-

---

17. For the feminist methodology, see especially chapter 4.4.

cording to the authors, should be transformed in the process. Instead, they are adopted directly and applied in practice. Nietzschean values become criteria according to which the authors rewrite Gospel narratives and dissolve Christian beliefs. All this reveals a close relationship between the novelists and this atheist philosopher.

But how are the extant manuscripts treated in Jesus-novels? How is the subtext created so that it can serve the purposes of adaptation and appropriation? In the following chapters we will discuss the roles of different groups of manuscripts in the writing process.

2. CANONICAL GOSPELS

In principle, an intertextual relationship can take almost any form from quotations to versions of more general pantextualism. It is important for the present investigation to define the former set of relations as precisely as possible. This concerns not merely direct quoting but also all kinds of exploitation and adaptation of New Testament material. A subtext is a particular selection of passages taken from the original source text, as noted, but this definition does not solve all the basic problems raised by the rereadings and revisions. There are many different ways of rendering the material that is used in an intertextual process.

But what is the Bible that the author exploits or even contests like? There are some relevant if general questions that need to be discussed briefly here. Do authors in their intertextual reading think that they are simply dealing with an ancient manuscript, or a book that has its own independent life in history? Or do they perhaps focus on an image of a doctrinal Christianity, which represents certain beliefs about God and human beings? In the investigated novels, it is not merely the Bible as a canonical standard that is the object of intertextual revision. It is justified to assume that different Jesus-novels do not work with one and the same "Bible." Instead, their source text in a more general sense appears to be Christianity, which bases its views on the canonical Scriptures. So the object of the intertextual assessment in each case is a slightly different view of God and his Word, or Jesus and his message. Therefore, the hermeneutical reality of understanding religion is important also for this study.[18]

---

18. Authors are not usually dependent on any particular translation, but Mailer often attempts to copy the style of the old KJV. See discussion below.

Hence, in theory, Christianity in the sense of a doctrinal entity could be represented for instance by authoritative Catholicism, rationalist Lutheranism, high-church Anglicanism, North American fundamentalism, or charismatic Brazilian Pentecostalism. Saramago uses the Bible to challenge Catholic tradition. Fredriksson, in turn, seems to wrestle with a Scandinavian Lutheran interpretation of Christianity. It is essential to treat this theoretical problem because it has important methodological implications. We must now develop some of the issues that were initially discussed in the Introduction. As the investigated novels intentionally produce polarisations they tend to create a subtext that suits their intentions.[19]

These methodological points of departure need to be taken into consideration when one investigates the author's selection of passages and construction of the subtext. One soon discovers that the selection is usually constructed with a purpose. There is ideology and even theology behind the decisions to choose particular passages and statements, and even more so as we consider the relocation of, for instance, Jesus' words into new contexts. The author makes the subtext an integral part of his or her rereading and new story. In many cases this is done quite skillfully.[20]

According to the premises adopted in the present investigation, constructing a subtext is part of a process of adaptation and appropriation. Since an author's intertextual strategy in selecting material has a particular aim, many passages—and in some cases most passages—in the investigated novels are revised by using different methods. Gospel stories are moulded in a way that changes their original meaning. Canonical words and sentences are placed into a new context, certain words and expressions are changed so that the original meaning is

---

19. Many details in Saramago's novel prove that he writes explicitly in the context of the Catholic Church. He deals with the saints and exploits Catholic martyrologies. Fredriksson, in turn, has no reference whatsoever that could be defined as Catholic. She writes in Lutheran Sweden where standard Protestant tradition prevails. Her view of Christian faith is rational and theoretical despite the fact that her own contribution derives from Gnosticism.

20. Cf. Hutcheon who says: "For an adaptation to be experienced *as an adaptation,* recognition of the story has to be possible: some copying-fidelity is needed, in fact, precisely because of the changes across media and contexts." Hutcheon, *Theory of Adaptation*, 167.

turned inside out, and some passages are turned into new paraphrasings that compete with the original text.

Ben-Porat, who is an expert on Saramago, calls this kind of adaptive intertextual rendering *prototypical rewriting*. The new text is written with the help of a source text, in this case the New Testament, but the original canonical text is but a tool in the hands of the author. The intertextual process is prototypical because the justification for the new interpretation, in spite of its unorthodox nature, is derived from the original context. In the adaptation, the few words quoted verbatim gain new meaning when seen in a new light and directed by the author's own narrative.

> Prototypical novelistic rewriting is, then, a retelling of a known story in such a way that the resulting text, the rewrite, is simultaneously an original composition and a recognizable rendition, involving a rereading of the source. Recognizable rendition requires the consistent use of significant original elements.[21]

For instance Saramago is not usually content just with altering the original canonical words to make them fit his own story. Neither is he content with quoting long passages of the Gospels as they are. Instead, he often uses the original context and picks up some extraordinary feature which, when developed in a new direction, creates an ironic reinterpretation of the original. Such interpretive appropriation serves his goal of writing a completely new narrative.

Saramago's novel is a good example to start with when assessing the nature of prototypical rewriting. He knows his sources well. Saramago appears to be a master of both biblical writings and theological doctrines. He quotes Old and New Testament texts like a scholar who knows his documents by heart. The basic setting of his story resembles that of the New Testament. The reader meets Mary and Joseph with their little baby, although the conception of the Jesus-child may not be completely divine and mysterious. The holy family stays in Bethlehem, a place that becomes crucial for Saramago's story. Herod's soldiers come, and the massacre and Joseph's guilt in not preventing it actually become a pedal point for the whole narrative. Jesus then wanders in the wilderness with the Devil and, afterwards, starts his mission by calling the disciples and

---

21. Ben-Porat, "Prototypical Rewriting," 93.

meeting Mary Magdalene. The concluding chapters of the novel, after the Devil-stories, present a complete summary of the canonical story.

As noted above, Saramago often accepts an original idea present in the canonical Gospel but, simultaneously, confronts the reader with an unorthodox adaptation. For instance he describes the virgin conception with much ambivalence. Joseph is involved in the event, and carnality is part of the narrative. At the same time, however, the story contains several mythical features that suggest that one could also be witnessing a divine event.[22]

> God, Who is omnipresent, was there, but pure spirit that He is, was unable to see how Joseph's skin came into contact with that of Mary, how his flesh penetrated hers as had been ordained, and perhaps He was not even there when the holy seed of Joseph spilled into the precious womb of Mary, both sacrosanct, being the fount and chalice of life. For in truth, there are things God himself does not understand, even though He created them.[23]

Such a description is typical of magical realism, which, in Saramago's work, intentionally disturbs the rationalist doubt that otherwise seems to direct the narration. The event is explained later in the story when an angel visits Mary.

> You must know, Mary, that the Lord mixed his seed with that of Joseph on the morning you conceived for the first time, and it was the Lord's seed rather than that of your husband, however legitimate, which engendered your son, Jesus.[24]

This additional information should not lead the reader astray, though. Saramago uses his subtext as a platform for his real revision. But ambivalence also appears in the text. The angel has to answer Mary's pertinent questions about God's real role and admit: "Well, it's a delicate matter, and what you're demanding is nothing less than a paternity test which in these mixed unions, no matter how many analyses, tests, and globule counts one carries out, can never give conclusive results." For Saramago, the belief in Jesus' divine origin is always a matter of faith, a dogma, not a biological or historical truth. In the first passage describing

---

22. "But as presented in the novel, this scene does not rule out the possibility of a divine origin of Jesus." Ibid., 95.
23. Saramago, *Gospel*, 11.
24. Ibid., 237.

the conception, treated above, Saramago has Mary use the words that, in the original Gospel story, are a response to divine revelation: "Thanks be to You, oh Lord, for having made me according to Your will." The narrator sees no difference whether these words are said to an angel or uttered in a prayer after intercourse. "Now there is no difference between these words and those spoken to the angel Gabriel, for clearly anyone who could say, Behold the handmaiden of the Lord, do with me as You will, might just as easily have used those other words."[25] Is Saramago playing with his own rationalism? The answer to this question is probably complex. As Saramago is inclined to think that we can never reach "real" history, this ambivalent feature may support his main argument. This question will be discussed in detail later.[26]

The next example is from the story where Jesus curses the fig tree. In the novel it is presented as a proper event in Jesus' mission. Originally in the canonical story, it has a theological or more precisely an eschatological meaning (Mark 11:12–14; Matt 21:20–22).[27] In Saramago's narration, however, Jesus' eschatology is questioned on the grounds of more humane morals. Mary Magdalene remarks that the figs could have helped the poor: "You must give to those in need, and ask nothing of those with nothing to give."[28] This makes Jesus hesitate, and he even tries to revive the tree but is unable to reverse the course of the divine mission here. By his curse he has simultaneously raised his hand against

---

25. Ibid., 11–12.

26. In magical realism, the narrative may well include miraculous elements. This has been Saramago's method in another book, as Henn notes: "With these two novels the reader is presented not with a 'real' world from which excursions are occasionally made into the realms of the fantastic or of magical realism, but largely the reverse." Henn, "History and the Fantastic," 112–13. One does not have to conclude that Saramago's goal is to write in the magical realism genre. Instead, he probably uses magical realism to sharpen his irony.

27. When compared with standard scholarly interpretation the contrast becomes clear. In the original story Jesus' act refers to exilic prophecies that bemoan the absence of good fruit in the tree Israel. The chosen people have fallen completely into sin and when God comes to look for fruit he discovers that the season is over: "there is no first-ripe fig for which I hunger." (Mic 7:1). This resembles Jeremiah's proclamation warning the people of Israel about the exile: "I will take away their harvest, declares the Lord. There will be no grapes on the vine. There will be no figs on the tree." (Jer 8:13 NIV.) In Jesus' teaching, thus, the event becomes a warning of judgment on Jerusalem and the Temple. See Wright, *Jesus and the Victory of God*, 333–34; Evans, *Mark 8:27—16:20*, 155–60.

28. Saramago, *Gospel*, 275.

the poor. Saramago's revision slightly misses the point since there were no figs in the tree to begin with. But in principle, this tree would never have borne fruit again and, in this respect, Mary's concern grows from the original event.

In Saramago's *Gospel*, the method of prototypical rewriting is also applied to the biblical concept of God. God in his story, as will become evident enough during the analysis later, is a bloodthirsty character who spreads violence around him. Ben-Porat remarks that, in Saramago's interpretation, this view of God is nevertheless not a reversal or revision. Instead, it is just a rewriting of the Old Testament picture of Israel's God. The adaptation is provocative but maintains the relationship between source text and hypertext. This God gets angry with David who has carried out a census of the people. David himself must choose between the alternatives for a fitting punishment. He chooses plague: "he reckoned that in three days, even with plague, fewer people would die than in three years of war and famine."[29] Furthermore, this is the God who accepts Abel's sacrifice and rejects Cain's offerings because there is no blood in them.[30] In a prototypical rewriting, thus, Saramago is able to pick a theme from the Old Testament and develop it when describing God's imaginative action. Saramago's message in the intertextual rendering is that the appropriation is based on a biblical prototype.[31]

Saramago applies prototypical rewriting further, to larger biblical themes that are based on Old Testament source texts. The story about the lost sheep provides a perfect example of this. Towards the end of his time with the Devil, Jesus' beloved sheep gets lost in the desert. Jesus goes looking for his lamb as the canonical predecessor proclaims in the parable.[32] The scene, however, is constructed in opposition to another biblical text. The desert, as well as Jesus' rambling on the mountains, are

29. Ibid., 100.

30. Ibid., 187.

31. Ben-Porat, even as a scholar, adopts a similar approach by adding the story about A'gag the Amalekite (1 Sam 15) whom Saul saved. In this story Yahweh appears as a violent divinity who demands killing and destruction. As a despot who sends the prophet and priest Samuel to destroy A'gag and Israel's enemies, God is paralleled with the one who, in Saramago's story, demands the blood of the sheep. 'Saramago's bloodthirsty power-craving God is a rewriting rather than an inversion of the biblical God, since his characterization foregrounds elements that exist but are largely ignored or explained away. Ben-Porat, "Prototypical Rewriting," 99.

32. Luke 15:4–6.

implicitly contrasted with Psalm 23. God is certainly not leading Jesus "in the paths of righteousness," and neither do we meet "green pastures" that a sheep might well seek—as Saramago remarks. Furthermore, it is unclear who the true shepherd in the narrative is. The source text itself is clear: "The Lord is my shepherd, I shall not want" (Ps 23:1–3). Saramago's description questions the biblical prototype in many ways; even the desert is desolate.[33]

> The desert in these parts is not one of those vast tracks of sand with which we are all familiar. Here the desert is more like a great sea of parched, rugged sand-dunes, straddling each other and creating an inextricable labyrinth of valleys. A few rare plants barely survive at the foot of these slopes, plants consisting of nothing but thorns and thistles which a goat might be able to chew, but which are likely to tear the sensitive chops of a sheep at the slightest contact.[34]

Combined with the idea of Jesus searching for his lost sheep, this description, once again, emphatically contrasts Jesus and God. Jesus finds his sheep but, simultaneously, God appears to him and begins to demand the slaughtering of the sheep. Instead of being the Good Shepherd, God proves to be the one who creates deserts. With his feet bleeding Jesus encounters the Divinity who demands killing and sacrifice. It is useless to search for any lost sheep as long as there is a God who destroys everything that has been found.[35]

The prototypical rewriting here is inversive, and Saramago is not content with just copying the biblical material. Saramago's approach even has a parodic tone. It does not fulfil all theoretically parodic criteria, but it certainly is an example of ironic adaptation where only the reader's knowledge of the original source text opens the hermeneutical intention of the presentation.[36] This confirms that prototypical rewriting is im-

---

33. Emery pays attention to the fact that Saramago reinterprets the shepherd theme, which, in the Bible, continually reappears. It becomes a constant theme of Davidic Messianism in Jer 23:1–5, and also serves as criticism against Israel's fallen shepherds in Jer 25:34. Emery, "Pasteur," 69.

34. Saramago, *Gospel*, 195.

35. Ibid., 196–98. I am grateful to Tiina Hallikainen for this analysis of Ps 23, presented in her MA thesis on Saramago, "Se oli näin," 83.

36. In agreement with Peña Fernandés, who writes concerning Saramago: "Esta intención paródica del autor veremos que se expresa en la realización de manipulaciones aditivas o sustitutivas en relación al hipertexto, en la *traducción inversa* de determi-

portant for Saramago's intertextual strategy, as Ben-Porat has suggested. Saramago uses original New Testament quotations whenever possible in order to find a biblical basis for his inversive writing. However, he is not always able to find a fitting quotation for his purposes. In these cases, he changes the original wording and leaves only the general tone to echo the canonical source text. This, of course, is less effective than direct quotation in making a literary impression.[37]

> En cambio la parodia realizada por Saramago, por su intención *irónica, satírica* e incluso *polémica*, es consistente en todo momento en su particular tratamiento y transformación de la tradición textual al la que se remite. [Instead, the parody made by Saramago is, for its *ironic, satirical*, and even *polemical* intention, completely consistent in its particular treatment and transformation of the textual tradition to which it refers.][38]

Saramago does use longer quotations and paraphrases of the New Testament, especially in the last part of his novel. These are not simple copies of the original, either. In the new story, the author controls the events. Every reference to the canonical Gospels, be it by a quotation, a paraphrase, or just an allusion, strictly serves his purposes. The subtext present in the novel's main section, the Devil-episodes, is quite short, but in the end of his book Saramago somewhat surprisingly includes a large number of biblical events from the canonical Gospel. It is typical of Saramago to work mainly by making a comparison with the original source text. He discusses large themes and issues, from the Bethlehem massacre to the Good Shepherd and the concept of God. In his work the constructed subtext roams far from its canonical source. It is merely a short selection, and it serves the author's own intentions. For him, it

---

nados pasajes y en la desviación del texto a través de un mínimo de transformación, que afecta sobre todo al aspecto semántico del hipertexto." Peña, *José Saramago o la intertextualidad inversa*, 24. [We see that the author's parodic intention is expressed in conducting additive or substitutive manipulations in relation to hypertext, in the inversive rendering of certain passages and in deviating from the text with minimal transformation, which especially affect the semantic aspect of the hypertext.]

37. Ben-Porat ("Prototypical Rewriting," 98) states that Saramago just follows the "rules of historical contextualization." According to my analysis Saramago does not always succeed in this. Instead, he is forced to change wordings and introduce extratextual hermeneutics in the revision. Therefore, it is proper to widen the horizon and speak of ironic or inversive rewriting which take subversive imitation into account.

38. Peña Fernandés, *José Saramago*, 24. Italics his.

is a tool to continue criticising the religion that grew from the original texts.[39]

Mailer's strategy is completely different from that of Saramago's. He seems to be extremely faithful to the canonical tradition and, therefore, some scholars assume he follows the canonical source text faithfully.[40] No estimation could be more biased, though. Mailer's use of long quotations inevitably suggests this, but it is radically misleading. Mailer's approach is inversive, he wants to criticise Jewish/Christian tradition. In this respect he seems quite close to Saramago. Furthermore, he adopts methods similar to Saramago's, and this mitigates any difference between these two authors.

Mailer's novel does differ from the others in that here the risen Jesus himself is the narrator. This solution has its advantages and disadvantages. It does bring an application of the divine-author discussion into the picture. As Bottum says, a novel's narrator "must speak as a god from outside the story." In Mailer's *Gospel* the play is twofold: we have the incarnate human character and the divine narrator, and we have the ideal first person narrator who speaks "beyond the grave of his own character." This dichotomy enables Mailer to work on the idea of incarnation. His Jesus is the Son of God from the very beginning, and there is no danger of making him a mere human being as other authors do.[41] However, the very same solution creates problems for the story. Wood criticises Mailer's *Gospel* for reading like a children's book. "Jesus lived and died, but he survived to tell the tale! No real harm came to him."[42] This is just a story. The Gospel narrative is a nice description of this divine person who visited the earth and now wishes to correct the mistakes made by his evangelists and rectify the errors that occur in the

---

39. "Saramago incorporates scriptural quotes to create a reinvigorating hybrid, one oscillating between a secular and a religious tone." Stavans, "Fisher," 676.

40. Crook ("Fictionalizing Jesus," 38) notes: "Mailer's narrative follows the gospel outline quite carefully: birth, John the Baptist, temptation, mission, healings, conflict, trip to Jerusalem, temple scene, Passover supper, arrest, execution, and resurrection, with many of the smaller events where you would expect them." No wonder Gelernter ("Gospel," 55) remarks: "his book is strikingly orthodox."

41. Bottum, "Mailer's Jesus," 53–56. "The identity and difference of character and narrator becomes a figure and a constant reminder of the mystery of the dual nature of the Savior."

42. Wood, "He Is Finished," 32. Cf. Manley, "Goth," 7: "However, there is one form of expression that no actor or author should ever attempt: the voice of Jesus Christ. Norman Mailer is not the only one to stumble badly on the road to Galilee."

religion bearing his name. In church history, such an authorial intention would be considered docetist.

Mailer often uses prototypical rewriting in the basic sense of placing a verbatim quotation into a new context. When treating Jesus' sayings about his family, Mailer transfers Jesus' eschatological words into the area of human relations. In the new story Jesus has chilling attitudes towards the other members of his family. His mother never really understands him. His brothers call him a disturbed person. All this is the background for Jesus' outburst: "Who is my mother? Who are my brothers?"[43] In Mailer's novel, Jesus calls all people his brothers because he is having a feud with his own family. This develops later into open hate:

> So I spoke not only with the Lord's anger but with my own. My family had left me divided. So I said: "A man's foes can be the members of his own household. Whoever would love father or mother more than me is not worthy of me, just as he who would find his life must first lose it. Yet he who loses his life for my sake shall find it."[44]

Jesus, the postmortem narrator for all of these passages, finds anger his main motive in this particular event. Jesus has quarreled with his family and wants to retaliate. These simple polarisations naturally aim at a discrepancy between the source text and the hypertext but, in addition to this, they also result gradually in a contradiction between the subtext and the hypertext. For instance, in the abovementioned passage Mailer fails to treat the loaded eschatological statement about losing one's life he quotes along with the sentence about one's family.[45]

Mailer no doubt writes a fifth Gospel. His criticism of the canonical evangelists is open and harsh:

> While I would not say that Mark's gospel is false, it has much exaggeration. And I would offer less for Matthew, and for Luke and John, who gave me words I never uttered and described me as

---

43. Mailer, *Gospel*, 90; a direct quotation of Mark 3:33.

44. Mailer, *Gospel*, 105; a quotation of Matt 10:37.

45. Saramago too refers to Jesus and his mother Mary's discussions and lets Mary state that she does not believe in him. This occurs in a passage where Frier has noted a slight change in the English translation. After telling his family about his stay in the wilderness and encounter with God Jesus asks them to believe him. I agree with Frier who translates Mary's answer: "I do not believe in you" ["Não creio em ti." Saramago, *O Evangelho*, 302.] Frier, "Outline," 373. The present English translation has for some reason put Joseph's reply in Mary's mouth. Saramago, *Gospel*, 229.

gentle when I was pale with rage. Their words were written many years after I was gone and only repeat what old men told them.[46]

As Mailer's risen Jesus tells his story in his own words, he assumes that he remains "closer to the truth" than his willing apostles. Apparently Mailer is serious here, and most of his critics so interpret him. This, of course, raises questions concerning biblical criticism to which Mailer here refers. He does assume that critical investigation has proven many of Jesus' words to be later additions—just as the rationalist authors of the nineteenth- and early twentieth-century Jesus-novels did. Mailer's scientific interest stops here, though. He never uses any new theories about Jesus, like Jesus as a stoic wisdom teacher or a fierce Jewish enthusiast. Instead, it is sufficient for him to quote the canonical Gospels directly and alter them only slightly in his work.[47]

Particular passages reveal the difficulties Mailer has with his source text. The most obvious ones concern the Sermon on the Mount. In Mailer's version Jesus quotes complete verses from Matthew 5. "Blessed are the poor in spirit," says the new, like the canonical, Jesus. "Blessed are those who thirst after righteousness." Mailer includes Jesus' eschatological consciousness about the new reality of salvation: "You are the light of the world." Then Mailer's Jesus proceeds to more difficult passages and has to use words "that they would not wish to hear." For Mailer this means words about perfect love that exceed common selfishness disguised as kindness.

> "If someone," I said, "shall strike you on your right cheek, turn to him the other cheek. And if a man will take your coat, give him your cloak as well." I could feel the desperation with which they sought to understand this, to believe this. "You have hear it said," I told them, "that you shall love your neighbor and hate your enemy. But I say: Love your enemy. Bless him who curses you. Do good to those that hate you. Pray for them who persecute you.

---

46. Mailer, *Gospel*, 4–5. This makes Wood later remark: "Mailer is not a novelist here; he is a very late, very bad pseudepigraphist. Though he does not mean to, he returns the novel to a piece of biblical writing." Wood, "He Is Finished," 34.

47. Allen criticises Mailer for this: "Extensive research on the historical Jesus has revealed countless fascinating alternatives to the 'facts' of his life that have accrued over two millennia. If Mailer had been willing to invest any significant time, imagination, or effort, he might have written a genuinely interesting—and genuinely provocative—novel, exploiting such possibilities." Allen, "Gospel of Norman," 77. Price ("Mailer," 9), however, assumes that Mailer has a solid point of departure in critical investigation.

Source Texts and Subtexts in Contemporary Jesus-Novels 59

Then, and only then, can you become the children of your Father. For He makes His sun to rise upon the evil and on the good, and He sends rain on the just and on the unjust. If you only love those who love you, what reward do you have? Be perfect, therefore, even as your Father in Heaven is perfect."[48]

It is easy to understand those critics who wonder why Mailer quotes all these passages. Where is the difference? If he is to create a new gospel with a brave new message, why is he copying the most elementary and unquestionably best known sermon about loving one's neighbor? Such questions are justified. As Mailer further includes the birds and the lilies, he apparently goes too far at the expense of consistency. But there is more. The trick is perhaps in the omissions. Mailer's Jesus skips the divine commandments. No hands are cut or eyes torn in this sermon (Matt 5:29–30).[49] No hell of fire is waiting for the sinners breaking God's precepts and hurting their neighbors. This is a new Sermon on the Mount, not the original. For Mailer, these elements probably belong to the material Matthew has made Jesus say. Their problem, in Mailer's story, is that they are contradictory: "some were the opposite of others."[50] Mailer the theologian provides a reduction of the apostolic deception. Hard sayings cannot belong to Jesus' ideal message, which is the message of love: "I sought to move them to love of God."[51] Nevertheless, this watered down version of the Sermon on the Mount has been crafted to be as generally acceptable as possible. Any post-Christian humanist can agree with the idea of loving one's enemies. Without swallowing the New Testament's religious enthusiasm whole, one can still accept the sermon as a most beautiful way to describe philanthropy and goodwill.[52] In this respect, Mailer's revised story does not aim too high.

Apart from the small changes, traditional material remains important for Mailer's story. Jesus meets the very same people that are

---

48. Mailer, *Gospel*, 113; on Matt 5:39–48, with just minor unimportant changes. Even the Lord's prayer is printed verbatim in the novel (114–15).

49. Jesus' words about the cutting off of a hand for the sake of moral purity has in Mailer's novel been transferred into the context of the story about the adulterous woman; see 2.1. below.

50. Mailer, *Gospel*, 111.

51. Ibid., 112.

52. It is true, of course, as Crook says, that at least in a formal sense Mailer's deliberate correction and commentary on the canonical story makes his novel meta-historical. He does raise the question of 'fiction versus history. Crook, "Fictionalizing Jesus," 37.

described in the canonical narrative. Furthermore, he is as powerful as the original character. In this sense Mailer's picture is quite conservative throughout the book. Mailer is in fact so traditional that his imitation of biblical language has inspired scholars to colorful criticism. Mailer adopts a now artificial language by writing a new gospel in old King Jamesian English and this, apparently, should strengthen an impression of loyalty to the source text.[53] Sometimes he uses short expressions such as "Often would I ponder," but the effect is deepened by Mailer's personal wisdom-sayings: "A good name is rather to be chosen than great riches";[54] or: "Fatigue of the spirit is like a twisting of the limbs; new pain enters into the old."[55]

Mailer does not appear to manipulate canonical materials as drastically as Saramago. Several direct quotations in his story actually work against his apparent purposes. His subtext is so extensive that it begins to create tension inside the story itself. The subtext's Jesus becomes greater than Mailer's Jesus. Hence, Mailer's use of original Gospel material is not completely consistent. He quotes more passages than he can use. In his story Jesus wonders at the pompous words he himself uses and often finds them distant. Mailer's Jesus is also a literary critic who keeps revising the canonical story and yet does not really succeed at it. Wood states that "Mailer's Jesus is constantly anticipating and foreshortening his story." Recurring comments reveal in advance what Mailer is about to write—and what the reader naturally already knows on the basis of the New Testament. "I was yet to learn that I would care about sinners more than for the pious," Jesus hints early on, and the reader is not certain whether he really foresaw this already or whether it is just the risen narrator who knows it in that phase. Here Mailer loses more than he gains. "It destroys what tang of discovery the narrative might have had, and makes it impossible for us to believe Jesus's self-doubt. For Jesus has

---

53. Bottum ("Mailer's Jesus," 53–56) remarks that "Mailer's semi-King Jamesian prose ought to have warned reviewers that the author is not attempting to write the sort of revisionist, anti-Christian account of the gospel" given for instance by Renan or Lawrence. Wood, "He Is Finished," 31: "The pith of reality has been spat away, and in its place is a spastic simulacrum of biblical style. Mailer uses a strange, abandoned version of King James English, as if a rival monarch had broken into the text and stolen all its gold."

54. Mailer, *Gospel*, 148. "Disastrously, Mailer borrows this style that is so inimical to the movement of a novel." Wood, "He Is Finished," 31.

55. Mailer, *Gospel*, 123. "The results run from awkward to ludicrous." Gelernter, "Gospel," 55–56.

already marked his route." Therefore, Mailer's Jesus does not act like a Messiah with a mission. "He acts like a fool who cannot keep a secret."[56]

Mailer's critics may not be completely right, though. In many passages the style could of course be better. Nevertheless, there is a possibility that Jesus' uncertainty is intentional and serves the author's purposes. The muddle created by quoting too much and using the New Testament passages too little belongs to Mailer's strategy by which he constructs his picture of Jesus. In his revision he makes good use of the subtext. Mailer's Jesus is a divided personality: "I felt as if I were a man enclosing another man within."[57] The Jesus-character in the story is a Janus-faced figure: he is simultaneously both the canonical, literary figure and his agnostic reader. Mailer makes his subtext part of a reader-response reception. It seems apparent that, in his intertextual revision, Mailer has written either his own ambivalence or a (post)modern criticism of Christianity into his narrative. Thus, Jesus' person in the story becomes the locus where biblical message and modern scepticism meet.[58] This ambivalence covers even Jesus' predictions of his own death: "'If I am killed, I will rise again after three days,' I said. But I did not know if I spoke the truth."[59]

Considering the tension between Mailer's doceticism and modern scepticism, it may well be that he is smarter than some of his critics. In his cunning scheme he exploits the divine narrator idea in order to question the whole doctrine of the incarnation. Jesus the narrator is alive only in the Christian story. If he could, he would write the whole story anew—but if he did, he would end up with a rationalist and sceptical

---

56. Wood, "He Is Finished," 32. This is accompanied by Mailer's irritating manner of expanding and explaining as if he could not trust the reader who evidently knows his or her Bible. Gordon remarks: "Mailer is like someone who wants to tell jokes but isn't sure people are getting them. He does exactly the opposite of what the New Testament does. It suggests; he armwrestles us to understanding." Gordon, "Superstar," 28.

57. Mailer, *Gospel*, 26. This particular theme will be investigated in detail in chapter 2.1.

58. I do not completely agree with Wood and Bottum, who make Mailer just a tired old author who has lost his touch. Mailer's writing should have been far more polished, and his ideas suffer from poor poetic presentation. Despite this, he does have a point, which becomes even clearer towards the end of the story. This will be discussed later in chapter 6.2. Neither is Mailer's ambivalence just a strategy to express incarnation. There is no humane version of "Jesus the pious Jew" present in this novel. Instead, the humanist face of the Janus-Jesus is that of agnosticism or even postmodern relativism.

59. Mailer, *Gospel*, 127. This sentence is derived directly from Mark 8:31, and the preceding discussion concerning the disciples' (especially Peter's) disbelief in Mailer's story is a free paraphrasing of the original passage, Mark 8:29–36.

criticism of the very story he is part of. The appearance of such a strategy in no way mitigates the problems Mailer has as a professional writer. His book leaves much room for criticism. But this view on Mailer's work recognises that he has both a plan and a point. This basic point of departure will be further confirmed by Mailer's interest in essential philosophical and historical problems concerning the problem of theodicy in particular. These issues will be addressed in later chapters.

This general interpretation also explains why the subtext is so extensive in Mailer's novel. When compared with the other Jesus-novels investigated here, Mailer's *Gospel* quotes many more passages from the New Testament. Given his hermeneutical goals, however, this does not mean that he is more faithful to the Bible than the others—quite the opposite. Using the method of focusing on two persons inside Jesus, Mailer questions the content of Jesus' original words. He is not that different from Saramago. For both of them the canonical Jesus is merely a literary character whose words and deeds can be reinterpreted and must be revised for a modern reader.

Feminist novels' use of the source text and construction of subtext differs essentially from the approaches of Saramago and Mailer. Fredriksson in particular is quite conservative in treating New Testament stories and Jesus' words, and Berlinghof adopts a similar method. Roberts' subtext remains sporadic and vague, while Rinser appears to be making many changes. The reason for Fredriksson's loyalty to the original source text must be that her main ideas for the altered picture of Jesus are derived from Gnostic gospels. Thus, many familiar events in Jesus' life are described quite in line with the biblical stories:

> But wherever they chose to rest, people assembled, appearing as if from nowhere, just standing there, the halt and the lame, the old bowed with their ailments, and the sick children with their sorrowing mothers. And as always, Jesus went from one to another, putting his hand on their heads and giving them health and new courage.[60]

Many biblical events are included in Fredriksson's story. The paralysed man is brought to Jesus; Levi the publican collecting taxes at the custom point is called to follow; the Tyrean woman's daughter is healed; the Roman officer in Capernaum finds his servant cured; the

---

60. Fredriksson, *According to Mary*, 120. This passage resembles the summaries given by the evangelists in the Bible; see Matt 9:35; Luke 8:1.

blind man is met at the gates of Jericho; and Zacchaeus is called sitting on the branches of a tree. All this creates a general picture of mere rewriting and copying without any particular prototypical rewriting. Even Lazarus is raised, although in Fredriksson's story he remains in a kind of interim state between life and death, remaining silent and avoiding people. According to Martha this was the situation after the miracle: "My brother seems still not adjusted to life."[61]

Thus, Fredriksson is seemingly faithful in reproducing several stories from Gospel material. She quotes Jesus' words strictly and refers to passages that describe his actions. All this, however, is done with a purpose. When compared with Saramago and Mailer, Fredriksson too appears to manipulate the material especially when selecting particular passages for her novel. In this respect she is closer to the former than the latter. This being said, one must admit that Fredriksson follows Gnostic gospels more than the canonical. Her picture of Jesus is not primarily constructed on a biblical subtext but on the process where Gnostic ideology goes beyond Christian tradition. Therefore, the main questions about intertextuality in constructing the subtext in feminist novels will be discussed in the next chapter.

Before moving into the area of apocryphal gospels there is one more problem to discuss. The question about the subtext is not merely a matter of investigating passages that have been included in the novel. One must also pay attention to the material that has been left out. In the narrative structure of the New Testament Gospels where synoptic material is actually rather unified, it is easy to discern thematic categories about Jesus' teaching. The canonical Jesus speaks of a new Torah (the Sermon on the Mount), conversion and salvation (the prodigal son; forgiveness of sins), fulfillment of prophesies (the ride into Jerusalem), and eschatology in its many forms (tribulations, resurrection, judgment, heaven). To what degree have these themes been introduced in the investigated novels?

It is somewhat surprising that, despite the seemingly faithful construction of the subtext and numerous quotations, these main themes do not appear in the new stories. The subtext does not present to us a Jesus who would have anything positive to say about the Torah. Instead, brief

---

61. Fredriksson, *According to Mary*, 167. Roberts keeps the raising of Lazarus and the scene where Mary washes and anoints Jesus' feet. These events reflect especially Jesus' loving attitude towards his close friends. Roberts, *Wild Girl*, 42–43.

allusions to Jewish law are usually superseded by the new Jesus' antagonism towards the Torah. This is apparently also the reason why there are no descriptions of real conversions in these novels. Even Jesus' disciples do not seem to know why they are following this teacher who, against all logical expectations, is uncertain of his own mission. Furthermore, prophecies are not fulfilled in these new stories. Authors may refer to Old Testament prophecies but usually only for the sake of irony. Great Jewish expectations turn into divine mistakes that only prove God's ambivalence toward his plans for humankind. And finally the novels' Jesus has no eschatology. Proclamation of the end of times, the nearness of God's divine judgment, and the joys of eternal life in heaven form an essential part of the canonical Jesus' message. In recent Jesus-novels these themes have not readily found their way into the subtext.

Mark's Gospel begins with Jesus' programmatic summary of his mission: "The time is fulfilled, and the kingdom of God has come near; repent, and believe in the good news" (Mark 1:15).[62] In the light of the abovementioned analysis even this essential core of Jesus' message is unknown to the Jesus-novels.[63] Its expressions no longer belong to the subtext that is constructed in the novels. Therefore, it is apparent that the subtext is usually only a collection of individual sentences that serve the authors' designs. Any impression of a wide and faithful adoption of Gospel material is false where the actual aims of the new author have been missed. This is why one must be extremely cautious when analysing the particular themes in chapters to come. Subtext, in these novels, is just a tool for the authors, not a real part of the source text taken into the novel.

Constructing a subtext thus appears to be a matter of prototypical rewriting. Authors may sometimes quote the canonical source as it is, but usually they adapt their material by, for instance, transferring it into a new context in order to change the meaning and make the canonical words serve their own purposes. Such exploitation of biblical passages aims at a recognisable rendition, as Ben-Porat calls it. For the literary

---

62. This short passage is key for Jesus' message. It proclaims the opening of a new era (*kairos*), bases salvation on God's present kingdom (*basileia*), demands repentance, and promises the gospel, the good news (*euangelion*).

63. Saramago quotes the passage at the moment when Jesus starts his public work. The content of the proclamation, however, no longer has anything to do with Jesus' message in the Bible—despite the verbatim quotation. In Saramago's story, nothing has been fulfilled and no one needs to repent. Saramago, *Gospel*, 307.

effect to function, the original text must still be recognisable. The new passage, however, often appropriates the original meaning and turns it into its opposite. Authors sometimes also alter the original wording in order to produce an ironic reinterpretation of the canonical passage. In the case of larger biblical themes the whole train of thought can be reversed. Here it is no longer easy to discern the original source text, so it must be detected through the intentionally opposing terminology used in the passage.

3. GNOSTIC WRITINGS

Ever since the unearthing of the Nag Hammadi manuscripts, Gnosticism has inspired many philosophers of religion as well as fiction writers. The English translation of the collection was published in 1977. Gnosticism as a religious phenomenon has always been well known since church fathers like Irenaeus and Tertullian wrote extensively against it. The texts themselves, however, had mostly vanished. Biblical scholarship has grappled with many apocryphal gospels before this, but the originality of the new texts is in the new mystical worldview they represent. Several Nag Hammadi gospels, such as the *Gospel of Philip* and the *Gospel of Mary*, speak of secret heavenly wisdom and give Mary Magdalene a special role in the revelation of a new message that canonical Scripture seems to be completely unaware of.[64]

To be precise, not all Nag Hammadi texts are now considered Gnostic. The collection of manuscripts found in Egypt is heterogeneous. Some writings reflect the ideas of some unorthodox Christian sects, some teach Gnostic cosmology, and some belong to mysticism in general and are not easy to classify. There is one influential reading, though, that has directed the interpretation of Nag Hammadi texts in the area of literature. Elaine Pagels published her feminist interpretation *The Gnostic Gospels* in 1979, and many authors appear to follow her guidelines. According to Pagels, practically all Nag Hammadi texts represent Gnostic ideas and are more or less related to Valentinian Gnostic religion. Pagels's Gnosticism gives women a central role in the Christian community and opposes male interest in orthodox doctrines. This is also how Jesus-novels treat the Gnostic gospels. Since these writings are

---

64. The collection *The Nag Hammadi Library* was edited by James M. Robinson. The manuscripts are dated mainly to the fourth and fifth centuries but also probably contain earlier traditions. Church fathers wrote against Gnosticism around 200 CE.

read or exploited as one block, it is useless to bring any stricter historical or theological analysis in the investigation of their intertextual relation. For the investigated Jesus-novels, *The Nag Hammadi Library* is a text that lives its own life in history.[65]

Some of the investigated novels refer openly to Gnostic gospels. In her introduction, Fredriksson describes the process that led to the writing of her novel and states that one particular question drove her from the beginning: "How did Jesus, whose foremost message is forgiveness and mercy, become the judgmental god?" After reading books on different religions she finally happened to find Gnostic writings. "One day I was looking for something in the Nag Hammadi Library and happened to come upon the fragment that remains of the gospel of Mary Magdalene." Mary's rejection of doctrines answered the burning question: "And it struck me: here is perhaps someone with ears to listen, eyes to see, and a mind to understand. The disciple whom Jesus loved the most."[66] The figure of Fredriksson's Mary is influenced by Nag Hammadi texts, even though the exact relation between her words in the story and the original writings is far from clear.

In *The Da Vinci Code*, Gnostic gospels form the basis of the whole train of thought of the book. The eccentric scholar Teabing is convinced that there were numerous gospels in ancient times and that the church rejected those that had preserved the most trustworthy teaching of Jesus. Manuscripts lie in his bookshelf, and he has devoted his life to their study. The story of the novel, then, is composed on the play between an implied gospel revision and a search for a Gnostic sect practising the religion of "the sacred feminine" as it is called in some passages.[67] All these novels share the basic argument: the new story is based on original and genuine gospels that the established church has rejected.[68]

But how should one define Gnosticism? What is the relation between the Gnostic source text, the subtext, and the narrative of the new Jesus-novel? There are certain features that one can use in an intertextual

---

65. See the Introduction in Pagels, *Gnostic Gospels*, xvii–xix.

66. See the introductory "Why Mary Magdalene?" in the beginning of *According to Mary*.

67. Brown, *Da Vinci Code*, 349.

68. According to D. Brown, Hilda Doolittle in her *Trilogy* constructs a Gnostic version of Christianity. New teaching is dependent on Mary Magdalene's figure there, too. Brown, "Modern Gnosticism," 356. Gnostic Christianity is also central to Margaret Atwood's *Alias Grace*, which is not a new gospel but a detective story. See Miller, "Grace," 182–83.

analysis. Based on the Nag Hammadi manuscripts (as one collection), one can say that Gnostic spirituality builds on a strict dualism between matter and spirit. This view then influences the conceptions of God and different divine powers. Standard Gnostic belief, if one may use such a definition, states that the material world has been created by an evil Old Testament God. Because of this creation, human souls live imprisoned on earth without saving knowledge (gnosis) about the divinity. Only the teachers of Gnostic secret wisdom can release innocent souls from this bondage. For instance, the *Hypostasis of the Archons* ("Reality of the Rulers") is a reinterpretation of Genesis 1–6 and explains the birth of the material world. One of the heavenly beings passes through the veil of heaven and creates "Matter." The being itself becomes "an arrogant beast resembling a lion." This divinity defines his own status according to Old Testament Mosaic commandments: "It is I who am God, and there is none other apart from me."[69]

Since salvation means deliverance from the despotic power of the evil God, the real nature of soul's heavenly origin must be taught to human beings:

> You, together with your offspring, are from the Primeval Father; from Above, out of the imperishable Light, their souls are come. Thus the Authorities cannot approach them because of the Spirit of Truth present with them; and all who have become acquainted with this Way exist deathless in the midst of dying Mankind.[70]

Gnostic soteriology openly opposes the biblical doctrine with its proclamation of the bondage of sin and God's unconditional forgiveness. In Gnostic thinking, all sin has been produced by the Creator of Matter. Salvation is gained through true knowledge, and it can be taught. Teachers of the new community transmit the secret wisdom to all who become initiated into the mysteries of gnosis. Moreover, salvation does not merely mean sanctification but divinisation. Christ for the Gnostics is not a person but a state of being, instead. Human beings can become Christ through gnosis.[71]

Gnostic cosmology also influences Christology in these writings, naturally, since Jesus as a human being cannot be divine in a theologi-

---

69. *Hypostasis of the Archons* 94.10–21.
70. Ibid., 96.19–27.
71. *Gospel of Philip* 61.30–31.

cal sense. Instead, he is united with a heavenly spirit called Christ, and because this heavenly spirit cannot die Christ departs from the person of Jesus before the crucifixion. This kind of Christology has not had much influence on the Jesus-novels, though. The question about anthropology is much more interesting. According to Gnostic thought the human body as "flesh" is in opposition to the soul. Salvation is a mental matter and merely a spiritual reality. The *Gospel of Philip* states: "Fear not the flesh nor love it. If you fear it, it will gain mastery over you. If you love it, it will swallow and paralyze you" (66:4–6). This is something Jesus-novels seldom agree with. Instead, Mary Magdalene's new Gnostic Christianity focuses on bodily existence and sexuality. Furthermore, when Brown lets Teabing remark in *The Da Vinci Code* that the rejected secret gospels describe "Christ's human traits," he is inventing a new story. Gnostic gospels are not at all interested in Jesus' earthly life or his human nature. Their mission is solely to proclaim the gnosis that makes spiritual human beings into Christlike beings.[72]

Jesus-novels quote and reinterpret most often from the text that tells the story of Mary Magdalene, the *Gospel of Mary*.[73] In this writing male apostles discuss with Mary about the message the risen Lord gave her after his resurrection. There are certain features that are often used in Jesus-novels in one form or another. The most important one turns out to be the rejection of doctrines. Fredriksson describes this in a crucial passage that is repeated several times in her story:

> Be of good cheer, the Son of Man is within you. Follow him, he who seeks him will find him. Write no laws of this that I have revealed to you. Write no laws as the scribes do.[74]

Fredriksson's passage refers to the first part of the *Gospel of Mary*:

> Peace be with you. Receive my peace to yourselves beware that no one lead you astray, saying, "Lo here!" or "Lo there!" For the Son of man is within you. Follow after him! Those who seek him will find him. Go then and preach the gospel of the kingdom.

---

72. Brown, *Da Vinci Code*, 317.

73. For the dating and structure of the *Gospel of Mary* (the Nag Hammadi manuscript BG 8502, 1) see MacRae and Wilson in *Nag Hammadi Library*, 471. It is actually a short compilation of two different fragments of eight columns. The middle part of the text is missing.

74. Fredriksson, *According to Mary*, 5.

> Do not lay down any rules beyond what I appointed for you, and do not give a law like the lawgiver lest you be constrained by it.[75]

The novel's subtext is not based on direct quotation. Instead, in her adaptation Fredriksson makes several changes in the Gnostic text. In the *Gospel of Mary* the quoted ideas appear in the discussion between Peter and Jesus, not Mary and Jesus. In contrast to what one would expect in such a polarisation, Peter does not oppose these words but, instead, witnesses Jesus saying them. This feature has an important role in the discourse of the Gnostic writing itself. In the first fragment, Mary appears merely as a comforting figure and does not take part in disagreements. Only at the end of the *Gospel of Mary* is Peter persuaded to accept Mary's view. There Levi supports Mary's message by saying: "Rather let us be ashamed and put on the perfect man, and separate as he commanded us and preach the gospel, not laying down any other rule or other law beyond what the Savior said."[76]

Furthermore, according to the *Gospel of Mary*, Jesus did appoint some rules for his followers. Only false "other rules" are prohibited here. It was important for the Gnostics to argue that the sect was really following Jesus' own rules. If Mary Magdalene was of use when presenting evidence for several uncanonical or unorthodox views, her name and role could be exploited. In Fredriksson's adaptation, however, feminist Gnosticism is a religion that opposes laws and doctrines in principle. She does provide a subtext that consists of certain clauses taken from the *Gospel of Mary*. Nevertheless, she also creates a hypertext where her appropriation deliberately changes the original text's meaning.

Furthermore, Fredriksson quotes another Gnostic discussion concerning, as she states, the relation between body and soul. The discussion explores what "man had to overcome while his soul was still in his body." Mary presents it in the form of a conversation between body and soul.

> The body says, "I did not see you." And the soul replies, "I saw you. But you neither saw nor recognized me." I asked him, "What are the sins of the world?" And he answered me, "There is no sin in the world. You create it yourself when you falsify reality."[77]

---

75. *Gospel of Mary* 8.14—9.4.

76. Ibid., 18.15–20. It is somewhat surprising that Fredriksson uses the latter part of the *Gospel of Mary* so little since the second fragment is the text where Mary speaks the most.

77. Fredriksson, *According to Mary*, 5.

An intentional adaptation and exploitation of the source text continues also here. In the *Gospel of Mary*, the discussion about the nature of sin belongs originally to the conversation between Peter and Jesus (column 7). In Fredriksson's novel it has been transferred into the context of a passage that, in the *Gospel of Mary*, describes another conversation between "desire" and "soul" (column 15).

> And desire said, "I did not see you descending, but now I see you ascending. Why do you lie, since you belong to me?" The soul answered and said, "I saw you. You did not see me nor recognize me. I served you as a garment, and you did not know me." When it had said this, it went away rejoicing greatly. [78]

In Gnostic theology, this mystical conversation between desire and soul belongs to the context of a (spiritual) heavenly ascension journey. Jesus' secret message concerns knowledge about the nature of such an itinerary. When the soul is ascending towards the heavenly realms it has to fight lower heavenly powers. Desire is one of these powers. According to the Gnostic text, desire had not previously recognised the soul, and so it is now astonished at the soul's ascension. Mary's teaching describes thus how the pupil of true gnosis will enter triumphantly into the light of the highest divinity.

Fredriksson's subtext inside her novel is completely different. It is a compilation of separate Gnostic clauses where desire has been changed into a concept of body. Therefore, in the intertextual reinterpretation we encounter a complete reversal of the original ideas. Gnostic dualism and flesh-hating spirituality is changed into praise of corporality. In Fredriksson's text the sin of ignorance means simply an alienation of soul from the body. Therefore, Jesus' new gnosis can restore this unity. Thus corporality, "flesh," and sexuality, which is part of it, have nothing to do with sin in Fredrikssons new reading. This is also what Roberts makes Jesus say about the body-soul relationship: "The body is the mirror of the soul." Such a reinterpretation is really an inversion of the original idea since in Gnostic thinking the flesh belongs to the realm of the evil creator God. For a Gnostic, true gnosis can never have anything to do with corporality.[79]

---

78. *Gospel of Mary* 15.1–11.
79. See Roberts, *Wild Girl*, 73.

Fredriksson is, thus, quite selective in her use of the *Gospel of Mary*. By composing a strongly reformed subtext she creates a feeling that original Gnostic writings would support the views of her Mary Magdalene. Mary's and later in the novel also Jesus' religious ideology is practically an inversion of Gnostic religion, though. Gnostic dualism is ignored and spiritual soteriology is turned into praise for corporeality and sexuality. All this emphasises Mary's extraordinary role in early Christianity and makes her relation to Jesus important. After all, it is Mary who taught Jesus bodily love and thus helped him to overcome the alienation between body and soul: "You loved and perhaps felt gratitude for teaching you bodily love, so increasing your knowledge of the condition of humankind."[80] One of the few features common to The *Nag Hammadi Library* and *According to Mary* is the concept of sin. For the latter, sin is a misunderstanding of life resulting from a false concept of God. This is parallel to the idea that sin belongs to the creation made by the Old Testament God.

Gnostic gospels appear to be important for the investigated authors and especially for feminist novels. There is something in Gnostic spirituality that suits the authors' designs well. In feminist novels Mary Magdalene's special role is naturally exploited to its full extent but also issues of religious content seem to be important. The exploitation and adaptation of Gnostic writings appear to be influenced by Pagels's monograph and feminist interpretation of Gnosticism, but the detailed assessment of these applications must be left to later chapters. What is important to note already here is that authors seldom use or quote Gnostic gospels as they are. Their new narrative is based on adaptation and appropriation. Intertextual revision is determinate also in the passages dealing with these texts.

4. APOCRYPHAL GOSPELS

Apocryphal gospels as such are usually not quoted verbatim in the investigated novels. Nevertheless, they seem to have affected the writing of some authors. Usually the apocryphal writings want to provide additional materials for instance about Jesus' childhood or the extraordinary virgin birth by describing Mary's condition. One of the best-known

---

80. Fredriksson, *According to Mary*, 6.

examples of these amendments is the story about the child Jesus and the birds. At the age of five Jesus is playing with clay on the Sabbath.

> When this boy Jesus was five years old he was playing at the ford of a brook, and he gathered together into pools the water that flowed by, and made it at once clean, and commanded it by his word alone. He made soft clay and fashioned from it twelve sparrows. And it was the sabbath when he did this. . . .
> But Jesus clapped his hands and cried to the sparrows: "Off with you!" And the sparrows took flight and went away chirping.[81]

After Jesus had made the sparrows a conservative Jew criticised Joseph for not preventing his son from working on the sabbath. Jesus answers with a miracle. This event is not directly referred to in these novels but the intention bears similar features. Authors present new information that is not known on the basis of the canonical Bible.[82]

One can find some direct links between ancient apocryphal gospels and the investigated Jesus-novels. Francisco Peña Fernandés has suggested that Saramago's picture of the Devil is dependent on apocryphal prototypes. In his description of Satan, Saramago apparently starts with Job 1:6, a passage where Satan enters the heavenly court with other heavenly beings. The original term denoting "the sons of God" provides a literary point of departure for the idea that there might be some kind of identity between God and Satan.[83] This picture, however, is then completed with an apocryphal conviction that the Devil's/Azazel's "portion" is on earth. According to the *Apocalypse of Abraham* this explains how the Devil is the source of all evil in this world: "Through you the all-evil spirit (is) a liar, and through you (are) wrath and trials on the generations of men who live impiously."[84]

Based on these kinds of passages Peña Fernández suggests that Saramago builds on apocryphal tradition. This is apparently true as

---

81. *Infancy Gospel of Thomas* 2.1. See Hennecke, *New Testament Apocrypha*, 1:392–93.

82. Saramago hints at an apocryphal tradition by using this story in his Jesus-novel, in a new context, though. Saramago, *Gospel*, 304–5.

83. The original term "sons of Elohim" in Old Testament texts often refers to angels but the number of different heavenly beings in the texts is large and the term may denote also other kinds of beings. Peña Fernández, *José Saramago*, 52. Bloom speaks about the "unfallen Satan of the book of Job" who also in Saramago's novel is able to go to and fro between heaven and earth. Bloom, "One with the Beard," 158.

84. *Apocalypse of Abraham* 13:7–9.

far as a general literary intention can be assessed. In a general sense Saramago's *Gospel* resembles apocryphal writings such as the *Life of Adam and Eve*, which presents free renderings of Old Testament stories.[85] In more particular issues Saramago has exploited apocryphal writings describing the life of Joseph or other members of Jesus' family.

> Over the next few years there were not many changes in the family apart from the arrival of more children, including two daughters, while their parents lost the last traces of youth. In the case of Mary this was not surprising, for we know how childbearing, and she had borne so many children, gradually saps any freshness and beauty a woman may possess and causes her face and body to age and wither, suffice it to say that after James came Lisa, after Lisa came Joseph, after Joseph came Judas, after Judas came Simon, then Lydia, then Justus, then Samuel, and if any more came after them they perished without trace.[86]

Such information is mainly derived from apocryphal material that is well known in Catholic tradition. Saramago spared nothing in searching for the alleged names of Jesus' sisters and brothers. His designs extend beyond family matters, but he uses this material in order to create a new argument about biblical history.[87]

For Peña Fernández, this literary strategy is in accord with the Jewish hermeneutical method of *derash*. The word denotes "inquiry" and expresses the seeking of new meanings through investigating similar occurrences. The method includes metaphorical meanings, which is useful in Old Testament adaptation:

> La intención, como hemos venido insistiendo, es marcadamente midrásica, de ampliación haggádica; al contrar la misma historia a través de un relato completamente nuevo que se remite constantemente a los textos que utiliza como referencia, los interpreta. [The intention, as we have been insisting, is markedly

---

85. Peña Fernandés, *José Saramago*, 31.

86. Saramago, *Gospel*, 93. Peña Fernandés refers especially to the *Gospel of Joseph* and the *Testament of Joseph*. For details, see Peña Fernandés, *José Saramago*, 42

87. "Sin embargo, el elemento en el que más se aproxima la literatura de Saramago a la literatura apócrifa antigua, cuyo análisis ocupará la mayor parte de este libro, es la utilización de material bíblico con la intención de crear un relato con un argumento *nuevo* y diferente." [However, the element that in Saramago's literature is closest to ancient apocryphal literature, whose analysis will also cover the most part of this monograph, is the use of biblical material with the intention of creating a story with a *new* and different argument.] Peña Fernandés, *José Saramago*, 16.

midrashic, with haggadic expansion; to contradict the very same history through a completely new story which constantly refers to the texts it uses as source, in order to interpret them.]⁸⁸

Saramago's desire in writing another apocryphal gospel is to provide new information about ancient history. His method serves his overall aim to expose God's devious plan to gain complete control over humanity.⁸⁹ In a general sense, Peña Fernandés is right when he says that the basic intention in Saramago's novel is similar to that of ancient apocryphal gospels. They both wish to create a completely new story by exploiting biblical material through adding, creating, amending, and revising the canonical tradition. In ancient texts the focus has often been on events of which the Bible remains silent. In this respect the recent Jesus-novels, including authors from Roberts to Mailer, follow their predecessors only partly. We do find extraordinary discussions between Jesus and the Devil in the desert and love scenes between Jesus and Mary Magdalene, but in addition to this, the prototypical rewriting of the Gospels aims at a deliberate revision of the extant stories of the New Testament.

Tunström's *Letter from the Wilderness* has also been intentionally constructed as an apocryphal gospel. It treats a period in Jesus' life of which the canonical text remains silent. Furthermore, Tunström wishes to shed light on certain aspects in Jesus' program that are left almost untouched in the Bible. What does Jesus think about liberation movements? How would he have expanded his criticism against institutional violence? What about handicapped people who are not healed? Tunström does not merely give a Scandinavian socialist rereading the New Testament. He is also a pseudepigraphist with a mission.⁹⁰

Apocryphal intention in these novels is not just a matter of using particular quotations or following ideas taken from apocryphal gospels. Instead, it can be held as a strategy applied now in a new context. We encounter apocryphal novels that wish to propose an altered picture of Jesus by presenting unknown material to the readers. Furthermore, di-

---

88. Ibid., 27.

89. Ibid., 29 "El *evangelio* de Saramago parece querer volver a conformar un *todo* con las Escrituras revisando su sentido por entero a través de la vida y obra de Jesús." [Saramago's *Gospel* probably wants to return and form a whole with the Scriptures revising entirely its meaning about the life and works of Jesus.]

90. Tunström, *Ökenbrevet*, 22, 76, 135–36.

rect links to ancient apocryphal gospels provide Jesus-novels with credibility and locate them in a millennial tradition.

5. QUMRAN SCROLLS

Qumran scrolls can no doubt be included as a source text that has been used in the novels investigated here but, in practice, these writings hardly ever appear as a subtext. The Dead Sea community interests many authors, and it is mentioned in many novels. Particular texts, however, are not quoted. This is easy to understand. The Qumran community represents conservative orthodox Judaism, whose religious beliefs are quite distant from the novels' aims. In spite of this, authors are fascinated by this sect that lived outside mainstream Judaism and opposed Jerusalem's priestly religion. This idea is available also to the investigated authors who contest the community's religious identity.

The community itself appears in many novels, at least briefly. Tunström brings Jesus into the monastery and makes him a novice. Mailer too suggests that Jesus wants to join the community but his journey is directed elsewhere. Tunström's Jesus never really joins the community, though. In his novel there is no reference to the strict conditions to be found in the Dead Sea Scrolls themselves.

> This is the rule for the men of the Community who freely volunteer to convert from all evil and to keep themselves steadfast in all he prescribes in compliance with his will. They should keep apart from men of sin in order to constitute a Community in law and possessions, and acquiesce to the authority of the sons of Zadok, the priests who safeguard the covenant and to the authority of the multitude of the men of the Community, those who persevere steadfastly in the covenant.[91]

The Qumran sect was led by priests, the sons of Zadok, named after the legendary first high priest of David's temple in Jerusalem. Therefore, the priestly holiness code was followed in the community. Every precept reflecting holiness in everyday life, be it following purity regulations or wearing a religious habit, was to be put into practice. Everyone requesting to be a member had to swear an oath ensuring such loyalty.

---

91. These are the conditions given for novices in the *Rule of the Community*, 1QS V, 1–3.

> He shall swear with a binding oath to revert to the Law of Moses with all that it decrees, with whole heart and whole soul, in compliance with all that has been revealed concerning it to the sons of Zadok, the priests who keep the covenant. . . .[92]

Tunström does not derive his presentation of the Qumran community particularly from the Dead Sea Scrolls. He is not building a contradiction between the historical sect and the new story. In his story there are several details that make this clear. Tunström's Jesus enters a community that is open and even quite liberal. People living at this Qumran never follow the original Qumran rules. The monks working as the kitchen staff are like ordinary Jews who do not obey priestly precepts, and Jesus' best friend is a political Zealot. Therefore, Tunström has not attempted to be historically accurate by using the Qumran community in his story. The Qumran community presented in the community rules and theological commentaries of the Dead Sea Scrolls is a conservative hierarchic society. Men in the community follow regulations and a strict daily schedule. It is a quiet monastery where speaking is allowed only in particular places—and sanctions for any violation are extreme. It is a place for learning and copying manuscripts. In a Mosaic community the interpretation of the Torah is a primary task. In Jesus-novels, we find none of these features.[93]

Tunström's description of Qumran appears to be a kind of abstraction of different Jewish sects. The monastery has its apocalyptical features but it is simultaneously a scholarly Torah institute where all kinds of views are allowed. Tunström does not depict it as a community practicing a true orthodox form of Judaism. Furthermore, several Zealots live in the community. They combat Romans in the area and Jesus, too, is drawn into this fight. All this is intertextual reading where the original beliefs of the sect have been changed.

An analysis of the novel's Jesus-character confirms this intertextual analysis. His theology and religious ponderings bear no resemblance to Qumranic views. Tunström's Jesus is not interested in purity regulations

---

92. 1QS V, 8–9. Josephus remarks that the Essenes must "swear tremendous oaths" in their community in order to practise piety towards God. This leads to an ascetic life and complete withdrawal from Jewish society and family life. See Josephus, *War* 2.137–42.

93. For Qumran theology and practices see VanderKam, *Dead Sea Scrolls*, 111–17; and the texts themselves: 1QS V,1–13; 1QS VI,24—VII,25. Cf. Tunström, *Ökenbrevet*, 96-97.

or proper service in the Jerusalem temple. Neither does he investigate the Old Testament or speculate on ancient prophecies. Tunström's Jesus does oppose the Essene sect that lives at Qumran, but he does not directly oppose the sect that one meets in the Dead Sea Scrolls. And the difference between the fictional Jesus and the fictional sect is nothing like the difference between canonical Jesus, the friend of sinners, and the Dead Sea Scrolls Qumran sect that despises the children of darkness.[94]

Mailer, in his *According to the Son*, makes Jesus' whole family Essenes. "Being Essenes we were, of all Jews, strictest in our worship of the one God and were full of scorn for Roman religions with their belief in many deities."[95] This depiction as such is also historically correct, and Essenes being the movement that is believed to have supported the Qumran community would make Jesus' upbringing conservative as well. This, however, is not a major theme in Mailer's novel. His Jesus has not learnt Essene doctrines at home and apparently dismisses his father's teaching, at least according to what the author makes Jesus say and do in the novel. So it is clear that even though Mailer has mentioned the Essenes in his presentation, he has not used this detail in his story.

This kind of treatment of conservative Judaism in these books is evidently intentional. The intertextual reading in Tunström's novel or in Mailer's book aims apparently at a revision of conservative Judaism. They are not simply altering Judaism into any form they themselves could accept—as they usually do with Jesus. Instead, they describe the Qumran community as a group that needs to be opposed. The re-envisioned community, especially for Tunström, is the place Jesus leaves after becoming frustrated with its precepts. Therefore, changing the historical picture of Qumran sect and the content of the Dead Sea Scrolls has no particular purpose. It seems that, certainly for Tunström and probably also for Mailer, the Qumran community merely serves as a symbol for the whole

---

94. Differences between Qumranian beliefs and Jesus or the canonical Gospels have been investigated in several books. See especially the collection *Jesus and the Dead Sea Scrolls* and the opening essay by James Charlesworth called "The Dead Sea Scrolls and the Historical Jesus."

95. Mailer, *Gospel*, 6. Stead makes Jesus study at Qumran and describes the situation quite correctly. Jesus lives in a cave, eats little and works long hours both in the garden and in the scriptorium. Stead, *My Name Was Judas*, 90–91. The problem with this story is similar to the difficulties one encounters in Mailer's story: How can the novel's Jesus come out of the loyal novitiate of an orthodox Jewish sect?

of conservative Judaism. There is no notable intertextual intention in the adaptation of the Qumran material in his novel.

Why, then, take Qumran as an example of orthodox Judaism? The reason for this may simply be that the findings at Qumran in 1948 were so exciting that any writer interested in ancient history would want to treat the Dead Sea Scrolls. This is also an easy way to give some extraordinary color to the narrative. Retreating from this hectic world like the Qumran community is a romantic idea as such, and it is inspiring to ask whether Jesus himself could have made such a move. Moreover, any novel can do with some secrecy, conspiracy, and even threat of violence. As a closed monastery, Qumran makes an intriguing setting for several interesting ideas in fiction. My assessment, however, is that the potentiality of these scrolls has not been exploited as it could have.

Some authors have Jesus visit the Qumran community but the sect has no particular impact on his ideas. This raises a provocative question: Could the historical Jesus have visited the monastery? Is there any parallel between the novels and the historical study of the Bible? Not really. Qumran piety, as can easily be seen in the extant community rules, was based on orthodox Judaism proclaiming soteriological dualism. In Qumran there were no friends of sinners, quite the opposite. Children of darkness were condemned as vehemently as possible in the Mosaic tradition. There is one theory in biblical scholarship, however, which claims that both Jesus and his brother James, the alleged Teacher of Righteousness of the Qumran texts and the later leader of the Jerusalem community, would actually have been the leading figures of the Dead Sea Essenes.[96] This explanation has remained an anomaly in scholarship, though.

Feminist novels are not usually interested in the Dead Sea Scrolls, and this, too, is easy to understand. As a male-dominated enclave with certain texts that disparage women, Qumran is a fortress of Jewish patriarchy.[97] The Qumran writings contain few or no details that could be exploited or changed into a new form acceptable to feminist authors. Gnostic writings with their occasional clauses about Mary Magdalene serve the purposes of such revisions better.

---

96. See Eisenmann, *Maccabees, Zadokites, Christians*.

97. According to Josephus, the Essenes, who are assumed to have inhabited Qumran, believed that no woman could be completely faithful to her husband. Josephus, *War* 2.120–21.

In Longfellow's The *Secret Magdalene*, Mary/Mariamne and her sister Salome are forced to leave home already at the age of ten. They are led to a Qumran monastery called Damascus in the book (apparently named after a Dead Sea Scroll with a similar name, the Damascus Document). There they spend time disguised as boys and their secret is safe because they are held to be young prophets with special gifts. This Dead Sea monastery is not really a place for orthodox conservatism following the precepts of the Torah, but an eschatological community expecting the holy war in the end of days. To be precise, the sect bears no resemblance to the original Qumran community at all. Instead, it is a centre for trade and medical help and even a kind of inn or tavern where people can come and stay. Since women can visit this place it is not a dark cave of patriarchy. In Longfellow's novel Qumran is merely a place that Mary/Mariamne can visit in order to grow into a young woman who will later become "Yehoshua's" best friend, still under a disguise and with the alias of John the Less.[98]

The Dead Sea Scrolls serve more as a source text than a subtext in the adaptation and intertextual rewriting of the investigated Jesus-novels. Authors use some ideas taken from the writings but they do not exploit Qumran customs or beliefs in detail. The Qumran of the novels is quite different from the community of the scrolls. I would not say, however, that these authors deliberately aim at an inversive rewriting of the Qumran texts. Instead, they ignore both historical accuracy and any real relation between the source text and their new narrative. For all these reasons, the community of Qumran has no prominent role in these novels, at least apart from Tunström's *Ökenbrevet*. Furthermore, feminist novels can make better use of Gnostic gospels and, therefore, this patriarchal sect is not given any importance in the story.

---

98. Longfellow, *Secret Magdalene*, 38–41.

2

Turning God-Incarnate into a Faustian Frivol

THE MAIN MESSAGE OF fictional gospels and Jesus-novels towards the end of the twentieth century is that Jesus should not be seen as the canonical Gospels see him. For Nietzsche, the biblical Jesus was but a literary invention. The life of Jesus needed to be written anew. The novels investigated here make an enthusiastic effort to do this. Jesus, in their descriptions, is not much of a hero. According to the intertextual adaptations of these new narratives, Jesus is an insecure adolescent or a wandering preacher without any clear message. He is more associated with the Devil than with God. Furthermore, his conceptions of a good life are derived from common sense rather than from the Scriptures in general or the Mosaic Torah. One of the most surprising features is that Jesus himself usually becomes only a co-star in this own story. He often plays a subordinate role while Mary Magdalene, Judas, or even the Devil stands in the limelight. The Nazarene of the novels, playing his minor part, is often cast as the opposite of a Saviour, a weak figure who creates problems instead of providing solutions.

1. DISCARDING JESUS' MESSIANIC IDENTITY

In the age of reason Jesus was still considered a great humanist or even a "comrade Jesus," as Ziolkowski has shown in his treatment of earlier Jesus-novels. Adaptation focused on some positive element in the canonical Jesus-story, and it served as a connecting link between the New Testament and its later rewritings. In recent novels this attitude has vanished. There may be some slight features left of Jesus' ethical thinking, for instance, or of his social responsibility but primarily, in these writings, the Nazarene has an uncertain identity and is more a restless nomad than a dedicated Messiah.[1]

Considered from a purely literary point of view one could assume that the canonical story already in itself calls for an inversion of the high Christology of the Christian narrative. If there is an incarnation, one is entitled to ask how human can the Son of God be if the ultimate limits of carnal existence are really tested. This is how Partridge starts his analysis on Mailer, who keeps emphasising Jesus' humanity:

> He offers a Jesus who *seems to be* exactly what orthodox Christian theology demands in its Christological doctrine of hypostatic union: a Jesus who is "fully man and fully God."[2]

Jesus-novels struggle with these two aspects. Practically all authors maintain the idea of Jesus' divinity, at least in the sense of magical realism where supernatural features are integral parts of the narrative and the work's rhetorical purpose. This, however, does not mean that these novels really describe the "hypostatic union" as such. Instead, this intention is rather a part of their literary strategy, and the outcome of the story is reductionist. Authors appear to be mostly interested in Jesus' human features, which is understandable since canonical tradition has already focused on the divine story.

Furthermore, the treatment of this christological question is affected by the Nietzschean conviction about the biblical figure being a literary invention. If Jesus is a product of a "Jewish" mind, the features of divinity and Messianism are mere theological themes also. It is easy to propose another invention in their stead.[3] In an intertextual adaptation that aims at reformulation or even inversion, there usually can be found a motivation that is dependent on ideological as well as religious convictions.

---

1. See Ziolkowski, *Fictional Transfigurations*, 55–56, 182–83.

2. Partridge, "Gospel," 66.

3. The background for this view is in nineteenth-century Germany with its rationalistic biblical criticism. It was originally based on a dichotomy between the alleged historical Jesus and the "Christ of faith" of the early church. Many monographs from that period based their titles on this dichotomy, the most famous one being Martin Kähler. See Kümmel, *Investigation*, 222–23. It is proper to note that this is one of the features already investigated by Ziolkowski. Novels building on some kind of historical reconstruction belong to the rationalistic tradition. Ziolkowski, *Fictional Transfigurations*, 142–43.

The intertextual relation between the canonical Jesus and the new figures in the novels is complex because tension in recent Jesus-novels is immense. Simultaneously, however, the subtext present in them supports the new picture that is constructed in the texts. Biblical quotations and Jesus' words that have been taken from their original context and placed in the new narrative support the author's altered view of the Nazarene. Thus, the novels appear as real intertexts for the New Testament, not just as new stories that merely borrow some ideas from the Bible. In addition to this, it is not merely Jesus' human nature that is experimented with in these novels. The opposition they provide is primarily religious or even theological, although readers seldom pay attention to these aspects. In the novels, Jesus often becomes a follower of the Devil. Hence one needs to assess why particular aspects of the Gospel narrative are subjected to such radical reinterpretation.

There are traits of inversive hermeneutics already in Nietzsche's treatment of the biblical Jesus. Nietzsche has an ambivalent relation both to the canonical and the historical Jesus-figure. His main objection is that the biblical Jesus has adopted every horrible Jewish conviction about a heavenly God who as a lawgiver suppresses independent and proud human beings. Because Judaism is the religion of slave morality, Jesus must be opposed simply because he is a Jew among other Jews. In spite of this, however, Nietzsche sometimes respects Jesus, or at least the new dismantled Jesus-figure who is freed from apostolic mythicisation. Even in a writing as enthusiastic as *The Anti-Christ*, the revised Jesus is called the only proper Christian in this world, after whom Christianity suffocates in its dogmatism.[4]

In recent Jesus-novels, the historical reconstruction of Jesus' life is usually constructed in Nietzschean terms. Jesus is not an embodiment of divine Wisdom who would astonish even his Jewish teachers with his devotedness to Jewish faith. Neither is he described as the firstborn of a large Jewish family living in a conservative Galilean village. In many of these novels, Jesus is living a hard and cold life without proper parents and without compassion from his relatives. Making Jesus a deprived child in a dysfunctional family aims at appropriating God-incarnate as one who no longer resembles the familiar iconic baby on the arms of the Madonna. The novels' Jesus is rather a representative of the rejected.

---

4. Nietzsche, *Gay Science*, § 137; *Anti-Christ*, § 39.

Tunström in his *The Letter from the Wilderness* focuses on Jesus' difficult relationship to his parents. In several passages the Jesus of the narrative grieves for the lack of warmth he has experienced at home. This focuses most clearly on his relation to his mother Mary. In the novel this can be seen in constant remarks like, "Mary was tired as usual and probably wanted to be rid of me." Mary shows neither love nor affection to her children.[5] Furthermore, Jesus' relation to Joseph remains distant, and he appears to be almost a fatherless child, even though this point is not stressed in the novel. It probably takes its cue from the canonical story where Joseph has a minor role.

When Jesus is leaving home and starting his journey to the monastery of Qumran, he wishes that Mary would express some kind of compassion however slight. It never happens even at the moment of departure, and Mary stays coldly distant. Later Jesus keeps repeating the situation in his mind and imagines a warmhearted and loving mother whom he never has had.[6] The problematic relationship is emphasised in the story since the family of John the Baptist, Jesus' cousin, is contrasted with Jesus' own family. John lives happily with his elderly parents, taking good care of them. He even carries his mother Elizabeth on his back in a willow basket once she no longer has the strength to walk. Envy grows in Jesus' mind.

> They belonged. It was not like at home. I thought: I wonder how it would feel to have mother's back so close to my own. Is it warm, does it feel secure? Those hands which have stroked my forehead. There were no hands like that at home.[7]

Tunström's Jesus is emotionally handicapped, which explains the development of the Jesus-figure in the narrative. On the one hand, it is possible that this kind of intertextual change stems from the fragmentary nature of the information given about Jesus' family in the canonical Gospels. On the other hand, the change is clearly deliberate since in the canonical Gospels it is precisely his mother Mary who accompanies Jesus even up to Calvary. In the original story Mary appears to love her son passionately until the very end. Given this difference Tunström's

---

5. See the translation by Martinus; Tunström, "Letter from the Wilderness," 12.

6. Tunström, *Ökenbrevet*, 75–76.

7. Tunström, "Letter from the Wilderness," 13. In the story Jesus even steals a moment of compassion from Elizabeth who on one occasion does not recognise Jesus and treats him like John. Tunström, *Ökenbrevet*, 50.

intertextual change clearly has a specific intention. It serves as an argument to downplay Jesus' Messianic identity.[8]

This is further confirmed by Tunström's description of Jesus' inner weakness and lack of calling. When, in the beginning of the story, a young Jesus and John play near Elizabeth's house, they invent a scene where Jesus attempts to become a novice in the Qumran monastery, represented by John. The tests are strict, and since Jesus must offer his money to the community, he also gives John some stones. Then, in their imaginative desert, John proclaims to Jesus about his Messianic mission.

> "Get down on your knees," he ordered in a harsh voice. "You are the new Messiah." At first I felt quite empty inside. Why did he say that? I could feel myself knitting my brows, trying to understand what he meant. Messiah! But that was someone else. Someone who was going to come. From the side or from above. A silly game. John would say anything as long as he could be in charge. I thought: now I have seen through you. Now it is not dangerous any more. But he had spoken strange words: as if a Messiah could emerge from inside. Grow inside that which was already. Like a foetus. As if one could carry something inside one, like a woman. But I was a man. I shrugged it off.[9]

Tunström constructs Jesus' inner convictions by using psychological elements. His feelings of insecurity result from his experiences in a cold family with distorted relationships. For Tunström, this is also one of the reasons why Jesus some years later wants to join the community at Qumran. A strict religious sect could evidently better meet the needs of a young man who does not yet know what he wants from life. He does have some kind of sense of calling but his mission is not clear. He apparently searches for a proper authority or model for his religious convictions. In this regard, though, the Dead Sea community cannot provide protection or reliable teaching since Tunström's Jesus quite soon abandons almost every teaching the sect offers. Jesus' inner insecurity is stronger than Jewish tradition.[10]

Saramago builds his story from somewhat different elements. In his novel Jesus lives in the shadow of his father's sins. The story is constructed around the bloodshed in Bethlehem. Joseph, working as a carpenter in Jerusalem, overhears soldiers talking about an attack on

---

8. For the original story, see John 19:25.
9. Tunström, "Letter from the Wilderness," 19.
10. Tunström, *Ökenbrevet*, 118.

this small town. Paralysed by fear, he tells no one, but only saves his own family by hiding in a nearby cave. From his hiding place he watches the massacre in panoramic view: the villagers are being slaughtered because of his inability to act.[11]

In a larger context this event serves merely as one example of divine violence revealing the true nature of God and his world. For Saramago, it becomes a key structural element in the story. Jesus too shares in his father's crime. The theme is developed from the days of Jesus' childhood. As a young boy he asks the scribes teaching at the temple whether children may inherit the guilt of their fathers. They must, answer the learned teachers, since this is how people have inherited the guilt of Adam.[12]

> The Lord said that parents will not die for their children or children for their parents, and that each man will be sentenced for his own crimes, True, but you ought to know that this was a precept for those ancient times when an entire family, however innocent, paid for the crime of any one of its members, But if the word of the Lord is forever and there is no apparent end to guilt, and as you yourself have just said, man is free so that he might be punished, then one has a right to believe that the father's guilt, even after he's been punished, doesn't cease to exist but is passed on to his children, just as all of us who are alive today have inherited the guilt of Adam and Eve, our first parents.[13]

Saramago is somewhat difficult to read since he prefers commas to periods. Even in a dialogue, another speaker's entry into the conversation happens only after a comma, not a new line, and different speakers are indicated simply by a capital letter. Given these factors, the reader must tread carefully to avoid confusion when following Saramago's thought. In this passage the scribe becomes confused because of Jesus' difficult and mature questions. He knows his Scriptures but cannot find a solution, and answer the boy's concern about deterministic fate: "Guilt is a wolf that eats its cub after having devoured its father, The wolf of which you speak has already devoured my father, Then it will soon be your turn."[14] Jesus participates in the horrifying inheritance of his father.

11. Saramago, *Gospel*, 74–76.
12. In Luke's story the boy Jesus in the temple discusses with the rabbis and asks them questions, which was part of the teaching method. "And all who heard him were amazed at his understanding and his answers" (Luke 2:47).
13. Saramago, *Gospel*, 156–57.
14. Ibid., 158.

Furthermore, the scribe has confirmed that God himself accepts the situation. Therefore, Jesus must abide by this divine precept and submit himself to God's will. Since guilt is transmitted through the generations, Jesus cannot escape his burden. After he has buried his father he inherits Joseph's nightmares as well as his sandals.

> I dream that I'm in a village which isn't Nazareth and that you are with me, but it's not you, because the woman who's my mother in the dream looks quite different, and there are other boys of my age, difficult to say how many, with women who could be their mothers, someone has assembled us in a square and we're waiting for soldiers who are coming to kill us, we can hear them on the road, they draw near but we can't see them. At this point I'm still not frightened, I know it's only a nightmare, then suddenly I feel sure father is coming with the soldiers, I turn to you for protection, uncertain whether you're really my mother, but you're no longer there.[15]

Jesus, in Saramago's novel, is no Messiah with a mission. Instead, he is a Sisyphus who has inherited an absurd burden, which he himself has not chosen. He is a victim of God's omnipotent despotism and if he has a mission, it is in opposing God's plans in this world. Saramago's story is constructed on the themes of Joseph's guilt and the inheritance of sins. These issues confirm universal determinism leading to the problem of theodicy: God commands everything, therefore it is ultimately just he who is responsible for every event that occurs in this bizarre world. This is Saramago's key idea, and later it becomes his ultimate premise for questioning the Christian concept of God. The massacre at Bethlehem is, therefore, not only a symbol of human evilness in Saramago's novel; it becomes a symbol for God's weakness. It is the shadow in the divine soul and becomes God's responsibility and even fault, which he himself cannot escape. God never sleeps "because He made a mistake for which no man would be forgiven."[16]

The only weakness in Saramago's idea of the hereditary guilt of Joseph—and Jesus—is that it is strained and inconsistent. Even though this main argument carries the narrative until the final discussions about God's devious plan to kill thousands of human beings in Jesus' name,

---

15. Ibid., 133–34.

16. Ibid., 94. The problem of theodicy as a theme will be investigated further in chapter 6.2.

the point of departure remains unclear. Why should Joseph be culpable for something that Roman soldiers do?[17] Unlike many of Saramago's ingenious literary inventions in the novel, this particular claim lacks justification. Is Saramago acting like a corrupt judge laying guilt on the victims? In the story, Joseph and his family no doubt belong to the victims of the assault even though they manage to escape the violent act itself. Herod is the same monster he is in the New Testament. Saramago never changes that feature in his narrative.[18]

Saramago apparently attempts to create a logical chain from God's divine predictions to the massacre at Bethlehem and in this way lay the groundwork for his master narrative about God's violent nature. The whole event, he suggests, can already be read from God's earlier prophecies. Moreover, it is first and foremost God who is responsible for the killing because he, as the guardian of children and provider of providence, could have made Joseph prevent it. But from a literary point of view, this is nonsense. Saramago's logical chain is broken before he can even proceed to the second step of his reasoning. He attempts to rewrite history and ostensibly let God correct his mistakes. In his magical realism Saramago sends Joseph back to Bethlehem and lets him hear the soldiers' plan. All the children in his village are in danger. In spite of the new situation and his opportunity to change history Joseph does nothing. He proves to be as weak as his God. Joseph, and later also Jesus, for some irrational reason—probably due to original sin—participate in God's sin. So, why send him? Saramago never makes use of the possibilities magical realism provides but, instead, introduces a *diabolus ex machina* by making hereditary sin a credible feature of his narrative.

Saramago's literary strategy is acceptable, of course. He moves freely between two worlds by giving Joseph and his God a second chance to improve history. Past and present are interwoven. In the story, then, the

---

17. It is possible that Saramago himself has attempted to use the theme that could be called "guilt of the survivors." This is a theme that appears in literature that deals with terror and oppression. Joseph's guilt in Saramago's story is not collective, though, and so is an insufficient explanation.

18. This is an annoying flaw. It casts a shadow on Saramago's excellent style and his extraordinary knowledge of biblical history, which easily exceeds that of many pastors and priests. We must remember Bloom who stated: "As Saramago's fierce critical admirer, I am reluctant to choose it over all his other novels, but it is an awesome work, imaginatively superior to any other life of Jesus, including the four canonical Gospels." Bloom, "One with the Beard," 155.

implied author's intention is good, but the real author appears to know better; "real" history intervenes and makes the effort futile. Hard facts destroy fiction. The children have already been murdered, and nothing can be done. Hence, there must be something wrong with the God who conducts such history.[19] The major flaw in this reasoning, however, is that the only god in this new story is Saramago himself. Should the reader ask why the omnipotent author does not make the new Joseph prevent the killing of the children, he could look only to the author. The Joseph of the new narrative takes orders only from the author, not from God. Thus the author becomes as bloodthirsty as Herod who, in the original story, attempts to destroy the Messianic King of the Jews. In developing his guilt theme Saramago ends in a blind alley.

Frier attempts to solve this by stating that the problem is not particularly in Joseph's guilt but in his *feeling* of guilt. It is Joseph's lack of rebelliousness that produces the horrible history the original Gospels witness to.[20] This is a plausible explanation and apparently Saramago's aim. This is not a question of consistency but a question of attitude. Divine history is discussed in human terms. By putting Joseph back into the original situation Saramago implies that he should have acted. The problem with biblical history and Christianity is that they do not rise against all the violence done in the name of some god or described in some Holy Scripture. This is precisely the Nietzschean rebellion. With his guilt theme Saramago shifts the blame onto the Christian church, which prevents this world from developing a tolerant philanthropy.

Saramago's Jesus, thus, is a Sisyphus-figure whose desperate mission is to resist God's divine plans. Apart from this, Jesus' person is not described in detail. If one wishes to conclude something about his personality through his actions, Jesus appears to be a post-Christian humanist whose values oppose those of traditional Christian morals.

Mailer takes another point of departure, however. He is especially interested in Jesus' mental growth and describes his ambivalence towards his calling. In principle, Mailer's Jesus in the *Gospel* is conscious

---

19. Fokkema notes that Saramago argues here mainly on the basis of the source text. "How could He have wanted to save the life of His son at the cost of the cruel murder of twenty or thirty innocent infants?" Fokkema, "Art of Rewriting," 397.

20. "The problem, therefore, is not one of Joseph's guilt as such, but of his *feeling* of guilt; ironically, it is Joseph's very lack of rebellion that leads him to accept the justice that he chooses to perceive in his own execution as a rebel." Frier, "Outline," 380.

of his exceptional identity, mainly because Joseph has told him about it, but he does not understand what his divinity could mean in practice.

> An even greater weight was upon me. That was Joseph's story concerning my true father. I could hardly see myself as the Son. After school, on days when we would scuffle with each other, I would lose such fights as often as I won. How, then, could I be the Son of the Lord? And this doubt left me in fear of His wrath.[21]

By writing this *Bildungsroman* Mailer wishes to describe Jesus' growth into his mature identity. He just does not succeed very well. His Jesus lags far behind the canonical original. The best Mailer's Jesus can achieve is some kind of college-based consciousness of a certain potentiality in life.[22]

There are some similarities between Mailer's construction and Renan's rationalist picture of Jesus, at least as Wood describes it:

> He is tempted—he is ignorant of many things—he corrects himself—he is cast down, discouraged—he asks his Father to spare him trials—he is submissive to God as a son. He who is to judge the world does not know the day of judgment....[23]

Wood is convinced that there is no difference between Renan and Mailer. "This is, essentially, Mailer's Jesus." There are recognisable similarities, of course, and Wood can easily refer to their somewhat similar writing contexts. "Renan was a Catholic who lost his faith. His book is a piece of learned kitsch, soft with surmise and invention. It is a disingenuous book, in which Renan, conscious that he is dismantling Christianity as he turns it into a myth, nervously compensates by idealizing Jesus."[24] It would be a mistake, however, to make Mailer just another rationalist who attempts to turn Jesus into a European humanist.

Despite the fact that Jewish Messianism is no longer recognisable in Mailer's picture of Jesus, one should not forget his conception of Jesus

---

21. Mailer, *Gospel*, 21.

22. So Gordon, "Superstar," 29. Partridge notes that Jesus "not only lacks knowledge of his position as God's Son, but he also is confused by the interference of his human nature." This leads to an imbalance between the alleged two natures: "If this Jesus is the embodiment of two natures, then the two natures are not equal, and the human keeps running interference on the divine." Partridge, "Gospel," 68.

23. See Wood, "He Is Finished," 32.

24. Ibid.

as a divided person, "a man enclosing another man within."[25] Mailer paints a picture where the canonical figure oscillates with the new version present in the story. He assimilates Gospel quotations in his own narrative where the renewed personality of the Nazarene appears to differ essentially from the original figure. Describing the process of humanisation requires a skillful adaptation of Gospel material into an altered context. Mailer's recurring quotations from canonical writings serve the construction of a new story, which no longer resembles the canonical original in the least.[26]

Mailer's revision can be detected in several passages. For instance, Mailer reserves the question about the desperate fate of offending hands and eyes, discussed in chapter 1, for the story about the adulterous woman. Facing the beautiful young woman Mailer's Jesus becomes conscious of his own lust. He recognises that despite the transgression this woman has committed, he cannot judge her. Mailer's theological inference is straightforward: who can be perfect? Jesus proclaims boldly to the Pharisees:

> And this time, I said aloud: "If thy hand offend thee, cut it off." When they looked at me, I told them: "It is better to enter the other life maimed than to have two hands to take into hell." Then I saw fear in their eyes. "If your eye offend thee," I told them, "pluck it out. It is better to enter the Kingdom of God and see only with the eye that is left than have both eyes look into the flames. In hell-fire, the worm that eats at your flesh does not die." I was amazed. I felt cleansed of disturbance toward this woman, and by my own words. So I also said: "He that is without sin among you, let him cast the first stone."[27]

Prototypical rewriting appears here in its pure form. Mailer merely combines separate canonical Jesus-words in a new way and produces

---

25. Mailer, *Gospel*, 26.

26. I agree with McDonald who says: "Mailer wants to coax the polemical energy of the gospel form away from its orthodox ecclesiastical theological agenda, and in order to do this he must both accept, for the purposes of the novel, the fundamental confidence of the gospel writers that Jesus is the Son of God, and free himself from the limitations which this 'proclamation of divinity' necessarily imposes on the direction in which he wants to take his 'gospel.'" McDonald, "Theodicy," 80.

27. Mailer, *Gospel*, 178. Here Mailer is using word for word quotations and the rewriting is simply a result of the new context as he combines the Sermon on the Mount with the story of the adulterous woman.

a moral judgment that opposes the one given in the New Testament. Jesus' paradoxical words expressing the human inability to maintain an integration of sexuality and love now justify immorality. In Mailer's story there is no longer any Saviour who brings forgiveness of sins to this world. We find only a human Jesus who struggles with his inner feelings just as his fellow citizens do. Divine absolution has turned into a brotherhood of sinners.

Also Saramago's Jesus gives his Sermon on the Mount, but there Jesus' words are dependent on God's greedy ambition and violent will

> Blessed be you poor, Jesus told them, for yours is the kingdom of heaven, blessed are you that hunger now, for you shall be filled, blessed are you that weep now, for you shall laugh, but just then God became aware of what was happening and although too late to retract what Jesus had said, He forced him to speak other words which turned those tears of happiness into grim foreboding of the black future ahead, Blessed are you when men shall hate you, and when they shall separate you from their company, and shall reproach you and cast out your name as evil for the Son of Man's sake.[28]

Saramago and Mailer use a somewhat similar technique in treating the Sermon on the Mount, but the former is more loyal to his basic idea of prototypical rewriting. Saramago exploits canonical material directly (Matt 5:3–11) and accommodates it to his own narrative. So Jesus' comforting sentences are contradicted with words of hate. This, of course, is possible only by omitting Jesus' original words about the heavenly joy of the reviled and the reward the persecuted will get (Matt 5:12). Both Saramago and Mailer aim at one definite purpose, though. This preacher of the Sermon on the Mount is no Saviour.[29]

Miracles occur in practically every Jesus-novel, and Mailer is not immune. This, however, does not yet make Jesus the New Testament Messiah. His Jesus is a Jewish healer like the Jewish preachers Honi and

---

28. Saramago, *Gospel*, 309. Preto-Rodas notes that Jesus' original shift from comforting promises to dire warnings is interpreted as God's direct orders. It is too late for God to censor Jesus' words but he can make Jesus add "other words." Saramago, review of *O Evangelho segundo Jesus Cristo*, 697.

29. In the context of the passage Saramago identifies with those who reproach Christians and thus the author stands in opposition to the Jesus-figure he creates. This tension is resolved only by making the violent God responsible for Jesus' last words in the sermon.

Hanina in rabbinic tradition.[30] There is a rationalist tone in Mailer's treatment of the original stories. His Jesus often doubts his own talents and power, and wonders how his miracles can take place. After calming the wind he remarks: "In truth, I do not know if I can say that this miracle was mine."[31] Occasionally Mailer becomes as sardonic as Saramago: "Even as waste will exist in all matters, so in the working of miracles, extravagance is best avoided."[32] And finally, the feeding of the five hundred bears marks of Renanian rationalism.

> I would lay one flake of fish and one bit of bread upon each tongue. Yet when each person had tasted these fragments, so do I believe that each morsel became enlargened within his thoughts (even as once in Cana I had been enlarged by eating one grape), and so I knew that few among these hundreds would say that they had not been given sufficient fish and bread. And this was a triumph of the Spirit rather than an enlargement of matter.[33]

In Mailer's story Jesus is, at his best, a representative of reformed Judaism, a rabbi who is well informed in Jewish traditions but who, simultaneously, is a reformer opposing even the basic doctrines of Jewish faith. Nevertheless, despite all his doubts, Mailer's Jesus continually receives different mystical messages from the Lord. One of the key messages is given after the crucial baptism by John in the Jordan: "Say not 'I am a child,' for you shall go to all the places that I send thee."[34] Jesus has no message of his own, though. He attempts to imitate John in his work, but he learns slowly, and the dualism remains. After the baptism Jesus's calling gains some clarity and purpose. "Now I knew the other man who had lived within the shell of myself, and he was better than me. I had become that man."[35]

---

30. Honi and Hanina ben Dosa were Jewish healers whose action has often been compared with Jesus' history. See Vermes, *Jesus the Jew*, 69, 72; *Jesus and the World of Judaism*, 8–9. For the scholarly discussion, see Koskenniemi, *Miracle-Workers*, 174. Furthermore, Jewish literature in New Testament times was filled with stories about Old Testament miracle workers. Ibid., 160–66, 189–91; and esp. 290–92.

31. Mailer, *Gospel*, 93. Like the Jewish scholar Vermes, Mailer appears to locate Jesus in the context of charismatic Judaism. Cf. Vermes, *Jesus the Jew*, 58–59. This kind of interpretation does not yet make Jesus divine, though.

32. Mailer, *Gospel*, 117.

33. Ibid., 116.

34. Ibid., 34.

35. Ibid., 35. Such uncertainty in Jesus' personality has inspired critics to give quite

Some scholars have assumed that Mailer, when attempting to cope with a figure who is "both a Jew and the Christian messiah," would end up with "a very Jewish Jesus."[36] This, however, is not true because Mailer's Jesus never grows into a proper Jewish teacher. He often ignores the Torah. His schooling must therefore have been inadequate. Even though Mailer's Jesus is depicted as an Essene and he is said to be somewhat interested in the Qumran community, he appears to know practically nothing of Essene orthodox Judaism. Qumran is the place where the standard of religious and theological knowledge surely is on the highest possible level. It soon becomes evident that his mother Mary is more interested in seeing Jesus in that community than Jesus himself: "She wanted me to join the desert community at Qumran, where the most devout are gathered."[37] Jesus' individual thoughts prevent him from making the final commitment and entering the monastery. He baulks at the hard discipline and unconditional authority prevailing in the group. "It was the Lord to whom I should submit myself for tests, not to this or that High Priest."[38]

If Mailer's Jesus is not an "ordinary Jew," how should one then characterise Mailer's picture of Jesus? Partridge reminds us that practically all alternative versions of Jesus have already been introduced in the course of doctrinal history. It is not easy for authors to create something essentially new as far as theology itself is concerned.

> According to orthodox Christian theology, Jesus is not a man on whom God bestowed supernatural powers (a heresy known as Adoptionism); he is not a man whose divine will overshadowed and replaced him (Apollinarianism); he is not a divine being who just appeared to be human (Docetism); he is not two per-

---

devastating analyses: "In his version of Christ's inner life he portrays the Messiah as a dopey, inarticulate guy who is not too sure why God has chosen him in the first place." Allen, "Gospel of Norman," 77. This criticism is justified because Mailer tries to hide behind his idea of Jesus' dualist personality, and this makes his picture of Jesus incoherent. Mailer's almost-canonical Jesus cannot simultaneously be a vagabond.

36. So McDonald, "Theodicy," 84. He identifies Mailer with authors who emphasise the genuinely Jewish substance and intention of the life and teaching of Jesus.

37. Mailer, *Gospel*, 59.

38. Ibid. Is Mailer's Jesus then just an ordinary Jew as in novels written by other Jewish authors? Langenhorst has analysed these novels and on that basis there is some similarity. Langenhorst, "Rediscovery," 90. Such a conclusion has some merit considering other analyses of Mailer's work, but it cannot be true. His Jesus is far from ordinary and accepts almost nothing his teachers suggest to him.

sons (Nestorianism); and he is not a deified man (Socinianism). Mailer's Jesus seems in some instances to fall into the Nestorian view and in others to into the Socinian view.³⁹

In his novel Mailer describes Jesus as one man yet two persons and, in the story, he repeats this anthropological dualism almost at the risk of stupidity. It is not certain, however, that this could be assessed as a theological conviction. Mailer is not seeking to present us with a Nestorian Jesus. Instead, this dualism is a literary device. It is guided by Mailer's main strategy in making the risen Jesus the narrator of the whole story. Therefore, Mailer's theological stance, if there is one, in portraying Jesus is that of Docetism. His Jesus keeps on telling a light story of how he, through certain unpleasant events, reached heaven where he now assesses his own history with an ambivalence that was typical of him on earth.

Mailer's solution creates problems, though. As Jesus is made the "real" narrator of historical events, Mailer claims authority. This is the true story from God's own mouth. But can one trust Jesus' story? Mailer's Jesus is uncertain and inarticulate. He knows little and proclaims even less. Furthermore, the status of revelation is vague. If Mailer wishes to present the reader with true revelation about divine things, why does he keep it at such a low level? Jesus' ambivalence in the story betrays the literary strategy. It leads gradually to Mailer's main thesis about the problem of theodicy. We shall return to this issue below when Mailer's "Manichean" concept of evil will be discussed.⁴⁰

In feminist novels the setting is somewhat different. In these books Jesus is more or less subordinate to women's control. Usually he has no great message or program to promote. Instead, Mary Magdalene teaches him many essentials. Nevertheless, as we saw already when discussing the construction of subtexts, feminist novels retain a rather conservative picture of the "historical Jesus." Fredriksson's Jesus heals the paralysed man and Tyrean woman's daughter. He calls Zacchaeus and teaches his disciples much like the New Testament tells us. Jesus gives his sermons and speaks about the lilies of the field as one would expect. Sometimes Mary Magdalene, of course, becomes "the disciple Jesus loved most."⁴¹

---

39. Partridge, "Gospel," 67.

40. See chapter 6.1.

41. Fredriksson, *According to Mary*, 119. Robert's *Wild Girl* tells mostly about Mary Magdalene, but Lazarus's rising from the dead is described quite biblically (p. 42).

The weightiest influence in feminist novels comes from the Gnostic gospels and, therefore, they focus on the resurrected Jesus. So Jesus' hidden message usually comes through Mary Magdalene. In the stories themselves Jesus hardly differs from the person one meets on the pages of the New Testament. Fredriksson has Jesus only vaguely reveal his Gnostic message to Mary before Easter. He prepares the ground for the emerging new message by telling Mary that most people live "outside their own nature." Man's "real nature" is of God and, therefore, people must learn to hear God's voice inside them.[42] Needless to say, in feminist novels Jesus hardly ever speaks about Torah or explains Mosaic tradition. The reason for this is evidently the antagonism towards law that is prominent in these novels. Neither is eschatology included in Jesus' teaching. Jesus' canonical words about the last judgment would have been too much for a Jesus-figure who hardly ever speaks against sin.[43]

In intertextual reinterpretations Jesus the theologian is often reduced to one simply seeking a good life. The new Jesus-figure is ready to abandon traditional dogmas, and his message is contrasted with canonical teaching. It is not easy for the authors to produce a coherent story on these premises, though. Especially in Tunström, Saramago, and Mailer, Jesus' Messianic identity is played down by making him an indecisive and even emotionally handicapped person without any clear calling even though, for some reason, he performs the role of a rabbi in the narratives. In a contradiction to the almost docetic pictures given in many conservative Jesus-novels of the past, where the divine Jesus had hardly any human features at all, the content of these new novels resembles the adoptionist view that was discussed above. For the most part, Jesus is seen as an average Jew who is *adopted* into a divine mission, but one can seldom speak of deification in the narratives. As a doctrine, it comes close to the Arian (from Areios) heresy where Jesus is considered to be merely a Jewish man without supernatural powers or a divine nature.

---

42. Fredriksson, *According to Mary*, 141. For the relation between Jesus and Mary Magdalene, see chapter 4.2 below. Furthermore, the Gnostic element will be discussed in 7.2.

43. Rinser's Jesus does speak about Old Testament history, warns his hearers not to fall into a similar disobedience as Israel in the wilderness, and even urges people to repent. There is not much biblical content left in this message, however, since for Jesus the positive counterpoint for human failure is just "das Reich des Friedens und der Liebe." [the Kingdom of peace and love.] Rinser, *Mirjam*, 137–38. There is no sin, salvation, or atonement in this message.

According to some of the novels, Jesus does perform certain miracles but it never amounts to more than a charismatic phenomenon typical of many religions. However, Mailer's docetic story told by the risen Jesus is so contradictory and so tied up with the idea of Jesus' mental growth that it really cannot be characterised by any of these simple patterns. The first result here thus suggests that the Jesus in these novels reminds us vaguely of Renan's Jesus the humanist, at least in the sense that he is a man among other human beings.[44]

However, this is not yet the whole truth. Even from the very start, the renewed Jesus-figure is no normative Jew.[45] Neither is he a philanthropist of the romantic tradition. The inversion of Jesus' character and the rejection of his Messianism are more profound. This can be seen in several different details. In spite of his failings Jesus in these novels is a rabbi, evidently because he worked as one in the original Gospels. This is how the intertextual change emphasises the turning over of previous hierarchies. Instead of just passing over the theme of Jesus' rabbinic profession, it is adopted as a tool for making him an incompetent teacher and an untrained shepherd. The new Jesus is a man with a crippled identity. His worldview is no longer based on the Old Testament, and he has no vision of the values of life. So, why teach? Just because the canonical figure did? The reader is entitled to ask for consistency in this particular regard since the Jesus of the novels does not seem to have much to give. Therefore, in many respects, the invented Jesus is merely a literary figure whose function is to serve the ideological purpose of the novel.

Nietzsche's Jesus would not have wanted to be a Saviour. In this respect there is a clear analogy between the investigated novels and Nietzsche's books. Moreover, most of the rationalist Jesus-figures appearing in nineteenth-century German scholarship or twentieth-century novels have no eschatological mission or soteriological function. When Jesus is demythologised, authors usually present some other rea-

---

44. Mailer's weakness, as Bottum claims, is in his inability to create a convincing story because fictional hypotheses are judged by their "literary and psychological persuasiveness." Mailer's story remains quite incoherent. "And Mailer's Jesus is never persuasive as either a human or divine character, weak and strong in a mix that seems more a muddle than a mystery." Bottum, "Mailer's Jesus," 53–56.

45. In this respect these novels no longer remind one of the Jesus-novels written by Jewish authors, which tend to present Jesus as an average Nazarean Jew. See Langenhorst, "Rediscovery," 90. Mailer's Jesus is not a normative Jew, even though his figure might resemble one at first glance.

son for his work and a new content for his proclamation, be it a moralist program or social work in general. What is distinctive for these recent novels, however, is that their view of the canonical Jesus is no longer positive. This is undoubtedly a Nietzschean feature. The description is based on a contradiction. The new Jesus of the novels becomes a kind of Zarathustra who no longer resembles his biblical predecessor. He does resist the heavenly King but he is not completely like Zarathustra, because he is weak and uncertain of his mission. Hence the first tentative conclusion suggests that the hypothesis of the present analysis is on the right track.

2. A PACT WITH THE DEVIL

The dissolving of Jesus' Messianic identity is the first Nietzschean theme, or at least an analogy for one, to be found in the investigated Jesus-novels. The most powerful expression of this theme is Jesus' transformation from an incarnated Son of God into a disciple of the Devil. In several novels the Galilean is reaching beyond good and evil. He does not necessarily become a disciple of the Devil in the sense many later figures in more ideological and distanced novels do. Nevertheless, he begins to resemble Zarathustra, who is convinced that gods do fail, and that even the concept of God may fail.

The Jesus of the novels often undergoes a Faustian temptation to gain transcendental knowledge without the help of his heavenly Father. This is how the mental life of the new figure is juxtaposed with the apparent omniscience of the Son of God prevailing in the canonical Gospels. Here again the intertextual change is Nietzschean since Jesus is now made to reach beyond good and evil.[46] The Jesus of the new story learns that to live life properly, one cannot follow God's guidance. In reality, for the authors, there is no divine Mosaic revelation. Or if there is one, it is to be confronted belligerently. The new master is the Devil, who becomes the real teacher of Christianity—or at least attempts to be become one.[47]

---

46. When Nietzsche rushes beyond good and evil he deliberately confronts Christian morality, which he calls slavish religion. Nietzsche, *Beyond Good and Evil*, § 62

47. See Partridge, "Gospel," 72: "For Mailer, however, the temptation scene is just the beginning of Satan's influence on Jesus—he can almost be said to become tutor to Jesus's tyro."

In Mailer's novel Jesus meets the Devil in the wilderness, just as one would expect while reading the canonical story. This is a rewritten story of Jesus' temptation. Jesus is being tested but not like the canonical figure. Many details are now different. For a start, Mailer's Devil is no monster. He is "as handsome as a prince." The Devil does not instill fear, either. Instead, he is a beautiful creature, which even Jesus acknowledges in the story: "The Devil is the most beautiful creature God ever made."[48] Mailer's Devil is the source of the temptations that necessarily belong to the narrative, but he does his work in an eloquent manner. From the very start Jesus trusts him and takes his difficult questions for granted. This is God's opponent, as Jesus knows, but he has also been God's most obedient servant. Therefore, it is precisely the Devil who, during their long discussions, makes Jesus hesitate about whether God is actually omnipotent or not.[49] Furthermore, some of the questions seem justified to Mailer's Jesus-figure. God evidently hates women, at least as far as the Scriptures are concerned. The Old Testament is filled with metaphors concerning whores, and Jewish rhetoric is filled with words such as whoredom, fornication, and harlot. This, according to the Devil, reveals that God is in fact just covering up his own lust, and Jesus agrees.[50]

This is why, states Mailer, God is simply filled with hatred of women. "Indeed, your Father has no inkling of women; His scorn for them is shared by His prophets, who speak, so they claim, with His voice."[51]

> "Does all this take place," asked the Devil, "in order to scorn Jerusalem? Say rather that your Father's language reeks of desire."
>
> "Your words are pollutions." I hoped to excite enough anger in myself to reply, but I could only repeat: "Your words are poisonous."
>
> Satan replied: "Your Father's tongue is as ripe with lust as my own."
>
> I knew confusion. Could I deny that my loins had quickened as I listened to the repetition of my Father's words?[52]

---

48. Mailer, *Gospel*, 45.
49. Ibid., 48.
50. Ibid., 53.
51. Ibid., 50.
52. Ibid., 53. Allen remarks that this dialogue betrays feminist concerns in the novel but, coming from Mailer with his reputation, these concerns "are aired by the Devil." Allen, "Gospel of Norman," 77.

Mailer's theology becomes apparent, then, in his treatment of the final example of temptation. Now the subtext is based directly on the canonical original. The Devil leads Jesus on the summit of mountain and tells him to jump. "Cast yourself out. Your Father's angels will carry you." Between the dichotomy of trust and will to power Jesus becomes conscious of the most crucial choice there is for a human being to make: "An abyss was below me. And I knew it would be there for all the generations to come." Jesus feels vertigo. "You will be consumed. Jump! You can save yourself. Jump!"[53] Mailer's Jesus does not jump. One might suspect that by this solution the author would in fact have returned to a more conservative path. This is how Mailer's work has sometimes been estimated, at least in a more general sense. However, the relation between Jesus and the Devil is more complex.

The last temptation is burned into Jesus' heart, and it follows him and his thoughts until the end of the story: "I wanted to, but I did not dare."[54] Later when working as a healer in Galilee, Jesus still remembers the temptation. Even when people are healed through his hands he recalls: "I could still feel the mark of cowardice on my own flesh." In a sense, Mailer's Jesus has made an existentialist leap, and this experience never leaves him.

> For it is cowardly to fear death as I had feared it. Now I would make amends by recalling my shame. That was just. I would not be proud of my good deeds. I would brood upon my hour with the Devil. Had I given some of my fealty to him?[55]

The Jesus of this story has then also sworn fealty to the Devil. He does not completely follow his calling in a mission for God. Hence Mailer's Jesus remains in ambivalence about his life. On the one hand the temptations have given Jesus inner strength so that he is ready to resist the Devil who "hates emptiness." On the other hand, there are still two different men inside the Jesus-character. He sees the seeds of cowardice in his heart because part of him is under the Devil's control: "But then, on this new morning I was not much afraid of Satan. He had captured only a small part of me."[56]

---

53. Mailer, *Gospel*, 54.
54. Ibid., 55.
55. Ibid., 92.
56. Ibid., 56, 57.

After these events, in Mailer's novel, this dualist figure of Jesus, almost like a Gnostic novice or the Devil's apprentice, gradually grows to meet new challenges. Jesus' power in the book is described as a mystical energy, which enables him to work increasingly powerful miracles. "If I could increase in my powers (and I knew that He would pass on many powers to me), perhaps the world of men might multiply in virtue with me." (*ibid.*) Discussions with the Devil had taught Mailer's Jesus some practical skills as well. Like Saramago's Jesus, the figure in *The Gospel According to the Son* learns from the Devil. Actually, he "steal[s] a few skills from the Devil."

> In truth, I could now employ Satan's manner when speaking. I would address strangers with the finest courtesy and the most intimate exhilaration, as if we shared among ourselves the wonder of many things unsaid.[57]

These tools enable Mailer's Jesus to promote his new message. The new figure is practically an autodidact in the sense that nobody other than the Devil actually teaches him. He does not appear to read the Tanakh, the Jewish Old Testament. He probably learns something from his Father, but most of the time this Father remains distant and unknown. The idea of Jesus' inner conflict in Mailer's novel is accompanied by the ambivalence that prevails in his social context. Jesus' disciples also experience personal crises concerning their calling. They lack any real conviction to preach the message of the kingdom. Instead, their attitudes and actions are tools for expressing the theme of uncertainty.

Even though Mailer's Jesus is somewhat uneducated in the Jewish faith, one should not be led astray in the interpretation of the work. The novel has a very precise aim. The author is well informed about Jewish Law and also knows his New Testament. In *The Gospel According to the Son*, meaning is constructed through goal-directed writing. Mailer constructs a human Jesus who fights his special calling and deals with religious issues common to any pious Jew.

---

57. Ibid., 68. "The idea of Jesus employing Satan's tactics is anathema to orthodox Christian theology, but it is an intriguing contemplation of power and influence." Partridge, "Gospel," 72. Furthermore, Partridge concludes, this means that there is a "transmission of power" in Mailer's story because Jesus stretched out his hand to the Devil: "And because I had wanted him to leave, I had touched my right hand to his, and knew in the same instant that I had surrendered a share of the Lord's protection." Mailer, *Gospel*, 68.

Somewhat surprisingly, it is precisely the idea of inner growth typical of Mailer's story that makes his novel inconsistent. His psychologising treatment is not perfectly in line with the extensive subtext present in the book. Mailer's picture of the uncertain figure of the new Jesus is in contradiction with certain quite impressive passages he quotes almost directly from the canonical Gospels. For instance, Jesus heals the sick and fulfils the promises and signs of eschatological salvation. Because readers still know the Bible rather well, the original figure breaks through the later description. Thus, Mailer becomes a target for the critique that has often been directed at Jesus-novels: it is not easy to create a new Jesus who has to compete with the canonical figure. The source text is quite good, and the inconsistency becomes evident when several passages of the original source text are taken into the subtext. Mailer's treatment of the Qumran scrolls does not mitigate his problems with inconsistency. Had Jesus really entered the community of the Essenes, he would have more closely resembled an orthodox Jew and not the religious Boy Scout appearing in Mailer's novel. Tunström actually makes a similar but worse mistake since his Jesus ends up living in the community. His problems are eased only by the fact that his story does not depend on a large subtext. One could grant Tunström the benefit of the doubt and venture that he deliberately presents an adaptation of Qumran teaching. This, however, does not seem plausible because he uses the sect as an example of a legalist group who wishes to follow the precepts of Moses. Therefore, the only apparent reason for Tunström to choose the Qumran sect is his goal of exploring a period in Jesus' life about which the Bible says very little.

What these authors are fundamentally discussing is Jesus' Jewishness. In this respect it is surprising that neither Tunström's nor Mailer's Jesus is a typical Jew. Both of these portrayals oppose Jewish customs and Mosaic faith. They are far from the Jesus-figures depicted by Jewish scholars in scholarly scientific investigations. For instance Geza Vermes, who has written several books on Jesus, describes him as a pious Jew who follows most of the precepts of the Jewish tradition.[58] This is not to say that the Jesus of the new novels has not adopted any Jewish doctrines. His concept of God is quite traditional. In fact, there are issues whose traditionalism may even surprise many readers. Some of Jesus' views on eschatology, for instance, derive directly from the Old Testament.

58. Vermes, *Jesus and the World of Judaism*, 30–36.

And even Jesus' resurrection, which is treated by Mailer for example, is a theme that many Jewish scholars accept. This is because the idea of resurrection as such is a completely Jewish belief. Jewish tradition speaks of several persons from Enoch to Moses and Elijah who have been assumed into heaven.[59] Mailer struggles with Judaism but he does not really know what to do with it. He seems sympathetic to both Jewish tradition and Jesus' teaching, but his grand idea of overwhelming evil makes positive conclusions impossible. Jesus becomes the Devil's apprentice.

In Saramago's *Gospel* as well, the Pastor/Devil has a prominent role. He appears in the story at every crucial moment in Jesus' life. As an angel disguised as a beggar he foretells Mary's pregnancy. As a shepherd he reveals Joseph's sin to Mary in Bethlehem. And as a Pastor he appears to Jesus and makes him his apprentice and disciple.[60] This anti-Christian figure is no Good Shepherd. His views turn out to be godless, and he never follows Jewish precepts, since he is "not a Jew."[61] Instead, the Pastor has skills that refer to his primary origin below in the fires of hell. He is able to heat a shepherd's wooden crook in the fire (without having it burst into flame) and hold the hot crook in his hand, but Jesus burns his hands and throws it quickly away. "How could the shepherd hold anything so hot?," Jesus asks himself.[62]

In Saramago's story Jesus' calling takes place here. In the intertextual inversion, ideas taken from prophetic callings in the Old Testament and expressions from the New Testament are diligently woven together in a new narrative speaking of Jesus mission.

> Will you take me with you to help with the flock, I was waiting for you to ask, Well then, Yes, you may join the flock. The man got to his feet, lifted his torch and went outside. Jesus followed. It was darkest night and the moon had still not risen. Gathered near the entrance to the cave, the sheep and goats stood around in silence, except for the faint jingling of bells from time to time. Patiently they awaited the outcome of the conversation between the shepherd and his latest helpmate. The man raised the torch exposing the black heads of the goats and the whitish snouts of

---

59. Jewish scholars are cautious with Jesus' resurrection, which is understandable, but in principle they hold it as possible because it is in line with Jewish eschatology. See especially Flusser, *Jesus*, 175–77, 271–74.

60. See especially Saramago, *Gospel*, 168–69.

61. Ibid., 174.

62. Ibid., 170.

the sheep, some scraggy with sparse hairs, others plump with woolly coats, and told him, This is my flock, take care not to lose even one of these animals.[63]

Despite some inconsistencies, like certain frightening elements in the meeting and the Pastor's contradictions of Jewish faith, the Jesus of the story decides to follow the new Shepherd. He becomes a disciple of the rabbi of darkness and stays as long as four years with him. During his period of discipleship, Jesus learns many things from his mentor. As a result, the roles of God and the Devil begin gradually to become intertwined, if not inverted. God has already been depicted as a greedy and violent figure in the novel. In contrast, the Devil is described as an honest teacher and a man of integrity. He is a freethinker, no doubt, and a cynical rationalist who opposes the God whom he sees as his greatest enemy. But as such a figure the Pastor begins to resemble a European intellectual who, frustrated in his Judeo-Christian tradition, attempts to construct a humanist morality through solidarity. He worries over the children of Bethlehem and detests any idea of religious sacrifice killing innocent animals. In this respect the Pastor champions the weak and rejected. He is not a completely Nietzschean nihilist.[64]

For Jesus, in Saramago's novel, the most obvious peculiarity in the daily life is that he never thanks Israel's God for his life or of the events he experiences. This too becomes an element that distances Jesus from Judaism.

> Now as we know, in a normal situation amongst ordinary people, Jesus would not have had to wait long in order to discover the extent of his master's piety, since Jews in those days gave thanks to the Lord some thirty times each day and on the slightest pretext, as we have often seen throughout this Gospel, without needing any further proof. But the day passed and Pastor showed no signs of offering prayers of thanksgiving, dusk fell and they settled down to sleep out in the open and not even the majesty of God's

---

63. Ibid., 169–70. Cf. the good shepherd, John 10:11; not losing one follower, John 6:39; and Jesus' word to the apostle Peter, "Tend my sheep," John 21:16.

64. Ben-Porat suggests that even in the depiction of Satan as the good shepherd, as "the ultimate reversal of roles," Saramago stays "within the possibilities offered by both the biblical text and the traditions surrounding it." Ben-Porat, "Prototypical Rewriting," 99. This cannot be completely true. It can be argued only in terms of Satan's heavenly origin, and this will be discussed later in this investigation. The reversal of these roles in Saramago's novel is a deliberate contradiction aiming at ironical rewriting.

sky above touched the shepherd's heart or brought so much as a word of praise or gratitude to his lips, after all, it might have been raining and it was not, which to all intents and purposes, both human and divine, was a clear sign that the Lord was watching over His creatures.[65]

For Mailer, one of the problematic questions concerning God's precepts is God's attitude towards women and sexuality. Saramago's Pastor also teases Jesus with similar ponderings. This point is worth noting since, in the New Testament, sexuality was not among the subjects with which Jesus was tempted in the wilderness. Saramago's main argument lies here: can God deny something he himself has created? "Can God disown what you have between your legs as something not of His making, just answer yes or no, No, He can't, Why not, Because the Lord cannot undo what He previously willed." According to the Pastor, God's alleged depreciation of carnality and sexuality leads to a contradiction in God's person. He has created something he later detests: "In other words, your God is the only warder of a prison where the only captive is your God."[66]

When discussing sexuality Saramago's Pastor finally breaks all Jewish (-Christian) taboos. If the biblical God fails here and is a captive in his own prison, then a naturalist view of the basic identity of all animals must be true. The way beyond good and evil must be followed consistently. "You must choose a sheep."

> What did you say, asked Jesus in bewilderment, I told you to choose a sheep, unless you prefer a goat. Whatever for, Because you'll need it unless you really are a eunuch. When these words sank in, the boy felt stunned, but worst of all, was the onslaught of horrendous sensuality once he had suppressed his embarrassment and revulsion. Covering his face with both hands, he said in a hoarse voice, This is the word of the Lord, If a man should copulate with an animal he will be punished with death and the animal be slaughtered.[67]

---

65. Saramago, *Gospel*, 173. Prayer was important for pious Jews. In addition to daily prayers, three times a day, the weekly prayer, called simply the Eighteen Benedictions (*Berakhot*), contained all essential elements of religious life. Schürer, *History of the Jewish People* 2:456–59.

66. Saramago, *Gospel*, 177.

67. Ibid., 177–78.

Jesus answers as his canonical predecessor does in the New Testament when responding to the Devil's temptations: this is the word of the Lord. The scene ends with a conflict that resembles the biblical original. "Yes, and now leave me alone, abominable creature, for you are not God's creature but belong to the Devil."[68] The Pastor has evidently offered Jesus "all the kingdoms" of hedonism. The canonical Jesus contested the Devil in the same way: "Jesus said to him, 'Away with you, Satan! for it is written, "Worship the Lord your God, and serve only him."' Then the Devil left him, and suddenly angels came and waited on him" (Matt 4:10–11).

The intertextual play goes further, though. It is less about taboos after all. When the Pastor leaves he speaks to his sheep: "God has forbidden that anyone should copulate with you, so worry not, but as for shearing you, neglecting you, slaughtering you, and eating you, all these things are permitted." The problem, for Saramago's Pastor, is not sexuality in itself. The purpose of this example was probably to surprise and astonish Jesus. Is killing less repulsive than copulation? In biblical thinking the sheep were created for use, and this fact, according to the Pastor, should make Jesus revise his ideology. So ultimately, in Saramago's *Gospel*, Jesus does not leave the Devil over this issue. After assessing his words, he follows the Pastor's voice as the young prophet Samuel followed God's voice in the temple: "I'm here."[69]

However, Saramago uses the slaughtering of the sheep theme to describe the final break between Jesus and the Pastor. After spending years in the wilderness Jesus meets God, who immediately demands a sacrifice. Jesus must offer his sheep if he is to become God's servant. Their new covenant must be confirmed by blood. "Can I bring my sheep, Oh, so that's what's bothering you, Yes, that's all, may I, No, Why not, Because you must offer it in sacrifice to Me in order to seal our covenant."[70] After a moment of hesitation, Jesus makes the offering by killing the sheep. There is a symbolism in his sacrifice since this happens to be the very same sheep that was earlier saved from being slaughtered in the temple—then pleasing the Pastor's ideology. Once again the plot twists: the new covenant has been sealed, and despite all Pastor's attempts to educate, Jesus now decides to follow God.

68. Ibid.

69. Ibid., 178. Cf. 1 Sam 3:4, "Then the Lord called, 'Samuel! Samuel!' and he said, 'Here I am!'"

70. Saramago, *Gospel*, 198.

When returning to the Pastor's camp Jesus openly tells him the events of the day. The Pastor briefly asks about the fate of the sheep, and Jesus must admit that he has offered it in sacrifice. Now the Devil appears as the real opponent of God. He raises his objections against the conditions of life and God's omnipotence. The rebellion familiar from Camus' philosophy of religion incites the spirit of this refusal: if there is a God who demands all this he must be confronted.[71]

This leads to the final conflict between the Pastor and Jesus. Pastor draws a line on the ground and cries:

> "You've learned nothing, be gone with you." [Nâo aprendeste nada, vai.][72]

The crisis is clear. The Pastor has not been able to save Jesus from the demands of the violent God and, therefore, Jesus has to leave. His period of temptation is over, and in Saramago's story, he has failed. It is actually God who has tempted and seduced him, not the Devil. There is nothing to be done. Thereafter Jesus must follow the precepts of God and begin his missionary work. The event thus anticipates the major reversal of roles in the novel. Already here God is a bloodthirsty beast who enjoys sacrifice while the Devil appears to be a gentleman who still can recognise good manners when he sees them. In Saramago's story, the Devil could have been Jesus' moral teacher but Jesus turned out to be an ignorant pupil.[73]

If there is a pact with the Devil in these two novels, what is its purpose in the story? Mailer and Saramago differ in their presentation. In both of these novels Satan is Jesus' teacher and the roles of God and the Devil are reversed. In Mailer's book Jesus learns that God's power is not unlimited. He is probably not the only God there is. Therefore, Jesus is able to learn from the Devil's manner of preaching. He can also make use of Satan's integrity described so eloquently in the story. Saramago's

---

71. So also Emery: "Ce passage est aussi le dernier moment où le Diable est encore prométhéen, ou en tout cas une représentation crédible de Prométhée, sur un point essentiel, celui de la liberté." Emery, "Pasteur," 81.

72. Saramago, *Gospel*, 199; Saramago, *Evangelho*, 265.

73. Frier notes that this is a key moment in the narrative, as well. "What Jesus needs to learn is that merely perceiving the inevitability of an event does not make that situation *ipso facto* one that should readily be accepted, and this incident thus comes to sum up the novel's surprising reversal of the traditional moral roles of God and the Devil." Frier, "Outline," 375. In a similar way Emery, "Pasteur," 80.

narrative goes beyond this. His Pastor contests violence and exploitation and attempts to teach his values to Jesus, as well. He wishes to save Jesus from the temptations of the violent God but Jesus never really adopts his pacifist ideology.

Nevertheless, in many respects Satan succeeds in the wilderness as far as the intertextual reading is concerned. His temptations are powerful, and Jesus becomes his disciple, at least for a short period. One probably should not speak of temptations at all since, in these novels, Jesus seems to be in the desert of the Enlightenment. He sees a new light and at least to some extent adopts a Nietzschean attitude towards the slavish religion of the fathers. The original story is turned inside out, and Jesus' temptations become a moment of education. It is as if he were in Paradise eating from the forbidden tree and gaining true knowledge about heaven and hell, and God and the Devil. After tasting the forbidden fruit Jesus' eyes are opened. If there is to be a Paradise, he must build it himself without divine guidance. According to Mailer's and Saramago's novels, Jesus then learns the Devil's way of speaking, begins to suspect that Israel's God is not the only god on the market, and finally starts to see the real face of the patriarchal Demiurge, the evil Creator of this world.[74]

Jesus' pact with the Devil is realised more on the level of a mutual agreement than in a direct discipleship. He never becomes a Devil's disciple in a literal sense. He neither proclaims the Devil's message nor mentions his name. But he clearly appears as a practical atheist. The novels are ambivalent on this subject, though. One could say that the Devil's teaching that Jesus adopts is atheistic, but Jesus' message remains religious. In this respect there remains a tension between rewriting and obedience to the source text. One could more accurately say that the biblical subtext extant in the novel becomes the culminating point where these two contradictory tendencies collide. The source text is quoted

---

74. Bloom asks: "Why is Pastor in the book?" The question is important, but Bloom's answer is perhaps insufficient as he says: "Evidently, only as a witness, I think one has to conclude." Bloom, "One with the Beard," 158. The Pastor no doubt appears as a witness to God's devious plans but there must be also other reasons for his character. Firstly, the source text tells Saramago to include the Devil in the cast. Secondly, the Devil is a fitting counterpoint to a violent God of history and thus a justification for a reversal of roles. Furthermore, since the Devil appears as Jesus' mentor, it is possible to create a Faustian story where Jesus through his novitiate can learn completely new things from the transcendental world as well as this *terra*, of course.

only in so far as it can support the aims of the author, and the subtext is being constructed so that it can agree with the critical view of traditional Christianity. Considering the results of the two preceding chapters together, one can say that in Mailer's and Tunström's novels this kind of ambivalence is obvious, while Saramago keeps leaning towards atheism. Roberts and Fredriksson, in their turn, maintain Jesus' religious program despite the fact that its content will be essentially changed, but this is probably due to the fact the Devil has no visible role in their stories.

It is obvious that Messianic idealism is completely inverted in these novels. As a disciple of the Devil, Jesus fulfils no prophecies. Instead, he goes through a process of inner development outgrowing traditional religion. He seeks independence from God, even though he appears to be dependent on the Devil. Authors could easily have made him look different. Instead of a Jewish Messiah he could be a violent Messiah or a Son of natural selection, and Saramago makes hints in that direction. But this would be too much. The new Jesus is a European humanist who wishes all people well. He reaches beyond good and evil; this is evident in several examples seen already in these short analyses, but there is a limit. There appears to be collective Messianism which resembles the Nietzschean "will to power." This kind of freedom from old slavish religion has an ethical purpose in the novels. Jesus never becomes a villain, as Nietzsche's *Übermensch* could when necessary. Usually the reaching beyond good and evil in these novels means simply sexual freedom, promiscuity. Most of the novels analysed here sport examples of this. In fact, other kinds of examples are hard to find. For instance Jesus' canonical temptations are turned into questions about sexuality or God's hidden lust. In most of the investigated novels this develops later into stories about Jesus sexual relationships.

The problem with these intertextual changes is that the Jesus-figure in the novels remains quite pale. Jesus has no clear mission and can no longer be called a proper Messiah of the Jewish people. He is ambivalent about the Mosaic tradition and the Devil's teachings and oscillates between them. He should learn the "will to power" but most of the time he seems to lack any will even of his own. Mailer's Jesus looks most of the time like a schoolboy and Saramago's Jesus has completely lost his way. This kind of Jesus is almost "the man without qualities." He no longer proclaims any real doctrine about salvation. This does not mean that the Jesus-figure does not have any proper role in the novels themselves.

The authors do use their character to create a narrative with a purpose. But in most intertextual revisions, Jesus generally remains insignificant and has nothing in common with his biblical prototype. One begins to suspect that these novels are not Jesus-books at all. Instead, his person has probably been selected in order to speak about something else.

3. JESUS AGAINST MOSES

Jesus' distance from Israel's God means simultaneously his deferral of God's word. This is a clear intertextual procedure that can be detected in the Jesus-novels. Judaism was a religion of the Torah, and Israel at the time of Jesus was a people of the Law. The canonical Jesus respects God's revelation and, in a famous passage from the Sermon on the Mount, he states that not even the smallest *iota* will disappear from the divine Law.[75] Furthermore, Jesus is called "rabbi" in the Gospels. He works as a teacher of the Mosaic Law educating his disciples in the knowledge of Israel's Holy Scriptures. For Jesus, the basic purpose of God's will and all the aspects of the Torah are embodied in the dual command of love and, more obvious still for a reader raised in the Christian West, the Golden Rule: "In everything do to others as you would have them do to you; for this is the law and the prophets" (Matt 7:12).

This is not what one finds in the novels. Here again they follow Nietzsche, according to whom not one justified or intelligent commandment exists in the Jewish Torah. Nietzsche went to great pains to separate biblical commandments and love: "What is done out of love always takes place beyond good and evil."[76] For him, all divine precepts were to be considered absurd and most of them even harmful for human beings. They were designed merely in order to please God, to extol his honor, and to ensure true devotion to him. Divine vanity is the basic motivation for teaching the Torah's commandments.[77]

Tunström's Jesus, who had drifted into a conflict with his legalistic teachers at Qumran, began to oppose the divine commandments. For him, a proper and sensible law could never be something that is transmitted merely in Jewish tradition. Justice must be based exclusively on

---

75. From the beginning of the Sermon on the Mount, Matt 5:18.

76. Nietzsche, *Beyond Good and Evil*, § 153.

77. See Nietzsche, *Gay Science*, § 135; cf. my Introduction above, section 5, on Nietzsche.

personal convictions and, thus, it belongs more to the area of feelings than the area of instituted rules.

> I do not believe those who say that they believe in Law and Scriptures. One cannot believe in a word. Word comes from the outside. Someone has merely told them that if you believe in *this*, you have faith. But what does it mean? I wish I knew. My body hurts all over so that I'm breaking into pieces. All contradictions, everything noble and everything mean, all mixed up, the whole thing.[78]

For Tunström the essence of faith is love, which is beyond morality. He contrasts love with Jewish tradition and the Mosaic Torah. He seeks for an experience that could assure him about the meaningfulness of life. Old Testament law cannot do this because, for Tunström, divine precepts have no power to engender the good things in life. In a sense, God does not speak to Tunström's Jesus. The only voice he hears is his own inner voice, which alone is able to access the reality of life and its goodness.

> I want—and I know that it is possible—that when faith becomes real it will once and for all sweep away everything, everything that is in its way: one can see trees before they become trees, birds before they become birds. One is just in a moment before. And love. One must surrender to love. Life will be seen in a new light. And nothing has been left outside. Do you understand?[79]

In the novel, these words mean also a final departure from Qumran and its Essene piety. It was a community of the Scriptures. The main purpose of the whole monastery was the preservation, copying, and teaching of the Torah. The Qumran caves saved dozens of writings and even commentaries on Old Testament books, which all testify to such a motivation in the life of the sectarians.[80] Love, for Tunström's Jesus, cannot be found in the Torah. The author understands Jewish law as just a collection of useless precepts that direct religious life and have

---

78. Tunström, *Ökenbrevet*, 118. "Det är så att de som svarar att de tror på Lagen och Skrifterna, dom tror inte jag på. Man kan inte tro på ett ord. Ett ord kommer utifrån. Någon har talat om det för dem, att bara du tror på *detta*, så har du tro. Men vad betyder det? Om jag visste det. Det gör så ont i kroppen på mig att jag håller på att gå i bitar. Alla motsägelser, allt högt och lågt som blandas, all historia."

79. Ibid.

80. For the nature of the sect, see Stegemann, *Library of Qumran*, 80–82, 104–5.

nothing to do with the problems of everyday life for ordinary people. This is why in the end the novel climaxes in Jesus' cry: "I say: what lacks is love."[81] Love, for Tunström, is the opposite of the rabbis' cold language of power. The language of love and caring is Jesus' new discourse and his Messianic message. What never changes is the opposition to the message of the Old Testament.

In Tunstöm's *The Letter from the Wilderness,* love is the opposite of the Law. This intertextual inversion appears in all the novels studied in this work. Israel's Torah is a metanarrative that needs to be rejected. In his *Gospel,* Mailer goes even further and, despite being a Jewish author, describes Judaism as petty legalism quite as the nineteenth century anti-Judaists did.

> Yet one cannot honor the pious. For no matter what care is taken to satisfy them by studious observance of the laws, they can never be satisfied. Indeed, how can one obey the Law absolutely? The laws of observance were written by men more pious than oneself. Therefore the Law, if by a tittle, has once more been broken.[82]

Jewish law, for Mailer, is a law of observance, and his Jesus attacks pious Jews who demand the observance of the Torah's precepts. But Mailer does not refer to a soteriological argument, as Jesus does in the canonical Gospels. The problem is not merely that people are unable to fulfil the commandments. Once again the problem lies in the fact that, according to Mailer, the Old Testament law of the scribes is the opposite of love. Jesus criticises the teachers of the Torah from this angle. "Dirt, to them, was a sea of sin. But where in any one of them could one find a love of God that was ready to sacrifice all that they had?"[83]

Moreover, in Mailer's description Jesus is not alone in proclaiming against the Scriptures. Even God himself, who in one instance speaks from the heavens, states that the sacred writings are not to be trusted. "And a strong voice spoke into my ear: 'The words of the prophets are not My words. My prophets are honest but full of excess.'"[84] For Mailer, the Scriptures are defective in two respects. Firstly, they do not recognise

---

81. Tunström, *Ökenbrevet,* 219.
82. Mailer, *Gospel,* 121.
83. Ibid., 122.
84. Ibid., 65.

genuine love and, secondly, they are full of human imagination, which exaggerates the original intentions of the heavenly Being.

Fredriksson follows the same path but adopts another kind of strategy. For her Jesus-figure, all doctrines are defective. For Fredriksson, there is no Torah that can be considered a divine revelation. Her Jesus rejects Israel's tradition almost completely. In the novel this view is naturally based on Jesus' own teaching. Jesus told Mary that his own father had taught him both practical skills as a carpenter and the basic knowledge of the Scriptures ever since his childhood. "And I learned the scriptures from him. The Torah filled my ears. I know it all, but the beautiful words have never really fastened in my heart."[85] The critique against the Torah is further confirmed by a skillful quotation taken from the canonical Gospels, crafting the subtext too to confirm the author's interpretation. Teachers of the law were to be held as enemies of good morals, and their message, as Nietzsche would say, a contradiction to life.

> Mary flushed as always when she was upset, and her voice rose as she went on, emphasizing every word. "Woe unto you, also you lawyers, for you lade men with burdens grievous to be borne. Woe unto you, lawyers, for you have taken away the key of knowledge: you entered not in yourselves, and them that were entering in you hindered."[86]

In the course of Fredriksson's narrative this theme has a special role since it gradually grows into the proclamation of doctrine-free Gnosticism. Before treating this issue more deeply, the essential feature to be noted here is the opposition between the Torah-teachers and Fredriksson's Jesus. Divine commandments are not considered defective because sin, the heritage of Adam, has made them ineffective for gaining salvation. Instead, all laws are seen merely as "burdens," which are useless and even noxious. The keeping of laws hinder people from entering the real kingdom of God.

But what is the kingdom of heaven for Fredriksson? The answer can be found in the wisdom of which Mary patiently reminds the apostle Peter: "The kingdom of heaven is within you." For Mary, the kingdom is "among us." It is the kingdom that is the opposite of the realm of the law,

---

85. Fredriksson, *According to Mary*, 101.
86. Ibid., 135.

the kingdom of love. "I've thought so much about it, about the love that was there among all of us who followed him." For Fredriksson's Mary, too, love is the opposite of God's law.[87]

It is probably worth noting that Saramago in his *Gospel* speaks little about God's law and ignores any ponderings about the nature of love. He does oppose God's Word with the Devil's intentions, as we noted earlier, but this does not lead to contradictions similar to Mailer's or Fredriksson's.[88] In fact, love does not belong to Saramago's vocabulary. He does not want to drift into theological debates about the nature of love or the true intentions of Jesus' original proclamation. Instead, he makes sure that he is in control in his straightforward attack of the Bible. This shows that Saramago is not particularly interested in the content of Christian beliefs. The world is a mess, and Saramago himself is not going to offer any easy solutions for the problems of human life. Most authors follow a different path. For them love, as the opposite of the Jewish Torah, is the answer. The old metanarrative must be rejected and replaced by a new solidarity and caring. God no longer has much to do with this.

However, as an intertextual strategy this is somewhat inconsistent. Assessed from a simple theological perspective understandable for any reader, the Torah and love are not opposites in the New Testament. Instead, Jesus in the canonical Gospels actually identifies God's commandments with love. This quickly becomes evident when one reads Jesus' most famous sayings, such as the Golden Rule, or the Sermon on the Mount. Other passages confirm this view. In the Gospel According to Mark, a scribe comes to Jesus and asks him about the Old Testament commandments: "Which commandment is the first of all?" Jesus' answer belongs to the best-known New Testament passages:

> The first is, "Hear, O Israel: the Lord our God, the Lord is one; you shall love the lord your God with all your heart, and with all your soul, and with all your mind, and with all your strength." The second is this, "You shall love your neighbor as yourself." There is no other commandment greater than these. (Mark 12:29–30)[89]

---

87. Ibid., 137.

88. See Saramago, *Gospel*, 177–78.

89. In a theological sense Jesus' answer is wise since he speaks his opponent's own language. Thus it would be very difficult for a Jewish scribe to disagree with him. This small detail confirms the fact that the identification of law and love was common in Judaism.

Here Jesus does not contrast his own message with Old Testament teaching but, instead, answers his opponent by referring to the most intimate Jewish beliefs. The first part of Jesus' answer is not precisely the first one of the Ten Commandments as such but recapitulates the essential *Shema*-confession (Deut 6:4) that was held in phylacteries and uttered three times a day during the daily prayers. The second part is a revision of Lev 19:18, "You shall not take vengeance or bear a grudge against any of your people, but you shall love your neighbor as yourself: I am the Lord." The idea of love being the essence of the Mosaic Law is thus not just Jesus' own conviction but the traditional teaching of the Old Testament itself. Hence, in the biblical context distinguishing between God's law and altruist love is unjustified.

A similar interpretation is later provided by the apostle Paul who summarises his understanding of the nature of the Mosaic Law by referring to love: "Owe no one anything, except to love one another; for the one who loves another has fulfilled the law."

> The commandments, "You shall not commit adultery; You shall not murder; You shall not steal; You shall not covet"; and any other commandment, are summed up in this word, "Love your neighbor as yourself." Love does no wrong to a neighbor; therefore, love is the fulfilling of the law. (Rom 13:9–10).

It is hard to believe that the authors of the Jesus-novels do not know these oft quoted passages. This leads to the conclusion that the authors' polarisations are intentional. The deliberate contradiction between law and love must be an intertextual move that aims at something particular in their work. And this is especially interesting when one considers the ideological opposition the authors want to follow. Old Testament law, the Torah in which the canonical Jesus wants to ground his message, represents *Sklavenmoral*. According to these Jesus-novels the law binds its followers to a slavish religion that gives nothing but burdens hard to bear. The Jesus of the New Testament was wrong. God's word has nothing to do with love. Genuine love must be detected and defined after the Jewish legalism present still in Jesus' teaching has been rooted out of and separated from pure faith.

Such a polarisation would be expected in an openly Nietzschean tradition, but in the context of twentieth-century history and ideological traditions it is surprising. A devastatingly negative view of Judaism was common before the Second World War but after the Holocaust everything changed both in philosophy and theology. After the war, biblical scholars saw and condemned anti-Judaistic attitudes, allowing for Jewish faith to be interpreted in a completely new light. In New Testament criticism, E. P. Sanders published his monograph *Paul and Palestinian Judaism* where he harshly criticised German scholarship's traditional picture of Judaism. During the nineteenth century and before the war, Judaism was regarded as a legalistic religion that had become estranged from life. The idea of a legalistic Judaism was commonplace in the writings of Weber, Schürer, and Bousset.[90] For example Wilhelm Bousset, in his *Die Religion des Judentums* (1926), describes early Judaism as "eine Religion der Observanz" (a religion bound by hereditary precepts).[91] This kind of attitude was common among scholars, and it directed research for well more than a century. According to Bousset, morality based in Old Testament law was destined to end up in a casuistic view of life.[92]

Why, then, do the Jesus-novels still adopt a negative view of the Torah? It would have been more accurate and tolerant to create a narrative where the original principles of Judaism were described more positively. There is more than one answer to that question. It is plausible that these authors are unaware of this discussion in the fields of biblical criticism and Jewish studies. A basic and general knowledge of European cultural history apparently does not provide sufficient information about a principal change in attitudes towards Judaism. The most obvious answer, however, is that the polarising tradition the authors have adopted in itself produces such an opposition. Nietzschean antagonism against Jewish slave morality is anti-Judaist, and any author accepting its implicit premises cannot help ending up with a negative view of the Torah—even though such a view can no longer be held as historically true.

---

90. See Sanders, *Paul*, 2–6, 33–34. Sanders's work was perfectly timed and soon blazed a new trail for New Testament studies in general. It inaugurated the new approach of post-Holocaust interpretation where negative views of Judaism were consciously put aside and scholars attempted to do justice to the ancient texts they were investigating.

91. Bousset, *Religion des Judentums*, 85; cf. 409.

92. "Durch den engen Zusammenhang mit dem Gesetz ist der jüdischen Sittlichkeit ferner der Charakter der Uneinheitlichkeit und kleinlichen Kasuistik aufgeprägt." Ibid., 137.

Furthermore, the authors' view of Jewish law proves that this common intertextual change has been made on theological premises. It is not just a literary strategy that one could employ on the basis of pure imagination. In many novels the subtext is skilfully constructed against the source text. The contrasting of the Torah and love is deliberate. The qualities ascribed to authentic love must, in this polarised situation, be taken beyond good and evil and contrasted with the traditional Christian view. Otherwise the whole narrative would be meaningless, and Jesus-novels would just be copying biblical ideas in a slightly altered form. Usually this is expressed by reducing love to eros. Thus, these novels adopt a discourse of discontinuity where the constructed opposition becomes the basis for a new picture of Jesus. Jesus becomes an enemy of Moses and begins to preach new freedom from the law. This first aspect concerns the novels' interpretation of the Torah. The contradiction becomes even more intense when their assessment of Judaism as a religion is the target.

4. TRANSFERRING JESUS OUT OF JUDAISM

Nietzsche was not too happy with Jesus' Jewishness. For him, the Jewish nature of the biblical character was delusive and dangerous while proclaiming the slavish propaganda of the former patriarchs. "Too Jewish," shouted Nietzsche. The founder of Christianity "was not refined enough in his feelings at this point—being a Jew." Such an anti-Judaist attitude was no coincidence but rather a consistent conclusion of Nietzsche's *Destruktionen*, which expressed his intention to distill the Jesus-figure from his traditional features. This is also why Nietzsche made Jesus proclaim against Judaism in *Beyond Good and Evil*.

> Jesus told his Jews: "The law was meant for servants—love God as I love him, as his son! What do we sons of God care about morality!"[93]

For this reason Nietzsche began to construct a new Jesus-character. He even spoke of Jesus as the sole Christian, after whose appearance everything in Christianity went astray. And naturally, his Zarathustra wished to be an exemplary saviour in whom the principles of the new race's master morality became flesh.[94]

---

93. Nietzsche, *Beyond Good and Evil*, § 164.
94. See especially Nietzsche, *Gay Science*, § 140; *Anti-Christ*, § 39.

Should Jesus be understood without his Jewish background? Should his value be assessed merely on later Western readers' terms and their subjective values? This happened widely in Protestant theology in the twentieth century. The figure of Jesus was adapted to the world of materialism and technology. Jewish features were separated from his "real" person. This kind of translocation was not explicitly anti-Judaist as such, for the most part, but it was accompanied by the distorted picture of Judaism that prevailed in scholarly tradition at that time. As we saw above, it perfected in the nineteenth century when a negative view on Judaism had been a commonplace. Judaism had been considered a religion of casuistic legalism leading to petty asceticism in everyday life. This conforms more or less with Nietzsche's view about Judaism.[95]

Recent Jesus-novels tend to fall into the same tradition of interpretation. They are not openly anti-Judaist but, nevertheless, they deprive the canonical Jesus of his Jewish heritage.[96] In many of the investigated novels Jesus is no longer a Jewish preacher with a Jewish identity. He does not follow Moses, as we saw above, and he does not even worship Yahweh, the God of Israel. Through transgressing and probably "erring," as Taylor would put it, he becomes a frivol who constructs his own life as he wishes. The features of the new life may be almost anything from anarchism to fervent socialism—but not Judaism.[97]

There are at least two different kinds of reinterpretations in the novels concerning this polarisation. In certain novels Jesus' Jewishness is played down by making him oppose Jewish traditions. For instance Tunström's Jesus still lives in the conservative community of Qumran, but the situation as a whole is inconsistent. The beliefs of the community are not precisely those of the historical Qumran and its convictions. And more importantly still, the Jesus-figure even opposes those beliefs. "I

---

95. See for instance Kelley, *Racializing Jesus*, 65–73.

96. When writing on Mailer, Gelernter notes: "Don't conclude that, because Mailer doesn't tell this story like a Christian, he tells it like a Jew. Jewish scholars have long rejected as impossible the Gospel account of the legal proceedings culminating in the Crucifixion, and Mailer is scrupulously faithful to the Gospels. The Gospels and the Jews disagree radically on the Pharisees: Jews see them as heroes and martyrs struggling to uphold the legal framework of Torah under the killing pressure of Rome. Mailer of course lines up with the Gospels, and it isn't clear that he understands what the normative Jewish view is." Gelernter, "Gospel," 55–56.

97. The reference is to Taylor's idea in his postmodern theology, see *Erring*, 8–10, 20.

do not want to follow the path of Truth. I believe that I must *be* the Truth."[98] Tunström probably does not intend any conscious destruction of Jewish precepts or biblical morality. He just replaces Jewish casuistic legalism with Western individualism. This is also what Nietzsche did in his more aggressive criticism. The essential point is in the reinterpretation through which Jesus is transferred from the Jordan Valley to middle-class Sweden.

Saramago too is active in stripping Jewish features from Jesus' person. The most impressive examples of this, quite naturally, can be found in stories about Jesus and the Pastor. As Satan educates his novice in the wilderness, main lessons concern God's violent nature and the uselessness of Jewish tradition. Saramago's Satan is no Jew, but neither does his Jesus appear as one, at least not as an orthodox Jew following God's divine precepts in his life. The novitiate culminates in Jesus' visit to the temple in Jerusalem. He actually does sacrifice a lamb but he has already adopted the Pastor's teaching about the slavish nature of such a procedure. Saramago's Jesus is no longer an obedient Jew with high calling. The final purpose of the story is to reveal God's essential thirst for blood. In this respect everything that the Jewish religion and Old Testament worship represents is described in dark colours. For Saramago, biblical Christianity is too Jewish.[99]

Mailer goes even further in this subject. Even as a Jewish writer he, for some reason, describes Judaism as a religion of petty legalism as we noted earlier. "Yet one cannot honor the pious. For no matter what care is taken to satisfy them by studious observance of the laws, they can never be satisfied."[100] Even though Mailer's Jesus also learns from Satan he is not as obedient a disciple as the Jesus-figure in Saramago's novel. In fact, towards the end of his story Mailer makes Jesus accuse the Jewish people of following Satan in their daily life and thus earning God's punishment. "Did the great wrath of my Father come from knowing that His chosen people might be more loyal to Satan than to Him?"[101]

In some of these novels, however, the reinterpretation is transferred to the realm of the so-called pagan religions. The Jewishness of the canonical Jesus is rejected especially by making his new message

98. Tunström, *Ökenbrevet*, 118.
99. Saramago, *Gospel*, 187, 191.
100. Mailer, *Gospel*, 121.
101. Ibid. 68, 131.

resemble Gnosticism or more generally some other Eastern religion. In Fredriksson's novel Leonidas first states that Jesus' teaching is identical with Egyptian wisdom: "His teaching was largely based on ancient wisdom."[102] Later Mary herself becomes a witness to this.

> Mary stood still as she gazed over the town and thought about how she had walked along the great avenues and listened to the Buddhist monks in their saffron yellow robes and heard the Zoroastrian wise men preaching. In Antioch, she had found Iranian thinking on the resurrection of the soul, Jewish philosophy, Babylonian astrology, and Greek philosophy. She had increasingly often stopped at the Indian wise men and listened to them speaking of the core of man being identical with God, even recognized it—Jesus could have said the same, although his words would have been different.[103]

For Fredriksson, Jesus' message does not grow out of the Old Testament or the Mosaic teaching of the Jewish tradition. It would never have resembled Pharisaic wisdom or Qumranic apocalypticism. As an intertextual collage, Jesus' teaching resembles rather the syncretistic message of the Zorastrians and the imaginative Buddhist monks Fredriksson refers to. Jewish faith and Jewish confession are no longer needed. If there is divine revelation, for Fredriksson, it can be found in any religion—except the one represented by the New Testament. The divinity of human beings is at the core of the new message and, therefore, any proclamation of human sinfulness would be a blasphemy against the new belief. In spite of the superficial pleasantness of such an open and tolerant attitude the result is unavoidable: Jesus' figure is intentionally transferred out of the sphere of Judaism.

(Post)modern authors are not in good company here. Nietzsche's anti-Judaistic if not anti-Semitic attitudes were well accepted and adopted in German Nazi ideological reinterpretation in the 1930s.[104] The most influential of these ideological writings was the book by Alfred Rosenberg (1893–1946). His *The Myth of the Twentieth Century* (*Der*

---

102. Fredriksson, *According to Mary*, 151.

103. Ibid., 155.

104. There has been discussion about Nietzsche's anti-Judaism, based on the fact that Nietzsche himself admits his racist attitudes in *Beyond Good and Evil*, 251. He was not free of this "sickness." But in the very same passage he repeats his worst prejudices against the Jews stating that they, whenever they wish to do so, could rise in power and take over Europe. For the problem in general, see my Introduction above.

Mythus des zwanzigsten Jahrhunderts) was published in 1930 and sold millions of copies. Rosenberg adapted Nietzsche's "wild proclamation concerning the superman" to his own optimistic views of the future of the humankind. It was time for all inferiority to be put into the past.[105]

Rosenberg's Jesus was no longer a Jew. He had not merely been distanced from Judaism or transferred to another position. He was not of Jewish descent. Rosenberg's racist interpretation, based on the suggestions of Houston S. Chamberlain, stated that coming from Galilee Jesus actually had to be an Aryan. Therefore, and quite according to the conventions of Nazi ideology, Jesus did not even resemble a Jew by appearance. He was tall, thin, and handsome with a long blond hair. This was also what Jesus had looked like Western art for centuries. For Rosenberg, both history and art proved that the real Jesus had actually been against Judaism from the very start.[106]

This is not far from the descriptions of the investigated Jesus-novels. Even though the motivation for such an interpretation is completely different in these two approaches, the genealogy of the concept is similar. A Jewish Jesus is not popular. If the figure of Jesus is to be transferred to the world of modern or even postmodern humanity, he must be cleansed of Judeo-Christian traits. Like Nietzsche and many liberal theologians in Germany, Rosenberg felt he knew how the picture of Jesus had become distorted in history.

> The great personality of Jesus Christ which should have been the point of departure for all descriptions, was soon after his death mixed with different kinds of Asian, Jewish, and African nonsense.[107]

The description given in the canonical Bible represented, for Rosenberg, in fact a perversion of real history. Therefore, biblical history should be written anew. This is what Rosenberg attempted to do, simultaneously criticising the views of the canonical text. If Nietzsche claimed that the New Testament was about to "Judaise" the whole world, Rosenberg took the next step. He naturally repeated that claim (*Verjudung*), but noted that the apostle Paul professed a kind of a racial chaos (*Rassenchaos*) that would result in a bastardisation

---

105. Rosenberg, *Mythus*, 581.
106. Ibid., 51, 672.
107. Ibid., 101.

(*Verbastardierung*) of Christianity.¹⁰⁸ How close is all this to the intertextual polarisation of the investigated novels?

This attitude has found its way into theology. There is a surprising analogy between Rosenberg's explanation of the deification of Jesus and that of German rationalistic theology in the early eighteenth century. Rosenberg had maintained that there must have been a historical development that gradually produced the idea of Jesus' divinity. Nietzsche had stated that it was the apostle Paul who invented a religion based on sacrifice and atonement. Rosenberg contributed to this by claiming that Paul had adopted a peculiar Chrestos-myth from Rome, this Chrestos being a liberator of slaves. As this idea was combined with irresponsible Old Testament interpretations, the emergence of a new theological doctrine was unavoidable. In Paul's proclamation Jesus became the Saviour of the whole world.¹⁰⁹

Such views were not news in the area of theology, where Hermann Reimarus (1694–1768), a deist and a religious individualist, had already in the 1760s suggested that the canonical story about Jesus' divinity could be nothing but a pious invention. Since the real historical Jesus, according to Reimarus, had been just a normal Galilean man with a political program, everything else in the Christian religion must be a product of deception. In his *Fragments* Reimarus states that, after the events of the Passover, the disciples stole Jesus' body and began to proclaim a message about his resurrection from the dead. Christian dogma, as well as our picture of Jesus, is based on a lie.¹¹⁰

These examples show that Jesus had been extracted from Judaism and transferred into the symbolic world of the Enlightenment long before the time of the investigated Jesus-novels. Nietzsche himself, in this respect, was but one minor representative of the new interpretation. For more than two centuries, both in theology and in Christian culture, the conviction that the canonical picture of Jesus was merely an invention has existed. It was the fruit of pious imagination or, to adopt Nietzsche's or Rosenberg's view, a Jewish delusion distorting the original message of the historical Jesus. Our Jesus-novels stand thus in a long line of reinterpretations concerning the historical figure of Jesus. These books

---

108. Ibid., 103.
109. Ibid., 101–2.
110. See Reimarus's text in Talbert, *Reimarus*, 153–54.

continue to separate Jesus from Judaism and reconstruct his picture according to the ideas of post-Christian Western thinkers.

In such an interpretation, biblical Christianity is merely a fable-based creation based on Jewish lies. This hermeneutical approach is based on an anti-Judaist dichotomy. This inspired Albert Camus later to proclaim:

> We must first of all realize that we can never confuse Nietzsche with Rosenberg. We must be the advocates for the defence of Nietzsche. He himself has said so, denouncing in advance his bastard progeny, "he who had liberated his mind still has to purify himself". But the question is to find out if the liberation of the mind, as he conceived it, does not preclude purification. The idea that comes to a head with Nietzsche, and that supports him, has its laws and its logic which, perhaps, explain the bloody travesty of his philosophy.[111]

After such comparisons, one can conclude that many of the investigated Jesus-novels have absorbed this anti-Judaistic stance. It is not intentional or even conscious but, nevertheless, it exists in the basic structure of the hermeneutical approach. The authors have clearly inherited this attitude from their culture and from the Nietzschean polarisation between the ostensible Jewish/Christian slave morality and Western humanism. This kind of anti-Judaistic tendency is not openly anti-Semitic, to be sure. The authors are not writing against race, but only against religion or morals. No writer would want to be proven guilty of actual anti-Semitism in the present cultural situation. But the tragedy of Western humanism lies undoubtedly in the fact that, from the days of Nietzsche, the freedom of the Faustian spirit has been tied up with an opposition to the Jewish/Christian slavish religion.

5. FROM DEIFICATION TO HUMANIZATION

What do the Jesus-figures of the novels represent? Why have they been constructed? The first answer to these questions is literary. Given that

---

111. Camus remains ambivalent in his relation to Nietzsche and must create a dualist hermeneutics in order to cope with his racist philosophy: "Cannot the killers, provided that they deny the spirit for the letter (and even what still remains of the spirit in the letter), find their pretext in Nietzsche? The answer must be Yes." Camus, *Rebel*, 67–68. Later in his book, Camus does admit that the idea of violence belongs to the core of Nietzsche's thinking; see chapter 6.2. below.

the theological theme of incarnation may already awaken questions about Jesus' human nature, some logical conclusions follow automatically. How does Jesus become conscious of his calling? He must have gone through some kind of inner process. What does he think about justice, and how does he argue for his ethics? Jesus can easily be planted into a Nietzschean context where a traditional justification of moral theory is questioned. What is his relation to women and sexuality? Jesus could easily be described as a person with sexual experience.[112]

The literary approach is a theoretical one, and it produces pure fiction. Some passages, for instance in Saramago's or Fredriksson's novels, express this kind of rewriting and imagining and do not really attempt to contest the canonical story but to expand it or test it. In this respect they are similar to Paul Park's *The Gospel of Corax*, which takes Jesus to India, or Dowling's *The Aquarian Gospel*, which makes Jesus a devout Hindu.[113] These fantastic presentations do not suggest that the historical Jesus had anything to do with Hinduism. Likewise, there are many invented passages in the investigated novels, even though their nature differs from that of Park's or Dowling's. Recent Jesus-novels never remain completely on this level, though. Instead, they are interested in a contradiction between Jesus and God. They spend much time making Jesus transgress divine Law.

The genre, as noted before, is often that of a *Bildungsroman* and the novels propose several different psychological explanations for Jesus' mental growth. These developments reflect the novels' weakest presentations. How does one get a passionate and believing preacher out of a deprived child? Or how does ambivalence in theological matters turn into great ideologies merely by listening to the Devil in the wilderness? Consistency does not seem to be the strong suit of these novels. For instance, according to Mailer, Tunström, and Saramago, the young Jesus

---

112. In scholarship Nietzsche has usually been seen as aiming at a construction of the psychological "type" (den "psychologischen Typus") of Jesus. See Benz, *Nietzsches Ideen*, 17f.

113. Park, *Gospel of Corax*, 257, for instance, describes Jesus' message as a kind of meditation. Dowling's Jesus, in turn, travels to Lahore and even teaches a Brahmic priest the following: "He taught him how he could control the spirits of the air, the fire, the water and the earth; and he explained to him the secret doctrine of forgiveness, and the blotting out of sins." *Aquarian Gospel* 37:7.

has a one-dimensional personality that contradicts the image of an educated Jew well versed in Old Testament history and cultic tradition.[114]

There must be another explanation for this. The character-less, impersonal Jesus must be a tool serving the purposes of the novels. He is raw material for artistic constructions. Jesus has first been cleansed of all his canonical characteristics so that he can be moulded into a new role, the one given by the authors. There is some analogy with the historical-critical study of the "historical Jesus" here. In the area of New Testament criticism, the discussion about the tension between history and faith has, itself, a long history. Not all scholars assume that the canonical Gospels describe history "as it really happened"—very few, in fact. Instead, since the beginning of the nineteenth century an influential tradition of Protestant scholarship has claimed that these stories are in fact religious fictionalisations. The Gospel of Matthew, for instance, has often been seen as fiction. The picture of the canonical Jesus has, thus, been considered a pious construction. He is a hypothesis that needs to be proven wrong. Historical criticism first deprived the canonical character of his specific qualities, his identity and his message. Then scholars attempted to reconstruct the real historical Jesus behind the texts. This logic begets a new question. Is the canonical Gospel's relation to the historical Jesus similar to that of, for instance, Mailer's novel's relation to the historical Jesus?[115]

Ziolkowski, when uncovering the cultural context for post-rationalist Jesus-novels, pays considerable attention to David Strauss who, already in 1835, attempted to solve the problems rationalism had created in the supernaturalist discussion.

> He had noted that many of the deeds and miracles attributed to Jesus were fulfillments of expectations pronounced in the Old Testament. Rather than accepting them on faith or explaining them away by rational means, he concluded that these elements were actually literary conventions added to the accounts of the life of Jesus by the authors of the Gospels, who wanted to make

---

114. Already Ziolkowski noted the fact that towards the end of the twentieth century, in novels written for instance by Lars Görling, Günter Grass, and Gore Vidal, the Jesus figure is presented in a new way and described as an uncertain individualist. Ziolkowski, *Fictional Transfigurations*, 225–26.

115. In Kümmel's history of research several chapters describe these changes. Kümmel, *History*, 120, 281. The precise examples of historicism in Gospel studies are given by Schweitzer, *Quest*, 78–81, 193–95.

of the historical Jesus a figure that corresponded in every respect to the predictions of the prophets. It is difficult to exaggerate the epochmaking brilliance of Strauss's two volumes, in which he elaborated this basic idea.[116]

According to Ziolkowski, Strauss was thus the first to distinguish systematically "between the Christ of faith and the Jesus of history." As the key word was "myth," this led to the stripping away of supernatural or Messianic elements in the story. In the paradigm of historicism, scholars believed that they knew the course of true history, and the interpretation of the Gospels turned into a quest for the "historical" Jesus. The Gospels themselves turned out to be "literary conventions." They were brought down from the religious heights of revelation into the world of human beings. From this perspective, the New Testament should be understood as fictional literature, just like Mailer's novels.[117]

It is tempting to shift into comparative literature and to compare Jesus-novels with a scholarly theory about the alleged "historical Jesus." In this case both the novel and the source text would be treated as fictional rereadings. Both would be considered interpretations of the original historical event about which there is, of course, no consensus among scholars. In scholarship, however, this resembles the fallacy of rationalism, which, in the twentieth century, developed into historicism. This theory was based on the conviction that a scholar could reach beyond ancient sources and decide the real nature of historical events, even if their speculations went against the existing documents themselves.[118] Such an approach has been abandoned in biblical interpretation. Materialistic reduction is not the primary task of biblical criticism. After linguistic analysis, investigations now focus on the content of the texts themselves.

However, the rationalist interpretation goes beyond the limits of intertextual analysis. The source text, for Saramago and Mailer and many

---

116. Ziolkowski, *Fictional Transfigurations*, 35–36.

117. In fact it was Reimarus who introduced the basic distinction between the historical Jesus and the so-called Christ of faith, as noted above, but this does not weaken Ziolkowski's comment. See Klein, *Reimarus*, 136–48. Ziolkowski is probably right in saying that some authors of the Jesus-novels followed Strauss's example.

118. Kaufman, in her analysis of Saramago's Jesus-novel, places Saramago in the Straussian tradition where authors aim at the humanisation of the canonical Jesus-figure. Kaufman, "Evangelical Truths," 451–52. I think this is only partly true because Saramago has no real interest in a "quest" for the historical Jesus.

other authors, is not any reconstructed picture of the "real" historical Jesus. Instead, the source text is simply the New Testament, which is a collection of manuscripts living its own life in history. Therefore the intertextual relationship in these novels is constructed between the texts. It is true that some of the ideas the authors exploit, like that of using Gnostic sources in the reinterpretation of the Christian faith, apparently come from the field of biblical criticism. The historical-critical method may have influenced the writing of the novels. But even here the counterpoint remains the same: the opposing pole is the canonical Bible with its Gospels describing Jesus' life.

Both a scholar and an author may, for instance, have a rationalist or materialist point of departure, but they proceed in opposite directions. A nineteenth-century historian wanted to reconstruct ancient history; the authors of recent Jesus-novel direct their work to contemporary rereading and revision. This is further confirmed by the fact that Jesus-novels do not really attempt to claim that the real Jesus resembled their reconstruction. Instead, they criticise the "historical" Jesus for not supporting the ideas that the new gospel promotes. The conclusion is undeniable. The authors of recent Jesus-novels, such as Mailer, Saramago, and Fredriksson, do not conduct historical-critical work. They do not attempt to reconstruct the historical Jesus. Claiming this would completely misconstrue the novels' purpose. They wish to present a new Jesus whose person contrasts with the canonical figure at every turn.[119]

It is actually Brown's novel *The Da Vinci Code* that, apart from theological textbooks, wishes to explain the mechanism of Jesus' deification. Because he is working in a different genre, Brown is able to speculate more than other Jesus-novels. Saramago too hints at making Jesus divine in the course of history but his remark remains vague. Brown's novel, however, provides a detailed explanation. The eccentric scholar Teabing claims that Christ's divinity was invented several hundred years after Jesus' death.

> "'Jesus' establishment as 'the Son of God' was officially proposed and voted on by the Council of Nicaea.'
> 'Hold on. You're saying Jesus' divinity was the result of a *vote*?'
> 'A relatively close vote at that,' Teabing added."[120]

---

119. Wood actually remarks that Mailer has "no interest in reality." Wood, "He Is Finished," 33.

120. Brown, *Da Vinci Code*, 315.

Sophie Neveu, Jesus' earthly heiress to be, for the first time in her life hears the real truth about Jesus' history. The argument is simple, and its premise is well known from any schoolbook treating the issue. In the Council of Nicaea (325 CE) the "creed of Nicaea" was written and after that, in the church that had just become tolerated and accepted in society, this creed about the Trinitarian God became the basis for formal Christian belief.[121]

It is a pity that *The Da Vinci Code* does not attempt to create a consistent narrative about this new theology, though. Brown identifies the real historical Jesus with the Saviour of the Gnostic gospels. These writings must be trustworthy because, according to the novel, the canonical Gospels were chosen from the vast group of eighty early gospels. Gnostic gospels, which the church soon abandoned, present Christ as a heavenly Spirit who can lead people to the sources of true wisdom. Jesus in Gnostic writings is merely a human being, as we saw in the first chapter, but Gnostic faith focused on Christ from the very beginning. Therefore, the Gnostics "invented" Christ's divinity already in those writings that Brown's Teabing quotes—and without voting.[122]

In *The Da Vinci Code*, thus, Jesus' divinity is the outcome of a conspiracy that the church supports. This is how Jesus can be married to Mary Magdalene and, as in Roberts's novel, beget a child. According to Brown's narrative, Jesus was later raised from the dead in order to tell Mary some heavenly secrets, but the reason for this is not mentioned. If his spirit, the Christ-spirit, has departed from the body and if, according to Gnosticism, soul is in principle imprisoned in the material body, why should Jesus the human being be raised from the dead? Gnostics do not accept bodily resurrection. Brown's novel does not rise to the theological level of Fredriksson's or Roberts's. The basic point of departure, however, is similar to that of other Jesus-novels investigated in this study. Jesus

---

121. The history of Christian creeds is interesting in itself. The relatively late Nicene Creed is based on the Roman creed that evolved around 200 CE. It is accompanied by the creeds found, for instance, in the letters of the martyred bishop Ignatius around 107 (see *Ign. Trall.* 9). These creeds base their presentation of Christian faith especially on Paul's letters in the New Testament (1 Cor 8:6; 15:1–5) as well as the "Great commission" (Matt 28:19). Kelly, *Early Christian Creeds*, 68, 102, 205.

122. Brown adds another conspiracy, now in agreement with the scholarly tradition Reimarus put forth in his time. "Constantine commissioned and financed a new Bible, which omitted those gospels that spoke of Christ's *human* traits and embellished those gospels that made Him godlike." Brown, *Da Vinci Code*, 317. One way or another, for Teabing, the present Bible is a forgery.

must be drawn back to this earth, and it is easiest to do this by making him an average Galilean man. As an intertextual procedure, this is a process of humanisation.

With the help of Jesus' renewed personality the authors are able to write a completely new gospel. This hints of Rosenberg, whose new interpretation was presented as the "fifth Gospel," but which was not a product of ecclesiastical synods. Instead, it was a gospel written by a superman and reflecting *Herrenmoral*. Only when the New Testament was purged of all negative attitudes, weeping and weakness of spirit, could it present Jesus as a hero for the present generation.[123] The Jesus-figures of Saramago, Mailer, and Roberts no longer speak against sin. In this respect these novels resemble their Nietzschean prototypes. This suggests that they wish to replace the canonical Gospel's Judaising pettiness with individual strength. Their Jesus can probably no longer be identified with the great Moralist of Renan's and Strauss's tradition, but they seek something more significant. As an opponent of God himself, the new Jesus is usually developed in the direction of an *Übermensch*, the so-called Superman who teaches a new ideology beyond good and evil.[124]

In this sense Saramago, Roberts and others also write fifth Gospels. They are rewritten in the same spirit as the older revisions, even though they follow new methods. The canonical image of a Jewish Jesus with his legalistic nomism and with his Messianic idealism is considered merely a distorted picture of Jesus the wandering free spirit who in the end listens to nothing but his own heart. Even though the Jesus-figure of the new adaptations often has a weak personality and remains in the shadow of Judas or Mary Magdalene, he shares in the values of an enlightened humanist. Ultimately this means he resembles the novel's author rather than his original predecessor in the Bible. In this respect Nietzsche's influence is immense. His Zarathustra never appears to be a monster but rather a proclaimer of altruistic love. The values the new Jesus represents resemble the common values of twentieth-century post-Christian Europe.

---

123. Rosenberg, *Mythus*, 659.

124. It is true as Kort noted that in previous Jesus-novels religious issues were usually presented by making the main character face the omnipotent God who is majestic and arouses reverence. This showed that there was something in this life that human beings could not control. Kort, *Narrative Elements*, 108. In the investigated novels the situation is reversed.

Turning God-Incarnate into a Faustian Frivol

In most of the investigated novels, Jesus appears as an average Jew who either wishes to contribute to human happiness, strengthen God in his struggle with the Devil, or even contest against God for the sake of greater humanity in this world.[125] Some traits of his divine nature remain in the story, but more as a strategic foil for his human nature. Some scholars go very far in such humanisation. Ricci, for instance, makes even Jesus' arrest and execution just the result of a misunderstanding. Jesus was a preacher and had a mission, even though there was nothing particularly divine in him. Judas no longer belonged to his group when the disciples went to Jerusalem and so the biblical information about the betrayal is wrong. The final conflict in Jesus' life was based on an unfortunate error as people took Jesus' joke about the building of a temple—a snow hut actually—at face value. Jesus was accused of rebellion, which, for the abovementioned reasons, was merely a misunderstanding and based on false rumors.[126]

In other words, these novels engage in a process of humanisation—one of Nietzsche's main missions. The new Jesus is an image of the modern man, sometimes even the postmodern man. Humankind prevails. This process is seemingly dependent on secularisation, but this point will be discussed later in this work. Here, Christology must make room for *Entmythologisierung* in a new way. Jesus really becomes a Faustian frivol. He learns from the Devil and wishes to attain true knowledge of life itself. This he cannot find in divine commandments, which merely restrict independent living. Therefore, Jesus' new values are "frightening" as Nietzsche said. They concern tradition, society, sexuality, family, and power. It is to these moral issues, therefore, that we now turn.

---

125. This is approximately how McDonald describes Mailer's Jesus: "Ultimately, Mailer portrays Jesus as a Judeo-Christian, left-conservative meliorist, a believer in, and preacher of, the power of human effort to strengthen the hand of God against the Devil and to realize the potential goodness in Creation." McDonald, "Theodicy," 88.

126. Ricci, *Testament*, 386. "The effect of Ricci's novel is brilliant: it shows how an extraordinary but thoroughly human person could come to have such fantastic things said or believed about him, and it makes this look completely natural." Crook, "Fictionalizing Jesus," 52.

3

Contesting the Moral Values of the Gospels

Nietzsche's depiction of Christian ethics as a slave morality is a key issue for investigating his influence on recent Jesus-novels. Contrast-novels that use extreme oppositions to juxtapose the narrative and its canonical source often focus on moral values. This does not mean that such themes are easy to discern, though. The Jesus of the new novels seldom appears as a nihilistic Anti-Christ opposing his biblical prototype. Admittedly, he is not an orthodox Jew or enthusiast but, at least in a general way, he seems like an ordinary Jew. In the intertextual readings of these works, however, the authors' strategies reveal their intentions to contrast the new gospels with their source text.

1. A REHABILITATION OF JUDAS

One of the most impressive, and probably also the most evident, examples of prototypical rewriting aiming at a reversal of traditional convictions is that of changing the image of Judas. Instead of being a historical archetype for a traitor, in some of these novels, Judas becomes the actual hero of the gospel. Especially in Mailer's *Gospel According to the Son*, Judas appears to be a committed Jew, a sincere believer and, moreover, a man of integrity. Such a perspective proves that something extraordinary is taking place in the literary strategy when Judas' role is changed. In the Bible, as a literary figure in the story, Judas is a traitor with his symbolic kiss and thirty pieces of silver.

With this choice, Mailer contributes to the so-called Judas-literature where Judas's person and role in the gospel narrative are reconsidered. Usually such novels attempt to rehabilitate Judas in the history of Christianity.[1] Judas-literature often grounds its historical point of depar-

---

1. On Judas-literature see the presentation of Pyper, "Modern Gospels of Judas,"

ture in Irenaeus, who in his *Against Heresies* cites a Valentinian Gnostic writing from the third century.² The writing was the *Gospel of Judas*, the original text of which later vanished. It was rediscovered recently in a manuscript, a papyrus codex, found in Egypt in the 1970s but published only three decades later.

Irenaeus discusses how, in the *Gospel of Judas*, the Gnostic heavenly goddess Sofia (Wisdom) combats with Old Testament God and protects revolutionary men such as Cain and Esau, as well as the men of Sodom, who all oppose the Demiurge, the Creator of this material world. Among Jesus' disciples Judas alone was given this secret knowledge. Therefore, quite consistently, the key to the proper understanding of Judas' betrayal lies in the Gnostic reading of canonical Gospel narratives. Its real nature will be revealed only to those familiar with gnosis, secret heavenly wisdom.

First of all, in Gnostic soteriology, Judas was Jesus' favorite pupil, and he alone understood Jesus' mission in this world. He learned the secret directly from Jesus himself that the Creator of this world was not the true heavenly God. Instead, he was a weak and evil Demiurge who had imprisoned the free souls of humanity in carnal bodies. Jesus' mission was to liberate people's souls and to elevate them into the heavenly realm. This is why Judas in his Gnostic gospel says to him: "I know who you are and where you have come from. You are from the immortal realm of Barbelo. And I am not worthy to utter the name of the one who has sent you." Jesus' task was commissioned by Barbelo, who was one of the heavenly divinities in the Gnostic pantheon.³

Judas' betrayal is described in the *Gospel of Judas* only indirectly. According to the narrative Jesus says to Judas: "But you will exceed all of them. For you will sacrifice the man that clothes me."⁴ With his act Judas wishes to help Jesus and to take part in the combat between the aforementioned two gods. There is no betrayal but an act of loyalty here. The logic of this act remains somewhat irrational, but this is only to be expected since two different ideas had to be joined together. Gnostic cosmology had to be linked with the extant Gospel tradition of the canonical New Testament. When Judas betrays Jesus he is merely cheating

---

111–22, esp. 112–14; cf. Cockerill, "Judas," 1090–91.

2. Irenaeus, *Against Heresies* 1.30.1.

3. Kasser et al., *Gospel of Judas*.

4. Ibid., 56.

the evil god of the material world. According to the story, the Demiurge believes he has been able to destroy the heavenly Christ-Spirit. He does not know that the Christ-Spirit has only temporarily possessed the body of the earthly Jesus. The Nazarene will be sacrificed, or in some Gnostic writings actually some other person is sacrificed on the cross, but this is a foil since the Christ-Spirit has already completed his mission on earth. He departs from the body of Jesus and returns to heaven right before the crucifixion.[5]

Even though the *Gospel of Judas* tradition has inspired Judas-literature in earlier periods, in recent Jesus-novels the Gnostic picture of Judas is usually not prominent. Transcendent cosmology has not inspired the imagination of the authors. The basic idea of changing Judas's role remains, though. In many novels Judas is as much a betrayed person as he is a traitor. Because the Jesus of the new narratives does not commit to the plans that have been agreed on together, he does not gain Judas's respect. This is something that Jesus-novels have in common with the more general Judas-literature. Moreover, in some novels the Jewish leaders betray Judas and crucify Jesus despite the promises that they have made before.[6]

Saramago's *Gospel* comes probably nearest to the theme of swindling familiar from the *Gospel of Judas*. In this novel, God's transformation into a violent despot thirsting for blood is noteworthy. Saramago's God resembles the evil Demiurge of Gnostic writings. Furthermore, his Jesus attempts to cheat this God in order to avert the prediction of the church's violent history. As Jesus realises that his options are limited and that his time has come, he schemes with his disciples about how to thwart God's plans. Saramago's solution resembles that of *The Gospel of Judas*. The Demiurge must be deluded. Therefore, Jesus wishes to sacrifice himself, not as a Son of God, but merely as a human being, a political pretender to the throne, and so to prevent the story of the death of God's Son. Evil powers are cheated, and God's plans are spoiled. In Saramago's reasoning Jesus' death must be made to look like the death of an ordinary Jewish citizen.

> The Son of God must die on the cross so that the will of the Father may be done, but if we were to replace him with an ordi-

---

5. For Gnostic soteriology see the Nag Hammadi texts, *Second Treatise of the Great Seth* 7.51–56; *Apocalypse of Peter* 7.81.3–24.

6. Cf. Pyper, "Modern Gospels of Judas," 112–13.

Contesting the Moral Values of the Gospels

nary man, God would no longer be able to sacrifice His Son, Do you wish one of us to take your place, asked Peter, No, I myself will take the Son's place.[7]

Saramago's rendering of the canonical story is analogical to the Gnostic *Gospel of Judas*, even though its details are different. If Jesus could avoid the fame of a martyr when dying, his followers would not become fanatic believers. Only in this way could the world be saved. This is where Judas enters the picture. Judas' role as a traitor transforms into the role of a loyal assistant. Someone must help Jesus and betray him to the authorities as a rebel. He must be sentenced as quickly as possible so that the divine despot has no time to react. While other disciples hesitate, Judas instantly understands the situation. He is willing to follow Jesus' orders whatever it may cost him.

There is actually a play between the source texts and Saramago's narrative here that cannot be understood only as subtext. During the supper Jesus says something to Judas and soon the latter leaves the room and vanishes. In John's Gospel, Judas does not speak, but Jesus says to him one of the key sentences of the passion narrative: "That thou doest, do quickly." (John 13:27, Authorized Version). In Saramago's story the disciples are having a supper as well. Here, however, it is Judas who speaks.[8]

> At that moment the voice of Judas Iscariot rang out loud and clear above the din, I'll go if you like. The others grabbed him and were already drawing daggers from their tunics when Jesus ordered them, Leave him alone and do him no harm. He then rose and, embracing Judas, kissed him on both cheeks, Go, my hour is yours. Without saying a word, Judas Iscariot threw the hem of his mantle over one shoulder and, as if swallowed up by darkness, vanished into the night.[9]

The event of the canonical Gospel is turned into the commissioning of an important task. The reversal of traditional polarisation is complete in Saramago's narrative. Judas becomes a loyal follower of Jesus, and the

---

7. Saramago, *Gospel*, 334. For the description of God's violent nature, see below in chapters 4.1 and 5.3.

8. In Stead's story, which has a somewhat different idea, Judas uses the thirty pieces of silver to hire a room, "make bookings at Passover," as Grylls notes in "My Life." See Stead, *My Name Was Judas*, 206.

9. Saramago, *Gospel*, 335.

one who perhaps best understands his strange mission. In the manner of the *Gospel of Judas* Judas simply does what he has been told. Also the meaning of Judas's kiss is reversed here. It becomes an expression of true devotion.[10]

The ideological reversal in Saramago's gospel is furthermore applied to every detail of Judas's history. Even Judas's suicide now serves the new plan. He follows his master to the death. "Dangling from a branch hung the disciple who had offered to carry out his master's last wish." Judas dies with the conviction that he—probably alone of the disciples—had not let Jesus down: "at peace with himself now that he had done his duty." This is further emphasised in the narrative through the information that Judas was not paid for his betrayal. According to Saramago's *Gospel*, he was not even in charge of the community's funds as the canonical tradition had erroneously stated.[11]

Saramago's Judas is not completely identical to the one of the Gnostic *Gospel of Judas*. There is no cosmology is Saramago's world, even though the mysterious element remains in his novel at several other occasions. It is mainly Christian history that motivates his altering of the canonical story. Judas becomes thus a tool for his criticism of God. Later, when I examine the problem of challenging traditional biblical theism, Saramago's view about the role of God will be discussed in detail.

But what if the traditional Gnostic view were right? Already in 1944 in his influential *Three Versions of Judas*, Jorge Luis Borges interpreted Judas's role in the story positively. The point of departure is based on certain premises typical of the philosophy of religion. If Judas was but a tool in God's hands, fulfilling prophesies about the Messiah, he must have had a Messianic role himself. Borges calls him another redeemer who acts with "enormous humility" in order to make way for Christ.[12]

Borges's writing is a short story in the form of a scholarly article by a fictitious Swedish author Nils Runeberg. Runeberg speculates on Judas's role in three different books and concludes: "*Ergo*, la traición de Judas no fue casual; fue un hecho prefijado que tiene su lugar misterioso en la economía de la redención." [So, Judas's treason was not accidental; it was a predestined deed which has a mysterious function in the economy of Redemption.] In Runeberg's final book Judas is even described

10. See Fokkema, "Art of Rewriting," 399.
11. Saramago, *Gospel*, 336–37.
12. *Tres versiones de Judas*, from Borges's text *Ficciones* (1944).

as a divine incarnation.¹³ In Borges's short story salvation is not possible without Judas's role. Thus he becomes a saviour who is ready to sacrifice his reputation and life for Jesus whom he loves so much. Saramago's picture of Judas appears to be a rewriting of Borges's idea, now written into a fully expanded story.¹⁴

Borges's and Saramago's witty speculations are clever, in the same vein as the *Gospel of Judas,* turning traditional Christian convictions upside down. They even seem theological by nature, grounding their reasoning in the essentially biblical idea of divine prophecies and God's deterministic salvation history. The idea of Judas actually being God's servant in the great plan of reconciliation is a perfect example of prototypical rewriting that takes the seeds for the new story from biblical ideas. Nevertheless, this is not theology. These novels and essays deliver fictions, which have not been constructed according to any theological standards. These authors move on a level that differs even from general biblical interpretation. In a theological analysis, Judas is not an exceptional villain among the disciples. Judas does "betray" Jesus and point him out with his kiss, but in the passion narrative he is just one example of how, in the end, all the disciples abandon Jesus and betray him. In fact, Peter's fall is usually considered worse than that of Judas. The cock crows for Peter, and the whole Christian tradition until the present day remembers his deception. When Jesus is arrested, everyone flees, one of them almost naked, leaving his linen cloth in order to avoid punishment (Mark 14:51). Most of the disciples stay away and only the young John follows Jesus to the Calvary with the women. Borges's literary invention is but a simplification that serves only his, and later Saramago's, rhetorical purposes.¹⁵

With C. K. Stead's *My Name Was Judas* all such interpretations change. This is a story told by an old man Judas who, apparently, never committed suicide.¹⁶ Instead, he looks back to the years he spent with Jesus, first as a friend and later as some kind of associate. He wishes

13. For the quotation, see Borger, "Tres versions." My translation ad hoc.

14. This was also the basic idea about Judas's role in Jens's book on the same issue, *Der Fall Judas,* 8. For Slavoj Žižek, Judas's fate reveals the perverse core of Christian tradition. For him, its "ethical knot" is unavoidable: "in order to fulfill his mission, was he obliged to have recourse to such obscure, arch-Stalinist manipulation?" Žižek, *Puppet and the Dwarf,* 16.

15. In Finnish biblical interpretation this view about Judas is a commonplace.

16. Stead, *My Name Was Judas,* 240.

to correct some mistakes recounted in the canonical tradition. Stead's Judas is a rationalist and a sceptic who refuses to accept the miraculous in Jesus' work.[17] This approach is not far from eighteenth-century rationalistic reductions where Jesus' life is described as the life of an average Jew in Galilee. There is neither sin nor atonement in Stead's novel. Furthermore, there is no resurrection because Jesus' body was removed by temple priests who wanted to prevent enthusiastic reactions to Jesus' death.[18] Judas himself leaves Jesus' group and later in Jerusalem keeps his distance from them. When Jesus is arrested Judas the sceptic believes that the event was no result of any divine plan but merely the inevitable conclusion to a purposeful man-made aim "to fit the prophecies."[19] Stead's Judas has no divine mission as the figure in the previously mentioned novels does, but nevertheless this portrayal is also a revision of the canonical original. The reason for the new interpretation is apparently similar to that of Borges's and Saramago's. Christian malevolence has blackened Judas's reputation, and now the author has the possibility to make things right.

Also in Ricci's *Testament* Judas's person and role are separated completely from the betrayal and, in accordance with the explanation concerning Jesus' arrest, Judas's nefarious reputation is the result of a misunderstanding as well. When Jesus arrives in Jerusalem, Judas no longer belongs to his group, but for a reason other than the one in Stead's story. Judas, who had been a rebel even before meeting Jesus, later rejoins his former group. Jesus' arrest, first of all, is based on a misunderstood joke about the building of the new temple. As Roman authorities are eager to prove Jesus guilty of planning a revolt, they decide to execute him because of his association with Judas.[20] Hence the explanation in later church history that Judas came to be blamed for Jesus' arrest and death even though in the new story he had nothing to do with it.[21]

In Mailer's *Gospel According to the Son* Judas is not Jesus' assistant but his opponent. The figure of the apostle here is a new construction,

---

17. For the scepticism, see ibid., 5: "I had rid my consciousness of gods, ghosts and demons." See also Wood, "Jesus." Cf. Grylls, "My Life": "Dismissing the demonised picture of himself, he also repudiates the sacred image of Jesus."

18. Stead, *My Name Was Judas*, 235.

19. So Diski, "Judas."

20. See Crook, "Fictionalizing Jesus," 45.

21. Ricci, *Testament*, 432–35.

fashioned in opposition to the canonical Judas. He is a gallant and handsome man. Even his looks impress the people he meets, including Jesus. He is enthusiastic and devoted, and this is why Jesus is astonished by his personality.

> With his dark beard, he was handsome. I wished him to be among my twelve even if I could not see what was in his heart. His eyes were too full of fire. Indeed, I felt blinded by the blaze of his spirit. Notwithstanding, I welcomed him. He claimed to love the poor, saying that he had lived among the rich long enough to despise them.[22]

This Judas is a man with high morals and who feels a deep social responsibility. Above all, he supports the poor and the oppressed. His independence is emphasised in the novel by the statement that, unlike with the other disciples, Jesus cannot see into his heart. Instead, he wonders "whether he might be Satan's gift to me."[23]

Mailer transforms several original features of the canonical figure into their opposites. Firstly, the canonical Judas with his thirty pieces of silver is a symbol of greed in Western culture (Matt 26:14). He betrayed Jesus for money. Furthermore, John in his Gospel makes Judas the keeper of the disciples' common purse—a feature that Saramago contests in his novel. The canonical Judas is more interested in having enough money for his personal needs than in Jesus' mission, as the story of Jesus' anointing with expensive perfume reveals.[24] Mailer's Judas, quite straightforwardly, is a defender of the poor. "I hate the rich. They poison all of us."[25] He also criticises Jesus for not really recognising the greed of the wealthy. In spite of this, Judas stays with Jesus. He is content with Jesus' proclamation according to which the kingdom of heaven is not based on earthly riches.

Secondly, the general Messianic hope of the disciples is thwarted in Mailer's gospel. From the perspective of the canonical Gospels, Judas belongs to the group of devout young men who await the renewal of the

---

22. Mailer, *Gospel*, 82.

23. Ibid.

24. In John's story Judas criticises Jesus for not selling the perfume and giving the money to the poor. John comments: "He said this not because he cared about the poor, but because he was a thief; he kept the common purse and used to steal what was put into it" (John 12:6).

25. Mailer, *Gospel*, 138.

world and expect to have a special role in the eschatological upheaval. They are the ones who, quite according to the claims of Jewish apocalyptic, will be granted heavenly thrones where they will rule the world side by side with their Messiah.[26] Judas in *The Gospel According to the Son* is disillusioned and has lost his apocalyptic hopes. Mailer's Jesus is somewhat surprised by Judas's social emphasis and his reluctance to accept the good news concerning the coming kingdom. Judas does not hesitate, though: "The truth, dear Yeshua, is that I do not believe you will ever bring us all to salvation. Yet in the course of saying all that you say, the poor will take courage to feel more equal to the rich. That gives me happiness."[27]

To the degree that the canonical Judas is deceitful, Mailer's figure is honest and trustworthy. In the novel the final opposition is constructed between Jesus and Judas. Jesus' uncertainty is contrasted with Judas's own mission.

> "If," I now asked, "I ceased to labor—by even a jot or a tittle—for the needs of the poor, would you see less of value in me?"
>
> "I would turn against you. A man who is ready to walk away from the poor by a little is soon ready to depart from them by a lot."[28]

This conversation prepares the scene for Jesus' betrayal. Mailer's solution is rather rationalistic. He makes Judas and Jesus quarrel about money. Also in *The Gospel According to the Son* the new setting is constructed around Jesus' anointing by Mary in Lazarus's house. When Judas notices the event he becomes "dark with anger." Mailer gives Judas a reason to incite discord. "Why was this ointment not sold by our Master and the money given to the poor? This is waste!"[29]

In this passage Mailer exploits his subtext skillfully. Jesus' answer to Judas follows the canonical Gospels almost verbatim: "The poor are with you always . . . and whenever you can, you may do them good. But me you will not have always." By locating Jesus' utterance in a new context Mailer is able to prove his point with a simple quotation from the Gospel of John (cf. John 12:8). As a selection of original passages from

---

26. This is the eschatological message Jesus teaches to his disciples in Matt 19:28.
27. Mailer, *Gospel*, 138.
28. Ibid., 139.
29. Ibid., 193–94.

the canonical Gospels the subtext increases the rhetorical effect of the new interpretation. Mailer's suggestion becomes a possible interpretation of the alleged original event and Jesus' words gain new meaning. Simultaneously, however, the subtext remains an intentional compilation of sporadic passages that serves merely as a tool for the writer's strategies.

The biblical quotation mentioned above is accompanied by Jesus' interpretative meditation on the anointing. Mailer makes Jesus speculate about his relationship to the poor. His moment of ambivalence was a temptation in the wilderness. "The love that had come from this woman's hands had given me a moment of happiness; so at this instant I did not feel like a friend of the poor."[30] From the point of view of the Judas figure in the story, Jesus worships an idol. So Mailer's Jesus is betrayed because he himself betrays the poor. The gallant Judas is justified in rejecting Jesus. In Mailer's gospel Jesus is not a victim of the sinful world. Rather, he is the victim of his own uncertainty. He could not live up to the standards he himself had postulated. The conclusion is clear: Mailer's Jesus causes his own death.[31]

The role reversal of Jesus and Judas is quite profound in Mailer's *Gospel*. The traditional features that Jesus has in the canonical Gospels are now ascribed to Judas. He is truthful and determined. He is a friend of the poor and sick. Even without any eschatological mission Judas, with his social gospel, is prepared to follow basic Mosaic ethics. His relationship to the God of Israel, though, is not very close. Rather, he is on a profane or mundane road, adhering mainly to the values of the materialistic world. Jesus, in turn, is weak and uncertain of his mission. His relation to God may be more intense than that of Judas's, but his life is a failure. Deep in his heart he is a traitor like the canonical Judas.[32]

The interpretation of the Gnostic writings hints at why, in these Jesus-novels, Judas is often made an exemplary and brave man. In ca-

30. Ibid.

31. Caldwell and Stearn, in their novel *I, Judas*, propose a somewhat similar reason for Judas's act. Here Judas is a patriot who attempts to force Jesus to accept his political messianic role and rise against the Romans. So the "betrayal" is merely part of such a strategy. In this novel Judas does not wish Jesus' death but the death of Israel's enemies instead. Ibid., 293.

32. This solution differs somewhat from that of more traditional Judas-literature. Mailer's Judas becomes disappointed mainly because the Jesus of the narrative does not accept his aims. Pyper, "Modern Gospels of Judas," 113.

nonical history it is actually Judas who is being sacrificed on the principal level. Jesus dies but he is later resurrected into heavenly glory. Judas, instead, sacrifices himself completely. He has no future. He goes to eternal fire for the sake of Jesus and his followers. Therefore a reversal of traditional hierarchies will do justice to Judas's exemplary courage.

It is easy to criticise the Gnostic gospels' "secondary rationalisations" in reconsidering Judas's role, inventing for him a new mission as an assistant of the heavenly Christ-Spirit. The Gnostics had their own cosmology and their peculiar soteriology, and the canonical narrative needed to be adapted to it. At first glance such a reasoning would seem to have little in common with later Jesus-novels. Similarities may, however, be clearer than what one might first expect. Jesus-novels also offer a rationalisation, even though it is not an enthusiastic and syncretic adaptation of Gospel material. In these novels both Jesus and Judas are given new roles that fit the ideologies of the readers. A new reading of the New Testament does not lead to its complete rejection. Instead, it means—according to some contemporary philosophers—rendering, assimilating, perverting, and consuming.[33]

The main reason for the change must be found in the intertextual dynamics. The canonical literary figure of Judas, the kissing deceiver, is an archetypal traitor, so the motives for his transformation cannot be merely poetic. If these authors saw Judas's original act as indifferent, they could have left it in. However, they emphasise the change. This leads to the conclusion that their modifications are ideologically grounded.

This centers on Judas's rehabilitation as a human being and a philosophical or political seeker. According to these novels, Christian tradition has done Judas wrong and suppressed his integrity and personal convictions. He should not have been considered inferior to any of the other disciples, quite the opposite. Christian history has made Judas a villain. In this respect, the canonical Judas is a direct victim of Christian slave morality. Throughout history he has been made a scapegoat for the evilness of Roman soldiers. In Christian tradition he has been held responsible for all the hostility directed towards Jesus.[34] Furthermore, according to the authors, Judas is a victim of false polarisation. Since

---

33. The changing of Judas's role is no novelty as such but rather a commonplace even in older Jesus-novels. See Ziolkowski, *Fictional Transfigurations*, 233–35.

34. Stead, *My Name Was Judas*, 49, for instance, makes it clear in his novel that other disciples branded Judas a traitor without any proof.

polarisations usually depend on ideologies, it stands to reason that his status must be the result of a constrained contradiction. When these violent cultural and linguistic oppositions are dissolved, Judas is allowed to be what he really must have been: a brave Jewish man and a good disciple. Therefore, it is no wonder that, in some of these novels, Judas surpasses Jesus and is described almost in a Messianic manner.

2. BASTARDS AND DRUNKARDS

Even though "comrade Jesus" has been one of the standard characters in twentieth-century Jesus-novels, in more recent books the idea of Jesus as a friend of the poor has been elevated to a new level. In several novels, different marginalised groups and deprived individuals appear in the core of the narrative. In certain texts Jesus himself belongs to these lonely and rejected people.

Tunström in his *The Letter from the Wilderness* describes Jesus' difficult relationship with his parents. In several passages Tunström's Jesus grieves over the lack of warmth he has experienced at home, particularly in relation to his mother Mary. In the novel this can be seen in constant remarks like, "Mary was tired as usual and probably wanted to be rid of me." Mary shows neither love nor affection to her children.[35] In the beginning of the narrative Jesus is leaving home in order to join the Qumran community and wishes that Mary would embrace him and show even the slightest sign of sorrow due to his impending departure. "I could see us both, arms around each other walking across the marketplace, embracing each other just when I was about to climb on my donkey, but she destroyed even that opportunity." Nothing happened. Mary kept her distance.[36]

The theme of rejection is prominent in Tunström's novel. The next deprived person in the story is another young disciple of the Essenes in Qumran, Johanan, the son of an Essene priest. As the son of a severe father Johanan had had "too little food and too little love." The problems of Johanan's family are further emphasised through the story of his brother who, after a mental breakdown, had become a beggar in Jerusalem.

So Jesus meets this child who has remained invisible and whose bitterness poisons his life and even makes Jesus' life in the community dif-

---

35. See the translation by Martinus; Tunström, "Letter from the Wilderness," 12.
36. Tunström, *Ökenbrevet*, 61.

ficult. Johanan's tragic experiences culminated in Sabbath meals, which had been, for him, moments of ignorance and abandonment.

> I could have borne his punches, his insults, had there not been these Sabbath meals. Because there I noticed that he did not *see* me. Do you know what it means when you are not seen?
> I shook my head.
> —The worst of all is to live so that you are not seen. My brother gets seen. He is a madman who is sitting by the Sheep Gate.[37]

As a rejected child Johanan is rebellious and, in the community of Qumran, he later becomes Jesus' denouncer. His envy of Jesus grows so extreme that he reveals Jesus' secret connections with the Zealots to Roman soldiers.[38]

There is even a third marginalised person in Tunström's novel. He is a handicapped child, an idiot, whose parents have abandoned him. After Jesus has fled from Qumran and the Roman soldiers, he meets this child by accident. Ultimately the idiot is left in Jesus' care.[39] This is the world Tunström describes. It is a cold world of deprivation and abandonment. Through his very personal experiences Jesus grows to become a saviour of the rejected and oppressed. He will be the Messiah who sees those with less than nothing.

This is not merely a social gospel in the traditional sense. Tunström's Jesus in not simply a "comrade Jesus" of leftist ideology. There is some class struggle in the novel concerning economic power, but it is not prominent. Instead, Tunström's novel is a quest for a particular voice. He attempts to give a voice to the marginalised. Abandoned and rejected people should be seen. Their discourse should be heard in the community. Their existence needs to be recognised. From a more theological perspective *The Letter from the Wilderness* is a gospel of the weak and in this sense close to the canonical Gospels. Nothing remains of the traditional good news, though. This is a deconstructive reading of Christianity. The message of the novel does not focus on the justification of sinners. Quite the contrary, this is a revolt of the righteous ones against sinners. Parents are not forgiven in this story.

---

37. Ibid., 152.
38. Ibid., 134.
39. Ibid., 167, 180.

The gospel of Mary Magdalene is also a story of a deprived child, this time a despised orphan who grows up in a brothel. The Magdalene in Fredriksson's *According to Mary* is a sad figure. Every possible feature of otherness is ascribed to her.

She is a stranger in her own society. Mary's father belongs to a group of Zealots fighting against the Romans. This is why her family's presence causes fear in the village. Furthermore, Mary's appearance is not Jewish enough. "But Mary did not seem particularly Jewish, noticeably fair-skinned and blonde as she was. And those eyes, a brilliant blue like the spring gentians flowering in the mountains."[40] She looks like a Roman. Mary herself understands that. When she sees a troop of Romans riding through the village she notices that there are men with yellow hair like hers. "She looked like the hated strangers." Because of this, her mother had constantly attempted to hide her hair under a headcloth.[41]

Her appearance even generates conflicts with Jewish purity regulations. At the fish market Mary is driven away from the vicinity of the fishing boats so that she, as a potential Gentile, would not make the fish ritually impure. Back home, Mary's brother announces the general opinion of the community: "Everyone says you're unclean, a child of sin."[42] Moreover, Mary's childhood ends dramatically and violently when Roman soldiers kill her parents and burn their house. Only Mary is able to avoid the massacre since her parents have enough time to hide her.

So Mary Magdalene in *According to Mary* is, in a sense, an icon of the Third World. At the age of seven this orphan or ostensible bastard is taken care of by complete strangers. She is brought to a whorehouse and her maintenance is paid for by a Roman soldier who has decided to take care of her. Such a fate belongs rather to an Indian or African orphan, not an adolescent Jew with a social network.

---

40. Fredriksson, *According to Mary*, 10.

41. Ibid., 19. Mary's appearance is clearly a tool for describing her sinful descent, not a symbolic bridge between Jews and Europeans. In post-Holocaust literature there is a tendency to avoid ascribing any "Aryan" features to Jews, and especially to Jesus, since this had previously been a tool for anti-Semitism. See Kelley, *Racializing Jesus*, 15–28; cf. Steigmann-Gall, *Holy Reich*, 33, 86.

42. Fredriksson, *According to Mary*, 21. There is a reference to Jewish purity regulations here. According to Jewish custom, food, vessels, and people become ritually impure after having been in contact with a Gentile. See Jewish regulations in the Mishnah, Kelim 1:1ff.; Yadaim 1:1ff.; cf. Mark 7:4.

In Mailer's *Gospel* marginalisation is described in quite a different way. Here Jesus' disciples are a bunch of vagabonds who have nothing much to do in life. They resent both the social conventions of the community as well as the religious regulations of Judaism. Some of them, i.e., fishermen, Jesus calls when they are working on the Sabbath. Jesus comments simply: "they did not keep a mark of the days on which work was forbidden."[43]

There is also an aspect of easy living in Mailer's *Gospel*. Rewriting the biblical idea that Jesus' disciples did not fast, Mailer describes a Jesus who is "happy to eat with sinners."[44] As a friend of sinners, Jesus and his disciples are treated to meals in the houses of the wealthy. Not all rich people are hospitable though, and Mailer's Jesus wonders why it is often the non-religious and not those interested in ritual purity who sympathise with the poor. Such speculation awakens the question, is Mailer raising this prominent debate from Reform Judaism in his novel? Discussion about the status of commandments and regulations has been a major issue among Jews in the United States for decades. Seen in this light, Mailer's book treats Jewish tradition as much as it treats Jesus and Christianity.

In Mailer's Steinbeckian narrative even Jesus himself wonders about how much he can drink wine. Sometimes life just seems too easy. Among the disciples, Levi appears to be an alcoholic.[45] At one moment Jesus actually reflects on why he associates with idle men:

> But there were many questions for me. Why did I seek out men who would rather eat and drink than pray? Was it that those who boasted of how they were children of Abraham did not believe that more would be demanded of them than good attendance at the synagogue? I would tell myself that a feast was being prepared in heaven where the pious would be cast out. Only the poor and the sinful would be invited to the banquet. And with that I would drink my wine and wonder at how much I drank.[46]

---

43. Mailer, *Gospel*, 70.

44. Ibid., 83–84. In the New Testament, Jesus' disciples did not fast and Jesus did not demand the following of purity regulations as the rabbis did (Mark 7:1–13). This, however, has usually been connected with his eschatological message of complete renewal, not with a simplistic rebellion against Jewish tradition.

45. Mailer, *Gospel*, 84, 133.

46. Ibid., 84.

In *The Gospel According to the Son* ordinary people living according to their personal desires and also living in sin in a traditional sense are considered more pious than priests and Pharisees observing the Mosaic Law. In this context, Jesus is really a Messiah of the marginalised but, nevertheless, this new role can be transformed and justified through prototypical rewriting. "A drunkard and a glutton. A devil equal to Beelzebub."[47]

The foremost sin in this world, according to these novels, seems to be deprivation. Morality is no longer primarily a matter of right and wrong, but a matter of pity. First of all, these writings focus on the psychological level of human relations. Those who are marginalised in these stories are those deprived of parental love. They are inconsequential people who have fallen through the cracks of the social network as well as social welfare. Tunström finishes his novel with the simple words: "what lacks is love." In a sense, these are novels of a fatherless age. There are, naturally, also discussions about political issues and Roman occupation, but they never take center stage here. These novels do not aim at a political metanarrative or a theology of revolution. Rather, they support a social gospel that wishes to focus on minority groups.

Such a theme may also be a symbol for the Heavenly Father-lessness of post-Christian interpretation. There is no transcendent Father behind this visible world. Life lacks love even inside the kingdom of God, or amongst the Chosen People. The materialistic world, where the new story firmly places itself, is also a place where social responsibility must be constructed anew. Such responsibility does not flow automatically from religious commandments. But simultaneously, as Nietzsche put it, it is colder in here than it used to be.

Secondly, however, the revised Jesus is not merely a friend of the sick and the disabled. His followers are below the acceptable social classes of the society. It may of course be that authors are just attempting to find the real environment for the canonical Jesus' work. Jesus not only walks among "people of the land," as the Jewish identification of ordinary people goes, but also among the despised outside the acceptable social classes, and he comforts those rejected by the society. He associates himself with the lowest orders and opposes mighty leaders.

---

47. Ibid., 84, 109; cf. Matt 11:18–19, "For John came neither eating nor drinking, and they say, 'He has a demon'; the Son of Man came eating and drinking, and they say, 'Look, a glutton and a drunkard, a friend of tax collectors and sinners!'"

This kind of polarisation, however, is not sufficient for the new stories. These novels want to go further. They often propose a polarisation that is almost a perversion of the canonical original. There are hints of this for instance in Stead's description:

> They came and went. Their number waxed and waned, increasing whenever a story of a miracle went about, and then declining until there was another. We were a ragged bunch. There were some lovely people among the followers, some strange and unwholesome people, and some who were stupid, thick as bricks, crazed, or stark mad.[48]

Such a view can be found in other novels as well. Jesus gathers around himself a group of idle vagrants who do not worry about daily life.[49] Some are drunkards, some have criminal backgrounds. No one cares less about religious ordinances than Jesus' disciples. This group is not an eschatological orthodox Jewish sect preaching the imminent revelation of God's wrath and the day of salvation. Rather, Jesus is depicted as a Master of the mob and a Rabbi of the rabble.

3. MAGDALENE'S LOVER

In the Western tradition of Jesus-novels it is no novelty to make Jesus an exponent of free sexuality. Since the writings of D. H. Lawrence and Niko Kazantzakis, an unorthodox treatment of sexual ethics has been commonplace. Most of the investigated novels continue in this vein. Christian faith is repeatedly accused of repressing sexuality and of demonising sexual behaviour. This clearly stems from church's traditional emphasis on the commandment against adultery and the obligation of fidelity in marriage. In Jesus-novels, Jesus is not very fond of family values. In fact, many stories describe his ambivalence about traditional family roles. His relation to his parents is rather difficult. Therefore, it is

---

48. Stead, *My Name Was Judas*, 113. See also Diski, "Judas."

49. There is an interesting parallel for such a view in the liberal theology movement. For instance in the Finnish discussion, Sakari Häkkinen joins these two themes together and makes Jesus both fatherless and the leader of a mob that consists of criminals and outcasts. Häkkinen, *Kenen poika*, 63. John Dominic Crossan compares Jesus with leaders of bandits and suggests that he may have been some kind of Robin Hood figure. Finally, however, Crossan emphasises egalitarianism and describes Jesus as a preacher of democratic idealism who ignored the ritual laws of Judaism. Crossan, *Historical Jesus*, 168–69, 263.

only natural that he never marries but instead is introduced to the world of sexuality through other experiences.

In Michèle Roberts's *Wild Girl* Mary belongs to the realm of abused girls mentioned in the previous chapter. Already as a small child she loses her mother. She is then raped and, as a result, becomes a prostitute. After years of wandering she meets Sibylla who introduces her "into the art of woman-love." Later Mary meets Jesus, and they become lovers. Jesus, however, is a subsidiary character in the story. Roberts is writing a gospel of Mary, and in this novel the canonical Gospels are not important. They provide characters and geography but not much more. Jesus is Magdalene's lover, and Roberts's novel focuses on detailed descriptions of their sexual acts. "Let me be the serpent, Mary, and you the tree. See me rising to coil round you, and enter you, and hide inside."[50]

It is somewhat surprising that in an openly feminist novel Mary is described almost solely as a prostitute. She is a one-dimensional character. A justification for this kind of feminist version of Christianity comes via a glorification of whoredom and a rehabilitation of brothels. According to Haskins, this really does not do credit to the character of Mary: "Such literary effusions surely do Mary Magdalene a disservice, as their creators fall into the trap that the earlier male writers have created for them: by portraying Mary Magdalene as a prostitute or courtesan . . . they merely reinterpret her as a primarily sexual being. . . . By doing so, they deny her a dignity in which her sexuality could be an integral part of her humanity, a dignity which accords the gospel figure her proper prominence."[51]

In Roberts's narrative the character of Mary, of course, grows beyond previous post-biblical prejudices. Roberts depicts her as an Eternal Feminine who, as Jesus' mistress, attains highest status in early Christianity. She gives birth to Jesus' child and becomes thus, at least symbolically, a new mother with a divine child beside Mary the mother of Jesus. These two Marys, in Roberts's new narrative, are also soulmates who understand the principles of female religion. Together they sing:

---

50. Roberts, *Wild Girl*, 82. Among Finnish Jesus-novels, similar themes occur as well. In Harri Sirola's *Jeesus* there is a provocative, naturalistic description of Jesus and Mary's intercourse. This time they meet in their youth, and Mary is described merely as a friend in a nearby village. Sirola, *Jeesus*, 139 (only in Finnish).

51. Haskins, *Mary Magdalen*, 386–87.

– I am the whore, sang the mother of the Lord: and the holy one.
– I am the virgin, I sang: and I am the mother.
– I am the midwife, she sang: and she who is sterile.
– I am the honoured one, I sang: and she who is scorned.[52]

But why is Mary a prostitute in these novels? There is, of course, a Christian tradition behind this, but it is rather late. In the source text one cannot find any references to Mary's profession. In Luke, there is one somewhat surprising notion according to which "seven demons" had gone out from her (Luke 8:2). On this basis one might assume that Mary Magdalene had been described as some kind of magician or sorceress, but this is merely a hypothetical inference based on the fact that such details are few in the canonical Gospels. Mary's name never appears in a context dealing with whoredom. In the original story of the canonical Gospels she evidently is not a prostitute.

Jesus-novels usually identify Mary Magdalene with the "sinful woman," whose story Luke tells just before his mention of Mary (7:36–50).[53] This "sinner," apparently a prostitute, comes into the house of a Pharisee, bathes Jesus' feet with her tears, and dries them with her hair. She also anoints his feet with an expensive ointment. It is easy to see how an identification was made through an association of literary elements. The passage is especially suitable for later authors because love is mentioned here. According to Jesus, "she has shown great love" (v. 47). However, there is a third person. In the Gospel of John, it is actually Mary, the sister of Martha and Lazarus, who anoints Jesus' feet and wipes them with her hair (John 12:1–5). This was the incident that provoked Judas to question the waste of expensive ointment. So we have three different persons who can be merged into one character. For instance, Roberts identifies Mary Magdalene as Martha's sister, despite the problem that the city of Magdala thus turns into Bethany.[54]

In Fredriksson's novel *According to Mary*, Mary Magdalene is an orphan whose parents were killed by Roman soldiers. She has nothing to do with Martha or Lazarus. This young Mary experiences sexual harass-

---

52. Roberts, *Wild Girl*, 64.

53. This is an interesting story told only in Luke, in 7:36–50. It is not mentioned in Matthew, even though other pericopes taken into the seventh chapter of Luke come from Luke and Matthew's common source.

54. Mailer, however, makes a conscious distinction between these Marys. Mailer, *Gospel*, 193.

ment, but in this case, somewhat strangely, without any intimation of rape. Mary, taken as a refugee to a whorehouse, lives a rather protected youth until she meets a young Roman boy who seduces her. After this event she becomes a professional prostitute who, according to the story, enjoys carnal pleasure and "likes men."[55]

When Mary runs across Jesus for the first time, the historical meeting is described in terms of sexual passions. Fredriksson's story clearly aims at a disturbing or shocking effect. These two meet in the mountains, in an out-of-the-way place. During a journey to another town, Mary has been left behind since the donkey of the travelling group has been injured. Therefore Mary has to spend a few hours alone by a small stream in the middle of nowhere. Jesus, by chance visiting Nazareth, happens to walk through the same district. The scene starts with a short conversation where Mary, despite the incidental nature of the moment, confesses her inner feelings and also admits that she has been working at a whorehouse: "I have been a whore in a house of pleasure in the City of Sin." Also Jesus tells Mary certain intimate features about his own life and reveals his solitude: "But nor have I ever felt I belonged."[56]

Then, quite straightforwardly, Mary touches Jesus' hand and desire is lit up. She starts to kiss Jesus and arouses his sexual lust. In the middle of all this, however, Jesus has to confess to an experienced prostitute: "I have never been close to a woman."[57] Mary is not confused but guides the young man into an act of intercourse. After experiencing an orgasm Jesus, usually omniscient and supernatural in the same narrative, opens up and rejoices over this new knowledge about human life he had been quite unaware of.

> Afterward, he rolled over on to his back and laughed. "I hadn't understood this."
> "That there is so much joy in your body?"
> He closed his eyes and did not answer.[58]

The interpretation of the passage is rather difficult. Not even the narrative's implicit goals illuminate why the first meeting between Mary and Jesus has been reduced to a brief encounter climaxing quickly in intercourse. In a more abstract, narrative sense, there are only two persons

---

55. Fredriksson, *According to Mary*, 74.
56. Ibid., 100–101.
57. Ibid., 102.
58. Ibid., 103.

who accidentally meet and who quite arbitrarily end up in a sexual act. The description could easily be a scene in a book of soft pornography with no ideological or religious aims. Simultaneously, however, from an intertextual point of view, this is supposedly the first meeting of Son of God with a person who is to become one of his closest followers. Should one assume that, according to Fredriksson, the most important intertextual change should concern free sexual relations? Undoubtedly, sex is in the core of the passage, and it is valued more highly than any deep relationship growing gradually between woman and man. Mary's role too, at least superficially, is constructed in terms of the fortuitous event. Mary and Jesus' meeting does not support Mary's integrity or womanhood. Neither is her personality or human independence emphasised here. Instead, the text as it is simply describes some man's joyful moment with a prostitute in the central Galilean countryside.

If one were to see it from an ideological feminist perspective, which is more than likely assumed considering both Roberts's and Fredriksson's general ideological aims, the interpretation should be much more positive. Some feminist writers have proposed that sexuality belongs to a woman's special way of experiencing the divine. The acts of intercourse described in Roberts's and Fredriksson's narratives become thus events where desire replaces male dogmatism. According to second-wave post-structuralist feminists' desire to transform patriarchal interpretations of God and the sacred, the ground for religious experience changes in these stories.[59]

Mary and Jesus' sexual relationship, however roughly described, becomes thus an ideal of a sacred marriage where an immanent, carnal rite reaching for the divine represents a deep unity with the Son of God.[60]

---

59. Thus for instance Pamela Anderson states that "myth and mimesis can serve as philosophical tools for feminists who endeavour to transform the patriarchal structure of empirical realist forms of theism. This includes structures which constitute sexual, racial and ethnic hierarchies of privileged vs less-privileged beliefs." Anderson, "Myth," 115.

60. Rowland in her Jungian interpretation applies the idea of sacred marriage in the interpretation of Roberts's novel: "Sacred marriage is a frequent motif for this process demonstrating Jung's belief that psychic narratives could embrace the bodily and sexual *and* the transcendent and spiritual with neither pole being the *real* explanation." According to her views, one application of this view can be seen in Roberts's description of Mary: "Therefore, in *The Wild Girl*, the narrator, Mary Magdalen's romance with Jesus [sic] is both psychic/religious and sexual. Bodily union becomes also a way of contacting her own psyche, inherently religious in Jungian terms. Thus sexuality becomes

This theme is essential also in Brown's *The Da Vinci Code*, where the tradition of Jesus' original (Gnostic) religion climaxes in the sacred marriage rite, which Sophie Neveu, a secret descent of Jesus, witnesses in the cellar of her own home.[61] The basic metaphor in the sacred marriage theme is that of a marriage, which creates some problems for a feminist interpretation. They seem unable to see that this metaphor contradicts the very independence they champion. Sacred experience is located in a relationship that maintains the most basic, even biological, identity of women and men. The divine is interpreted through heterosexual intercourse, and not a trusting and loyal relationship, but also it is also associated with whoredom and casual sexual encounters. Women remaining objects of desire and lust cannot then easily be transformed into subjects with deep, spiritual experience. This observation leads to another conclusion. The inverting of the conventional hierarchy of sexual lust may actually be the intention of the novels. After the death of the sign there are no prostitutes in the world. A description of sexual intercourse in such a religious context justifies sacred "whoredom" because all binary oppositions need to be reversed.[62]

However, strictly on the basis of the story, one can easily end up with a completely different conclusion. According to Fredriksson's narrative, Mary is an innocent victim, an orphan in trouble, who in her unhappy life has drifted into a whorehouse where she is constantly and repeatedly misused by an endless stream of men. Roberts's Mary has a similar history. Later Fredriksson's Mary meets Jesus, the famous Nazarene who, in principle, could accept her as she is and respect both her personality and her sexual integrity—as the canonical Jesus does, for example, in the story about the adulterous woman (John 8). In the intertextual reading, however, Jesus turns out to be merely one of those horny men running after Mary in the house of Euphrosyne. Even the Son of God cannot resist the physical temptation Mary arouses. Therefore, instead of respecting her personality, he almost attacks this completely unknown woman he has just happened to meet in the woods and practically rapes her

---

a rite, a 'sacred marriage' in which she experiences through her body the immanent sacred." Rowland, "Sacrifice," 163.

61. Brown, *Da Vinci Code*, 410–14.

62. This is probably why P. Anderson refers to the figure of the "seductive female" appearing in many myths, such as Circe in Homer's *Odyssey*, and Eve in the Old Testament. Anderson, "Myth," 115.

on the grass. Mary has simply gotten one more client for herself. One cannot escape the conclusion that Fredriksson's narrative, in its present form, legitimises male power and fails to defend any originally intended feminist values.[63]

The second-wave feminist approach appears to be the primary strategy later in these novels, though. Jesus and Mary Magdalene become partners so that Mary gradually learns the secret wisdom of Jesus' message during their journey together. Their relationship is close and tender, and they apparently love each other. Therefore, the sexual intercourse marking the beginning of their relationship receives a positive interpretation. Mary is the heroine of the narrative. Through meeting the errant wanderer who feels like a stranger in this world and is uncertain about his calling, she becomes his saviour and teacher. The omniscient Son of God who, elsewhere in the same narrative, knows even the thoughts of the people he meets, is actually unaware of real love, which depends on carnal joy. In this passage it is actually Mary Magdalene who is an omniscient expert, and she also brings meaning to the earthly life of this God Incarnate.[64]

This kind of intertextual interpretation obviously contests traditional Christian sexual morals. Biblical theology has emphasised the unity of sexuality and marriage. Sexuality has usually been inseparable from marital love and fidelity. All this is now considered slavish morality having nothing to do with real love as described in Fredriksson's novel. According to the writer, love and tenderness are dependent merely on a touching psychophysical experience. Love is a feeling, mostly a subjective feeling, a peak experience, which Jesus becomes acquainted with only through Mary's help. Instead of biblical family values, deep personal relationship, or even sexuality's connection with reproduction, the sexual relationship between women and men becomes mainly an orgiastic event. Given this perspective, Fredriksson should be located in the sphere of rather early Scandinavian feminism despite the fact that she has also adopted poststructuralist views. In earlier forms of feminism, female independence was defined in terms of one's right to make

---

63. One of the most difficult ideological problems with the second-wave feminist interpretation is that it is unable to criminalise sexual harassment and even rape. When the exploitation of women is justified in the glorification of whoredom, there is no return to higher values concerning personal inviolability. This must be taken into account in any ethical reading of these novels.

64. Cf. for instance Fredriksson, *According to Mary*, 121.

decisions about one's own body and sexual relationships regardless of male conventions and patriarchal social orders. Mary, in the story, takes initiative and, at least in this respect, remains independent in spite of the other factors that may be discerned in the meeting of these two persons and Mary's role in the sexual act. In fact, it is not easy to decide who is exploiting who in the given situation.

Mary Magdalene is Jesus' mistress also in Saramago's novel. Actually the Magdalene is the only remarkable female figure apart from Jesus' mother in the whole narrative. This Mary too is a common prostitute whose house outside the town of Magdala is known all over the district. Jesus, after hurting his feet during the journey, happens to stop at Mary's fence and stays in the house so that Mary can heal his wounds. Almost immediately Jesus falls for Mary, and she becomes his teacher. In this respect these novels are fairytales that do not go into any trouble in developing the plot in order to acquaint Jesus with Mary. Saramago's introductory words resemble those in Fredriksson's novel: "I have never been with a woman." Mary knows her business, and after their first act of intercourse an enthusiastic and intensive week of sexual pleasure follows.[65]

Jesus' relationship with Mary Magdalene is described with biblical expressions. Saramago makes several allusions to the beautiful Song of Solomon in the Old Testament. The key words Gilead, Heshbon, and Bath-Rabim establish the connection. At first the reader is ready to assume that the purpose in quoting these loving sentences is to describe Jesus and Mary's relationship with the best passages the Bible can offer. This, however, is probably not the case in Saramago's presentation.

> Jesus said, your tresses remind me of a flock of goats descending the mountain slopes of Gilead. The woman smiled and remained silent. Then Jesus said, Your eyes are like the pools of Heshbon by the gate of Bath-Rabim. The woman gave another smile yet continued to say nothing. Then Jesus slowly turned to look at her and said, I have never been with a woman.[66]

65. Saramago, *Gospel*, 211–14.

66. Ibid., 211; This is a free combination of different verses; see Song of Solomon 4:1; 7:4. Cf. Ben-Porat: "The love scene between Jesus and Mary Magdalene [...] is articulated in the language of the Song of Songs, which inscribes it within the biblical tradition, and consists of the same motives that appear in conversion stories in the Gospels: she washes her feet, anoints his wound with medication, allows him to see her flowing hair, and offers him love." Ben-Porat, "Prototypical Rewriting," 97.

Then Mary answers with words borrowed from the Song of Solomon (sometimes also called the Song of Songs according to the opening words of the canonical book):

> Awake, north wind, and come, you south, blow upon my garden, that the spices thereof may flow out, let my beloved come into his garden, and eat his pleasant fruits. Then together, Jesus's hand resting once more on the shoulder of Mary, this whore from Magdala who dressed his sores and is about to receive him in her bed, they went indoors into the welcome shade of a clean, fresh room.[67]

Saramago's quotation is twofold and ambivalent, though. He chooses to use words that in no way express freedom or emphasise Mary's independence. Instead, in the Old Testament's openly patriarchal setting behind the Song of Solomon women are private property and in the novel, as well, Mary does not open her own garden to anyone but lets the royal man enter his garden and eat the fruit that justifiably belongs to him. If this ambivalence is intentional, it is difficult to discern Saramago's basic purpose in selecting precisely these words. Saramago probably wants to contrast the beautiful Song of Solomon's poetry with street language referring to the "whore from Magdala." In the end it is the whore who wins.[68]

Thus, even this seemingly nice description of the loving relationship is based on irony. Religious discourse is dragged down to a purely physical, non-transcendent level. Carnal love among real human beings surpasses all religious euphemisms of patriarchal sexism. For Saramago, it is all about words: there are no whores or pools and gardens. Neither are there any true precepts or eternal divine commandments against non-marital sexuality, not even for Jesus the Son of God. And when the discourse changes, religious behaviour changes.[69]

---

67. Saramago, *Gospel*, 211–12. Song 4:16. In the preceding passage, Jesus' description of the naked Mary follows the canonical source text, Song 7:1–3.

68. Frier sees open criticism here: "The fact that Mary Magdalene is an outcast from society if anything increases her stature in this depiction of a community which has frequent recourse to prostitution while officially condemning it." Frier, "Outline," 374. Biblical moral codes are deliberately contrasted with Saramago's own ethics.

69. I disagree with Frier, who, following Orlando Grossegesse, assumes that Jesus' union with Mary Magdalene "represents a taste of heaven on earth for Jesus." The event in Saramago's description may well be meant to express Jesus' extraordinary experience but the contradiction remains. Frier further suggests that Saramago's language derived

What is Mary's function in the narrative? It seems that her primary role is to introduce Jesus into the art of carnal love. The principle of free love is one of the few issues that is never questioned in Saramago's narrative. A consequence of this is that Mary as a woman is denied her own dignity and reduced to an object of male fantasy. Saramago's novel is then a very male writing, one could even say macho, in a negative sense. Mary in the novel is the archetype of an obedient prostitute. In the story's romantic descriptions, Mary Magdalene listens endlessly to Jesus and appears to be the only person on earth who really understands him. She offers herself completely to Jesus and asks no favour in return. In her unselfish love she actually turns to monogamy and becomes faithful to Jesus. In all this she demands no commitment—and also gets none. She is no housewife. Social institutions and conventions are rejected completely in Saramago's novel.[70]

In these descriptions of Jesus' sexual life there is a certain Faustian element. This is true especially in Saramago's story. After staying as a disciple of the Pastor in the wilderness for a lengthy period, Jesus makes a silent deal with the Devil and strives to learn the essentials of human life according to the Pastor's advice. As an ancient prototype of Faust, Jesus finds his Margaret/"Gretchen" and learns about carnal love under her guidance. In such a role he furthermore resembles the Master in Mikhail Bulgakov's *The Master and Margarita*, who is left in a tension between the Devil and the woman, another Margaret, that has been led into his life.[71]

Fredriksson's Jesus, too, is a Faustian character, and he is even the one who seduces his Gretchen in the woods. In neither one of these novels, however, does the so-called lustful relationship end in tragedy, as was the case in Goethe's drama. Neither is the maiden, Mary Magdalene, an innocent woman but a prostitute who is more experienced in sexual matters than Jesus. These novels do not follow Faust's story in detail. Instead, the Faustian element in these novels inverts the original story.

---

from the Song of Songs has its original eroticism restored to it and thus "escapes completely the traditional virgin/whore dichotomy." Frier, "Outline," 374. My conclusion is that Saramago deliberately plays with that dichotomy in order to change discourses.

70. See especially Saramago, *Gospel*, 216.

71. In Goethe's drama it is Faust who seduces Gretchen, but that is not the case in Saramago's narrative. Mary Magdalene seduces Jesus and teaches him the secrets of eroticism. The setting is quite different from that of Fredriksson's, as will be seen below.

A pact with the Devil justifies post-Christian values that overcome those of the Jewish/Christian tradition.

Jesus is the Magdalene's lover in many of the investigated novels. Feminist novels depict him almost as a gigolo who has nothing to do with Jewish moral values or marital convictions. This is merely a byproduct in the novels, though, as it was for Nietzsche. Nietzsche was convinced that Christianity is a religion that hates sexuality and considers it shameful. He did not completely support promiscuity, however, and neither do the Jesus-novels. The latter's main purpose is to support feminist values and create a story where traditional repressive conceptions about sexuality are inverted. Their success is dubious, however. When attempting to express women's very immanent experience of the divine through sexuality they—probably by accident—legitimise traditional roles including the male reduction of women into mere sexual objects. The only escape from this paradox is in a poststructuralist interpretation where the whole concept of prostitution is inverted. This, however, makes the authors unable to defend against women's exploitation by referring to moral values.

4. DIFFICULTIES WITH SLAVE MORALITY

When attacking moral codes and inverting moral hierarchies, several authors alter the conventions of the canonical text through their intertextual reading. Jesus is described as a renegade who questions the slavish morality of mainstream Judaism. Traditional polarisations, such as the Christian image of Judas, are reversed without hesitation. Hence these descriptions can be seen as hints of nihilist leanings. Even though many of the Jesus-novels treated here seem to be rather conservative at first glance, the investigation of their views on moral hierarchies reveals clear examples of Nietzschean hermeneutics. The corrected gospel story opposes the canonical Gospels and implicitly accuses them of slave morality, in the Nietzschean sense. According to the new readings, the New Testament makes its readers feel guilty for a way of living that should be regarded as normal. Christian ethics demonises natural desires. Therefore, biblical texts have imposed moral values that are no longer acceptable for modern or postmodern people.

What is important for the present investigation is that these novels call for a change. In the new narrative, post-Christian values prevail. Jesus is living according to the principles of personal freedom even though this should drive him into a conflict with the representatives of Jewish slave morality. The authors' stories are not neutral and descriptive but normative. They depend on moral values, despite the fact that these values differ from those of the original narrative. The most obvious contradiction can be found in values concerning sexuality. Quite in the manner of Nietzsche, some of these novels identify Christian morality as bourgeois puritanism and therefore oppose it as an expression of restrictive pettiness. There are other kinds of examples, as we have seen. The act of Judas is explained as one of integrity. The roles of Jesus and Judas are in fact reversed and, in Mailer's interpretation, it is Jesus who betrays his own mission. Furthermore, the treatment of different attitudes towards the marginalised are used to critique conservative Christian ethics. This, however, is the field where the exploited principles mostly resemble those of traditional Christianity.

In what sense, then, is the Jesus-character of the new narrative making a deal with the Devil? These novels stand in the long tradition of Faustian literature where the line between good and evil is speculated upon and where the values of the good life are sought apart from biblical ethics. In many of the investigated novels, Jesus becomes a figure somewhat parallel to Goethe's Faust. Jesus is now frustrated with the wisdom of previous teachers, not in false scientific knowledge but in the vanity of Jewish wisdom and Mosaic morality. Tunström's Jesus no longer believes in divine commandments and Fredriksson's Jesus does not want to make laws. They are like Goethe's hero who wishes to attain deeper knowledge through the help of the expert in lust, Mephistopheles himself. So, in Saramago's novel the Devil becomes Jesus' teacher, and in Mailer's Jesus adopts Satan's rhetoric. The Son of God has found himself a malicious mentor who begins to educate him in the principles of the good life.[72]

In these Jesus-novels, Jesus wishes first and foremost to attain human happiness, as did Goethe's Faust. Unlike in traditional morality, however, these novels do not reject the Devil's advice as temptations. According to Saramago and Mailer, Satan's teachings will not lead to personal tragedy, but rather to Faustian new knowledge. Therefore, the original narrative about doctor Faust is inverted. The summit of ecstasy does not lead Jesus to the point where he would lose his soul. Instead, in the new narrative the Devil becomes a Messianic figure who brings good

---

72. Cf. Saramago, *Gospel*, 169–71.

tidings for enslaved humanity. In several novels, Jesus finds his inner conviction, his soul, through a long process under the Devil's direction.

This kind of imagery serves the authors in making Jesus a Nietzschean frivol, a method also used by the postmodern philosopher Taylor. By inverting traditional conceptions of law, guilt, and mercy, Taylor looks for a nihilist affirmation of a new experience of life, an "affirmation of centerlessness," which justifies an "exorbitant erring" without absolutes.[73] As God is dead, in the traditional sense of the concept, human beings are open to a new spectrum of meanings.

> When becoming no longer needs to be validated by reference to past or future but can be valued at every moment, one has broken (with) the law. Such transgression does not breed guilt and sin. In this case, lawlessness proves to be inseparable from grace—grace that arrives only when God and self are dead and history is over. The lawless land of erring, which is forever beyond good and evil, is the liminal world of Dionysus, the Anti-Christ, who calls every wandering mark to carnival, comedy, and carnality.[74]

Taylor's idea of Dionysian life derives from Nietzsche's early carnivalism. In a postmodern context, it is further justified (if such a word is proper here) with the death of meaning. The theology of deconstruction is based on empty signs. "Within this profitless economy, the mark that is the currency of frivolity is always empty."[75] This results in a new humanity, new kinds of personalities. Taylor's lot, evidently, coincides with the Nietzschean noble species. People living beyond good and evil create *Herrenmoral*, which finally leads to Dionysian happiness. Noble species feel that they can construct values themselves. They do not need other's approval.

> The noble type of person feels *himself* as determining value—as he does not need approval, he judges that "what is harmful to me is harmful per se," he knows that he is the one who causes things to be revered in the first place, he *creates values*.[76]

---

73. Taylor, *Erring*, 156–57.

74. Ibid., 157–58. He adds: "The death of God, in other words, unleashes the aberrant levity of free play" (158–59). The Nietzschean source text is in *Twilight of the Idols*, 112: "Affirmation of life even in its strangest and sternest problems, the will to life rejoicing in its own inexhaustibility through the *sacrifice* of its highest types—that is what I called Dionysian."

75. Taylor, *Erring*, 158–59.

76. Nietzsche, *Beyond Good and Evil*, § 260. What is tragicomic in Nietzsche's view

The narrator especially in Saramago's novel is himself a strong personality with a "will-to-power." He is in control, and he also plays with history as he wishes. Despite his rejection of God as the guarantor of human signification, he does not fall into fatalism. Instead, this narrator lauds strong personalities—the best example of these being the Devil—and approaches his issues in terms of ethical egoism.[77] In Mailer's novel the great personality is Judas, and in feminist novels naturally Mary Magdalene. It is noteworthy that not one of these novels makes the Jesus-figure himself a great personality with a will-to-power, even though his morality opposes the precepts of the Jewish/Christian tradition.

The exaltation of human dignity is a feature familiar to nihilist theology. There a similar view has been applied for instance to the reinterpretation of Adam's fall. "We must not denigrate the human being who ate of the tree of knowledge in the Genesis story. We must learn rather to celebrate the creative leap into a higher humanity."[78] If there is to be any standard for human life, it must be found in the human being himself or herself, not in any transcendent principle or divine authority. In this respect, the new morality present in recent Jesus-novels fits well in the Nietzschean tradition prevailing both in twentieth-century philosophy and negative theology.

It should be remembered that nihilism has always been a matter of morality. Both Nietzsche and Camus proclaimed that God must be abandoned in the name of higher morals. Later poststructuralist nihilism, too, has turned out to be a program of rehabilitating minorities and combating violent patriarchy. This is precisely what recent Jesus-novels do. Mailer remains more conservative in his ethics but Saramago and the feminist authors intentionally transgress the boundaries of Christian ethics.

---

is that as he attempts to define his new nihilist version of grounding the process of ethical decision making, he uses the most common Christian idea of the Golden Rule, derived directly from Jesus' teaching. What is harmful to me cannot be good for other people either. As noted already in the Introduction, this ambivalence in ethical theory made Nietzsche describe Zarathustra's proclamation almost in Christian terms.

77. Cf. Schlechta's analysis of Nietzsche's morals in "Nietzsche," 1478. In Western cultural history this nihilist interpretation of the grounds of morality is complex since Martin Heidegger revised Nietzsche's ontological views in his existentialist philosophy. This later philosophical trend, in turn, has affected many authors and intellectuals in Europe.

78. Spong, *Sins of Scripture*, 174.

In their zeal for humanity's progress, Jesus-novels hardly ever reflect on the darker side of human autonomy. Nietzsche was well aware of the logical conclusions of his thinking: the *Übermensch*. For him society was but a scaffold by the help of which the elite could proceed to a higher mode of being. "Egoism" belonged to the nature of the noble soul. Therefore Nietzsche, in his nihilism, arrived at hard and frightening values. Little did he know what these ideas would produce in the minds of a passionate audience, when the scaffolds would be crowded with executioners.[79]

The investigated Jesus-novels abandon this particular Nietzschean passion, and this also creates a tension inside the story itself. They revert into the compassionate religion of pity that Nietzsche so profoundly hated. These protectors of the marginalised drift into an implicit conflict with Nietzsche because they attempt to "preserve too much of what needed to be destroyed," as the great nihilist said. In their sympathetic attitude they are obviously upholding "sickness and suffering."[80] In Nietzsche's own estimation, then, these novels would apparently belong to literature that promotes the decline of the European race and thus remain completely inside the boundaries of Christianity. This, of course, is an embarrassing result, questioning the consistency of the novels.[81]

Furthermore, there are interesting analogies for these views in the area of liberal theology. Some authors have adopted quite a similar view of treating New Testament texts and Christian values. For instance Don Cupitt, intentionally following Nietzsche's ideas, states that Christianity is a slavish religion. New theology can be constructed only after the oppressive religion has first been rejected.

> The notion that religious ethics is a "slave-morality" was greatly elaborated by Nietzsche in numerous books.... he gave a kind of psychological explanation of how a slave-morality was foisted upon the ancient world by the guile of early Christian apologists.[82]

---

79. Nietzsche, *Beyond Good and Evil*, § 258–65; *Twilight of the Idols*, 101–3.

80. In their descriptions the Jesus-novels, Mailer's in particular, are kindred spirits with Vermes, who with his "Jewish" version of Jesus emphasises his extraordinary ethics and defence of the despised. Vermes, *Jesus the Jew*, 224.

81. See especially Nietzsche, *Beyond Good and Evil*, § 62. For Nietzsche, Christianity modeled the most destructive arrogance one could imagine. In its attempt to break those who are strong, it drives Western culture to self-destruction (ibid.).

82. Cupitt, *Crisis of Moral Authority*, 115.

According to Cupitt slave morality is promoted in the church by "*Master-servant imagery*." Christian faith is profoundly distorted because it proclaims a Jewish concept of God. The biblical Yahweh forces people to submit to his law. "Unhappily, no way has yet been found for a religion substantially to break with its past or modify its basic imagery."[83] This is why Nietzsche's critique against Christian tradition must be held as correct in both the present church and radical theology. "So far as we can tell, there is no objective personal God. The old language is still used, but the modern believer should use it expressively rather than descriptively."[84]

Cupitt does recognise the problems implied in the adoption of Nietzschean premises. Hence he simultaneously attempts to save the church from nihilism. He is convinced that Nietzschean master morality does not inevitably lead to tyranny. Instead, master morality can, somewhat paradoxically, lead back to an altruistic love of one's neighbour. This move is quite close to the developments of the investigated Jesus-novels, which usually end up with rather conventional ethics.

> This is surely indistinguishable from Nietzsche's own much-misunderstood master morality. The true master is the one who does not need a slave. The will-to-power is not struggle, and not competitive. It is a will to discriminate, to differentiate qualities and to create meaning . . . Jesus similarly distances himself from the reactive, at least in many of the texts attributed to him. He says, "Judge not, that ye be not judged": that is, precisely do not measure yourself against your neighbour, do not make comparisons, respect persons, be envious, plan anxiously, seek recompense or nurse grievances.[85]

For a reader of the canonical New Testament such an interpretation raises questions. The same question needs to be posed to Nietzsche who in his *Zarathustra* returns to similar conservatism: Why should one abandon Christian ethics just to return to the ideals of the Sermon on the Mount? Liberal criticism directed against the biblical message tends to acquire its rhetoric from the writings it wishes to contest. Cupitt falls into this trap, as do the investigated Jesus-novels. One of the foundations for Cupitt's romanticising reinterpretation of Christian faith may be in

---

83. Ibid., 120.
84. Cupitt, *Taking Leave of God*, 101.
85. Cupitt, *Long-Legged Fly*, 80.

Kantian cultural Protestantism. Ever since the first days of rationalism and the emergence of Immanuel Kant's philosophy of religion, the essence of Christian faith has been seen as ethics. This means that the Jesus-novels' relation to such a Kantian tradition needs to be assessed as well.

The investigated novels are Nietzschean in their zeal against Christian *Sklavenmoral*. They contest biblical views of family and sexuality. Moreover, they make the Gospel's descriptions of Judas's fate and Mary Magdalene's role look like discriminatory oppression. The disciples, in turn, appear in a new light. Jesus' followers are "stark raving mad" or complete drunkards. For these authors, humanity is not at fault. If there is someone to blame it is the biblical God who should have known better. The opposition towards biblical values is not consistent, though, since the authors are not willing to follow Nietzsche consistently to the ultimate conclusions of his "frightening values." Instead, in many cases they end up contradicting Nietzsche by supporting a religion of pity. They return to humane values that no longer differ, for instance, from the Sermon on the Mount—an ideological problem that is well known already from Nietzsche's own works. These novels are moralistic by nature; they defend the oppressed. Thus they appear to promote the very "sickness and suffering" in this world that Nietzsche so vehemently hated.

4

Challenging the Biblical Role of Women

According to many of the investigated novels' claims, women have been enslaved under the patriarchal dominion of men in the church. When emancipatory feminism rereads and rewrites the Gospels, the Jesus-narrative becomes a story where Jesus either defends feminism or steps aside as female apostles enter the scene.

1. DEFINING FEMINISM

Feminism as such is not one of Nietzsche's themes but critique of patriarchy is Nietzschean without hesitation. A rigid vision of mutual exclusivity between an allegedly repressive male attitude and experienced freedom has clear Nietzschean sources especially when the former is named after the famous biblical forefathers, the patriarchs. For the novels, the case is even easier since male dominion in the narrative is simultaneously a Jewish/Christian phenomenon.[1]

According to feminist Jesus-novels, Christianity is a religion of men. "As always, the victors wrote the history, the evangelists," remarks Fredriksson in the introduction to her novel. This is reminiscent of Pagels's conclusion in her *Gnostic Gospels*: "It is the winners who write history—their way. No wonder, then, that the viewpoint of the successful majority has dominated all traditional accounts of the origin of Christianity." Since the aim of feminist novels appears to be some kind of rehabilitation of the allegedly female-friendly Gnosticism as the true

---

1. Diethe notes that "many early German radical feminists, such as Hedwig Dohm, Lily Braun, and Helene Stöcker, were firm Nietzscheans." Nietzsche's idea of the *Übermensch* was useful since the German word "Mensch" denotes "human being," not just "man." Diethe, *Historical Dictionary of Nietzscheanism*, 89. She continues: "The liberating potential it offered to women cannot be overemphasized."

cradle of Christianity, one is entitled to expect that this orientation is related to a more general feminist theology as well.²

How to define feminism? This is a genuine problem for our analysis of certain novels that wish to support the religious activity of women. There is no standard feminism in Western history, neither is there one feminist philosophy that could serve as a point of departure for the investigation. A struggle for equality or democracy in society may be called feminism, since society has been ruled by men for centuries. This, however, is not what the novels seem to represent. Rather, they combat some kind of male interpretation of religion. This is quite in line with feminist theology from the 1980s and 1990s.

In the area of philosophy, as well as in literature, there are several phases that can be called feminist. One of the most famous of these is Simone de Beauvoir's early existentialist feminism. Roberts and Fredriksson do not seem to be existentialists, though. Instead, their novels have more in common with second-wave feminism, as it is usually called. Writers like Germaine Greer and Kate Millett, drawing on the theoretical work, for instance, of Julia Kristeva and Luce Irigaray, contest male values and male conventions in cultural analysis. They also establish the terminology suggested by their predecessors.

> Certain themes, then, dominate second-wave feminism: the omnipresence of patriarchy; the inadequacy for women of existing political organizations; and the celebration of women's difference as central to the cultural politics of liberation.³

Irigaray writes that we need to "reinterpret everything concerning the relations between the subject and discourse." After the linguistic turn it is necessary to redefine the language we use in our culture. This can also reveal certain power structures. The status of women in society is inferior because their person and identity has always been defined through the identity of men.

> Man has been the subject of discourse, whether in theory, morality, or politics. And the gender of God, the guardian of every subject and every discourse, is always *masculine and paternal*, in the West.⁴

---

2. Fredriksson in her foreword for the novel, "Why Mary Magdalene." Cf. Pagels, *Gnostic Gospels*, 142.

3. Selden et al., *Literary Theory*, 129.

4. Irigaray, *Ethics of Sexual Difference*, 6–7. Italics original.

According to Irigaray, there are thus certain violent features in patriarchal culture. In her critique on Spinoza she writes that women "would need to pass through man in order to have a relation, for herself, to man, to the world, and to God." The world of men violates both the rights and the identity of women. Only a dismantling of such structures can give women the right, similar to that of men, to conceive of themselves "without anything else."[5]

When these ideas are applied to feminist theology, religion becomes part of male-dominated history. For example the Bible is now treated as the production of male identity, "masculine and paternal," as Irigaray would have said. In her monograph *In Memory of Her* (1983), Elisabeth Schüssler Fiorenza laid the foundation for a feminist deconstruction of patriarchal Christianity. Her book became the measure for theological feminism for years. Furthermore, this means that second-wave feminism established its position as the most influential form of feminism in Protestant theology.

> The historical-theological insight that the New Testament is not only a source of revelatory truth but also a resource for patriarchal subordination and domination demands a new paradigm for biblical hermeneutics and theology.[6]

According to Schüssler Fiorenza, all "early Christian texts are formulated in an androcentric language and conditioned by their patriarchal milieux and histories."[7] Furthermore, the canonisation process of early Christian writings preserved the patriarchal texts of the New Testament. According to Schüssler Fiorenza, however, other kind of texts were also preserved, at least partly, and this proves that the *progressive patriarchalisation* of the church did not happen without opposition.[8]

This is also what Fredriksson states in her *According to Mary*. This world was not prepared to accept Jesus' original message when he lived and taught. For Fredriksson, Jesus "came too early into the world." Jesus' original message lost the struggle, and patriarchy, Jewish laws, and Greek logic took the opportunity to distort the whole idea of Jesus' new religion. Fredriksson is not the first one to suggest such degeneration.

---

5. Ibid., 88–89.
6. Schüssler Fiorenza, *In Memory of Her*, 30.
7. Ibid.
8. Ibid., 56.

Before her, Schüssler Fiorenza had already painted an idealistic picture of an egalitarian origin of Christianity. Authentic Christian faith gradually came under male dominion in the course of history. A parallel for such a romantic view of Christianity's (de)evolution as a religion can be found in German theology, where neo-Kantians such as von Harnack interpreted the genesis of church dogma as a process of deterioration. According to von Harnack, the construction of church doctrines corrupted the authentic, lively experience of the early *ecclesia* and turned it into rationalistic dogmatics.[9]

Schüssler Fiorenza's feminist interpretation of the genesis of Christian doctrines is somewhat stereotypical, too. According to Schüssler Fiorenza, dogmatic orthodoxy is a male intrigue against women's leadership, which, in turn, was condemned as heresy by the early church. "Therefore, feminist studies in religion must question the patristic interpretative model that identifies heresy with women's leadership and orthodoxy with patriarchal church structures." This is one of the key arguments later in Roberts's *The Wild Girl*, where Mary gets extremely angry after hearing from Peter that women have a different vocation in the church.[10]

When some of the Jesus-novels treated in this investigation are called feminist novels this means that, according to the present analysis, they contain features of second-wave feminism that are further related with Elisabeth Schüssler Fiorenza's ideas of feminist theology. No novel can be completely feminist, though. The novels will be investigated cautiously in order not to ascribe merely general qualities to them and to avoid unfounded accusations that merely produce a label without presenting detailed analysis. There are feminist elements in these novels but their nature will be identified only through a well-grounded investigation.

2. JESUS VS. MARY MAGDALENE

In feminist Jesus-novels, the contrast between Jesus and Mary Magdalene is not explicit. They are lovers, and there is no rivalry between them in

9. Fredriksson, *According to Mary*, 138. Concerning Harnack, see note 96 in the Introduction.

10. Schüssler Fiorenza, *In Memory of Her*, 53. Cf. 55 (citing Robert Kraft): "This development became necessary because there was 'never a single, pure, and authentic Christian position as later "orthodoxy" would have us believe.'" Roberts, *Wild Girl*, 133.

either their thoughts or speeches. Initially, the person of Jesus is not even depicted negatively, at least in his relationship with Mary. On some occasions one might even state that the story sounds rather conservative were there not this extraordinary love affair with the Magdalene. Jesus is presented as a teacher of wisdom or even divine love; he performs miracles and heals the sick. Such conservatism, however, is true only of the subtext inside the novel itself.

The character of Mary Magdalene stands out mainly when the story is compared with the original Gospel story. Mary naturally plays the leading role in Roberts's, Fredriksson's, Rinser's, and Berlinghof's novels but she also has a special status in Saramago's work. Especially in the feminist novels, Jesus stays in the margins and Mary becomes the actual creator of Christianity or at least the leader of one version of it. The new gospel works on two different levels. It presents a novel combination of carnality and heavenly wisdom. Jesus, despite being an omniscient Messiah, has no knowledge of carnal love. Hence Mary becomes his teacher. Furthermore, since Mary gradually becomes the true source of Jesus' secret wisdom, she simultaneously becomes a representative of Jesus' original faith. This is the new covenant of the feminist novels, and it no longer has anything to with the New Testament.[11]

Jesus' role is changed already through the demythologising of his character, as we saw in previous chapters. In feminist novels it is usually Mary who corrects the mythical views that surround Jesus in the male-dominated community. In these books Jesus does perform some miracles and heals the sick, and the raising of Lazarus is discussed usually in every novel. The general picture of Jesus' work, however, is explained in terms of the Western naturalistic worldview. For instance in Roberts's *Wild Girl* the feeding of the crowd in Galilee is merely a miracle concerning women's work. Jesus tells his disciples to organise food for people who have been away from their homes for hours. "People called it a miracle afterwards. I called it good housewifery." It is actually Martha who organises the disciples, "sending us hither and thither amongst the crowd." The food is fetched from near by homes: "and within what seemed only a short further space of time we were all

---

[11]. "Reintroducing a woman who has been left out but could have been present there is, therefore, the acceptable and simple filling of a gap." Ben-Porat, "Prototypical Rewriting," 98.

sitting down to feast on bread and dried fish and fruit that people ran back to their homes to fetch and then to distribute."[12]

According to Fredriksson, Jesus still heals the sick. Fredriksson hesitates slightly as she gets caught up in psychological explanations, but the result remains the same: people feel healed.

> The rumour that Jesus was again out on his wanderings had spread and everywhere people gathered around them. Once again the unhappy, the sick and the despairing crowded around the Master and as usual, he went straight out among the tormented, relieved them of their guilt and cured their illnesses. Mary watched his acts of faith healing as if seeing them for the first time.
>
> His immense presence is what achieves the miracles, she thought. He meets them all individually, sees their suffering, senses their question: "Why does life treat me so badly?" The moment he gives his hand to the sick, they are in total fellowship.
>
> Presence is perhaps the innermost form of love.[13]

In such therapeutic work Jesus' importance is more in pastoral counselling than in showing the power of God that is usually the focus in the canonical texts. In Fredriksson's *According to Mary*, not all of the biblical miracles really happened, though. For instance, the picture of Mary Magdalene herself in the canonical tradition was false. When Simon Peter asks Mary if demons were driven out of her (cf. Luke 8:2), Mary quickly remarks: "Did Jesus say that?" After this Mary turns to Paul, who is also present: "You see how the myths already flourished even when he was alive. I was not possessed by any demons." Mary is now the transmitter of true historical information, and she corrects Christian tradition when necessary.[14]

The main argument, in several feminist gospels, for the Magdalene's special status comes from Gnostic tradition, despite its modified form in Gnosticism. Mary is presented as Jesus' lover and this makes her a trusted person par excellence. In *The Wild Girl*, the setting compels Peter to ask:

---

12. Roberts, *Wild Girl*, 76.
13. Fredriksson, *According to Mary*, 142
14. Ibid., 104. As noted before, according to the canonical Gospels Mary Magdalene was not a harlot, but there was a story that Jesus had driven demons out of her when they had first met.

– Why do you love her more than any of us? Simon Peter burst out, his face red with anger: you know what she's been. It's not right.

Jesus sat up and looked at him.

– Why not ask why I don't love you in the same way as I love her? he replied.

Simon looked sulky.

– Men can't show love in that way, he muttered: it's an abomination, and unclean.

– Mary loves me completely, Jesus answered him: body and soul. Our kisses demonstrate that we are lovers of each other and lovers of God, nourishing each other, conceiving and giving birth between us to God.[15]

Jesus' straightforward answer gives a heavy emphasis to Mary's role. Carnal love is a tight bond, and it also gives Mary an extraordinary status among the disciples. Human love and divine love become one. After this, it should be apparent that no one else can reach such nearness with Jesus, not even the apostles of the canonical tradition.

Fredriksson, in her *According to Mary*, makes Mary Magdalene the beloved disciple in a similar manner. Since Mary becomes Jesus' mistress she gets the opportunity to hear his innermost thoughts that others have no knowledge of. "This is Mary, a woman I met and came to love."[16] Roberts is more straightforward in turning the roles of Jesus and Mary around. When Mary becomes Jesus' mistress and decides to accompany him, it is actually Mary who is the strong personality in their relationship. "Jesus forgave me nothing, because he said there was nothing to forgive. . . . He told me I was courageous and strong, with a gift for loving and for happiness."[17] Berlinghof makes the most radical move of them all. In her novel Mirjam's/Magdalene's love turns Jesus' message into its opposite. His concept of God, religion, and salvation are changed. Mirjam becomes thus the source of Jesus' so-called actual message, which is immediately rejected by Jesus' former disciples.[18]

Based on the well-known exegetical distinction between *Historie* and *Geschichte* (in German), i.e., the true historical Jesus and the Christ

---

15. Roberts, *Wild Girl*, 58.

16. Fredriksson, *According to Mary*, 113. In the canonical gospels the beloved apostle is of course John, see John 20:2.

17. Roberts, *Wild Girl*, 45.

18. Berlinghof, *Mirjam*, 380, 396.

of faith or the believer's Jesus, many feminist Jesus-novels distance their Jesus-character from the Jesus of the canonical Gospels. The argument goes as follows: Faith has always glazed the person of Jesus with mystery and mysticism, and myths flourished already during Jesus' lifetime. The male apostles participated in this mystifying process. Real history, according to the novels, must be quite different from the distorted picture blind faith has drawn that can now be seen in the canonical Gospels. Therefore, at least in part, Mary's new religion is a demythologised version of the biblical story. In this respect these novels do not differ from the rationalistic Jesus-novels that were written under the influence of deistic ideology or rationalistic biblical studies in the nineteenth and twentieth centuries.[19]

There is also another tension. It can be found in the contradiction between the source text and the subtext, and the subsequent spin given by the intertextual modification. Since Mary is the primary transmitter of the Jesus-tradition, one meets the real Jesus only through her words. This is where the feminine features of Jesus' proclamation come to fore. Jesus' message is centered on inner feelings. One should not worry about the morrow: "Consider the lilies of the field . . ." The core of Jesus' message, for Mary, was trust.[20]

Therefore, the essential difference between the biblical Jesus and the novel's Jesus can be seen in the intertextual construction where both biblical ideas and Gnostic views or themes are merged together with certain feminist convictions. There is no traditional soteriology in these novels. For Fredriksson, for instance, the general problem is that people live "outside their own nature." Religious renewal is a matter of psychological growth. They have not yet found their innermost nature, which is the basic foundation of their personality. They have not heard God's voice within. Mary Magdalene's Jesus sounds like a Buddhist who attempts to make people aware of their true nature. We do not see much meditation in these novels, but since all religions are said to aim towards the same end, such methods are acceptable in this process of growth.[21]

---

19. This distinction was often exploited in rationalistic Jesus-novels, see Ziolkowski, *Fictional Transfigurations*, 143, 148. Demythologisation here is only partial, though, since many feminist novels add mystical spirituality to the women's version of Christianity. See chapter below 7.

20. Fredriksson, *According to Mary*, 121.

21. Ibid., 141. This is the message of Berlinghof's Mirjam, too. What should be found in religious experience is the innermost essence of human beings ("im Innersten meines Wesens"). Berlinghof, *Mirjam*, 363.

Saramago in his *Gospel* too gives Mary Magdalene a primary role. He makes Mary Jesus' closest friend and mistress. They share both their uncertain feelings about everyday life and their humane convictions about morality. Again Mary becomes Jesus' teacher in the art of eroticism, as we have seen before. In the canonical Gospels Mary's role is not significant, but she does follow Jesus and belongs to the group that remains loyal to him. Hence there is a fragment of truth in the prototypical rewriting.[22]

In Saramago's story, Mary is kind and tender, and it is perhaps right to say with Fokkema that she becomes a wise companion: "The stylistic device of reversal makes Mary Magdalene into a wise and loyal companion of Jesus."[23] This, however, is nothing like Fredriksson's solution, which makes Mary the sole transmitter of Jesus' original teaching. Saramago's description remains patriarchal in the sense that, in the story, Jesus visits a whorehouse and then continues his journey. The only difference is that Mary really becomes his concubine.

> Who is that woman, asked James, Her name is Mary and she's with me, replied Jesus. Is she your wife, Well, yes and no, I don't understand, That doesn't surprise me.[24]

In this play of different readings and in the intertextual rendering of "texts," the picture of Jesus remains pale. He does not have a very clear message, but Mary often has one. Jesus speaks in Mary's voice when he focuses on inner feelings and the importance of one's real nature. The biblical subtext both in *The Wild Girl* and in *According to Mary* remains a collection of sweet words emptied of all the eschatology and hard proclamation against sins that fill the canonical Gospels. In a sense, this is not a feminist Jesus but, rather, a feminised Jesus speaking in the novels. He is not a man defending equality and transforming the role of women.

---

22. "The rules of historical contextualization fulfil, in this instance, the same legitimating task that the poetic style of the Song of Songs fulfils in the love scene. Fulfilling the conditions of prototypical rewriting in his treatment of Mary Magdalene, Saramago succeeds, by his sophisticated use of literary and historical codes, in maintaining maximum fidelity to the original text while reversing its function, thus forcing the reader to consider a different signification of the original as well." Ben-Porat, "Prototypical Rewriting," 98.

23. Fokkema, "Art of Rewriting," 399. See Saramago, *Gospel*, 216–17.

24. Saramago, *Gospel*, 246.

Instead he becomes a collection of attributes commonly understood as feminine or female.

One should not think that feminist novels with their new picture of Jesus are satirical, though. Presumably this is a natural result of raising Mary's position among the disciples and of a Gnostic reinterpretation of the canonical tradition. But is there something more behind this? One might further state that this kind of strategy aims at inverting conventional views about male and female qualities. In a poststructuralist feminist reading this might be the case. If Jesus, in the midst of the strong and dominating men in these stories, appears as a feminised person, this would go far in proving the novels' case. Truth about real life is mutually exclusive with all values associated with male behaviour, and the Son of God himself has proven it. It must be assumed, though, that this has not been the primary purpose here. Instead, it is just a secondary result since the prioritisation of Mary, clearly, is the important aim of the feminist novels. This is also achieved in these books. A novel written like this is no longer a gospel about Jesus, it is a gospel according to Mary.

3. AGAINST THE PRIMACY OF THE APOSTLES

For feminist Jesus-novels, historical Christianity turns out to be a male-dominated, patriarchal religion. It is ruled by men who, admittedly, have followed Jesus but who also have destroyed his message. Christianity as it is, as an institution, is not merely a community of men, it is also a counterfeit religion. It has betrayed Jesus' extraordinary message and turned it into a typical male ideology. And, according to the novels, the apostles in particular were guilty of this betrayal.

The elements of true Christianity, feminist novels state, are different. It is somewhat surprising then that gender identities are described in rather conventional terms. Women in the novels are sensitive to human relations. They are interested in questions of psychological growth and problems of personal independence—the only proper questions relevant for a true religion. Religion must be useful to human beings. It must not build walls or draw boundaries. Roberts and Fredriksson proclaim that religion must not separate people from each other. Every definition and every doctrine draws a line and, therefore, all definitions of religion or even of God are wrong.

Men, in turn—apostles like Peter and Paul—are dogmatic. They are interested merely in systems and doctrines. Their world is almost mathematical, constructed of formulas and hierarchies. There was a reason for this, according to many authors, and it will be discussed in the novels in due time, but first the fact of male dominance must be treated. According to feminist novels, Jesus as a true embodiment of humanity is more feminine than his followers have been able to admit. Only Mary Magdalene, who appears as Jesus' lover and concubine, has true knowledge about Jesus' innermost feelings and attitudes. And, furthermore, she has met with Jesus after his resurrection. Therefore, all heavenly wisdom has actually been entrusted to women. These are the features that recur in passage after passage in feminist Jesus-novels.

In Roberts's *The Wild Girl*, Jesus himself is a promoter of feminist religion. He teaches the equality of male and female and supports women instead of oppressing them. Women also have a special role in his group, as one might expect from a Jesus-movement described as "Gnostic." After Easter a fissure starts to open since the male apostles begin to organise the new church according to their own vision. Mary questions the one-sided new direction the community is taking.

> Tell me why I may not be a priest, I cried: tell me why I may not go forth and baptise as you will do in the Lord's name. Tell me why I may not offer the supper of bread and wine as he bade us do.[25]

The whole course of history is facing a feminist judgment here. The male world is about to take over the church, and Peter is securing his elevation to extreme power in the new hierarchy. Peter's arguments sound positive and convincing, though. Women cannot have a primary role since, in this "wicked and corrupt world," women are constantly at risk of being abused by men. Mary attempts to break the pattern but is destined to fail: "If we were priests, I said through my tears: it would be far less likely to happen. Our role and status would win us respect, and would protect us from harm."[26] Even though women, according to Roberts's story, have worked as preachers in Jesus' lifetime, this could never happen again. Men shall change the loving compassion of the female gospel into a cold dogmatic system and turn the church into a battlefield of religious power.[27]

---

25. Roberts, *Wild Girl*, 131.
26. Ibid., 132.
27. "The antagonism between Peter and Mary Magdalen shown in the *Gospel of*

In Fredriksson's novel as well the male-dominated church is a place for power games. Mary's protector Leonidas warns her about this game: "It's all about power, about the power the new church is to be based on."[28] This is how the figure of Mary is pushed to the fringes of early Christianity. She is not an ordinary member of the congregation. In the story, she is actually an outsider as she has been all her life, according to the novel. The famous apostles Peter and Paul are but sectarians building their own religions, sectarian because Mary has the original message Jesus entrusted to her.

Finally, in the story, Mary Magdalene confronts these two apostles. Peter has grown into a patriarch of the church and writes against women in his patriarchal letter:

> When I translated your letter, it became so clear, she said, turning to Simon. "You wives, be in subjection to your own husbands . . ." you wrote. Did you ever hear him say that? No! He said . . . there shall not be woman or man here. He is the only man I have ever met who regarded women as human beings, with respect. He did not protect them. He never made fun of them . . .[29]

Originality is a weighty argument. The message of the new gospel is more acceptable than the canonical text. The opposition remains the same throughout the story. According to Fredriksson and her new Jesus-figure, Jesus himself had founded a community of equality even adopting some feminist ideas. The male apostles, though, kept copying old Jewish attitudes and hierarchies. When reading Paul, Mary refers to her own experiences in the synagogue. Quoting some of the most negative expressions she can find, she opposes the traditional conviction: "Women, the gateway to the Devil."[30] The Pauline church, i.e., the male-dominated patriarchal church, has adopted and transmitted oppressive structures from Judaism to Christianity. Gradually, in example after example in Fredriksson's *According to Mary*, the apostle's violent

---

Thomas and *Gospel of Philip* is used here to demonstrate how the misogynist and flesh-hater Peter becomes the head of the orthodox Church. The feminine element, all loving and sexuate, represented by Mary Magdalen, is cast forth, proscribed from performing as preachers, prophets and priests, as they had in Christ's lifetime." Haskins, *Mary Magdalen*, 385.

28. Fredriksson, *According to Mary*, 157.

29. Properly quoted from 1 Pet 3:1 (AV). Ibid., 92–93.

30. Ibid., 198. This is one more example of the figure of the "seductive female" treated by P. Anderson ("Myth," 115).

patriarchy begins to be identified with the standard Jewish practice of religion. The only place where equality prevails, in Fredriksson's novel, is in a Gnostic-sounding feminist congregation where women are allowed to preach.[31]

Rinser is the most conservative these authors. For the most part, she presents Jesus' life as the canonical Gospels do, but simply from the perspective of the female disciples. Rinser's contribution is usually in certain expressions and ideas that are added to Jesus' original speeches like, "The truth is a sharp knife."[32] One can find traces of doctrinal expansion in Rinser's book, though. Her Jesus-figure states, for instance, that "The Eternal is both Father and Mother."[33] But even here Jesus' metaphorical speech remains on a general level and does not aim at a proclamation of a Heavenly Mother as such. Rinser's feminist ideology becomes explicit mainly on the last pages of the novel.

Mirjam gets angry with Paul's letters where the role of women is undervalued and women are almost entirely neglected in the hierarchy of the emerging church. According to Mirjam, the Jesus-movement could not have begun without women. They supported Jesus and his disciples, they fed them, they gave them money for everyday needs. Women followed Jesus to Golgotha and escorted his body to the grave. Women were also the first witnesses of Jesus' resurrection and were commissioned to preach his victory. But in the letters of male apostles, there is not a word of all this. Women had been rejected completely.[34]

The male version of Christianity, for Mirjam, was not a success. It would soon become a political power, a state religion where Jesus would be made a Caesar in sacral clothes. Men wanted only to conquer the

---

31. Fredriksson, *According to Mary*, 156.

32. "Die Wahrheit ist ein scharfes Messer." Rinser, *Mirjam*, 155.

33. "Der Ewige is Vater und Mutter." Ibid., 161. For Fulkerson feminist criticism is not merely a matter of language. She recognises, of course, that this has been a common point of departure in the movement. "Feminists have identified specific language or, more precisely, phrases and constellations of symbols in the Christian tradition (the dominance of male symbols, agents and pronouns and the paucity of female images or stories, ideals of subordination for women) with the problem of sexism. The dominance of male imagery for the divine in the Christian tradition is a paradigmatic instance of the claim that language is powerful and harmful for women when it only valorizes maleness." Fulkerson, "Subject," 133. She notes, however, that meaning and use cannot be inseparable and, therefore, the main focus must be on misogynist intentions, not particular words (134.)

34. Rinser, *Mirjam*, 329.

world in Jesus' name. Their visions gradually betrayed Jesus' message of peace and love. Instead, holy wars would enter history. Hence in Rinser's novel the male world is violent. The male church distorted Jesus' original religion, and only women could renew it. In the final pages Rinser thus participates in the feminist program, which is more clearly part of the adaptation in Roberts's and Fredriksson's novels.[35]

Berlinghof, however, creates one of the starkest contrasts imaginable between Mary Magdalene and Jesus' disciples. Her Mirjam makes Jesus actually resign from his office as a rabbi and a teacher. Jesus denies his messianic mission and renounces his earlier proclamation. After Jesus has learned to love Mirjam, everything he has taught his disciples becomes meaningless. He has just been leading his followers astray. This is something that makes his followers furious, and Jesus' announcement nullifying his work as a teacher leads to a severe conflict. Finally, in Jerusalem, it leads to Jesus' arrest and imprisonment.[36]

In Berlinghof's *Mirjam* one no longer meets a struggle about Christianity or a feminist substitution for male doctrines. Male-dominated Christianity is false from the very start. There is no sin, nor is there any salvation. There is no Messiah, and the patriarchal God is just a false image of some kind of creative power behind the true essence of humanity. All Jews and all Christians should just return home and look for the divine in their ordinary life, in the miracle of life as such.

According to feminist gospels, thus, Christianity in its present form is a religion for men only. Even though arguments change, the purpose remains the same. Christianity was founded by male apostles who did not really understand Jesus' teaching or the nature of his values. This is why these novels focus on a severe confrontation between the male apostles and Mary Magdalene. In these stories, the misogynist apostles establish patriarchal orthodoxy and secure their own power in ruling over the community. Women, in turn, are silenced and have no part in the hierarchy of the institution. Mary Magdalene remains the only figure who is able to confront the leaders, and her message gives birth to a Gnostic congregation which preserves Jesus' original message.

---

35. Ibid., 330.

36. Berlinghof, *Mirjam*, 392: "mein Lehren und Wirken euch mehr in die Irre als näher zu Gott geführt hat." [My teachings and deeds have led you astray, not nearer to God.]

4. FEMININE RELIGION REPLACES MALE DOGMATISM

But what is feminist religion like? It is to be expected that in feminist novels, religion will be defined in opposition to a male-dominated patriarchal way of understanding spirituality. There is no generally accepted view about male religion here, though. These novels do emphasise a stereotypical difference between women's concentration on experience and men's appeal to hierarchies, but this kind of dichotomy is not consistently written into the novels themselves. The most general feminine quality of the newly constructed Christianity is usually taken from Gnostic writings, but here again there is no unified view of Gnosticism that can be detected in the novels. Instead, each novel constructs its own version of Gnosticism and sometimes also distinguishes between Gnostic enthusiasm and the Magdalene's feminist spirituality.

There is, for example, some ambivalence between a critique of doctrines and a complete abandonment of doctrines in the novels. One of the most elementary of Christian doctrines, Jesus' virgin birth, is questioned in Fredriksson's *According to Mary*. In the novel it apparently belongs to the sphere of *demythologisation* familiar from other parts of the novel. Virgin birth does not fit in the rationalistic worldview of the new gospel. In the words of Leonidas: "I realize there is bound to be lively myth making around Jesus. But sometimes it seems to be taking on distasteful expressions. Like the virgin birth." The final authority, somewhat curiously, comes from Paul the apostle: "I never speak of it," said Paul. "But I know the legend flourishes in many circles." Mary then confirms the issue by answering Barnabas's question about Jesus' origins. "He once said his father, Joseph, was a good and rightminded man."[37] In Berlinghof's *Mirjam*, Jesus is the youngest of Mary's children and hardly born of a virgin in the traditional sense.[38]

Even though one can find severe critiques against certain doctrines in Fredriksson's novel, the question concerning structures and rules appears to be rather difficult. In the final part, there is a long discussion or a series of discussions concerning doctrines. This is probably necessary since the novel's approach, like that of all the investigated feminist novels, is normative. If one is to make changes to the structure of traditional

---

37. Fredriksson, *According to Mary*, 149. The reference to Paul hints at the scholarly dispute concerning the apostle's relation to the idea of the virgin birth. Fredriksson is well informed about issues in the scientific investigation of the Bible.

38. Berlinghof, *Mirjam*, 288.

Christianity, one must necessarily rely on values that exceed those found in the extant writings. From this perspective it is understandable that Fredriksson remains ambivalent concerning the nature of doctrines.

In several discussions with Paul, Peter, and Barnabas, Mary Magdalene confronts the orthodoxy of the male apostles. She is convinced that Jesus—the Gnostic Jesus of the Nag Hammadi texts, that is—was especially opposed to laws and rigid structures of thinking. Barnabas, in Fredriksson's story, first expresses his sympathies but simultaneously hesitates about whether the new kind of teaching could be accepted at all: "Your interpretations of the teachings of Jesus are interesting, but difficult to understand. People need simple rules and promises they can understand." Mary answers with a combination of Gnostic slogans and Jesus' canonical words: "New laws, you mean?" This is something Jesus explicitly forbade.

> Woe unto you, also you lawyers, for you lade men with burdens grievous to be borne. Woe unto you, lawyers, for you have taken away the key of knowledge: you entered not in yourselves, and them that were entering in you hindered.[39]

This time the intertextual effect is gained through placing a verbatim quotation from Jesus into a new context. Jewish scribes whose office was the teaching and interpreting of the Mosaic Law are identified with dogmaticians constructing doctrines. This kind of contradiction is repeated several times in *According to Mary*. The origin of the new teaching is, as noted before, in the message Jesus revealed to Mary after his resurrection.

> You know how often he was critical of the scribes and the men of the law. The last time I met him, in a vision after his death, he said it again. "Write no laws on what I have revealed to you."
> Peter was uneasy now, and Paul raised objections. "You can't build new teaching without any structure or system."[40]

In the intertextual setting, this is one of the key moments when the source text is confronted with the rewritten gospel of the novel. Mary admits that this is what people do; they build social as well as mental structures. Simultaneously she is convinced that this, in fact, is the heart of the problem: "But we turn all reality into a system, even what is invis-

---

39. Fredriksson, *According to Mary*, 135.
40. Ibid., 104–5.

ible. And as we are Jews, it becomes a Jewish system, based on laws and the hundreds of interpretations of them." Following the hermeneutics of twentieth-century existentialist theology, Fredriksson complains that each time a real religious experience is written into the form of a doctrine it becomes just a mythical description of an unspeakable event. Being Jewish in a Jewish community, the apostles would thus merely continue the Jewish tradition of constructing laws and making Jesus' religion a Jewish system.[41]

This is clearly the heart of feminist criticism of male Christianity. A dogmatic view of religion, for this ideology, contradicts and violates religious experience's real nature—the myth. As Pamela Anderson states: "Myths are not a product of instrumental rationality; in fact, they are what is excluded by formal reasoning."[42] Myths are used for refiguring traditional concepts. This is why also Fredriksson and Roberts use the patriarchal myth of Jesus' male-dominated group of disciples in order to refigure it into a women's community, which Fredriksson introduces at the end of her story. This also explains why Mary Magdalene in these stories opposes doctrines. It is necessary to make room for women's experience and feminine interpretation, and this is done by inverting the previous myths.[43] Their new religion cannot be based on dogmata and it must not sound like a catechism, because in that case it would not differ from the male version of Christianity. There is no logical reason why doctrine as such should be a male invention, though. A merely historical argument does not explain problems with the content of religious belief. The reason must be that this is the only way to introduce a feminist version of religious experience.[44]

---

41. Ibid., 105. This is the hermeneutical program of existential interpretation, developed especially by Rudolf Bultmann. See Kümmel, *Investigation*, 372–74.

42. Anderson, "Myth," 116.

43. Anderson explains: "As an example, the Adamic myth can be described as a symbolic narrative which founds both the religious culture and sexual identity for men under patriarchy, while marginalising women after Eve. But myths are narratives which, although configuring into a meaningful unity the heterogeneous experiences of concrete men and women, always remain open to refiguring." Ibid., 116.

44. As a theological or theoretical question, this is a well-known instance of circular reasoning. Contesting a doctrine anthropologically, for instance, (as is the case here) or soteriologically (as will be the case in the chapter discussing sacrifice) means the adoption of another doctrine based on different values. Therefore, there is no escape from doctrine, however strongly one wants to emphasise the importance of myths.

A similar new revelation can be found in Berlinghof's *Mirjam*. Her Jesus, after becoming conscious of real love in a real world, begins to proclaim the complete freedom of human beings. "You don't need any rabbi, priest, or a temple." None of the traditional Jewish elements of religious life are necessary for a genuine religious experience. "You don't need any doctrine." All one needs to do is to listen to one's heart.[45] Christianity should not adopt Jewish dogmatism as its foundation.

This kind of setting is quite interesting considering the aims of these novels. The identification of doctrines with Mosaic Law or even with law as a theological concept, namely as a demand and an absolute ideal of pure love, makes doctrines a Jewish phenomenon. According to Fredriksson, thus, the dogmatic male interpretation of Christianity is a sign of the Judaisation of Jesus' religion. Berlinghof also sets Mirjam and Jesus' religion of freedom in opposition especially to Jewish and Jewish-Christian spirituality. Here, once again, we encounter a polarisation that Nietzsche himself could have written, namely, the claim that Jesus gave in to Jewish tradition. "Too Jewish," Nietzsche wrote. Jesus accepted all Mosaic doctrines concerning law, sin, and God as a heavenly judge. Therefore, his ideas and his program were not noble enough: "he was a Jew."[46]

Behind Mary Magdalene's innocent pursuit of religious freedom and undogmatic independence there is, in Fredriksson's novel, an intentional contrast with Judaism and all that it represents: "You Jews with all your laws."[47] The opposition between the original source text and the novel is not merely an opposition between a patriarchal gospel and feminist Jesus. Instead, at least partly, it is a confrontation between a dogmatic Judaism and a de-Judaised version of Christianity. This does not mean that *According to Mary* is openly or consciously anti-Judaist—quite the opposite. The role of the Jews in Jesus' trial, for instance, is rewritten in favour of the Jewish people. But this means that, influenced by the Nietzschean tradition of confronting the alleged biblical slave

---

45. Berlinghof, *Mirjam*, 392: "Ihr braucht keine Rav, keine Priester und keinen Tempel! . . . Ihr brauch keine Lehre."

46. Nietzsche, *Gay Science*, § 140. The difference between Fredriksson and Berlinghof is probably that the latter rejects "Lehre" (doctrine) on the familiar grounds of German, Protestant western rationalism. From this perspective any doctrine in any religion would be condemned as futile. Fredriksson, however, makes doctrine a Jewish system.

47. Fredriksson, *According to Mary*, 138.

morality, Fredriksson gives in to branding dogmatic Judaism, as well as early Jewish-Christianity, as a violent and slavish religion.

Furthermore, from a theological point of view, the whole discussion is futile. There is a confusion of categories behind the first argument and, therefore, the arguments are directed towards the wrong objects. The identification of law and doctrine is a mistake, which probably derives from an effort to annihilate the general conception of doctrine in the first place. There is a Lutheran tone in this hermeneutical move since a distinction between "law" and "gospel" is a well-known Protestant dichotomy. Originally, it was used to make a distinction between the demands of law or the commandments, and faith as a free gift of the gospel. A confusion of these two would lead to an oppressive legalism. In Fredriksson's novel this dichotomy is applied to the contrast between inner experience and Christian doctrines. Protestant writers are more likely to exploit this kind of reinterpretation but authors like Saramago and Mailer never even touch upon it.

In addition to the fact that such a distinction is invalid, Fredriksson herself is inconsistent. Since individual laws, as such, are value-based precepts, practically everyone uses them. Fredriksson never abandons them but her novel, based on a feminist morality, is filled with implicit and explicit laws. The author in no way rejects laws as such. Theological doctrines, in turn, are systematised convictions about the nature of religion and here again, Fredriksson has adopted several solid conceptions about the reality of religious experience. Given these inconsistencies, does her novel really represent the reorientation that her characters insist upon?

But to go this far would mean treating *According to Mary* as a purely theological or philosophical writing, which it is not. Suffice it to say that the intertextual inversion detected in the novel betrays a Nietzschean antagonism to Judaism and the implications of this procedure may well be unconscious. The main purpose of the novel, namely, is to present a Gnostic-sounding feminist version of women's experience of religion. This is where the content of the feminist gospel becomes explicit. There are doctrines in these novels even though they are different from those of traditional Christianity.

In Roberts's *The Wild Girl*, Mary's message is quite different from that of the male apostles. As the Gnostic gospels claim, she gained her knowledge from the risen Lord right after the resurrection. From the very beginning, Roberts's novel states, there was a disagreement between Mary and the prominent men of the church. There was a battle over language, as it has been described, and men were about to spoil Jesus' original message. The words of the Lord would be twisted and distorted by men's patriarchal zeal. Since male Christianity was one of doctrines and hierarchies, the feminist version of Jesus' faith should be its opposite.

This is one of the crucial points concerning the ideology of the feminist gospels. The books are not just promoting inverted patriarchy. The feminist version of Christian faith is not matriarchal. It does not bear the marks of some kind of female understanding of spirituality. Instead, the feminist form of religion is usually pluralistic polytheism or even pantheism. If there is a so-called feminist argument behind this view, it is in favouring diversity and avoiding exclusive analytic definitions.

> I found that I had stored up all his teachings in my deepest heart, and that now I was ready to turn them over and take them in again, in a way that had not been possible before when I was so full of my own needs and strivings. This provided me with great comfort. I found, too, that I was able to join together the teachings of Jesus and the knowledge I had gained from my dreams. I threw loops of understanding between them. I wove them together into a complicated web which kept on changing, and no longer minded that the loose threads dangled and were untidy.[48]

The polarisation between male and female Christianity in Roberts's novel is quite conventional in its classifications. The male approach preserves, does not change, and remains static. Men's faith is based on doctrines and hierarchies, and it has a destination. The female approach, according to Roberts's book, is the opposite of this: renewing and changing, dynamic and inventive. Feminist faith is based on experience, and it is a continuing journey, seemingly without any deeper purpose. In this respect one should probably not say that Roberts's story of the Magdalene represents merely historiography that puts emphasis on written processes. Instead, in line with other feminist gospels, it claims interpretive power in the very world of discourse.[49]

---

48. Roberts, *Wild Girl*, 146.

49. When Linda Anderson defines poststructuralist historiography she notes that feminist historical narratives question the masculine subject as a real source of meaning: "By claiming a privileged relationship to the 'real,' historical narratives are thus really claiming interpretive power in a world of discourse, a power, which as feminists

Roberts's feminist religion supports polytheism, at least in a sense that there seems to be no clear distinction between different religions. At the time of Jesus' resurrection, for instance, Mary has a vision of the Queen of Heaven in a dream:

> I am the Ancient One. I am She who has many names. I am Ishtar and Astarte, Athar and Artemis and Aphrodite. I am Isis, busy with the work of re-membering my husband, and I am Inanna, she who descends from heaven to marry the shepherd Dumuzi and make him king after harrowing hell and reuniting heaven and earth. You have seen me as the witch Hecate, ad as her sister Demeter, mother and nurse. But I am also Persephone, borne off by Pluto into the underworld, there to eat the pomegranate seed and bring the human and the divine together again.[50]

In *According to Mary*, Fredriksson likewise builds a picture of a new Christianity mainly with the help of Gnostic writings. She too makes polytheism the essence of Christianity by paralleling Judaism with other Middle Eastern religions. Moses is made the soulmate of Hammurabi, and the writings concerning the Egyptian Osiris are made the source of Jesus' own teaching, since "His teaching was largely based on ancient wisdom."

> Lord of the Truth, before Thee I convey the truth. . . . I have annihilated the evil within me. . . . I have never killed, nor caused any tears. I have not let any go hungry, nor made any afraid, nor spoken in a haughty voice to call attention to my name. And I have never turned away God in his revelation.[51]

Both Roberts and Fredriksson substitute polytheism for the biblical monotheism. All religions are equal. Also Berlinghof lets her Magdalene, Mirjam, value different gods equally: "she made no distinction between religions and their followers." Even though it is clear that, in the minds of convinced Jews, this would be blasphemous and Israel's God could not be paralleled with false gods, Mirjam believes that inner conviction is all that matters.[52] After his so-called conversion Jesus proclaims that

---

have gone on to suggest, is indissolubly linked to the repression of difference in both language and culture and the positioning of the (masculine) subject as universal source of meaning." Anderson, "History," 131.

50. Roberts, *Wild Girl*, 125.
51. Fredriksson, *According to Mary*, 150.
52. Berlinghof, *Mirjam*, 41.

every man and woman can find God on their own. In the end, however, Jesus is finally inclined towards complete pantheism. Since God does not dwell in earthly buildings, he is everywhere, in every flower and every tree, even in every snake and every scorpion, in every created being.[53]

In these Jesus-novels, the feminist reading of Christianity is presented as the original form of Christian faith and Jesus' own teaching. It is usually depicted as the opposite of men's schematic dogmatism. True love does not need doctrines. The reading is somewhat dependent on a poststructuralist opposition, at least in their substituting of God the Father with polytheism. A heavenly pantheon with numerous male and female gods and multifarious kinds of divine beings is undeniably the most extreme counterpoint to the patriarchal Pater of the Bible. More importantly still is that the new Christianity is actually something Mary Magdalene taught Jesus. In this respect, feminist interpretation of Christian faith is in fact women's religion. It is based on women's experience of the divine. Jesus, in these novels, is but a servant of female spiritualism as explicated in the stories.

5. WRITING WOMEN INTO HISTORY

If the contesting of biblical moral values and the defence of the marginalised were two of the first expressions of Nietzschean hermeneutics in Jesus-novels, the next one can be found in the writers' conceptions of the status of women in Christianity. The treatment of women in biblical source texts is no doubt considered an example of Christian slave morality. The approach of the novels is that of emancipatory feminism, proclaiming the decline of patriarchal society.

But why should such an approach be called Nietzschean? Are we not witnessing merely a feminist reading of the Bible? As we stated earlier, the idea of Nietzschean influence must be understood on a rather general level. An approach may be called Nietzschean if it relies on a strict opposition to the biblical writings and if it further considers Christian views harmful to the people adopting them. In other words, the influence of Nietzschean ideology is evident if the views of the church are believed to support slavery and spiritual violence.[54]

---

53. Ibid., 394.

54. As noted already above, early German radical feminism built on Nietzsche since his "destructions" provided a useful tool for opposing traditional gender stereotypes and roles. Diethe, *Historical Dictionary of Nietzscheanism*, 89. There is, therefore, a di-

Several Jesus-novels fulfil these preconditions. Their basic intention reflects a true Nietzschean enthusiasm against the greatest possible fortress of patriarchal dominion one can imagine, namely Christianity. According to their interpretation, women of the Western world have suffered under the slavery of male apostles. Now it is time to write women into biblical history so that a complementary view could bring balance and provide a feminine understanding of religion. This is not standard political feminism aiming at equality in society. The problem is not even in the fact of male dominion in human relationships. Rather, the problem is found in the false, oppressive religion that needs to be reformed. And this, as said, is a true Nietzschean project. Roberts and Fredriksson write women into history each in their own way, but both with an intention.[55]

Fredriksson's *According to Mary* oscillates between pure fiction and honest historiography. She joins authors who want to write women into history. As Linda Anderson has said, ideologically loaded novels do not merely attempt to convey new meanings. They also construct history, in this case from a feminist point of view: "According to this radical critique historical narratives do not reveal meanings that are in some sense already 'there'; rather they construct meaning much as fictional narratives do."[56]

In Fredriksson's novel Mary's historical task of promoting feminist Christianity without "stability and structure" grows into a programme that contradicts the whole of Western cultural history and church tradition. "You have an almost impossible task," remarks Leonidas to Mary after she has completed her disputations with the prominent male leaders of the Jesus-movement. "The trouble is we human beings can't think unless we have a model, a pattern." For Fredriksson, surpassing this desire for a pattern is the real revolution of Christianity in its original, Gnostic form. Furthermore, it is probably also the essential difference between men and women and their ways of comprehending (or better: experiencing) their existence on earth. As Barnabas then asks Mary if she is able to think in new ways, she answers: "Jesus did." In the story

---

rect link from German feminism to Schüssler Fiorenza to Fredriksson. It is justified to assess this line of feminism as Nietzschean both for historical and ideological reasons.

55. Cf. White's conclusion about Roberts's literature in general: "Michèle Roberts's novels implicitly propose the act of, or quest for, narration as a means of reconstructing feminine identity." White, "Borders," 72.

56. Anderson, "History," 131.

of *According to Mary*, this is Jesus' original message and his original programme.[57]

Men, in turn, have a "weighty inheritance." Leonidas goes on to ponder the difficulties the new message will meet in the world where it will be proclaimed: "You Jews with all your laws, we Greeks with our naive faith in logic and reason. And last but not least, the Romans who live in their blind faith in Roman order and discipline." Preconditions for the success of a new, unsystematic religion are so bad that Fredriksson makes Leonidas sigh over the slowness of cultural evolution: "Sometimes I've thought Jesus came too early into the world."[58]

Male-dominated history will not accept Jesus' feminine message. The gospel of the church shall inevitably be distorted and assimilated into patriarchal ideologies. It shall preserve Jewish laws, construct doctrines with the help of sound logic and proper reasoning, and finally guard the result of all this with orthodox discipline. Mary and Leonidas also notice that Peter, Paul, and the rest of the male apostles are well prepared to execute this programme in the church. They are patriarchy's "willing promoters" who will make Christianity a logical system of dogmas and rationalistic truth. Saramago might go so far as to say that these apostles were ready to follow the violent precepts of the evil heavenly Being all the way to the Inquisition's raising of pyres. False doctrine would necessarily produce a church that violates the joyful life-experience of free souls. Christianity, once again, is seen as a system of *Sklavenmoral*.[59]

For these writers, religion and any other necessary institutions concerning human life are not systems of knowledge. These authors do not depend on analytical tools. These feminist novels rely on Derridean hermeneutics where the "transcendental signified," stable concept, or *logos*, as Derrida says, is denied. Real culture and especially truth about human beings is not a matter of thinking or understanding. It is a matter

---

57. Fredriksson, *According to Mary*, 138.

58. Ibid.

59. Cf. Haskins commenting on Roberts: "The studied simplicity of the Magdalen's prose style is equalled only by the simplicity of the ideas of equality and love, and the what-might-have-been if patriarchy hadn't taken over. In the end, Michèle Roberts' interesting use of much Christian feminist thinking and research into the figure of the Gnostic Mariham is overwhelmed by the romantic elements of the novel which do much to defuse its argumentative power." Haskins, *Mary Magdalen*, 386.

of experience and truthfulness to one's "innermost core," as Fredriksson said. Because Jesus made "the world new" he was a "subverter of society."[60]

The difficult problem in such poststructuralist interpretations of history is that when written history becomes only ideological schematisations of the past, mere forced patterns that need to be dismantled and inverted, and when meaning vanishes into the sea of rivaling discourses, truth claims also become futile. The schemata of genre and power themselves are dissolved in the death of the sign. Thus feminist authors find themselves in a difficult situation where history as such is about to disappear before women get the opportunity to write themselves into it. As Linda Anderson has said, feminist authors are left between the death of history and the remaining danger of accepting patriarchal categories.[61]

The poststructuralist difficulty with language is related to the "ethical paradox" belonging to the same movement. Scholars, and especially feminist scholars, are stuck with the problem that if words are mere prisoners inside the language system and values are but violent binary oppositions that have no basis in reality, it becomes impossible to combat patriarchy just by creating one more binary opposition. This is, for instance, what Fulkerson has noted in her feminist treatment of discourse.

> Despite the notoriety of poststructuralism as the procedure that reduces everything to textuality, or what I would prefer to call signifying processes, a poststructuralist turn to discourse will do more consistently what feminists have always tried to do with the insistence that language is more than mere semantics: that *it has reality effects*.[62]

Fulkerson cannot really solve the problem because she needs the deconstructive force of poststructuralism. This is why she makes the most common move there is in this tradition. She emphasises sociological structuralism. She is convinced that, despite all criticism against the "transcendental signified," and opposing the phenomenological conviction that meanings are constructed in contextual occasions, language

---

60. Derrida, *Of Grammatology*, 49. Fredriksson, *According to Mary*, 138.

61. "The fear that post-structuralist theory could be disabling for women, making history disappear even before we have had a chance to write ourselves into it, needs to be set against another danger: the constant danger that by using categories and genres which are implicated in patriarchal ideology we are simply re-writing our own oppression." Anderson, "History," 134.

62. Fulkerson, "Subject," 135.

does reflect "social processes."⁶³ This is the most common sociological view on structuralism presented in many dictionaries.⁶⁴ The theoretical difficulty with this solution is that, when giving up poststructuralism, feminism turns into ideology and loses the "ontological" theory of patriarchy. This does not mean that women could no longer combat male domination, but it does mean that feminism has to formulate new grounds for its views.⁶⁵

Hutcheon reminds us that both postmodernism and feminism are dependent on values they refer to or defend. Therefore, the "political" nature of such position leads to "political confusion" because of its "double encoding." One cannot exclude all values in order to defend certain selected values. This contradiction shows that postmodern feminism has its own nonnegotiable metanarrative.

> While feminisms may use postmodern parodic strategies of deconstruction, they never suffer from this confusion of political agenda, partly because they have a position and a 'truth' that offer ways of understanding aesthetic and social practices in the light of the production of—and challenge to—gender relations. This is their metanarrative.⁶⁶

All this is not simply mere theory, though. Constructing a new history means simultaneously that the extant tradition will be criticised severely. This results in a new understanding of Christian tradition and the history of the church. According to Roberts and Fredriksson and the other feminist authors, history has gone astray. It is not merely a false discourse. In the end, this is not just a question about words. We do not

---

63. Ibid., 136. Alicia Ostriker justifies poststructuralist hermeneutics by saying that biblical texts both forbid and invite feminist revision of religion. "The questioning of authority, including divine authority, has been built into Judaism in several different ways." Ostriker, *Feminist Revision*, 57. What may seem "outrageous, blasphemous, and irreligious about woman's re-imagining of the Bible" is, for her, a feature of biblical texts themselves.

64. *Penguin Dictionary of Sociology* and *Blackwell Companion to Social Theory*, s.v. structuralism.

65. White also notes this difficulty and places Roberts among the authors who actually resist the very tradition radical poststructuralist feminism relies on. Quoting Patricia Waugh she writes that many women writers are now drawing on postmodernist narrative techniques in ways which "resist the nihilistic implication of much of the theory." White, "Borders," 76. They are said to use disruptive forms to re-imagine our world, and this should be something that is able to escape the ethical paradox. This cannot be true because such technique reinforces the paradox.

66. Hutcheon, "Incredulity."

Challenging the Biblical Role of Women 189

just happen to have a distorted story about Christianity and Jesus' legacy by chance. Instead, feminist authors are witnessing a fraud. Christianity in its present form is a deception, as Professor Lüdemann in the radicalised German tradition stated in the twentieth century in a heated theological debate over the historical Jesus.[67]

The feminist approach also deliberately confuses the relation between source text, subtext, and novel as an intertext. Since all previous history is considered the result of patriarchal oppression, no document can be taken as a proper source for a feminist reading of history. Such historiography apparently results in a free restructuring of extant history and even in biased rendering of ancient documents. In a sense, the aim is to reveal the male intrigues that the documents reflect.

This is where the feminist Jesus-novels become identical with feminist theology, and it is apparent that the former have learned from the latter. When New Testament texts are considered resources for patriarchal subordination, there clearly must also have been a true history, a proper picture of Jesus, and a proper basis for a religion. In this respect, feminist Jesus-novels have more passionate, ideological motivations than any of the other investigated novels, perhaps excluding Saramago. At least as far as the novels are adopting a feminist theological approach, there is a committed striving for a religious revolution.

Writing women into history is an intentional project of feminist Jesus-novels. The authors apparently follow poststructuralist feminism in attempting to create stories where women have been given important roles in emerging Christianity. The theoretical problem with this is its dependence on the "ethical paradox" already detected in poststructuralist theory itself. Feminist theories appear to have metanarratives of their own. This leads to an ideological question about combative feminism, which in many ways accompanies the discussion concerning feminist Jesus-novels.

---

67. Lüdemann, *Grosse Betrug*, 8. Lüdemann became famous for his accusations that are quite similar to those found both in feminist theology and feminist Jesus-novels. According to Lüdemann, Gospel stories are only inventions and reflect mere religious fantasy. Therefore, the whole phenomenon of Christianity is historically based on a deception carried out by ignorant men. Lüdemann challenged the Church to question its fundamental doctrines, quite in the manner the investigated feminist Jesus-novels do.

6. DISMANTLING PROGRESSIVE PATRIARCHALISATION

Can fictional novels be held responsible for initiating a particular ideology or theology? Feminist novels appear to make an open statement against Christian patriarchalisation. For instance, in *According to Mary* Fredriksson co-opts many statements directly from Schüssler Fiorenza, and her treatment of early Christianity closely resembles that of Elaine Pagels. However, different feminist views produce different interpretations, even in theology. Irigaray opposes the view where female identity is seen merely as a function of man's life, while in Schüssler Fiorenza's estimation men's interest in doctrinal definitions corrupts the original, free, and egalitarian church. Put together, these two ideas result in a conclusion that in the early church women were subordinated violently under the prescriptions of restrictive Christian doctrines. It is quite apparent that this view has been adopted by Roberts and Fredriksson.

For instance, Fredriksson follows Schüssler Fiorenza, according to whom early church history gradually turned into a struggle between various groups, Montanists, Gnostics, and others. In such a situation, doctrinal clashes began. The "orthodox" church, as it is now called, won the struggle as the "gradual patriarchalisation" provided the means for coercive subordination and domination. In Fredriksson's *According to Mary* this kind of reconstruction is written into history; Mary Magdalene even attends the meeting of a Gnostic group that has been developing her own teaching about Jesus.[68]

In Schüssler Fiorenza's idealistic view these other groups were egalitarian and acknowledged the leadership of women, tracing their authority especially to Mary Magdalene. Schüssler Fiorenza's interpretation is unfortunately dependent on the so-called Gnostic fallacy, basing its arguments on an anachronistic interpretation of Gnostic writings. The Nag Hammadi texts are some 150 years younger than the writings and traditions of the New Testament, and the role of women in these texts is not egalitarian. Mary Magdalene is in these writings merely a receiver of heavenly knowledge, the secret gnosis, not a congregation leader. Montanism, in turn, was a movement around from 200 CE, and can hardly provide evidence of the life of the "original" early church.[69]

---

68. Fredriksson, *According to Mary*, 156.

69. Schüssler Fiorenza, *In Memory of Her*, 54. She wrote the monograph in 1983 when the investigation of Gnostic writings was still influenced by the views of the old history-of-religions school.

Nevertheless, Schüssler Fiorenza's views have had a strong impact on postmodern novelists rewriting the origins of early Christianity in a feminist light. In Jesus-novels one can see traces both of her views about the doctrines as expressions of patriarchal dominion and of her conception that Mary Magdalene had a special role in the alleged egalitarian, anti-dogmatic *ecclesia*. Clearly both in feminist theology and in the novels, these features are the result of a new construction of history. It is not just that women needed to be written into history. Instead, new feminist history had to be constructed from the ground up since the sources had been contaminated by patriarchy.

Another feature that has found its way into postmodern novels concerns women's experience of religion. As Rosemary Radford Ruether has indicated: "The uniqueness of feminist theology lies not in its use of the criterion of experience but rather in its use of women's experience, which has been almost entirely shut out of theological reflection in the past."[70] So it is not just the psychological notion of experience versus doctrine that should be raised by feminist awareness. Rather, one should speak directly about women's experience, women's way of seeing things in the world and in religion.

Not surprisingly, Ruether's post-Christian feminist theology also wants to liberate traditional Christianity from its patriarchal, monotheistic tradition. Ruether replaces monotheism with polytheism and suggests a syncretic form of religion. This is in line with the feminist novels. According to Roberts and Fredriksson, it is not woman's experience of spirituality that should be given a primary status in the church. Patriarchy should not be replaced by matriarchy. A true rejection of the patriarchal Heavenly Father means the adoption of pluralistic polytheism. Consequently Ruether states that feminist spirituality is "reassessing pre-Christian religion." According to Ruether, myths and cults of goddesses provide "alternative resources" for women's identity. Why this should be done is not evident on the basis of Ruether's statements. The only logical way from feminist premises to syncretism is in a Nietzschean rejection of the biblical God. This view seems to be well received in postmodern Jesus-novels.[71]

---

70. Ruether, *Sexism and God-Talk*, 13. This view is naturally related with the idea that, according to postmodern historiography, women who have been rejected in historiography should later be written into history; cf. chapter 1 above.

71. Ibid., 39. In Pamela Anderson's terminology this means the refiguring of myths. Religious language, expressing itself in myths, can also be seen as a process where "a

The reason for avoiding full-blown matriarchy may be in postmodern hermeneutics itself. Taylor has noted that the pattern of patriarchy cannot be destroyed by replacing it by another kind of hierarchy. "The death of the Father God does not, of course, end the regime of patriarchy. The humanistic inversion of divinity and humanity leads to a worldly representative of the omnipotent Father."[72] In this respect Nietzsche, whom Taylor honors in principle, was wrong. The introduction of the *Übermench* means actually the worst possible patriarchy one can imagine.

In the manner of philosophical feminism, thus, these theologians deplore the traditional roles of women in existing religious organisations and Christian theology. They also contest the patriarchal language of theological discourse. In feminist Jesus-novels such seeds fall on fertile soil. For instance Roberts in *The Wild Girl* states: "We have lost the knowledge of the Mother. We do not fully know God if we drive out this name of God."[73] Rinser, in turn, states: "The Eternal is both father and mother."[74] Finally, Fredriksson contrasts women's and especially Mary Magdalen's (Gnostic) interpretation of Jesus' message with the doctrinal religion of men. At the end of the story women explicitly state the narrative's feminist point: "Perhaps it's important that we also submit our testimonies?"[75]

Later, Grace Jantzen, a third-wave feminist, as one might call her, challenges the relevance of traditional Christianity altogether by exploiting Nietzschean terminology. In Jantzen's deconstructionism religious binary oppositions are dissolved. In her *Becoming Divine* she states that the problems of this world result from the violent hierarchies of the patriarchal world. Evil is a male invention. Patriarchy, in turn, is legitimated by the Jewish/Christian religion, which proclaims that God is a man. Feminist deconstruction attempts to dissolve such patterns.

> It means also considering both how traditional theistic doctrines of power, mastery, and hierarchical patterns of domination feed

---

certain mythopoetic activity constitutes the energy behind variable, mythical representations of religious meaning." Anderson, "Myth," 116.

72. Taylor, *Erring*, 28.
73. Roberts, *Wild Girl*, 111.
74. Rinser, *Mirjam*, 161: "Der Ewige ist Vater und Mutter."
75. Fredriksson, *According to Mary*, 220. This is naturally what the whole story in this novel is about, i.e. the testimony of Mary Magdalene.

into the ideologies propping up the structures of domination and reinforce racism, sexism, poverty, and homophobia.[76]

The problem of evil, thus, is mainly a result of the Bible's message. Theistic religion creates patriarchal power structures that generate everything from racism to homophobia. Christianity is the cancer of this world—as previously atheists would have said. In her criticism Jantzen aims at "a deliberate replacement of the traditional masculinist projection of God with a feminist pantheist projection," which, in turn, would "disrupt the polarized and hierarchized symbolic of western modernity."[77] By referring to Derrida, Jantzen suggests that the deconstruction of traditional hierarchies means precisely a change from theism to pantheism. "Pantheism rejects the split between spirit and matter, light and darkness, and the rest; it thereby also rejects the hierarchies based on these splits."[78]

The new polarisation of deconstructionist feminism is quite tense. The Bible with its theistic God is the source of evil and at the heart of the subordination and oppression in the world. The so-called pagan religions have always provided a more humanist alternative to Christianity. Their polytheism or pantheism leaves room for different kinds of religious experience and offers several different objects of identification. The role of women is also more open and acknowledged in pagan mysteries than in restrictive doctrinal Christianity. Therefore, traditional Christian faith should be replaced by its previous opposition and rival.

This, for some reason, seems to be the case in the polarised feminist Jesus-novels, too. There is no clear or evident reason why beliefs and doctrines should be rejected as tokens of male imagination. The only plausible explanation is that feminist rewriting plays with myths, which are not a product of men's instrumental rationality. This, however, does not solve all the problems of consistency. The plot thickens further as it is evident that, in these novels, Christian doctrines are simply replaced

---

76. Jantzen, *Becoming Divine*, 264.

77. Ibid., 265. This is a huge step forward from the thoughts of Schüssler Fiorenza who still remarked that, "such a feminist *memoria* of the suffering of Jesus Christ and of the innocent victims of patriarchal oppression must be careful not to ascribe this suffering and colonialization of women to the positive will of God, the heavenly patriarch, and to claim divine revelation and the agency of the Holy Spirit as the theological justification of such suffering." Schüssler Fiorenza, *In Memory of Her*, 32.

78. Jantzen, *Becoming Divine*, 267.

by new Gnostic doctrines. The literary motivation for such a decision may be in the conviction that male doctrines are life-denying while feminist-Gnostic views are philanthropic—and really not doctrines at all. This being the case, the contesting of male-dominated Christianity, with its male apostles and male distinctions producing separation and racist rejections of other religions, is just another Nietzschean line of attack where the Judeo-Christian tradition is seen as the source of discrimination and chauvinism.

5

Dissolving Sacrificial Religion

According to many recent Jesus-novels the stories of the New Testament and the message of Christian faith are not only patriarchal and restrictive. In the estimation of several authors, they are also violent. The novels denounce God who "thirsts for blood." One of the key issues in this discussion is the idea of sacrifice. The problem itself, however, is in the new understanding of human nature. According to the basic Nietzschean view, one must not understand human beings as sinful.

1. SACRIFICE AND VIOLENCE

As the desolate fate of Judas, for Slavoj Žižek, expresses the perverse core of Christianity, so has the idea of divine sacrifice been assessed as twisted. It is often considered an inhuman and a distorted dogma. Bishop John Spong describes the theology of Christ's death "a cruel act of divine child abuse" on the hill of Calvary.[1] For Spong, such a portrait of a sadistic God only "validates violence" and produces a sadomasochistic religion. "The punishing God is thus replicated in the punishing parent, the punishing authority figure and the punishing nation. Violence is redemptive. War is justified. Bloodshed is the way of salvation."[2]

This is quite the view that Nietzsche promotes in *The Anti-Christ*. He writes about the absurd problem of God demanding his Son's death. How could God allow something like this? According to Nietzsche, the early church solved the problem with its new soteriology: "God gave his

---

1. Spong, *Sins of Scripture*, 171. For Žižek, see chapter 3.1 above.
2. Ibid., 172–73.

son as a *sacrifice* for the forgiveness of sins." For Nietzsche, this is the most barbaric form of sacrifice. "What appalling paganism!"[3]

A common-sense argument apparently supports such a view, at least as far as a sacrificial cult is concerned. The slaughtering of a sacrificial animal is a violent event. Why should the divine Being be so cruel that he would demand death on the occasion of approaching him? Where should one draw the line? Does the biblical God also demand human sacrifice, the killing of devoted adults or even children, as did other Semitic gods in ancient times? Many of the recent Jesus-novels attack the biblical story vehemently. As the biography of Jesus' life necessarily culminates in his famous death, the meaning of such divine suffering needs to be addressed.

The problem of sacrifice is crucial especially in Saramago's novel. Speculation over Jesus' death begins already when the child Jesus is taken into the Temple of Jerusalem and Joseph buys two doves as a sacrifice. This is the first piece of evidence revealing the nature of the God who accepts such sacrifice.

> Any ironic or irreverent disciple of Voltaire will find it difficult to resist making the obvious remark that things being what they are, it would appear that purity can only be maintained so long as there are innocent creatures to sacrifice in this world, whether they be turtle-doves, lambs or whatever.[4]

As such a disciple of Voltaire, the author describes the temple as a huge slaughterhouse where these "innocent creatures" are slain in great numbers. The description intends to be sarcastic, even despite its historical basis. In the temple, sacrificial animals were slaughtered daily, and in considerable numbers. There was a practical aim too apart from the worship or cult. Most of the meat was eaten, and so to describe the event as the slaughtering of animals for food production is correct. The religious meaning was combined with its more practical purposes. Part of the sacrifice, in particular the cereal offerings (bread) and drink offerings (wine), provided meals for the priests serving in the temple. For a bourgeois Western reader such a tradition can induce culture shock since the context has vanished and we live in an era when slaughter is associated exclusively with meat production. The further idea that death

---

3. Nietzsche, *Anti-Christ*, § 41.
4. Saramago, *Gospel*, 67.

may have a theological meaning has no doubt become unfamiliar to modern readers.[5]

Saramago deepens the intertextual tension by presenting a detailed description of the butchers' tables:

> Within the Court of the Israelites there is a furnace and a slaughterhouse. On two large stone slabs larger animals such as oxen and calves are killed, also sheep, ewes and male and female goats. There are tall pillars alongside the tables where the carcasses are suspended from hooks set into the stonework, and here one can watch the frenzied activity as the butchers wield their knives, cleavers, axes and handsaws, the air filled with fumes rising from the wood and singed hides, from the vapours of blood and sweat. Anyone witnessing the scene would have to be a saint in order to understand how God could condone this appalling carnage if He is, as He claims, the Father of all men and beasts.[6]

Why is Israel's God a God of sacrifice, a God of slaughter, and a designer of the massacre of the children in Bethlehem? The reason, for Saramago, is simple: God loves carnage. In this "Menippean" satire, as it has been called, Saramago exploits prototypical rewriting unceasingly. In order to produce an inversion of the biblical metanarrative he does not need to change everything in the historical narrative. He only needs to stretch certain features to the limit so that they become absurd for modern readers. At this point it is not the story that has changed, it is the reader. After creating a black-and-white polarisation, Saramago is able to present statements about God that the readers believe without hesitation.[7]

God's guilt in the narrative is related to his inner nature, the essence of his divinity. The intertextual change here turns the idea of holiness around. God is no longer a heavenly Judge, in front of whom all sinful

---

5. On the details of the sacrificial cult of the Old Testament see, e.g., Anderson, "Sacrifice," 870–86.

6. Saramago, *Gospel*, 68.

7. Pál notes that this is a common feature in Saramago's novels: "The post-modern practice of juxtaposing heterogenous elements, the vulgar and the sublime, indicates the influence of the *menippea* in our days, which is the survival of the antique 'menippean satire' with its carnivalesque atmosphere. So we can explain the presence of carnivalesque elements in Saramago's novels because the Portuguese writer, who permanently queries the traditional form of novel, that is telling a story, has the opinion that the novel of our days has to deal with the ultimate questions of life and death, and it is one of the main characteristics of the *menippea* as well." Pál, "Traditions," 332.

flesh of creation will be destroyed, as was the case in the original story. This is the main point of the new metanarrative. God is guilty of violating the environment. He disobeys the laws of protecting nature. He may still be the male Demiurge of the Old Testament, but now he is implicitly battling against the female goddess Gaia who represents and protects the material world with its plants and animals. Sacrifice, of course, no longer has anything to do with sin. Nietzsche's project is completed. There is nothing left but slaughter and carnage.

Such a recoiling from Jewish sacrificial cult is typical also of Fredriksson's novel. The idea of sacrifice offends Mary's concept of religion as spiritual growth. According to the narrative, religion has actually degenerated and gradually turned into a system of horrors.

> Mary had heard Leonidas say that Christians saw the death of Jesus as a sacrifice. But she had not realized the breadth of that teaching. For many years, she had brooded over why He had chosen that terrible death on the cross. The people of this new teaching did not have to brood. They had the answer. But then she remembered that Passover in the great temple in Jerusalem, the house of God turned into a slaughterhouse, the animals bellowing, blood flowing.[8]

Such a view also serves the larger narrative of the novel. Since Mary herself, in Fredriksson's story, knew almost nothing about Jesus' sacrifice and the idea of his atoning death, there apparently had been a earlier, more original period when people had been directed to religious meditation. Presumably it was an idealistic proto-Gnosticism, which had always been there. As Mary Magdalene now aimed at a reformation, she only needed to regraft religion onto its spiritual roots. In this scheme animals are holy and to be valued in the same manner as humans. The holiness of the heavens has been transferred to earth.

A similar theme appears in another feminist Jesus-novel. Nature is divine also in Roberts' *Wild Girl* where, however, the female goddess and Gaia-figure is identified as the third person of the triune Christian God: "the Holy Spirit who is Sophia but also the name of the Mother who is earth, matter and soul married and indivisible."[9] In these kinds of contexts sacrifice no longer has a cultic function. Rather, it must be abandoned on the basis of other values, for instance those of respecting

---

8. Fredriksson, *According to Mary*, 89.
9. Roberts, *Wild Girl*, 111.

animal rights. Roberts's denial of religious sacrifice differs thus from that of Saramago, even though the theme of rejecting violence in any form seems to be a connecting factor.

In Saramago's novel, the criticism is developed even further. The Jesus of the story is displeased with God's intentions. He has spent much time with the evil Pastor and learned his lessons. Therefore, Jesus becomes a Sisyphus who begins to defy heavenly powers. He is a rebel who struggles to free himself from the determinism of divine providence. This leads him first and foremost to oppose cultic sacrifice. Later when Jesus happens to visit the Jerusalem temple, he still has a lamb with him to be slaughtered in the court of the shrine. Before entering the temple area, however, he begins to hesitate. The idea of the necessity of such an innocent animal's death becomes untenable for him. The animal looks at Jesus and starts to bleat "in that nervous, tremulous way young lambs do before being sacrificed to placate the gods." So Jesus decides to save the lamb.[10]

Why was the sacrifice necessary? Saramago repeats his criticism against sacrificial cult. Even from the beginning, Abel's animal sacrifice surpassed that of Cain's. This led gradually to the continual killing of animals in the temple: "they all offer the same sacrifice, and how that fat spits and those carcasses sizzle while God in the sublime heavens inhales with satisfaction the odours from all that carnage." This is what Jesus now doubts. His lamb does not need to die. Suppressing his fear of punishment Jesus disobeys.[11]

> For a moment, fear of punishment made him hesitate, but suddenly in his mind's eye, he momentarily saw the horrifying vision of a vast sea of blood, the blood of the countless lambs and other animals sacrificed since the creation of mankind, for that is why men have been put on this earth, to adore and offer sacrifice.[12]

So the Jesus-figure of the narrative agrees with the narrator. The latter has already defined God as utterly opposed to rational thinking and decent conduct. He is the source of evil and a flesh-eating beast who treats both animals and human beings as he wishes. This God is like a monster from Greek mythology and the reason why Jesus starts this odyssey of fleeing from his sphere of influence. It is only natural that,

10. Saramago, *Gospel*, 186.
11. Ibid., 187.
12. Ibid.

later in Saramago's novel, resisting sacrifice becomes a major theme of the narrative.

This produces other kinds of conflicts in the course of the story, though. A tension grows between Jesus and his teacher the Pastor, i.e., the Devil, who has opposed the idea of sacrifice from the very start. During the years they spent together, the Pastor succeeded in preventing Jesus from sacrificing to God. On one occasion, however, Jesus happens to meet God in the wilderness, and he demands that Jesus offer a lamb as a sacrifice. Because Jesus is to become God's servant, their covenant must be confirmed by a sacrifice.

After a moment of hesitation Jesus agrees to this and is willing to offer the lamb. The situation is complex, though, since the lamb Jesus has with him is the very animal the Pastor saved from God's hands earlier. Later Jesus tells all this to the Pastor who instantly asks about the fate of his lamb. Jesus' confession to Pastor leads then to a crucial conflict between them. At this culminating juncture, Jesus is taken back under the wing of the heavenly God.[13]

Jesus too, in Saramago's story, shall be a victim who is sacrificed for God's designs. There is a part for Jesus in God's plan: "That of a martyr, My son, that of victim." A martyr's death must be painful and ignominious so that believers may be moved to a great fervour.[14] Believers, in this parody, are guided merely by their feelings, and in their enthusiasm they aim merely at ecstatic experiences. Saramago uses this to make sacrifice a symbol for God's violent nature and to justify his abandonment of God's terrible kingdom with its future history. A false view of God produces only suffering. In the narrative, the Christian God is condemned in the name of love and compassion. The main charge, after all these preliminary speculations dealing with Jesus' life, concerns Christian history, the life of the church. God's kingdom will not be a kingdom of peace. What will the community be like when it lives under the providence of a God who loves sacrifice? In a crucial discussion towards the end of the book Jesus insists on knowing the future agony of the church: "how much death and suffering Your victory over other gods will cost, how much suffering and death will be needed to justify the battles men will fight in Your name and mine[?]"[15]

13. Ibid., 198–99.
14. Ibid., 282–83.
15. Ibid., 290.

The divine Being of the narrative confesses to Jesus that an assembly, a Christian church, will be founded, but its foundations will be dug out of flesh. It demands "abnegation, tears, suffering, torment, every conceivable form of death known or as yet unrevealed." After this confession follows a horrible list of countless ways of dying. It starts with the fate of the first disciples and then develops into a list following the oldest, Catholic martyrologies. As the number of Jesus' followers begins to grow, God wants hundreds of new victims.[16]

> Let's start with someone whom you know and love, the fisherman Simon, whom you will call Peter, like you, he will be crucified, but upside down, Andrew, too, will be crucified on a cross in the shape of an X, the son of Zebedee, known as James, will be beheaded.[17]

The unending list contains descriptions of torture and horror. Some are stoned to death, others skinned alive. There are people killed by spears or people sawn in half. These lists have a crucial role in the hermeneutics of the novel. Metanarratives change once again. The biblical battle between God's kingdom and the godless world is transformed into a battle between God and humankind. After the apostles, a new period begins, "an endless tale of iron and blood, of fire and ashes, an infinite sea of sorrow and tears." A traditional list of the martyrs of the church is then presented in alphabetical order. "Adalbert of Prague, put to death with a pikestaff with seven points, Adrian, hammered to death over an anvil, Afra of Augsburg, burnt at the stake, Agapitus of Praeneste, burnt at the stake hanging by his feet." The almost five pages long list is devastating—and even here God has only begun his presentation. After the letter C, God says: "from now it's all much the same with few variations," but the list goes on. [18]

It is not that much easier to stay alive, though. Fearing temptations, saints torment themselves with fasting and prayers. Saramago's picture

---

16. Traditions of martyrs have a special role in the history of the Catholic Church. See, e.g., *The Book of Saints*. Saramago at least partly follows the martyrologies of the Church.

17. Saramago, *Gospel*, 290.

18. The list has produced problems for translation because an alphabetical order should be preserved since it is mentioned especially in the beginning, and it is thus a vehicle for the proper impact. Saramago, *Gospel*, 291–92. The English version differs slightly from the original; see Saramago, *Evangelho*, 381–82.

of a pious life is not easy or peaceful. Believers will mortify their flesh with "suffering and blood and grime," they will use "hair shirts and flagellation." The most holy ones will retreat to caves as hermits, or climb to the top of high pillars and live there for years. Here even the Devil takes part in the discussion. "Note from what He has told us that there are two ways of losing one's life, either through martyrdom or by renunciation."[19]

As the Devil enters the discussion, he wants to wash his hands of these kinds of horrors: "these punishments were not invented by the Devil who is talking to you."[20] For the present story, Christianity is not merely Nietzschean *Sklavenmoral*, even though this faith as a negation of life surely spoils human happiness with all its restrictions. But Christianity is the ultimate source of violence, spreading horror all around it. This is further confirmed by referring to the Crusades and, of course, the Inquisition. Thousands of heretics and infidels will be killed in the name of Jesus. The Devil becomes even more defensive. "No one in his right mind can possibly suggest that the Devil was, is, or ever will be responsible for so much bloodshed and death."[21]

Simultaneously, however, the Devil maintains his biblical office. He is a prosecutor who accuses people in the heavenly court. The boat on the Sea of Galilee turns into a courthouse and a grueling cross-examination is conducted. God is on trial. The Devil appears as Satan (Nfc), "the accuser," as the Hebrew word originally denotes.[22] Here the Devil has the same role as in Zechariah 3. "Next I saw Joshua the high priest standing before the angel of the Lord, with Satan standing at his right hand to accuse him." On the Galilean ship there is no rescue for the present captain, though, as there was for Joshua in the Old Testament story. Now the accused has to confess every sin he has committed and reveal his devious plan to expand his territory by bloodshed.[23] Satan's

19. Saramago, *Gospel*, 295.
20. Ibid., 296.
21. Ibid., 297.
22. Bloom assumes that Saramago "seems to take us back to the unfallen Satan of the Book of Job" and, therefore, he should have another kind of role. "And yet Job's Satan was an Accuser; Pastor is not." Bloom, "One with the Beard," 158. Quite the opposite, Saramago's Satan on the Galilean boat is precisely an Accuser, only the object has changed.
23. Zech 3:1. Saramago exploits all the possible functions the Devil has in the Old Testament. This theme will be discussed further in chapter 6 on theism. Satan, "the great dragon," appears as an accuser also in Rev 12:9–10, where the Messiah, quite unlike Jesus here in Saramago's story, throws him down to the earth.

accusations find their proper addressee, and Saramago is able to prove his case against the divine Despot.

As God and the Devil switch roles, Jesus cries: "Father, take from me this cup, My power and your glory demand that you should drink to the last drop, I don't want this glory, But I want the power." Jesus' painful prayer in the garden of Gethsemane is transposed to a new context (Matt 26:39). His agony is not the weight of sin he bears on behalf of fallen humanity. He is suffering because of God's sins. This is confirmed by the Pastor, who ironically remarks: "One has to be God to enjoy so much bloodshed."[24]

Quite persistently Saramago focuses on sacrifice's dependence on violence. Why should one accept that violence provides atonement through a sacrifice? Saramago's hermeneutical point of departure leads inevitably to one conclusion. Since he no longer gives cultic sacrifice a theological interpretation, theology is replaced by rationalism. It is necessarily the event itself that needs to be assessed, and when Saramago focuses on it, it turns out to be violent. If the temple has turned into a slaughterhouse, the only criteria exploited here concern feelings such as sympathy. Violent actions cannot be right or righteous or good because they are so negative. What the world lacks is sympathy, and so the church or Christianity as such appears to be a religion of destruction and aggression.

All this leads to a crucial hermeneutical question. Is Saramago really aiming at a theological disputation? Frier is convinced that the religious controversy over Saramago's novel has been generally misled. According to his conclusions, the biblical material is used only metaphorically. Saramago's "fundamental meaning" is about power. Therefore, Frier assumes that the author's main intention is to denounce crimes committed in the name of Christianity.[25] This is an essential

---

24. Saramago, *Gospel*, 298. Fokkema interprets this: "Such pungent remarks are rare in the novel and certainly less frequent than the many ironic commentaries inserted in the text which, however, have a similar, or perhaps an even more devastating effect. The whole novel, notably its later part, is a running indictment against the Catholic Church, but the tone of exposing the senseless abnegation and bloodshed is subtle and rational." Fokkema, "Art of Rewriting," 398. It is difficult to assume that all this was done solely in the spirit of literary entertainment.

25. Frier, "Outline," 369. "I would argue, therefore, that if *O Evangelho Segundo Jesus Cristo* is to be seen as being in any way an attack upon Christianity, then it can be so only in the secular sense of an angered denunciation of crimes committed in the name of Christianity, rather than as a philosophical rejection of its core doctrines."

question for the hypothesis of the present analysis. Is Saramago writing merely on issues of power? Not merely. Nobody can question Frier's observation that Saramago obviously writes about crimes committed in the course of the church's history. The devastating lists of martyrs—both of the church and its adversaries—prove this without doubt. However, Saramago is not content with describing church history. He employs a Nietzschean device in attacking the ideological or religious system itself. For Saramago, there is a reason for the violent tradition, and it is precisely in Christianity's false view of God. It is the biblical God, as Saramago assumes he has proven, who has always demanded sacrifice. Divine history is filled with victims and incomprehensible suffering.

God, in this context, becomes a monster. From the very start, then, he is a man-eater who merely aims at destruction. While in the biblical story, it is the Devil who is the deceiver and conspirator who attempts to ruin souls, in the new story this role is reserved for God. For Saramago, the core of Christian faith is perverse. In his view the biblical God is destructive. The whole novel seems to emphasise this one point: The Christian God is a violent God who demands sacrifice. And the story confirms the hypothesis. Violence accompanies both Jesus' and his disciples' lives. The history of the church is that of coercion and murder.

In this respect Saramago's criticism begins to resemble Camus' "rebellion" in his fight against absurdity. For them both, real sublimity in life is to fight corruption to the point where even God must be denied.

> Thus Catholic prisoners, in the prison cells of Spain, refuse communion today because the priests of the régime have made it obligatory in certain prisons. These lonely witnesses to the crucifixion of innocence refuse salvation, too, if it must be paid for by injustice and oppression. This insane generosity is the generosity of rebellion, which unhesitating gives the strength of its love and refuses injustice without a moment's delay. Its merit ["honneur"] lies in making no calculations, distributing everything that it possesses to life and to living men.[26]

For Camus, the absurdity of life means sin without God. His examples comprise injustice and oppression as is the case in the quotation above. In a Nietzschean tradition, however, it is quite difficult to reject slave morality and still cling to a rebellion against absurdity. The journey

---

26. Camus, *Rebel*, 268. The French word générosité means sublimity, which naturally is just the Nietzschean term for the "honour" of new life.

beyond good and evil should not allow such a move. Camus—and no doubt Saramago too—appear to substitute grace with rebellion. The combat itself is considered redemptive. According to such idealism the rebellious human being is able to conquer evil.[27]

In Saramago's case there is similar ambivalence, especially concerning intertextuality. His inversion is incomplete because it never touches on biblical warnings and condemnations against violence to say nothing of the recurring proclamation of love in the original narrative. On the other hand, such preciseness in assessing these novels is unnecessary because they are not theology. Both the author and his narrator retain the freedom of narration. In the end, it is the (implied) author who is omniscient and knows every detail in the world he is creating. He knows the truth about God and the true nature of the sacrifice. The intertextual change wants to question even the good aims of the original story. The polarisation in these novels abandons the Nietzschean adaptation of the idea of sacrifice, not sacrfice's meaning in philosophy of religion or theology.

2. QUESTIONING THE BIBLICAL VIEW OF HUMAN NATURE

In a theological sense the questions about sin, atonement, and sacrifice are essentially linked with the question of human nature. A crucial problem among Western humanists from the Enlightenment onwards has been that of the church's position on the subject of sin. In a naturalistic worldview there is no point in speculating over transgression, absolution, and atonement. Why should one speak about sacrifice when there is nothing to atone for?

In Saramago's novel the sinfulness of the human race is a metanarrative that simply is false. If Nietzsche cannot find any relevant meaning for sin, neither can Saramago. For Nietzsche, sin is but a Jewish invention, based on a false concept of God and a distorted view of human nature. Even speaking about sin uses the language of slaves. As Christianity adopted this discourse it became an heir to the same perversion. As Nietzsche drastically puts it, Christianity was about the "to Judaise" the

---

27. Frier notes: "This spirit of refusal to accept the inevitability of what exists and the notion of the ongoing perfectibility of God's creation, in a sense the spirit which always says 'no', is as essential to succeful human existence as are the qualities more traditionally associated with goodness. . . ." Frier, "Outline," 376.

whole world. The crucial problem is that sin has no essence. Nietzsche assumes that it is all about God's honour. An act of sin is merely an offence to God, wounding his honour. "Every sin is a slight to his honor, a *crimen laesae majestatis divinae* [lese-majesty]—and no more."[28]

Saramago tells a tale about a second creation. In the beginning the Devil has witnessed the birth of Adam and Eve and learned how it was done. He repeats the process and creates an underworld for himself.

> And since the Devil, whom God had initially befriended and looked on with favour, causing people even in this world to comment that there had never been so close a friendship, since the Devil had witnessed the birth of Adam and Eve and learned how it was done, he then repeated the process and created man and woman for himself in his underworld, but with the one difference that, unlike God, he forbade them nothing, which explains why there has never been such a thing as original sin in the Devil's world. One of the old men even dared to suggest, And since there was no original sin, there was no other kind of sin either.[29]

Since the Devil forbids man and woman nothing, there is no such thing as original sin. And apparently, as the story informs the readers, no other kind of sin either. There are several ways this story depends directly on Nietzsche's ideas. Firstly, the concept of sin has no empirical justification. Secondly, humankind would do just as well without God interfering in its businesses. Thirdly, God's commandments have been prescribed merely to give him honour. And fourthly, no real ethical problems are addressed when discussing the nature of sin.

Just as this story, in Saramago's narrative, is a random tale of some old men visiting Nazareth, neither does it belong to the core of the Devil's teachings. Nevertheless, it soon becomes a hermeneutical guide for treating the problem of sin. The Devil begins to question Jesus about sexual matters. If God has created what men have between their legs, he cannot disown his creation. According to the Pastor, this means that God is inconsistent when he criminalises nakedness and speaks of defilement. So it is not the Pastor, but the double-dealing Creator who is in trouble. "In other words, your God is the only warder of a prison

---

28. Nietzsche, *Gay Science*, § 135.
29. Saramago, *Gospel*, 176.

where the only captive is your God." Sin is God's invention and no other ostensible verification of its existence.[30]

Fredriksson too, abandoning the theology of sacrifice, treats the conceptions of sin and human nature in her novel. After meeting with Paul the apostle, Mary reads his letters and finds strange passages speculating on sin and atonement. "For the wages of sin is death, but the gift of God is eternal life through Jesus Christ our Lord." The text is magnificent and makes an impact but, according to Mary, it has nothing to do with the teachings of Jesus. Mary cannot make Paul's vision fit in with the man she knew intimately. For her, Christianity is a religion of love and heavenly gnosis, not one of laws. Speaking of sin, in this setting, sounds negative, despite all the empirical evidence of cruelty described even in Fredriksson's story itself. In Fredriksson's novel there are "sins" in the postmodern, feminist sense, and they are severely reviled, but they are no longer biblical sins. They are Nietzschean sins, meaning sins that restrict human life in general and women's experience of life in particular. Male Christianity, for Fredriksson, is mainly a denial of life. God, therefore, has nothing to do with the remission of sins—unless Jesus' sending should be seen as a crusade against the patriarchal world of men.[31]

The scene is altered in Mailer's *Gospel* because, for him, Jesus is a moralist. He does take the reality of sin into account. There may be several reasons for this in the logical structure of the narrative itself, but Mailer presents one simple reason in the text: "Indeed, how can one obey the Law absolutely?" The traditional Jewish concern over obedience, a burning issue for every pious Jew from the days of Jesus ben Sirach, is important to Mailer's Jesus as well. When meeting with John the Baptist, Jesus confesses his sins to John—despite the fact that at the

---

30. Ibid., 176–77. This is also how Fokkema interprets (and adopts) Saramago's view: "If one starts thinking about it, one wonders how the idea can have survived the Enlightenment and the worldwide diffusion of democracy. It is unclear what it means to say that everyone is leading a life of sin." Fokkema, "Art of Rewriting," 400. The paradox with this statement as well as Saramago's narrative begins with Saramago's reasoning, which is based completely on the horrible wrongdoings described in a four to five page list in the novel. Violence is so devastating that even God must be dethroned since it occurs at all. The only way to solve this problem would be to claim that violence is not a sin. This would be a difficult task since both the Decalogue and Jesus' Sermon on the Mount denounce it as a sin. Fokkema's paradox appears regularly in atheist literature.

31. Fredriksson, *According to Mary*, 199. Comments are on Rom 6:23 (AV), quoted here verbatim.

time he does not really know what to confess.[32] Now, when standing before the Pharisees, Jesus teaches them about the Law in its deepest sense.

> What comes out of a man, however, can defile him. From a man's heart issue evil thoughts, adulteries, fornications, murders, thefts, covetousness, wickedness, deceit, blasphemy, pride, even the evil eye.[33]

One could speculate that Mailer quotes Jesus' words under the weight and pressure of the source text. This interpretation, however, cannot hold because the idea of human corruption is essential for Mailer's larger narrative. He needs the concept of sin in order to describe the devastating combat between good and evil forces in this world. This feature will become evident later when investigating Mailer's view on divine righteousness.[34] In this respect Mailer differs essentially from the other authors. But within Mailer's own narrative, one contradiction remains. Mailer is not a theologian and is unable to make his negative view of human nature fit his new gospel story. He has no use for the conception of sin later in his "soteriology," since Jesus does not die for fallen humanity. If there is forgiveness in Mailer's novel, it is based merely on divine goodwill like in numerous other religions—not on Jesus' sacrificial death for sins. This reflects Mailer's confused conception of human nature and shows that in general he differs little from Saramago or Fredriksson, despite his severe quotations about sin.

But what about reality? Why should one adopt moral values? Why do the authors claim or at least imply that one should defend the marginalised or support feminism? Committing oneself to a particular moral value implies the exclusion of some kind of negative human behaviour. Why is it necessary to condemn violence? Authors of the Jesus-novels end up with the painful problems Camus once tackled so meticulously. Through his atheistic moralism, Camus arrived at the concept of absurdity. As the problem of evil deprives us of a coherent concept of God, morality can no longer be justified by referring to divine power or eternal laws. But Camus never abandoned creation. For him, the world was

---

32. Mailer, *According to the Son*, 33.
33. Ibid., 121–22.
34. Mailer's view will be investigated in chapter 6.1. below.

paradoxical, but not completely irrational. Human beings are morally corrupt, not insane. Therefore, the world is to be defined as absurd.[35]

With his discussions on absurdity Camus wished to explain the cruelty of human life. Especially since he was writing during the Nazi occupation and participating the French resistance, he searching for a role for the existentialist figure of Sisyphus he had invented earlier. In this work he paved the way for the later authors of Jesus-novels: he began to write moral theology. According to Camus, "the absurd is sin without God." Ultimately, he had no other alternative to describe the state of the world and human nature. The paradoxical nature of life is close to what the Bible calls sin.[36]

In his speculations about the absurd, Camus had referred to Kierkegaard, who had also spoken about the basic absurdity of human life.[37] There is, however, an essential difference between these two. Kierkegaard, often described as an existentialist, was a rather conservative theologian. He accepted the idea of Adam's sin. Responsibility is not to be transferred to God, at least as far as we are speaking about the crimes of human beings. But there was absurdity in meeting with God. In his *Fear and Trembling* Kierkegaard stated that there is absurdity in the relation between God and human beings. Starting with the biblical story of Isaac's sacrifice Kierkegaard attempted to understand God's demands. He did not go in the direction Saramago took later but, instead, remained in the paradox. God demands Abraham to sacrifice his son. His only son should be made a victim on divine authority. For Kierkegaard, there are no rational answers or philosophical solutions for this paradox. Therefore, God's demand is absurd. For Kierkegaard, this is the only possible way to approach God. There is but fear and trembling. God is Almighty and just in all his commandments.[38]

Which line do the Jesus-novels adopt? What is absurdity for them? The novels, apparently, remain ambiguous on these questions. This world is full of horrible things, and human beings are both violent and

---

35. According to Sprintzen, Camus actually tried to justify the rationality of the world and make it seem coherent so that human beings could feel "at home" in this life. Therefore, Camus was constantly guided by a "hunger for unity." Sprintzen, *Camus*, 57.

36. Camus, *Myth of Sisyphus*, 42.

37. "Nothing more profound, for example than Kierkegaard's view according to which despair is not a fact but a state: the very state of sin." Ibid., 42.

38. Kierkegaard, *Fear and Trembling*, 55, 139.

deceitful. This world even without God is a difficult place. But just like atheist authors throughout the Enlightenment period, these novelists do not worry overmuch about unpleasant things. In a Nietzschean interpretation, unpleasantness is necessary only insofar as it can be used against the concept of God. After that, writers no longer take any pains in pondering the problem of evil. Therefore, these novels reflect an attitude similar to Spong's in his death-of-God theology:

> We are not fallen, sinful people who deserve to be punished. We are frightened, insecure people who have achieved the enormous breakthrough into self-consciousness that marks no other creature that has yet emerged from the evolutionary cycle. We must not denigrate the human being who ate of the tree of knowledge in the Genesis story. We must learn rather to celebrate the creative leap into a higher humanity.[39]

The setting in Jesus-novels, thus, is quite complex. Many of them seem merely to adopt a Nietzschean critique against the biblical concept of sin in order to justify European humanism and probably in order to promote the idea of a pure, Faustian will to life freed from Christian restrictions. But a comparison with Camus' work introduces the idea of existentialist ethics, which, no doubt, plays a crucial role in post-Hitler Western literature. It is insufficient for the writers to suggest a superficial view of good life when facing the horrors of everyday life. Therefore, their analysis of the human condition often takes Camus' turn, the rebellion.

3. REJECTING THE DOCTRINE OF ATONEMENT

Two of the abovementioned features, the identification of sacrifice and violence, and the abandonment of the concepts of the Adamic fall and humanity's sinfulness, lead consistently to a crucial theological presupposition in several of the investigated novels. Jesus' death cannot be an act of atonement. Atonement is neither needed nor expected. It does not bring well-being to humankind. In fact, as a doctrine, it even fails to help people be at peace with themselves and, rather, deprives them of their dignity.

A rehabilitation of human dignity was naturally Nietzsche's main mission. Already in his nihilistic theology he had suggested the abandon-

---

39. Spong, *Sins of Scripture*, 173–74.

ment of Christian rhetoric concerning reconciliation and forgiveness. For Nietzsche, the idea of atonement was "barbaric." It had corrupted all Christian dogmatics. The adoption of even this one false point of departure resulted in the corruption of many other details. This is where the Apostle Paul enters the picture. He begins to formulate a system that, according to Nietzsche, created the dogma concerning atonement.

> From this time forward the type of the Saviour was corrupted, bit by bit, by the doctrine of judgment and of the second coming, the doctrine of death as a sacrifice, the doctrine of the *resurrection*, by means of which the entire concept of "blessedness," the whole and only reality of the gospels, is juggled away—in favour of a state of existence *after* death.[40]

Such views have been repeated later especially in the death-of-God movement. According to Spong, Christians must rid themselves of the violent views of Christian dogma. He states: "Jesus did not die for your sins or my sins." Such a view ties people to a conviction that only validates our own violence, i.e., that bloodshed is the way of salvation.[41] A Nietzschean influence is thus easily seen in the Faustian tradition of postrationalist theology. It is no wonder, then, that such conceptions find their way to literature, as well. Jesus-novels are perfect areas for testing these ideas in the sphere of culture.

Therefore, it should not be a surprise for readers to find a rejection of the idea of atonement for instance in Fredriksson's feminist novel. In the new gospel of Mary Magdalene all rules and dogmas belong to the theoretical world of men. Men cannot think if they are not allowed to exploit patterns and models. Men are stuck in hierarchies and organisations. The world of women, instead, is dynamic. It is not in need of doctrines. "Mary had heard Leonidas say that Christians saw the death of Jesus as a sacrifice." This was the teaching of Peter and his friends, quoted according to the canonical writings. "Christ also has once suffered for your sins, the just for the unjust, that he might bring us to God."[42] Fredriksson's intertextual solution here is that of harsh contra-

---

40. Nietzsche, *Anti-Christ*, § 41.

41. See Spong, *Sins of Scripture*, 173.

42. Fredriksson, *According to Mary*, 89. This is a direct quotation from 1 Pet 3:18 (NKJV); cf. NRSV: "For Christ also suffered for sins once for all, the righteous for the unrighteous, in order to bring you to God."

diction. The source text is opposed in the intertext where Mary's own theology is contrasted with Peter's teaching.

In the novel, the teaching about sacrifice does not suit Mary. She is convinced that the old temple is only a slaughterhouse, and that her lover would never have taught in favour of such a system. Patterns cannot save anyone. Instead, God should be approached without any dogmas. The risen Jesus Mary meets with firmly dismisses religious laws. According to Mary's new gospel, Jesus makes no distinctions between religions on the basis of particular dogmas. Furthermore, there is a problem with the patriarchal system of Christian faith. It is based on power structures designed by men. And this, apparently, is related to violence.[43]

Saramago's position here deserves special mention since one of his main goals is to make Jesus prevent God from creating the doctrine of atonement. Furthermore, Jesus must do this on his own because, in the story, the Devil is unable to make a deal with God about reconciliation. Now Jesus must attempt to cheat God by creating a plot that enables him to avoid sacrificial death. This is the only way the violent future history of Christianity can be changed. The strategy is as follows. When Jesus understands that his final days are at hand he must appear as a common human being. So the Son of God will not die on the cross but a mere Galilean peasant will. This will supposedly destroy God's plans. I discussed this duplicitous act earlier as well when treating when Judas's fate.

> I myself will take the Son's place, For the love of God, explain yourself, An ordinary man, perhaps, but a man who was prepared to proclaim himself King of the Jews, to incite the people to depose Herod from his throne and expel the Romans from the land, and all I ask is that one of you go immediately to the Temple and say that I am this man and that if justice is swift perhaps God's justice will not have time to stay that of men, just as it did not stay the executioner's axe as he was about to behead John.[44]

Therefore, when facing his judges, Jesus consistently answers with clauses referring to political resistance. Saramago once again makes a clever change in the intertextual reading. The source text corresponds roughly with the subtext even though the intention is now turned inside out. "I am King of the Jews." The elders attempt to change the subject by

---

43. Fredriksson, *According to Mary*, 105.
44. Saramago, *Gospel*, 334–35. Cf. chapter 3.1. above.

asking the crucial question: "And second, that you are the Son of God." Jesus replies immediately: "Who told you that I claim to be the Son of God." By insisting on his political aims Jesus keeps to his plan and confirms his fate at the hands of the Romans.[45]

In the story, Jesus even attempts to hurry things when he is taken from one prison to another: "anxious to keep his appointment with death, lest God should look this way and say, What's going on, are you backing out of our agreement."[46] The death sentence is certain, though, and nothing prevents it. Saramago's story culminates in presenting an inversion and practically a perversion of the canonical story. Jesus himself asks Pilate to write an inscription above the cross. The text must state the political reason for Jesus' sentence. Pilate agrees to do this and writes: "Jesus of Nazareth, King of the Jews."[47] The use of a direct quotation from John 19:19 emphasises that the very charges of Jesus' sentence should actually work against the doctrine of atonement.

Divine predestination appears to direct Saramago's history, though. Eventually, everything goes according to God's plans. Jesus cannot escape his heavenly will. At the moment of his death he hears a heavenly voice: "This is My beloved Son, in whom I am well pleased." God has won.

> Jesus then realized he had been brought here under false pretences, as the lamb is led to sacrifice and that his life had been planned for death since the very beginning. Remembering the river of blood and suffering that would flow from his side and flood the entire earth, he called out to the open sky where God could be seen smiling, Men, forgive Him, for He knows not what He has done.[48]

For Saramago, Jesus is not a victim in the sense of being a sacrifice for the sins of the world. Instead, he is the victim that has been sacrificed in order to please the bloodthirsty Despot. He is a victim of God's ambition and jealousy. Like Nietzsche, Saramago proclaims that human rebellion is an offence to God, a slight to his honor, a lese-majesty. Therefore, Jesus' cry on the cross is a plea for his real executioner: He

---

45. Ibid., 337. In the canonical Gospels, when Pilate asks Jesus "Are you the King of the Jews," Jesus merely answers: "You say so [*sy legeis*]." Mark 15:2.
46. Ibid., 338.
47. Ibid., 339–40.
48. Ibid., 341.

knows not what He is doing.⁴⁹ This climax clearly confirms Saramago's basic message. The violent God, the God of the church's raw history, must be rejected in the name of morality. Saramago's crusade against slave morality ends in this final contradiction. There is no acceptable reason whatsoever to adopt Christian faith or even allow the church to continue proclaiming its destructive message.

The original feature in Saramago's intertextual change is that he builds a contradiction between the subtext and the (implied) author. Other authors usually make changes when assembling the subtext and make it serve their new designs. Saramago does not merely oppose the canonical tradition, the source text. The "ironic disciple of Voltaire," as he might be called, has first created a new gospel as a subtext and then subverts it in his criticism.⁵⁰ New Testament history as a whole, even as a revised subtext, is a story of God's devious plan to please himself through Jesus' sacrificial death. No matter what the original Jesus may have said or what the Gospel writers or apostles may have inferred in their theology, in Saramago's story all these statements belong to God's coercive history. Therefore, only the author is able to unmask truth and in this sense the real history behind the texts.⁵¹

Mailer, in his *Gospel*, avoids treating the idea of atonement. He finds no real meaning for Jesus' death. In a certain sense this is consistent with his "Docetic" narrative since his story is told by the risen Christ. This resurrected Messiah never really suffered because he was always aware of his future glory. God never rejected or abandoned him. Therefore, for Mailer, Jesus never defeats sin on the cross. It is all a cosmic game.⁵²

> For my Father saw how to gain much from defeat by calling it victory. Now, in these days, many Christians believe that all has

---

49. Jesus' original prayer on the cross can be found only in Luke 23:34: "Father, forgive them; for they do not know what they are doing."

50. This is an expression Saramago uses; see *Gospel*, 67.

51. Fokkema remarks that, for Saramago, there is no original sin to be reconciled. "Original sin requires unconditional surrender to powers one does not know. It is related to eternal revenge and repeated repentance. I cannot but conclude that it belongs to the pre-history of modernity, on a par with blood feud. It is based on the notion of collective guilt, just as racism [*sic*]." Fokkema, "Art of Rewriting," 400. Fokkema points out several oppositions that derive directly from the Nietzschean tradition: modern–postmodern, Christian–humanist, religious–secular.

52. "The cross of Christ did not defeat Satan. There has been no atonement for sins. In fact, Mailer's gospel seems to have no use for Jesus' death on the cross other than as a deception." Partridge, "Gospel," 73.

been won for them. They believe it was already won before they were born. They believe that this victory belongs to them because of my suffering on the cross.[53]

Through this new "satanic" manner of preaching, turning things upside down, the criticism of Mailer's novel focuses on the core of Christian picture of Jesus. Christianity's salvation history, according to this story, is false. Religion proclaiming defeat as victory is based on a lie. Due to such a tension there is also a contradiction between Judaism and Christianity in this novel. Christian hope in reconciliation is in vain and can help no one who is searching for truth.

Atonement, in the Nietzschean tradition, is a useless concept. The investigated Jesus-novels usually abandon the whole concept and place it along side other life-denying and oppressive beliefs that enslave free and strong human beings. Since the picture of Jesus as a sacrifice represents, for these writers as well as for Nietzsche himself, inhumane paganism, there is no need for redemption in the new community the novels construct. Perhaps a more important argument here, however, is anthropological. For the authors, there is no point in depicting human life as sinful. It may be imperfect and clumsy but there is no essential problem with humanity. Anybody claiming this is guilty of denigrating both the human mind and the will to power.

4. RELIGION AS A GAME OF POWER

There are many questions concerning the hermeneutical principles behind inversive adaptations of Gospel material. As a literary concept, inversion invokes speculation about its opposite as we have seen already with Jesus' incarnation/carnality and asceticism/promiscuity. As could be expected, the idea of sacrifice also inevitably provokes reinterpretations. Is this violent action at the core of Christian faith? What happens to the structure of a religion when the idea of sacrifice is completely inverted? This analysis shows that many of the recent Jesus-novels treat these questions with passion. For Saramago, for instance, they provide a key theme that governs the dynamics between God, the Devil, and Jesus.

There is a Nietzschean overtone in how the investigated novels deal with sacrifice, violence, and power. From a nihilistic perspective, the New Testament imposes power structures on human relations,

---

53. Mailer, *According to the Son*, 241.

starting with its so-called slave morality. If violence is considered redemptive, as such a perspective claims the Christian faith holds, there must be a violent core in this religion from the very start. On the one hand, this is a straightforward philosophical argument. On the other, it is one of the clearest claims of many of the investigated novels, especially for Saramago, Roberts, and Fredriksson. As a violent religion, canonical Christianity constantly veers towards producing violence anew. Nietzsche ceased "painting" pictures of the Crucified One. The abovementioned Jesus-novels end up with a similar conclusion.[54]

Such an approach is echoed by the ideas of French poststructuralism. According to Lyotard, power games in society are conducted through language games. Lyotard assumed that the structures of language reflect the structures of social reality. Therefore, an analysis of language will also affect politics and the construction of one's view of society—as well as religion. The rules of the game belong to the discourse itself. There is no justification of meaning outside the game. Each statement is merely a move in the game. For Lyotard, language creates an illusion of reality, or an ideological view of social relations. Hence the militant description of communication we referred to earlier: "to speak is to fight."[55]

According to the poststructuralist or postmodern analysis, modernism legitimised itself through metanarratives such as capitalism, Christianity, or even Marxism. These approaches did not use science or technology to save the Western world but rather, took it to the brink of disaster. This is why the legitimation of knowledge should be arranged without traditional metanarratives.

> In contemporary society and culture—postindustrial society, postmodern culture—the question of the legitimation of knowledge is formulated in different terms. The grand narrative has lost its credibility, regardless of what mode of unification it uses, regardless of whether it is a speculative narrative or a narrative of emancipation.[56]

Therefore, in Lyotard's world, the era of traditional polarisations has ended. There is no longer a class struggle, no argument about economics or capitalism, and no imperialistic wars over the colonies. In

---

54. For Nietzsche's vision, see *Gay Science*, § 313. The passage was treated above in the Introduction, section 5.

55. Lyotard, *Postmodern Condition*, 10.

56. Ibid., 37.

a postindustrial society, postmodernism fights over ideological power and legitimation of knowledge. This is a struggle between discourses. It is easy to see this kind of approach in postmodern Jesus-novels as well. The traditional Christian metanarrative is not the only truth about life and human beings. To write a Jesus-novel is to fight.

The conception of knowledge has changed, too, and this too may have influenced literature and different authors. According to Lyotard, scientific knowledge has usually presupposed or implied the use of merely one language game. He wants to replace this with an idea of narrative knowledge. Science is not only a matter of truth claims or criteria of justification. The ethical and the esthetic are also essential components in our understanding of knowledge. This is why it is possible to present assessments and prescriptive statements in scientific investigation.[57]

Since in the scientific community the new generation has been convinced that the conditions of knowledge have changed and that no single interpretation or school must be allowed to dominate the whole field, there is no reason why this view could not be transferred to the area of literature. Authors of the Jesus-novels may well question biblical power structures in order to present their own view about religious truths. More often than not then the tone is contemptuous or even arrogant because any verbal act takes part in a struggle.

Jesus-novels provide an opportunity to see at least a version of the French poststructuralist approach in action. The theme of divine violence illuminates a new aspect in the motivations in these novels' intertextual change. Quite in the manner of the theologian Spong or other adherents of the so-called death-of-God movement, Saramago and the other writers present the biblical God as a Heavenly Despot. He is like the evil and violent *demiurge* of the Old Testament, described in several heretical writings of the early church. These Gnostics claim that the biblical Yahweh desires the deaths of his creatures, enjoys suffering, and incites violence.

The intertextual change of the novels plays with the roles in the biblical story. In the civilised world of the Enlightenment it is not the human race that needs to be reconciled with the heavenly Judge. Rather, it is the sacrifice-demanding heavenly usurper who is in need of reconciliation when facing the modern world that has just found its mature independence from religious exploitation. Therefore, for instance in

57. Ibid., 18–20.

Saramago's *Gospel*, it is the figure of God that is contrasted with the honest Devil who renounces divine madness.

The treatment of Christian faith as a power game becomes thus a strong argument for the hypothesis that many of the recent Jesus-novels are Nietzschean. It is not a matter of a few analogous points. Rather, the whole treatment of religion as a phenomenon, and biblical Christianity in particular, shows that the adopted premises are derived from Nietzsche. Therefore, it is not a question of being able to identify certain direct quotations or even similar terminology, e.g., that of slave morality. It is about analysing the basic hermeneutical motivation behind the intertextual changes taking place in the rewritten Gospel.

What is quite original in the general attitude governing the vast number of modern Jesus-novels is that, strictly speaking, now for the first time these novels adopt atheist rhetoric in their presentation. They correspond with the "Christian atheism" promoted by Thomas Altizer and other theologians in the liberal theology movement, as they call themselves. For both of these groups, authors and theologians, it seems to be important to confront ecclesial power structures, "the whole grand system of psychological terrorism," as Don Cupitt calls it, where individual citizens submit to the command of biblical precepts and Christian morals.[58]

Furthermore, many of the investigated novels betray a Nietzschean mission to liberate the world from Christianity similar to the liberal movement's: "Our task, then, is to redeem people from the old masochistic 'orthodox' Christianity by curing them of the sense of sin, restoring their self-esteem and vindicating Christian action."[59] This is mainly what the Jesus-figures in Mailer's and Saramago's novels are doing. There is a secular reformation taking place in the story. Traditional Christianity and the religion of the source text, the canonical Gospel, is violent and leads to a masochistic orthodox faith. The new gospel written in a post-Christian time provides a new worldview where the world is in fact freed from religion itself.

This is also what Altizer suggested in his Christian atheism. It was a program for an ideology after the death of the biblical God: "Furthermore, we shall simply assume the truth of Nietzsche's proclamation of the death of God, a truth which has thus far been ignored or set

---

58. Cupitt, *New Christian Ethics*, 59.
59. Ibid., 20–23.

aside by contemporary theology."[60] In this movement the new salvation, too, was defined in Nietzsche's terms. "Only when God is dead can Being begin in every Now. Eternal Recurrence is neither a cosmology nor a metaphysical idea: it is Nietzsche's symbol of the deepest affirmation of existence."[61]

A theological adaptation of Christian doctrine, analogous once again to certain Jesus-novels and especially that of Saramago, is found in Stephen Moore's postmodern theology. He has applied Foucault's poststructuralist ideas in his deconstructionist interpretation of biblical writings.[62] Moore states that the idea of a propitiatory sacrifice retains an ideology of violence at the core of the Christian faith. It must be confronted in the name of ethics. Therefore, a "transformational" (deconstructionist) interpretation must reject essential elements of Christian teaching and oppose the church's traditional dogmas.[63]

Moore keeps company with Saramago also in maintaining that the basic problem with the idea of retributive punishment for sin is that it attributes absolute power to a monarchical God. By referring to Foucault he claims that the institutions of surveillance and control have only one purpose. "Discipline has only one purpose, according to Foucault: the production of 'docile bodies.'"[64] According to Moore, this violates the autonomy of independent human beings. "Who stands to benefit from this attribution? To appeal to one's own exemplary subjection to a conveniently absent authority in order to legitimate the subjection of others is a strategy as ancient as it is suspect."[65]

Therefore, in his adaptation and rewriting, Moore opposes the biblical concept of retributive punishment for sin, as well as the ideas of

60. Altizer, *The Death of God*, 95.

61. Ibid., 99.

62. Moore, *Poststructuralism*, 91. Quoting Foucault, Moore first remarks that every human relation, to some degree, is a power relation. From this point of departure Moore then applies the former's criticism concerning "discipline and punishment" in theological analysis. This results in a dismantling of the pattern of violence in the story of redemption and particularly in the sacrificial death of Jesus.

63. "Is the issue of power, an issue all too close to the surface in the punitive interpretation, the power of one person over the body of another, a power never more evident than in the relationship of the torturer to the victim—and never more disturbing, perhaps, than when the torturer is God and the victim God's Son?" Moore, *Poststructuralism*, 108.

64. Ibid., 109.

65. Ibid., 110.

redemption and atonement. In principle, he rejects the whole biblical view of salvation and reconciliation. For him all this is but a Christian "power technique." Seen from a Nietzschean point of view it maintains and supports coercion and enslavement. Here we have a deconstructionist pattern for the overturning of hierarchies and the dismantling of dogmatic structures. Similar strategies are exploited in deconstructive Jesus-novels, where the assumption of a violent God is rejected and traditional hierarchies of the Christian message are turned inside out.

In addition, one may state that the new interpretation found in these novels actually mixes theology with fiction. Identifying sacrifice with violence as such leads to the reduction of the primary theological idea of redemption. The original dogma of the church naturally did not consciously imply any irrational violence but, rather, aimed at justness and the idea of condemning, for instance, violations of human rights. The punishment itself was dealt with in a complicated way that left also room for forgiveness. In a theological sense, animal sacrifice was interpreted in terms of substitution, and the death of Christ, respectively, was considered a vicarious death. Therefore, a novel treatment of the theme merely on the brute level of violent actions without theological presuppositions introduces a new hermeneutical approach. This can and may, of course, be done in fiction. One might even state that this is what fiction does. It exploits traditions taken from the surrounding culture and provides new adaptations and new interpretations.

What makes this move complicated is that, in these novels, fiction becomes theology again. Authors never remain in the sphere of the materialistic world. They return to the area of soteriology. This can be seen in the conviction of several novels, according to which violent sacrifice cannot be seen as an element of redemption. In an ideological rewriting of the gospel, motivation for the revision or even inversion of the original source text, i.e., the canonical Gospels, comes from a new understanding of "salvation," namely, a new view about what makes a good and satisfactory life, and a new view about humanity and the meaning of life. The proof for this kind of explanation can be found in the intertextual changes itself made in these novels. These novels do not collapse into relativism or even into pessimistic nihilism. Rather, they promote an atheist utopia of a good life without the biblical concept of God.

This is one reason why many of these new Jesus-novels resemble the proclamation of the death-of-God theology. They reject the "psychological terrorism" that the Bible represents. Any allusion to violent actions must be rooted out from orthodox post-Christian humanism. The aim of an alleged "original" religion and the outcome of cultural evolution is, according to the novels, a philanthropic society from which most signs of traditional historical religion have been removed. As one can read especially in Saramago's novel, the violent history of the extant church itself produces the deconstruction and even destruction of canonical, orthodox Christianity. This is precisely what radicalised Protestantism with its death-of-God movement has been suggesting in its daring reinterpretations of the Christian faith. As apparent rewritings of the gospel story, the Jesus-novels reflect a similar ideology even though they formally remain in the field of fiction.

The rejection of the Christian dogma of atonement is a clear sign of a Nietzschean influence in Jesus-novels. The whole idea of a contrast between the biblical slave morality and pure humanist *Herrenmoral* is based on a conviction that perfectly good and innocent citizens must not be accused of leading immoral lives. From a Nietzschean perspective, he or she must not be thrown into slavery under an oppressive God who jealously protects only his own honor. Sacrifice, in this context, becomes an act of violence that can only be considered absurd. All this is part of an atheistic rhetoric, though. It is repeatedly used in contemporary atheistic discussions about religion. This raises a question: Why do these novelists adopt an atheistic discourse? Why do authors need to end up with an inversion when contesting the sacrificial religion of the Bible? These novels differ essentially from the idealistic moralities of the twentieth century. "Comrade Jesus" was no atheist. Our new Faustian disciple of the Devil undoubtedly is—at least of the so-called Christian atheism ilk. Growing out of Nietzschean soil, many of these novels openly embody poststructuralist values. Traditional images have been destroyed. Metanarratives have been subverted. The sacralised violence of the canonical New Testament has been replaced by a secularist utopia of optimistic humanism—which gradually grows into a new metanarrative of its own.

6

Attacking Biblical Theism

It would have been perplexing had the concept of God itself been neglected in the critical polarisations of the investigated novels. Knowing Nietzsche's pervasive influence, we are entitled to expect that one of his most famous statements would appear in Jesus-novels in one form or another: "God is dead. We have killed him. Do you not smell his corpse yet?" The postulations of different authors on the question of God and his status vary. For some writers, there is no longer any room for God in the sphere of religion and for others the biblical or Christian God must be rejected even if he exists.

1. YAHWEH AND HIS RIVALS

Starting with a somewhat disguised questioning of God's status, Mailer's *The Gospel According to the Son* relativises God's divine omnipotence by attacking the "omni" in the depiction. "Everything" does not seem to be under divine control in this world. Rather, according to Mailer, there is a struggle between God and the Devil, and Jesus is taken into the sphere of this tension. In the story, God's opponent clearly has a good grip on the Nazarean. Jesus has fallen into Satan's temptations and, on several occasions, he follows Satan's directions as much as the precepts of God. The story in this novel is mainly directed by Jesus' inner struggle, not by the christological dogmas of the church.

Mailer further ascribes the features of basic weakness and ambivalence to God himself. This becomes apparent in his treatment of Jesus' crucifixion and death. The Jesus of the narrative has betrayed the poor. Therefore, he stands fairly accused, at least to the degree that he follows the Devil and fails to defend the weak. And Jesus' temptations in the desert are seen as a point of departure that leads inexorably to his final end.

Jesus clearly does not defend the Devil in the story, but he is a symbol of weakness. And in Mailer's novel, this becomes a "divine" feature in Jesus' personality.

There is no special reason for Jesus' trial and sentence in this novel. According to Mailer's story, he is not dangerous in any political sense, and he poses no threat to the Romans. Neither is he in any great opposition to the Jewish leaders of his time. He is just a failure. Even Judas has more integrity than he does. At the scene on Golgotha the Son's real face is revealed, and this poor messianic figure with all his weaknesses is brought forth as the image of God. "Yet I knew. By these hours I had lived on the cross, I knew. My Father was only doing what He could do. Even as I had done what I could do. So he was truly my Father."[1]

Nailed to the cross, Mailer's Jesus once more prays for a miracle. All he receives is silence. This experience teaches him about theodicy. His heavenly Father cannot help him. The God of Mailer's novel is a weak God in a broken world.

> There was no answer. Only the echo of my cry. I saw the Garden of Eden and remembered the Lord's words to Adam: "Of every tree in the Garden you may eat freely, but from the Tree of the Knowledge of Good and Evil, you shall not eat."
>
> Let my Father's voice strike Golgotha and His thunder become as loud as His voice, but pain had driven me to believe what one must not believe.
>
> God was my Father, but I had to ask: Is He possessed of all Powers? Or is He not? Like Eve, I wanted knowledge of good and evil. Even as I asked if the Lord was all-powerful, I heard my own answer: God, my Father, was one god. But there were others. If I had failed Him, so had He failed me. Such was now my knowledge of good and evil. Was it for that reason that I was on the cross?[2]

It is not quite clear what Mailer's aim is in this passage. On the one hand he may simply be addressing a general Jewish concept of God but, on the other, he may also be focusing on a tension between Christianity and Judaism. If this is mainly an intertextual reflection on Old Testament convictions, the emphasis is on the person and nature of God himself. However, Mailer is actually writing a novel about Jesus, and this is not to be ignored. He must also be commenting on the figure

---

1. Mailer, *According to the Son*, 233.
2. Ibid., 231–32.

of Jesus. Jesus' character here cannot be being used merely as a secondary instrument in order to write on Judaism. There are other elements in Mailer's description, however, that help in assessing the nature of his reinterpretation.

One should not be led astray in the interpretation of the passage just because there is one ostensibly clear target in this statement. Mailer's Jesus is actually criticising the most profound and essential confession of Jewish faith, the *Shema Israel*: The Lord our God is one Lord.[3] This is the Jewish confession read in daily prayers, and it can be considered the highest possible expression of Jewish devotion. It is the text kept in the *tefillim*, leather boxes, that are strapped on the left arm and to the forehead for prayer. This confession is in the minds and in the hands of the Jewish people, pointing to the heart, as expected and commanded by the Mosaic Law. Mailer certainly is making a point here.[4]

As the *Shema* is here interpreted in direct and complete contrast to its original content, both Jewish faith and the God of Israel become trivialised. Therefore the deconstruction of the great Jewish metanarrative culminates here. Israel's God is merely one god. One among many. He is not God Almighty. Rather, he is just one alternative. He is as weak and uncertain as his Son. In this respect Mailer's *Gospel According to the Son*, despite its seemingly superficial approach, has a deep theological or at least religious stratum, and its criticism is severe. The novel questions Judaism, and it questions both the core of Jewish/Christian tradition and the church's faith. When assessed from the point of view of Jewish tradition, it verges on blasphemy. Earlier, I discussed Mailer's so-called conservative reading of the New Testament in the novel's initial chapters, but now Mailer's intention becomes clearer as he contrasts the novel's subtext with its final conclusion.[5]

---

3. See the Deut 6:4 (AV), following original Hebrew wording. In the NRSV the passage reads: "The Lord is our God, the Lord alone."

4. It is uncertain whether Mailer is referring to the Hebrew word depicting God, but that too is possible. The Hebrew word *elohim* is in fact plural [gods, rulers, angels] and therefore, the basic point of departure for the speculation about several gods may also be linguistic by nature.

5. Allen pays attention to this: "Mailer's only radical departure from Christian tradition—possibly the book's only valid raison d'etre—is not in his interpretation of Christ, but of God. Mailer's God is fallible, the death of his Son a defeat rather than, as it is interpreted by Christian theology, a victory." Allen, "Gospel of Norman," 77.

Jesus' insecurity and the anxiety he experienced before his calling were consistently leading in a philosophical direction. During and through his journey Jesus had learned that the traditional Jewish concept of God had no substance. He was on the mount of temptation: all he had left was existential insecurity, and possibly, a leap.[6] A similar criticism is directed at the Nazarene. Jesus with his divided mind will be raised from the dead and some of the darkness of life will be left behind. The great divide has not been overcome. God is a weak God, and his Son is no saviour of this world.

> Nonetheless, the truth is more valuable even than the heavens. Thereby, let it be understood: My Father may not have vanquished the Devil.[7]

Mailer himself has called this battle of heavenly powers a Manichean feature in his writing.[8] Mailer has always been esteemed as a master of describing violent characters in violent stories, but this is his *tour de force*: he transfers earthly battles to a heavenly field, as Johnston remarks: "Mr. Mailer, in effect, projected the violent moral universe of his fiction into heaven, to the point of suggesting that God himself does not know the outcome of the battle with Satan."[9] However, this Manichean structure is not as clear in the novel as it is in historical documents.

> A Manichean perspective is dualistic, with the forces of good and the forces of evil engaged in a never-ending struggle over control of the universe and the human soul. For Mailer, however, the matter is more complex, particularly if one allows for the notion of "free will," for the idea that individual human agency and judgment can serve one side or the other of the struggle.[10]

It is apparent that, for Mailer, God is not all-powerful but rather one of the forces in the universe. The basic nature of the cosmological combat is ethical, of course. Mailer appears to be describing a "Manichean

---

6. There have been more modest assessments, such as that of Bottum, "Mailer's Jesus": "His attempt is not blasphemous (indeed, Mailer doesn't know enough theology to be either pious or impious)." On the contrary, Mailer seems to be very conscious about the intertextual polarisation he is making.

7. Mailer, *According to the Son*, 241.

8. See Johnston, "Revised Nonstandard Version," 16.

9. Ibid. For the comment on Mailer's interest in violence, see Gelernter, "Gospel," 56.

10. McDonald, "Theodicy," 80–81.

gridlock" between good and evil. The struggle can also be described, as Partridge does, as "between the pretty good and the mostly evil."[11] Human beings are a separate force in this triangular relation between God and the Devil. This makes human beings into double agents of a sort in the cosmic battle.[12] In this respect Mailer portrays a common, garden-variety humanism where human life is seen as an inner struggle over moral questions and where people are tempted from both sides but where the control remains in their own hands.

The idea of a heavenly battle also means that, in spite of his sympathetic personality and even his identity as the Son, Mailer's Jesus is not a divine Messiah, the conqueror of sin and Satan. He is merely a Jewish Jesus. The Jesus of the New Testament is too much for the writer of the novel. Mailer is not far from modern Jewish scholars who accept many of the Jewish features in Jesus' life, and even accept the idea of resurrection when interpreted according to the Old Testament tradition. Even Jesus' resurrection can be accepted, as long as its interpretation remains in the context of Jewish theology. What is then important is that Jesus must not be regarded as one who makes atonement and brings reconciliation.[13]

Eventually, in the novel, God appears to be "as clever as Satan." He probably learns the Devil's way of speaking, as Jesus had done. God makes a new move in the eternal struggle and begins to preach defeat as a victory. After the Jewish concept of God has first been turned inside out, any other concept can be reversed as well. In this respect also the *Gospel According to the Son* transforms the roles of God and Satan, and Mailer's presentation veers close to that of Saramago's.

In his almost Manichean dualism Mailer apparently attempts to find a sophisticated way to think about God. As an intertextual change, however, his solution is a complete denial and denigration of the traditional Jewish concept of God. He makes his Jesus reject the *Shema Israel*, belief in one Holy God. Mailer himself probably wishes to emphasise the human perspective, thus producing one more Promethean narrative about mere people combating divinities. This literary transformation, however, joins the post-Christian hermeneutical front where both God's goodness and his authority are questioned.

11. Partridge, "Gospel," 73. Partridge also refers to an interview where Mailer explained his cosmology by saying: "For me, the concept that God is doing the best that He can do is a more beautiful and troubling concept than that He is all-powerful." Ibid.

12. So Rosenbaum, "Mailer was the Rage."

13. For such a view, see for instance Vermes, *Jesus the Jew*, 59–60, 224.

2. THE PROBLEM OF THEODICY

The ethical problems both Mailer and other authors of recent Jesus-novels face are huge. As I noted in the introduction, Mailer appears as the spokesman for Holocaust agony and believes that the memory of the concentration camps affects "the unconscious mind" of almost all post-war novelists. This memory is visible at the end of the book, where Mailer lets the risen Jesus say:

> My Father, however, does not often speak to me. Nonetheless, I honor him. Surely He sends forth as much love as He can offer, but His love is not without limit. For His wars with the Devil grow worse. Great battles have been lost. In the last century of this second millennium were holocausts, conflagrations, and plagues worse that any that had come before.[14]

The Second World War and the Holocaust have revealed a "demonic dimension of evil," as it has been called.[15] McDonald argues that, for Mailer, this means the appearance of a new sort of terror: a fear that in this world things are not going to end up well.

> The effluence of this terror is in itself, in Mailer's view, a strong intimation of the size of the divide which has opened up between the traditional notion of a good and omnipotent God and historical evidence of irredeemable evil.[16]

Things are not going to end up well in Mailer's and Saramago's novels. The problem of evil appears in these books in a traditional form

---

14. Mailer, *According to the Son*, 240.

15. Cf. Mailer's *The White Negro*: "For the first time in civilized history, perhaps for the first time in all of history, we have been forced to live with the suppressed knowledge that the smallest facets of our personality or the most minor projection of our ideas, or indeed the absence of ideas and the absence of personality could mean equally well that we might still be doomed to die as a cipher in some vast statistical operation in which our teeth would be counted, and our hair would be saved, but our death itself would be unknown, unhonored, and unremarked, a death which could not follow with dignity as a possible consequence to serious actions we had chosen, but rather a death by *deus ex machina* in a gas chamber or a radioactive city; and so if in the midst of civilization–that civilization founded upon the Faustian urge to dominate nature by mastering time, mastering the links of social cause and effect–in the middle of an economic civilization founded upon the confidence that time could indeed be subjected to our will, our psyche was subjected itself to the intolerable anxiety that death being causeless, life was causeless as well, and time deprived of cause and effect had come to a stop." Reprinted in *Dissent*, 2007; see Mailer, "White Negro."

16. McDonald, "Theodicy," 82.

familiar from the philosophy of religion. If this is a world created by an omnipotent and almighty God, why is there so much suffering in people's lives? Where is providence, and why does God not prevent evil? These become the burning questions in Mailer's *Gospel*, where the Devil attempts to shake Jesus' conviction about God's omnipotence. The issue concerns the problem of theodicy specifically. Can God's goodness still be defended? No, it cannot, Mailer claims, because evil in this world is not a result of temptations, decadence, and sin. The Devil should know. Instead, God himself must be the source of violence.

> Your Father would send you forth to improve the hearts of men when His own heart is caked with the blood of those He has slaughtered. His love of all He has created is choked by His curses.[17]

The divine being the Devil describes here is the God of hosts, a militant figure who continuously sows suffering in this world he allegedly created. In Mailer's novel, agony over the Holocaust directs the treatment of theodicy. It drives the author to his idea of Manichean dualism. It is not that the Devil should not be trusted. For once, the Devil is right. For Mailer, the world is filled with evilness because God is unable to win the cosmic war against Satan.[18]

Mailer and Saramago, who also makes full use of this theme, follow in the lines of Albert Camus who, especially in his *L'homme Revolté* (*The Rebel*), attacks the religious concept of God on the grounds of theodicy. For these writers the question about God is less about his existence as such. Instead, it is a question of the justification of his power, the problem of God as almighty. If the present world that looks like a house of horrors has a God, he has no ground to claim universal rule.[19]

Camus starts his theological criticism by quoting Dostoevsky. Already in *The Brothers Karamazov*, Ivan Karamazov had demanded that God be put on trial for his works: "If evil is essential to divine creation, then creation is unacceptable."[20] The point of departure here is the standard claim of rationalistic atheism. Thanks to the modern worldview,

---

17. Mailer, *According to the Son*, 52.

18. In *The White Negro* Mailer writes: "The Second World War presented a mirror to the human condition which blinded anyone who looked into it."

19. For Camus in general, see Lottman, *Camus*; Onimus, *Albert Camus and Christianity*.

20. Camus, *Rebel*, 50.

our interpretation of the premises of human life has changed as well. Naturalism's monistic premises hold that whatever this world appears to contain must derive from one source only. If there is a God, everything in our life must be caused by him. So, should one find evilness in human life, it must be the creation of the divine Creator. This logic both for atheist philosophers and our authors is undisputed. It grows from the Nietzschean spirit where the Jewish God of the Bible is the original source of human suffering. Furthermore, for Camus, this leads inevitably to metaphysical rebellion. Nietzsche is needed for further ideological conclusions: If this world really has a God, he must be dethroned.

> The rebel defies more than he denies. Originally, at least, he does not deny God, he simply talks to Him as an equal. But it is not a polite dialogue. It is a polemic animated by the desire to conquer. The slave starts by begging for justice and ends by wanting to wear a crown. He too wants to dominate. His insurrection against his condition is transformed into an unlimited campaign against the heavens for the purpose of capturing a king who will first be dethroned and finally condemned to death. Human rebellion ends in metaphysical revolution.[21]

Theodicy is a traditional subject in the philosophy of religion. In the naturalist tradition it has as well-known form, undoubtedly familiar to Camus. Either God is omnipotent and we cannot be responsible for evil, or we are responsible but God cannot be held omnipotent.[22] In both literature and philosophy there have been numerous variations of this conundrum but the result is always the same. If, as Christian tradition holds, there is a God in this corrupt world, according to this branch of philosophy he must inevitably be evil. Thus, Saramago in his diligent elaboration of the theme borrows a common idea that in itself shows no originality. The way he applies it in his novel is remarkable, though.

In the European literary tradition, this theme also derives from Nietzsche, whom Camus quite openly follows. Nietzsche stated that even if there was a God one should reject him in the name of morality. "If any one were to *show* us this Christian God, we'd be still less inclined to believe in him."[23] This question logically and consistently follows the

---

21. Ibid., 31.

22. Camus, *Myth of Sisyphus*, 55.

23. Nietzsche, *Anti-Christ*, § 47. Sprintzen states that Camus deliberately continued Nietzsche's ideological programme. "Joining with Nietzsche's effort to contribute to a

problem of sacrifice, treated in chapter 4.1 above. As the question concerning the meaningfulness of sacrifice enters the area of theistic speculation, it becomes crucial for defining the nature of God. There have been enough victims. First and foremost, God wished to kill his own Son. The question that everyone from Nietzsche to Camus to Saramago ask hits the core of the Christian message: Why does one need the death of the Son of God? For Nietzsche, it proves the biblical God's essentially "pagan" nature.

> – And from that time onward an absurd problem offered itself: "how *could* God allow it!" To which the deranged reason of the little community formulated an answer that was terrifying in its absurdity: God gave his son as a *sacrifice* for the forgiveness of sins. At once there was an end of the gospels! Sacrifice for sin, and in its most obnoxious and barbarous form: sacrifice of the *innocent* for the sins of the guilty! What appalling paganism![24]

According to Nietzsche, the foundation for the whole Christian religion is based on flawed inference. Jesus' death is seen as a sacrifice to God. One incorrect conclusion turned religion into barbarism. This view then found its way into radicalised theology. According to Spong, Christians have been bound to violent beliefs. Following his own logic, he gives a provocative reinterpretation of the cross: "the holy God involved in a cruel act of divine child abuse that was said to have occurred on a hill called Calvary." How could a true divine Being allow such a thing? It must be a false conclusion, promulgated by the first followers of Jesus who wrote the New Testament.[25]

Saramago never calls God a divine murderer of children, but his intention is similar to that of Spong. From the very start God is the Despot who kills children in Bethlehem. In Saramago's world there is no difference between the hands of human criminals and the hand of God. The Almighty must be considered responsible because he does not prevent awful and cruel events. The biblical God looks the same to Spong and

---

transvaluation of values by unmasking everything by which the nihilism of our age was being hidden from itself, Camus sought to describe that lived but inarticulate nihilism that is at the root of contemporary transcendent faiths." Sprintzen, *Camus*, 56.

24. Nietzsche, *Anti-Christ*, § 41. See also Fleischer, "Nietzsche," 516.

25. See Spong, *Sins of Scripture*, 171–73. He states: "This interpretation of Jesus as the sacrificed victim is a human creation, not a divine revelation." It was shaped by the disciples only later in the first-century world.

Saramago. He is a God of bloodshed. He enjoys seeing victims, and he leaves them on their own. Revealing this is Saramago's intention when he makes the Devil speak against God and his thirst for blood.

Why, cries Saramago's Pastor, doesn't God remove the causes of suffering and help people in their agony? The answer is simple: because God himself produces all this suffering. It is a result of God's nature. God is evil, and he entertains himself by torturing an endless number of victims in all possible contexts and situations.

> And as if holding a sword and shield before him, he exclaimed, The Lord alone is God. Pastor's smile faded and his mouth became twisted and embittered, Certainly, if God exists He must be only one Lord, but it would be preferable if He were two, then there would be a god for the wolf and one for the sheep, one for the victim and one for the assassin, a god for the condemned man and one for the executioner. . . .
>
> God does not live, God exists, These fine distinctions escape me, but I'll tell you this, I wouldn't want to be a god who guides the hand of the assassin clutching a dagger while presenting the throat that is about the be cut.[26]

In his Nietzschean zeal Saramago is quite determined. God, if he exists, is a threat to humankind. He must be fought until the end. All humanists from Camus to Spong agree. If the sheep knew what would be done to the lambs on the sacrificial altar, they would rise against the despotic God: "their mothers would howl like wolves if they were to know." This, for Saramago, is the real solution to the problem of theodicy.[27] Traditional philosophic solutions were on a similar track. If God does not stop suffering, he must either be weak or not all good. If God cannot deal with the real evilness in this world, he is worthless. There are probably greater forces above him. Mailer remarks that the biblical God may not be the only one out there. Saramago refers to a heavenly pantheon where real decisions are being made. No individual God can rebel against the great laws of the transcendent.

Bloom, in his interpretation of Saramago's anti-theodicy, maintains that Saramago subverts St. Augustine's theodicy of time. Augustine views God as the supreme Good. As God exists beyond time so his dealing with evil is independent of human history. Evil on this earth, for

---

26. Saramago, *Gospel*, 174.
27. Ibid., 174.

Augustine, is an act of choosing the lesser good, and so the existence of supreme Good is safeguarded in principle. In his omnipotence, God accepts the reality of evil for a time but this is only a part of the greater Good that will appear at the end. The existence of evil, therefore, does not threaten God's essential nature but is a problem that will be solved only over a longer period of time. Actually, the whole of salvation history, for Augustine, is a story about the theodicy of time. God has sent his Messiah to eliminate evil and simultaneously to create a new community by preaching reconciliation in his church.

Saramago in his novel, according to Bloom, puts God on trial for his slow responses in history and his callousness to human suffering. "If time is God, then God can be forgiven nothing, and who would desire to forgive him anyway?"[28]

> Power is God's only interest, and the sacrifice of Jesus employs the prospect of forgiveness of our sins only as an advertisement. God makes clear that all of us are guilty, and that he prefers to keep it that way. Jesus is no atonement: his crucifixion is merely a device by which God ceases to be Jewish, and becomes Catholic, a *converso* rather than a *marrano*.[29] That is superb irony, and Saramago makes it high art, though to thus reduce it critically is to invite a Catholic onslaught.[30]

Saramago's views suggest that one must choose between God's weakness and his evilness based on these ostensibly new premises. In the traditional discussion of theodicy, theologians were well aware of the possibility that God may not be good at all. God may himself be responsible for the evilness of this world. Our understanding of the nature of religion may have been completely false.[31] In order to approach

---

28. Bloom, "One with the Beard," 157.

29. *Marrano* is a strong word here, meaning a Crypto-Jew in the Catholic tradition, but a "pig" in Spanish.

30. Bloom, "One with the Beard," 157. Frier adds: "Saramago would emphasize the human experience of suffering within time and would therefore see this as being incompatible with any notion of God as a representative of the Supreme Good." This confirms the problem of theodicy: "To Saramago, therefore, supreme Power cannot be said to coexist with the supreme Good in an imperfect world, and the very fact of human suffering requires us to condemn any God who is so dismissive of human experience . . ." Frier, "Outline," 372n20. Both Bloom and Frier, despite their earlier claims, finally assume that Saramago really opposes the Christian concept of God, not merely the church's violent history.

31. Such reasoning is a standard in recent atheist literature; see Dennett, *Breaking the Spell*, 295; Onfray, *Atheist Manifesto*, 197–98.

the latter alternative, one needs to explore other philosophical directions and speculate on different worldviews. Many feminist novels depend on Gnostic writings, and there the dualist concept of divinity attempts to solve the abovementioned problem. According to the Gnostic view, the Creator-God of this world, the demiurge, is evil by nature. His material world is a rebellion against the world of light as such. Therefore, Gnostic elements in feminist Jesus-novels inevitably bring along a belief that human beings must be saved from the hands of the evil god—even though the authors never seem to exploit this feature in their narratives.

One should probably adopt another approach to this question, though. This perspective on the problem of evil depends on a deterministic worldview. God is responsible for suffering because he is the deterministic Creator of this world. He is the author of the script, and we are merely actors. Everybody's life is both planned and realised under his providence. In a historical sense, this is actually not a Christian view but, rather, a Hellenistic or magical view of religion. It belongs to the world of Moira, Fate, who directs all life. According to this view the world is one huge machine wherein all parts fit. There is neither free will nor individual autonomy. Therefore, it is possible to observe planetary movements and make valid inferences about human life. It is a world of horoscopes and fortune-tellers.

There are only few references to such a worldview in the investigated Jesus-novels. Fredriksson does mention other religions, the Zoroastrians, and Indian wise men, and also refers to Babylonian astrology. According to Mary Magdalene, a Christian can also recognise such ideas, and Jesus himself "could have said the same."[32] Usually authors remain inside Judeo-Christian tradition, though. This creates a confusing picture, since both anthropology and soteriology are altered in these novels. These authors practically never refer to Adam or the fall. Do they thus imply that the world as it is is good, and that all religions reflect the divine realm in a similar manner? The reader is to assume that people in this secularised, evolutionist world still live in some kind of paradise. The authors face one of the oldest problems of philosophy of religion. If all religions claim that God has created this world, and if the very same Divinity determines everyone's life every day, everything that happens must happen according to his will. How could one explain evil, and I mean the very evil the feminist Jesus-novels skilfully describe with all

32. Fredriksson, *According to Mary*, 154–55.

the violence and abuse of power that social life involves, in such a deterministic world?

Furthermore, this view collides with the idea of individual freedom. The latter is defended almost in all of the investigated novels quite clearly. In practice, it is the main reason why God can be opposed. Human beings are able to decide for themselves. It is also the reason why struggles may emerge between God and human beings. It is a contest of wills. The inclusion of all these mutually exclusive ideas reveals that these novels do not aim at a consistent philosophy. These are not scientific analyses. The idea of human freedom may well exist alongside determinism. These works only attempt to write a Nietzschean revision of the New Testament. If this effort demands the adoption of deterministic ideas, they are merely part of the strategy of writing, not necessarily part of a particular philosophy.

Should one expect theological reasoning from these authors? This is a persistent question with probably more than one answer. Making an inversion of some generally accepted conviction could be just a literary test a writer could present to readers interested in such imaginativeness. In subjects where deep inner convictions are involved in the writing process one probably should expect accuracy, even theological. This concerns especially our novels since they are deeply ideological to say the least. And so is the problem of theodicy.

One essential question always accompanies the traditional problem of theodicy. Once one abandons the view that God can influence this world and prevent violence, the divine Being must be removed from reasoning altogether. There is not much point in accepting creation and providence just in order to judge God guilty every time the question of evil is addressed. If there is no God, there is no God at all. The problem lies in the difficulty that even when such a removal has been executed, the first argument about the evilness of this world remains. If violence in this world is so horrible that even God must be killed to make it comprehensible, what happens to our view of human nature? All this evilness must be the product of human actions.

It would have been quite interesting to see the authors deal with these kinds of questions. All the speculations about hammerings and burnings, all those saws and spears, the endless tale of iron and blood, are in fact laid on the shoulders of these Sisyphus-like human beings who become settlers claiming land in the new world. What if there are nothing but wolves? The novels give no answer. The Pastor in Saramago's novel, for instance, never becomes a true social Darwinist, congratulating humankind for its excellent achievements in natural selection. He prefers innocent sheep to wolves. The Nietzschean *Übermensch* never really stands up and takes charge. Even Nietzsche's own Zarathustra was eventually a romantic traditionalist who preached altruistic love on the fields of Galilee. And Camus warned that the rebel, the new man or *Übermench*, must not become one more despot: "in no case, if he is consistent does he demand the right to destroy the existence and the freedom of others."[33]

The Jesus-novels remain silent on these basic questions. They usually content themselves with returning to humanistic values or political solidarity. There is a hint of absurd existential moralism in these novels, and many of them are not far from Camus or Sartre. Once God has been rejected, the problems of this world suddenly seem less dire. Despite the ambiguity of such a procedure, one should note that this too is a real Nietzschean solution: It was not sin that made this world a terrible place. It was Christianity with its *Sklavenmoral* and its negative view of humanity. The only slavish ideology oppressing human beings was biblical Christian faith. Christianity was the primary sin this world must exorcise. Here the Nietzschean inversion was complete.

Insensitivity towards real ethical problems or questions raised by the philosophy of religion probably explains why both Mailer and Saramago remain confused in their treatment of violence and denigration. Mailer in particular, who in his post-Holocaust apology fiercely opposes anti-Semitism and on the very same basis rejects the goodness of God, fails to defend Judaism. His *Gospel* is openly anti-Judaist, rejecting divine commandments and the Torah and opposing faith in the Old Testament God. Both Mailer and Saramago, even if unconsciously, adopt Nietzsche's attitude toward Judaism, playing with the ideas of a bloodthirsty Divinity with his senseless religious precepts.[34]

33. Nietzsche, *Zarathustra*, 14; Camus, *Rebel*, 248. In atheist literature these kinds of issues are well known. For instance John Gray in his *Straw Dogs* (110–11) states that in the natural world life should not be amusing at all. Human beings are aggressive and violent, and this is something an atheist must cope with. For him human beings are mere weapons-making animals.

34. Kelley has shown that in many issues Western culture and even theology involve anti-Judaist attitudes, which are usually unconscious and unquestioned. By this he means especially the denigration of Jewish beliefs and the Old Testament concept of God. Kelley, *Racializing Jesus*, 87, 125, 223.

When following this logic through, one should ultimately turn to Camus, one of Nietzsche's reluctant followers, who had praised rebellion for decades. After living through the agony of the Second World War, his views were destined to change. The world around him appeared to misuse or at least misunderstand the nihilist tradition he himself was engaged in. In *The Rebel* he picks up Nietzsche's own hesitation and suggests that the new worldview is not yet clear. "The *Will to Power* ends, like Pascal's *Pensées* of which it so often reminds us, with a wager. Man does not yet obtain assurance but only the wish for assurance which is not at all the same thing."[35] Camus, who posed murder as the most difficult of all philosophical questions, has to admit that, in a Nietzschean tradition, there is no nihilism without violence.

> In a certain sense, rebellion, with Nietzsche, ends again in the exaltation of evil. The difference is that evil is no longer a revenge. It is accepted as one of the possible aspects of good and, with rather more conviction, as part of destiny. Thus he considers it as something to be avoided and also as a sort of remedy. In Nietzsche's mind, the only problem was to see that the human spirit bowed proudly to the inevitable. We know, however, his posterity and the kind of politics that were to be authorized by the man who claimed to be the last anti-political German.[36]

In his last novels, then, Camus ends in pessimism. In *The Fall* (*La chute*) he presents readers with a penitent judge who has dedicated his life to judging miserable human beings. The hero Clamence criticises himself and all his postwar existentialist friends for taking God's role in their moralistic attitudes. Here we see in flesh what Camus said earlier in *The Rebel* about *homo homini lupus* becoming "*homo homini deus.*" At his worst, which may paradoxically also be his best, a human being is not merely a wolf, but a god.[37] Clamence becomes a secular priest who shows compassion but grants no absolution for sins because all he wants is his own vainglory. Hence, in his last will he admits that there is no rebellion without a burden of the absurd.[38] Camus recognises the problem Mailer and Saramago evade, but he has no solution for it.

---

35. Camus, *Rebel*, 66.
36. Ibid.
37. Camus, *La chute*, 89–90. For the quotation see *Rebel*, 115.
38. Onimus summarises a common conclusion when saying that Clamence is a caricature of the existentialist moralists in Camus' own time. They had become scho-

There is another alternative, though. The problem of theodicy can be solved by splitting the concept of God in two: Demiurge and Sophia, Vishnu and Shiva, Yin and Yang. It is possible that just like the rebellious Catholic Camus, and the secularised Anglicans Robinson, Cupitt, and Spong revising eighteenth century deism, Saramago, Mailer, and Tunström actually represent 'atheist' Christianity. They do not abandon the concept of God completely, because this would deprive them of the premise that makes the world and also reasoning as such sensible. God is necessary at least as a counterpoint. Thus these authors return to the world of the second-century heretic Marcion and Gnosticism. It is a spiritual cold war, where the destructive Demiurge is needed as the negative pole of their elliptic cosmology.[39]

Because of their dualism, the Jesus-novels do not wish to do away with the biblical God but merely to combat him. These works are still rewritten New Testaments. After all, Anti-Christ rhetoric pertains to the figure of Christ. Similarly, atheism is not intelligible without theism. Camus is an expert on this, and in a sense many authors follow him. He would even say that the metaphysical rebel is not an atheist. "The metaphysical rebel is, therefore, certainly not an atheist, as one might think him, but inevitably he is a blasphemer."[40] This is an arrogant adaptation of the Nietzschean death-of-God philosophy.

This is probably one of the reasons why Roberts and Fredriksson return to Gnosticism. Apart from the Gnostic figure of Mary Magdalene there are other things that can easily be adopted. These writings enable modern authors to oppose the male God of the Old Testament with a new feminine figure. This same feature helps Saramago to hold God responsible. Quite in the manner of Gnostic writings, Saramago depicts the Lord of Israel as an evil God of this material world. He is an Old Testament Despot who tortures all the living. The problem of theodicy has been solved. If humankind wishes to live a free and civilised life, state

---

lastics, presenting their cruel demands to people. Onimus, *Camus*, 93. In fact, Camus may be referring to the whole European intelligentsia which, in his view, is still tied up with the absurd, avoiding true rebellion. Cf. Mailer who states in *The White Negro*: "in a bad world there is no love nor mercy nor charity nor justice unless a man can keep his courage."

39. In Marcion's theology, the God of the Old Testament was evil and only the merciful God of the New Testament should belong to the doctrines of Christianity. See Kraft, "Marcion," 741.

40. Camus, *Rebel*, 30.

the Jesus-novels, it needs to destroy the biblical view of God and remake religion. Be this just a literary invention written to entertain readers or a true conviction of the author, these novels fit well into twentieth-century Western cultural history with its rebellious philosophers and liberal theologians' new "gospel of Christian atheism."[41]

The problem of theodicy appears thus to be one of the crucial issues behind the ideological speculation of recent Jesus-novels. Its appearance is catalysed by the Holocaust agony that affects these authors. Their reception of the Nietzschean tradition is ambivalent because it can be interpreted both as illness and cure. In a critical reading of twentieth-century cultural history, it has been considered one the main sources for Europe's violent inheritance. In Jesus-novels, however, it has become the justification for a rejection of the heavenly Despot who demands sacrifice. This alternative does not solve the problem of theodicy, though. Instead, it generates several new questions, which will be discussed later, especially in the ethical reading of these novels.

3. GOD AND THE DEVIL AS HETERONYMS

In Saramago's pantextual synthesis neither the description of God nor the description of the Devil follow the lines of canonical tradition. In his inversion it is actually the Devil who plays a leading role in Jesus' life from the very beginning. In the beginning he announces Jesus' birth to Mary and later he reveals to Mary that Joseph is guilty of allowing the Bethlehem massacre. As a shepherd, he later makes Jesus his disciple in the wilderness. He is a dark angel who is substituted for the biblical angels and who reveals heavenly secrets to human beings and especially to Mary.[42]

Jesus' relation to the Devil is special since he spends five years with him in the wilderness. During this time Jesus' conception of God starts to change as he listens to Pastor's cynical lessons and learns some cruel facts about Israel's God. Gradually the roles of God and the Devil begin to change in the story. God appears to be greedy and violent, while the Devil turns out to be honest and open in his pessimistic realism. Admittedly, he is a liberal materialist-rationalist, opposing anything

---

41. The last reference is to Altizer's provocative (Nietzschean) study *The Gospel of Christian Atheism*, from 1966; see chapter 6.5. below.

42. See for instance Saramago, *Gospel*, 11, 16, 81. Cf. chapter 2.2. above.

hints of God. But as such a character he simultaneously resembles the western intelligentsia who, frustrated with Christian tradition, attempts to find some kind of moral responsibility through solidarity. He is open and fair and, surely, consistent in his statements.

This is why the Devil continues to oppose God based on moral reasoning. As seen in previous analyses, the Devil's criticism against Christianity focuses on sacrifice because it reveals God's essential ruthlessness. On the level of Saramago's "omnipotent author," the case is clear from the very start: the Devil has all those properties that in the canonical tradition belong to Israel's God. Here we have an inverted salvation history. Satan attempts to save humanity from the evil temptations of the violent and bloodthirsty God. Saramago plays chess with only with the black pieces. He is convinced that his game is both justified and victorious. As the roles of God and the Devil begin to get confused in Jesus' mind, Pastor plays with words. What do we find inside a human being? Is it possible to find a king inside a slave? And what about the Devil?

> Slaves exist to serve us, so perhaps we should open them up to see if they carry slaves inside, or open up some monarch to see if he has another monarch in his belly, and I'll bet if we were to meet the Devil and he allowed us to open him up, we might be surprised to find God jumping out.[43]

The sentence expresses Pastor's quick imagination, and the narrator then comments on the strange relationship these two figures have with each other. Pastor is still capable of provoking Jesus with his remarks. But the narrator himself surpasses even Pastor's ideas: "After all, Pastor might have gone even further and suggested that on opening up God one might find the Devil inside."[44] If one does not act like a God, one should not be revered as a God. And if one acts like a divine being, one should not be doomed to the lowest circles of hell.[45]

These speculations prepare way for Saramago's final scene at the lake Gennesaret. Jesus spends a traditional forty days—doing another

---

43. Saramago, *Gospel*, 181

44. Ibid.

45. "If psychological profiles were done today from the dialogues, 'God' would be characterised by words such as macabre, vengeful, bloodthirsty and unforgiving, while the 'Devil' would be characterised by words such as charming, amiable, rational and kind to animals. Could the altered mind of Jesus have led Him to be mistaken as to who was 'God' and who was 'Devil'?" Pires-O'Brien, "Novel View," 187.

fast—at the lake in a small fisherman's boat. This wet desert is a place for new temptations, but this time it is not the Devil who puts Jesus to the test, but God himself. The setting is confused, however, when the Devil swims to the boat as an Old Testament Leviathan and climbs on board. As the Devil sits in the boat, Jesus makes an astonishing observation. God and the Devil resemble each other completely.

> This is the Devil whom we have just been discussing. Jesus looked from one to the other, and saw that without God's beard they could pass for twins, although the Devil looked younger and less wrinkled, but it must have been an optical illusion or mistake on Jesus' part.

In Saramago's story the Devil's fate is tied to God's fate. "My son, never forget what I'm about to tell you, everything that concerns God also concerns the Devil."[46] But why twins? Why does Saramago need this new reasoning? The character of the Devil has a dual role in the narrative. Satan is naturally a fallen angel. Originally, in the Bible, he is not a hero. He comes from the abyss and represents and also embodies evilness. This is why God, as his twin, may also be described as a violent character. But of these two the Devil, apparently, is the prodigal son. He has converted from his evil ways and gradually begins to find his divine nature. On the lake, it becomes clear that God wishes to make Jesus a martyr for his kingdom.

> And what is this part You've reserved for me in Your plan, That of martyr, My son, that of victim, which is the best role of all for propagating any faith and stirring up fervour.[47]

There is a detailed strategy behind this plan. Only through Jesus' martyrdom he will become a figure whom millions will follow. "It is only fitting that a martyr's death should be painful and, if possible, ignominious, so that believers may be moved to greater fervour and devotion."[48] This, however, is the place where the inverted characters rise against each other. As noted earlier, the Devil wants to wash his hands of God's divine horrors.[49] Such insanity could not have resulted from Pastor's

---

46. Saramago, *Gospel*, 281.
47. Ibid., 282.
48. Ibid., 283.
49. In chapter 5.1.; cf. Saramago, *Gospel*, 296.

Attacking Biblical Theism

intentions. Instead, in order to show that "the Devil also has a heart," Pastor makes a proposal.

> I propose that You should receive me into Your Heavenly Kingdom, my past offences redeemed by those I shall not commit in future, that you accept and preserve my obedience as in those happy days when I was one of Your chosen angels, Lucifer, You called me, the bearer of light, before my ambition to become Your equal consumed my soul and made me rebel against Your authority, And would you care to tell Me why I should pardon you and receive you into My Kingdom, Because if You were to do so and grant me that same pardon which one day you will promise so readily right and left, then Evil will cease at once, Your son will not have to die, and Your Kingdom will extend beyond the land of the Hebrews to embrace the entire world.[50]

Suddenly the Devil's history is laid before the eyes of the debaters. Saramago's magical realism is, after all, sensible only if the biblical story of Satan's origin is held to be true. He is a fallen angel, and God is the omnipotent ruler of heaven and earth. The intertextual situation is interesting. Both God and the Devil have actually two different roles. Firstly, their relation is comprehensible only if the biblical story is authentic. Secondly, however, their antagonism is effective only if they really are twins or at least intimate familiars having a common violent background with selfish intentions. Only on these premises can the Devil be made a repentant villain who wishes good for humanity. And Pastor's repentance seems honest. There is good and evil after all. And conversion is reasonable. All previous rejections of religious customs now evaporate. The future of this world is dependent on true repentance and commitment to the sanctification of life. In this way the Devil can appear as Satan "the accuser" who rises against God. God's world could be saved if only God himself would act according to his own precepts. The door is open, and the Devil is prepared: "Good will prevail everywhere and I shall sing amongst the lowliest of the angels who have remained faithful."[51]

This, however, is not an option for God. He will not pardon the Devil. At which point the whole situation ends up in a paradox. He needs his counterpart and adversary, and his role is dependent on oppo-

---

50. Saramago, *Gospel*, 299. Cf. Fokkema: "The book is not a celebration of the Devil, nor of paganism, but it questions the irrational horror of so-called revealed truth." Fokkema, "Art of Rewriting," 398.

51. Saramago, *Gospel*, 299. For the etymology concerning Satan as an accuser, see chapter 5.1. above.

sition. "Because the Good I represent cannot exist without the Evil you represent."[52] In the end we are just prisoners of different language games. The basis of religion is in the construction of a cosmic opposition: "unless the Devil lives like the Devil, God cannot live like God, the death of the one would mean the death of the other."[53]

Such a result is somewhat confusing. Were all this be taken as philosophical reasoning instead of entertainment, the presentation would be consistent. However, since the final argument is again based on dissolving morality, the reader witnesses the return of Nietzsche. Good and evil, God and the Devil, salvation and damnation are but arbitrary constructions that usually stand for evil and violence in society. All this is relativistic. Without a constructed evil there is no need for any god either. This is one of Saramago's shortcomings. How could God be condemned as the father of violence if there is no essential evil at all? At this point, one should not demand too complex a speculation concerning philosophy of religion from Saramago.

Finally, the discussion on the boat climaxes when a new voice enters and raises the whole scene to another sphere.

> It strikes me that you are not to blame and should anyone hold you responsible you need only to reply that if the Devil is false then he could never create a true god, Then who will create this hostile god, asked Pastor. Jesus was at a loss for an answer and God, who had been silent, remained silent, but a voice came down from the mist and said, Perhaps this God and the one yet to come are one and the same god, Jesus, God and the Devil pretended not to hear but could not help looking at each other in alarm, mutual fear is like this and readily unites enemies.[54]

The official English translation is not accurate here, since the original text refers to Pessoa and his ideas. Translated from the Portuguese, the central sentences above read as follows:

> Jesus was at a loss for an answer and God, who had been silent, remained silent, but a voice came down from the mist and said, Perhaps this God and the one yet to come are merely heteronyms, Whose, or of what the second voice asked curious, Pessoa, This is what the answer sounded but it may also have been, Person [De

52. Ibid., 300.
53. Ibid.
54. Ibid., 297.

quem, de quê, perguntou, curiosa, outra voz, De Pessoa, foi o que se percebeu, mas também podia ter sido, Da Pessoa.].[55]

Whose heteronyms? The reference to Fernando Pessoa and his heteronyms, different alias personalities, transfers the story onto a literary platform.[56] Characters of a narrative are usually fictive but Pessoa and Saramago have gone one step further and made even their implied authors fictional creations. This pattern can also be taken on the level of philosophy of religion. If there is some kind of god writing the great metanarrative of history, one cannot be certain of the true nature of his personality. God and the Devil may well be twins or even just synonyms for one single personality. Seen only from behind, God may really look like the Devil. One should probably note that, for Saramago, the idea of heteronyms here is merely a device for presenting God as evil. Pessoa's original idea is slightly distorted in this reinterpretation.

In Saramago's novel, God and the Devil are not identical but, instead, Saramago's God starts to resemble the canonical Devil and Pastor the canonical God—or at least his best features. Mailer in his Manichean dualism still credited God for the good things in life, even though he was not able not remove all evilness from this world. Saramago goes in the opposite direction. The purpose of the novel is to attack biblical theism, at least in a literary sense if not theological, by making God responsible for all the violence both his Word and his deeds on Good Friday incite.

This, however, is the also point in Saramago's story where the reality of heavenly beings is questioned. Religion is merely a form of discourse. It is a closed system where signs are defined by other signs. The only voice the rowers hear, namely the voice that proclaims a revelatory truth about heteronyms, comes from beyond the world of the text. It is the voice of the *Author*.[57] Only the author knows about heteronyms and is

---

55. Saramago, *Evangelho*, 389 (translation ad hoc). Pessoa in Portuguese means "person," hence the justification for the wordplay; see below.

56. Fernando Pessoa (1888–1935), a Portuguese author developed several different artistic personalities, heteronyms. He also published many book on different names and the personalities he created even had their unique style of writing. Many of the convictions of these personalities contradicted each other on purpose. Saramago has been continuing this game, and he also wrote a whole novel on one of Pessoa's heteronyms, Ricardo Reis. Passoja, "Jälkeläiset,"100–102, 121–22.

57. Saramago's works have been called "secondary literature" because, "instead of a mimetic description of reality he creates a fictive, artificial reality where his narrator and his characters can act, and the action is frequently interrupted by the digressions of the narrator." Pál, "Traditions," 333.

able to control the destiny of gods and devils. In an intertextual reading this reality must be the world of reception. Present readers of the Bible, like Saramago and other authors, decide which gods are real and which are not. They decide who is good and who is evil. Biblical *persons* are just religious readings of history, and they can be questioned. When the difference between God and the Devil is dissolved, humanists are freed from the power of the Christian God as well.[58]

Some scholars adopt Saramago's hermeneutics in their reading of his novel. For Bloom, Saramago, despite his straightforward depiction of a violent God, is no apostate.[59]

> Saramago's God can be both wily and bland, and he has a capacity for savage humor. No one is going to love this god, but then he doesn't ask or expect love. Worship and obedience are his requirements, and sacred violence is his endless resource. Baruch Spinoza insisted that it was necessary for us to love God without ever expecting that God would love us in return. No one could love Saramago's God, unless the lover were so deep in sado-masochism as to be helpless before its drive.[60]

Bloom too assumes that the biblical story is a language game. There is no divine revelation that should be taken into account in interpretation or even in rereading. Treatment of the conception of God is a matter of natural theology. Who could love the God of Christian history, the God of the Inquisition, the God of the Holocaust? Bloom acquiesces to Saramago's deconstructive revision. This leads to Nietzschean rhetoric where worship and obedience are God's only "requirements." They have no meaning or justification. Against the simplest and most fundamental element of the Christian story of salvation these critics write that no one can expect God to love us. Finally, this ends in the Nietzschean cry bishop Spong and the death-of-God theologians made so famous: only pitiful sado-masochists could love this kind of God.[61]

---

58. Stavans suggests that Pessoa's idea of heteronyms may even be regarded as a hermeneutical key to the whole novel: "In Saramago's portrait of Jesus and the Holy Family, Pessoa plays a fundamental role: The Messiah, the owner of a divided self, lives in a fractured world where reality and fiction are thoroughly commingled, heteronyms of each other." Stavans, "Fisher," 676.

59. Bloom, "One with the Beard," 155, where he states that "only a bigot or a fool would judge Saramago's *Gospel* to be blasphemous."

60. Bloom, "One with the Beard," 155–56.

61. Spong, *Sins of Scripture*, 172.

But why is this not blasphemy? Is Bloom right about Saramago? This must be a matter of definition. When discussing blasphemy one can move on different levels: Does the story hurt the religious feelings of devout believers? Does it contradict the doctrines of the church (for instance the Nicene Creed)? Does it directly attack God himself? As regards the first level, Saramago and Mailer have aroused fierce discussion where the authors have been accused of blasphemy. As regards the second level, many of these novels differ in form and content from ancient creeds. And as regards the third level, it would be impossible to state that making God and the Devil heteronyms or presenting the God of the Bible in a Manichean perspective would not be an attack on God. Therefore, the question about blasphemy is surely dependent on who you ask.

But when we ask the question on the literary level, it appears in a somewhat different light. Do some of these novels, and Saramago's in particular, aim at deliberate blasphemy? It is quite difficult to assess answers to this question. Feminist novels aim at new mysticism and in no way attack God himself. Mailer is rather conservative even in his critical treatment of the problem of theodicy. And Saramago's novel can in a literary sense be considered just an imaginative criticism against the violent history of the Catholic Church, exploiting all possible literary tools at hand—even the church's Holy Scriptures.

This, however, is but half of the story. Bloom's positive account would be completely true only in a world where values would be only values of distance between linguistic signs. The mistake is in a deconstructionist reading of Saramago. His values in particular are not merely arbitrary instances of a system. Saramago's Jesus is a Sisyphus who opposes God. The author's critical approach would be incomprehensible without values. This makes Saramago a proud rebel who deliberately questions the biblical concept of God or at least his authority.[62] This is probably what Bloom does, too. He is inclined to think that, from the days of Spinoza, there is just one justifiable concept of God.[63] His refer-

---

62. This is true at least if we read Saramago with Camus: "The metaphysical rebel is, therefore, certainly not an atheist, as one might think him, but inevitably he is a blasphemer." Camus, *Rebel*, 30.

63. Bloom himself is certainly a poststructuralist, even though he is "barely a deconstructionist" as Hartman's gentle and also self-critical classification points out. See the comments on Yale critics in Hartman, "Preface," ix. Blasphemy, for Bloom, is just a word that will be deconstructed in a reading where religious discourse will be assessed

ence to Spinoza shows that Bloom and Saramago never really abandon positivist historicism. In their secularised ideology they preserve every materialist postulate the age of reason and the grand scientific metanarrative posed—as do ideologues in the so-called postmodern movement.

Somewhere God dies. In Saramago's novel the heavenly Being is alive and well in the boat where divine plans are revealed to Jesus. But in the intertextual revision God and the Devil become heteronyms in a greater story of which only the author is master. Biblical *persons* become mere readings of history. In Saramago's Nietzschean interpretation God is a cosmic misunderstanding. He is merely a literary figure, a fictionalisation, which, unfortunately, has been constructed on false Jewish premises. He is a dark *person* whose oppressive precepts are imposed on innocent people. He treats human beings as puppets who carry out his horrible plan of expanding the Jewish/Christian power structure to the whole world.

4. THE GOD-SIGN AS A DERRIDEAN SIMULACRUM

It is possible that Saramago, with his mysterious identification of God with the Devil, is actually building on Derrida and his idea of deconstruction. For Saramago, God and the Devil "could pass for twins." As heteronyms, the signs of God and the Devil have identical meaning or even the very same meaning. In a Saussurean sense, thus, they actually become similar signs. Nevertheless, they are just signs, they are units in a system which cannot reach beyond its limits. Derrida, naturally, had developed Saussure's theory in the direction of poststructuralism. Therefore, in order to understand any possible relation between Derrida and Saramago, one needs to become at least slightly acquainted with Derrida's poststructuralistic theory.[64]

For Derrida, the linguistic system is autonomic. It is merely a system of signs where a process of distancing and deferring, *différance*, pro-

---

anew. He might even call Jesus' Freudian rebellion against the patriarchal God patricidal, which is to be expected in any reformation. See for instance Bloom, *Influence*, 30. Cf. Selden et al.: "They experience an Oedipal hatred, a desperate desire to deny paternity. The suppression of their aggressive feelings give rise to various defensive strategies." Selden et al., *Guide*, 179. But then again, Saramago's leftist fight against the Catholic Church would also be such an Oedipal fight.

64. The relation between Saussure and Derrida is somewhat problematic since the latter reinterprets the former's ideas about structuralism. See, e.g., Derrida, *Of Grammatology*, 30–35, 51.

duces new signs according to a natural tendency to produce oppositions. There are no other empirical reasons for linguistic signs, according to Derrida. Therefore, all signs are produced merely inside the system and all signs refer only to other signs in the system—not to reality. In Derrida's theory, God and the Devil would be but signs, and this is probably what Saramago also intends. As opposites these artificially constructed signs are bound to each other by the power of *différance*.[65]

This means that, for Derrida, the sign has no longer a theological or metaphysical meaning. Language cannot reach beyond language. Derrida is a radicalised phenomenologist. He states that it is very difficult for language to describe sensory data, to say nothing of descriptions of the metaphysical. Therefore, theological signs and the God-sign remain inside language. And what is more important, they remain inside the discourse of a particular religion. The God-sign, thus, is merely a sign belonging to a dead discourse. It is a *simulacrum*, in Derridean terminology, a picture of an object that never actually existed.[66]

Saramago seems to follow Derrida in this argumentation. In a deconstructive act the forced *différance* between the signs disappears and these signs merge into one. God becomes his opposite. As the original difference between signs in a linguistic system of signs, according to Derrida, is being produced by the system itself, in a cultural and religious system this process becomes now a feature of a structuralist system of beliefs. Saramago apparently sees religion, and in this case Christianity, as a discourse that produces meanings by the help or dynamics of *différance*.[67]

In a rather philosophical deconstruction, such differences of meaning and linguistic polarisations are finally dissolved. Derrida actually stated that even the concept of permanent meaning, the idea of logocentricism, has always been a theological concept. To believe that language

---

65. Derrida developed his theory especially in his *Of Grammatology*. His concept of *différance* is a French neologism built on the words of difference and deferring. Thus, for Derrida, it simultaneously means both conceptual difference and the process of distancing. See *Of Grammatology*, 49–51; *Margins*, 22–23.

66. See for instance Derrida, *Margins*, 23–24.

67. Saramago, *Gospel*, 297. Krysinski states that Saramago's "polysemantical" narration plays with archetypes: "Cette narration polysémantique construit tout un théâtre où se jouent les archétypes de l'humain. Ils engagent la vie et la mort, la violence et la douceur, la lutte avec l'autre et l'acceptation de l'autre." He assesses these archetypes as binary oppositions. Krysinski, "Observations," 407.

really has a stable referential meaning implies a conviction that there is a created universe with a divine origin. This is what Derrida proclaimed in *Of Grammatology*: "The sign and divinity have the same place and time of birth. The age of the sign is essentially theological."[68] If one is to assume that the justification of the so-called transcendental signified (the *logos*) depended on the Christian concept of God, the concept of God, said the deconstructionists, was inevitably dependent on a sign.[69]

If religion is only a structuralist system, a mere discourse or even a play that in itself produces meanings, then all its signs are to be dismantled. In a deconstructive reading, i.e., in Saramago's intertextual reading of the canonical gospel, the God-sign, which was originally presented as the opposition of the Devil-sign, was seen in a new light. The linguistic opposition was dissolved, and the signs were now seen merely as bipolar expressions of one and the same phenomenon. The difference—including the theological difference—between God and the Devil is, for Saramago, a construction produced by the power of *différance*, a violent act of language itself. It is not a product of reason or a proper interpretation of reality.[70]

This is evidently why God and the Devil, for Saramago, are only heteronyms: "everything that concerns God also concerns the Devil."[71] There is one problem, though. Saramago is not very consistent with his deconstructionist ideology. This is something that he shares with several postmodern writers. Meaning, for Saramago, has not vanished into relativism. He has not rejected value as such. Rather, as the author-god of his own world he introduces values that surpass those of traditional Christianity. He presents values that are strong enough to reject a whole

---

68. Derrida, *Of Grammatology*, 14. The statement as such is usually linked with Nietzsche. Derrida's theory about meaning cannot be treated here in detail. Actually he had adopted Husserl's idea according to which the whole dichotomy between lexical meaning and referential meaning had to be rejected. Therefore, his understanding of the so-called referential meaning was reduced to the naming of phenomena. Derrida, *Speech and Phenomena*, 18–22.

69. See for instance Raschke, Preface, viii, in *Deconstruction and Theology*. This book was a theological imitation of *Deconstruction and Criticism*, a collection of essays by Yale critics following Derrida, written in 1979.

70. This is also how Don Cupitt explains, in the Derridean tradition, the nature of religious language: "It's all signs: the words of Jesus, the stories of him, the iconography, the rituals, the commentaries and the lives all add up to a river of signs. The church is the Christian tradition, which is a river of signs." Cupitt, *Long-Legged Fly*, 146.

71. Saramago, *Gospel*, 281.

religion, if not the whole of Christian culture in the western world. What Saramago does not consider in his frenzied rewriting of Christian history is the question that had already been posed to Nietzsche and his numerous followers: If there is no God, at least in the sense of a Divine Omnipotent Ruler, why should violence be considered as negative? Nietzsche was ambivalent when facing this problem. He promoted a fierce mode of behaviour and despised empathy and pity. This, however, is not what Saramago does in his novel.

Thus there must be a literary and also a linguistic level in Saramago's critique against religion. Other authors do not seem to construct their polarisations in quite this manner. Mailer's negations are too theological, and Fredriksson bases her oppositions mostly on feminist readings. One might hear a poststructuralist tune behind literary feminism but, all things considered, they are in the background of Fredriksson's writing. She does not deconstruct divine signs but, rather, presents a reinterpretation of patriarchal tradition. Saramago is the only one of these authors who really exploits poststructuralism in his critique.

While some authors wish to replace the alleged patriarchal discourse of the New Testament with a feminist language game, Saramago aims at a complete deconstruction of Christian views of God and divinity by reading later church history back into the original gospel. This results in an iconoclasm where no element of Christian faith is left intact. Saramago's *Gospel* actually begins with an analysis of an icon or an altarpiece. The author meditates and speculates on the features of a picture he is looking at. He sorts out his impressions:

> Beneath the sun we see a naked man tied to a tree trunk with a cloth tied round his loins to cover those parts we call private or the genital organs, and his feet are resting on a piece of wood set crosswise, to give him support, and to prevent his feet from slipping, they are held by two nails driven deeply into the wood. Judging from the anguished expression on the man's face, and from his eyes which are raised to heaven, this must be the Good Thief. His ringlets are another reassuring sign, for it is well known that this is how angels and archangels wear their hair, and so it would appear that the repentant criminal is already ascending to the world of heavenly creatures.[72]

---

72. Ibid., 1.

Saramago's commentary on biblical history is limited to a picture. It is a stiffened, frozen code, the decoding of which is merely a matter of subjective imagination. Saramago's work takes this as its hermeneutical approach. The impressions produced by the icon/narrative are usually assessed first but, in addition to this, the author also gives the reader an ideological evaluation.

In the description of the sacred picture, focus shifts next from the thief to Jesus himself.

> In this place known as Golgotha, many have met the same cruel fate and many others will follow them, but this naked man, nailed through his hands and feet to a cross, the son of Joseph and Mary, named Jesus, is the only condemned man whom posterity will honour by inscribing his initials in capitals, for all the others will soon be forgotten.... Shining above his head with a thousand rays brighter than those of the sun and moon put together, is a placard in Roman letters proclaiming him King of the Jews, surrounded by a wounding crown of thorns like that worn without their even knowing, or any visible sign of blood, by all those men who are not even allowed to be sovereign of their own bodies.[73]

This approach leaves no connections to actual history. There is no reality outside language or image—the sign. Saramago does not seek to understand the religious conceptions of Jews or the first Christians. He is not interested in the devotional identity of the New Testament era. This will be confirmed later in the story by several examples. In Saramago's gospel only the reader's (or author's) inner feelings and experiences are essential. Truth is in reception. In front of the icon of those crucified, one can only say: "these are things of this Earth [*coisas da terra*] which will persist on Earth, and from these things the only possible history will be written."[74]

Saramago's interpretation, of course, cannot be the only one possible for the whole world. There is a deliberate rhetorical contradiction in his statement. In the history of Christianity there have been several possible stories, and many of them are criticised in Saramago's novel. If some of these stories establish priority, it must be those who receive

---

73. Ibid., 5.

74. Ibid., 6; *Evangelho*, 20. "What marks this novel with a Saramago stamp is the essential belief, shared in all his narratives, that the only possible story is the one that belongs to this imperfect world (*terra*). That is why his Jesus represents human struggle, and his story ends with death." Kaufman, "Evangelical Truths," 457–58.

a reader-response based adaptation. According to Saramago, it is a deconstructive reading of an icon. This is why it becomes, paradoxically, the "only" possible reading. A link between the source text and the hypertext is destroyed. The original metanarrative vanishes because it is no longer included among the accepted possible readings. This is how Saramago produces his reduction and reaches an ultimate secularisation. All characters or signs in the picture are merely *"coisas da terra,"* things of this earth. He states that a proper reading must be constructed in terms of the immanent world. There may be an allusion to Nietzsche's famous statement in *Zarathustra* here: "*Let* the Overhuman be the sense of the Earth!"[75]

Such a poststructuralist, reader-response approach mainly concerns the content, in other words the message, of the Scriptures. As a historiography, Saramago's novel does take history into account in a much more traditional way when he describes the social environment or religious sects. Actually, Saramago is rather skilful with general historical information. There are several quite detailed reconstructions of New Testament history in the story.[76] It is also worth noting that most of the information in these passages has been taken from the Bible itself. History as such is not unattainable. Therefore, Saramago divides historical materials in two categories. His purpose is literary. The only petrified code concerns the "religion" that needs to be confronted in the narrative.[77]

There is a parallel development for this line of interpretation in radical theology. In the collection *Deconstruction and Theology,* where Yalean postmodern theories were applied to theology, Thomas Altizer

75. Nietzsche, *Zarathustra*, 12.

76. There is, for example, a decent description of the temple and a skilful description of the Roman army in Sepphoris; Saramago, *Gospel*, 66–67; 109–10.

77. As a short excursus it is useful to refer to a tension in the semiotic tradition that may enlighten the difficulties Saramago and Mailer have in their presentation. In the French tradition of phenomenological (post)structuralism, the arbitrariness of the sign was emphasised and, gradually, this led to a conviction about the autonomy of language and a belief in a closed language system. This theory, developed especially by Derrida, maintained that there can be no natural connection between sign and reality. All meanings must be conventional and relative. Meanings were considered as values inside the system. Derrida, *Of Grammatology*, 44; *Writing and Difference*, 280. In sociological structuralism, however, from the days of Claude Lévi-Strauss there evolved a conviction that language reflects social structures of reality. Sociological structuralism was discussed in chapter 4.4. above.

along with other deconstructionist theologians states that the concept of God is inevitably dependent on a sign.[78] Altizer combines Derrida's thoughts with his previous death-of-God theology. According to Altizer, Derrida simply developed Nietzsche's and Hegel's critique against the idea of presence. In this tradition of decentering—focused on meanings as well as doctrines—Derridean *différance* played the same role as Altizer's theology of reversal.[79]

> Indeed, Derrida's Hegelian conception of logos or presence is at once a conception of a totally incarnate Word and a universal or catholic word which is the ultimate source and ground of all actual meaning and identity. So it is that it is against this very background and foreground of the totality and universality of presence or logos that Derrida establishes his impossible project of recovering that "trace" which is sublimated and erased in pure and total presence. True, this project is made possible by the end of history or the death of God, but it remains an impossible project, and is so because of the total and ineradicable effects of the very actualization of a total presence.[80]

With the help of Derrida Altizer constructed his somewhat paradoxical theology of absence, where the idea of the death of God was paralleled with the movement of *différance*. In the same manner as the "trace" (a Derridean term) conceals its origin, a consciousness about God defers actual divinity beyond the horizon of the observer. Furthermore, a sign corrupts the trace because it replaces it with a conventional unit of a sign system. Similarly, says Altizer, the speech about God replaces the original trace of divinity in theology.[81]

> Derrida is the one in our time who has most fully recovered or restored the purely iconoclastic identity of the Book, and therewith the purely aniconic identity of pure writing or trace. That trace is the concealment of the origin, a concealment which is the unnameable movement of *difference-itself*, which Derrida strategically "nicknames" *différance*, and which can be called writing

---

78. See the Raschke, Preface, viii.
79. Altizer, "History as Apocalypse," 148.
80. Ibid., 154.
81. The "trace" is an intuition of reality, an illusion of a representation which reality produces in the mind. According to Derridean phenomenology it is not yet a sign. The trace produces a sign. But because the sign is already an arbitrary unit of a semiotic system, its meaning has to be something other than the object itself.

only within the *historical* closure of absolute knowledge. So it is that it is the death of God which makes possible the return of *difference-itself*, a pure difference which is lost with the advent of history or consciousness, and a difference or *differance* which is the true "other" of God.[82]

For both Saramago and the radical theologians of the death-of-God movement there never was a personal God to begin with. All we face is otherness and mute signs. The God-sign preached and taught in the Christian tradition is merely a *simulacrum*, a fictive picture on the wall or an icon that has never had any object or referential counterpoint in any reality. The Christian church, for Saramago, has only ever been a human organisation with a violent system that ruins personal happiness and tortures people. For him a truthful reading of this kind of history dismantles the Christian interpretation of human life.

Existentialist rebellion resolves in the paradox that is born when, after all these skillful deconstructive acts in Saramago's novel, God finally wins. The Devil's Promethean combat has no effect. Even Jesus fails on Good Friday. The Christian God is the God of history. His every prediction is fulfilled in later history just as Saramago's long lists of martyrs have already proven. The inference has been circular from the very beginning. The novel's critical approach and the Devil's warnings would have been futile would God not have won in the end. All that is left is a persistent fight against the violent church, which has chosen to worship a monster and whose doctrine is a denial of life.

5. APPLICATIONS OF DEATH-OF-GOD THEOLOGY

So God is dead. Nietzsche's ghost haunts all late twentieth-century Jesus-novels. In the adaptation of the novels, God may not be dead as a character in the narrative, but he is dead in terms of his authority and power. As Nietzsche said, even though God's existence could be proved, he should be rejected. In the very core of these novels' narratives there is nihilistic enthusiasm questioning and also neglecting the traditional, biblical view of God. The polarisation produced by the intertextual ap-

---

82. Altizer, "History as Apocalypse," 155. Cf. Ward: "Derrida's work provided these death-of-God theologians with an anti-metaphysical account of language. Language pointed to itself, not to any realms or personages, revelations or hierarchies above, beyond or outside the secular world it constructed." Ward, "Postmodern Theology," 77–78.

propriation climaxes in making the Creator look like the opposite of life.[83]

This revolt may be guided by the paradoxes induced by the problem of theodicy, or it may be a result of emancipatory opposition to God as a paradigmatic Man in heaven. Whatever the reason, God is on trial in these novels. During this analysis, it has become apparent that nihilist atheism is not merely a matter of selected lines in the dialogue of certain novels. Instead, it can be detected in the intertextual strategy by which the canonical Gospel is contrasted with the novel's new story. This is also the hypertext's rhetorical aim, especially in Saramago's *Gospel*.

> No disinterested reader, free of ideology and of creed, is going to forgive Saramago's God for the murder of Jesus and the subsequent torrents of human blood that will result. Joyce's Stephen speaks of the "hangman God," as some Italians still call him, and that precisely is Saramago's God.[84]

Saramago's destruction or deconstruction, whatever the epithet, is complete. He has been able to conduct his readers to a point where they will never forgive God for giving his son as a sacrifice for the sins of humanity. In his Nietzschean zeal he does not merely attack the dark eras of the Catholic Church, although he gives them much attention. His narrative culminates in a metaphysical *coup d'état* where God's divine authority is abandoned.

Similarly, many of the investigated Jesus-novels can be easily located in the widely spread death-of-God ideology, which, apart from literature and the arts, is present both in philosophy and theology. Antagonism towards the Christian concept of God is part of Western cultural history. Jesus-novels belong to a long tradition of secularisation and, therefore, it is easy to find different parallel movements both in philosophy and theology. As noted, poststructuralist speculation about meaning has repeatedly exploited religious terminology. Especially for French philosophers the idea of a transcendental signified is essentially based on a belief in God as a Creator. Poststructuralists contest the

---

83. This antagonism is partly dependent on cultural change as Stavans notes concerning Saramago's novel: "As a literary genre, the novel retains a loyalty to the secularist and even cynical views it was born with during Erasmus's age; any historical figure metamorphosed into a novelistic character thus becomes an expression, a mirror of the container it inhabits." Stavans, "Fisher," 676.

84. Bloom, "One with the Beard," 163.

Author-God whose theological meaning should be seen as a fixed meaning of the text. Meaning, for them, has a multidimensional nature and this is why religious speech or the contemplation of metaphysics must be freed from any theological premises.

In theology, the death-of-God movement provides a perfect parallel to this ideology. Its most famous forefather is John A. T. Robinson, who, in his *Honest to God*, introduces the principles of Nietzschean theology. Robinson cannot yet be considered a poststructuralist like many of his later followers, but he is a Nietzschean by conviction. Robinson contests the idea that God is a person. He opposes the long theological tradition that holds that "the language of transcendence" referred to God as a personal being, wholly other to human beings, dwelling in majesty. "It is precisely the identification of Christianity—and transcendence—with this conception of theism that I believe we must be prepared to question."[85] For Robinson, Nietzsche is a critic *par excellence* of theism.

> But, earlier, men like Feuerbach and Nietzsche, whom Proudhon correctly described as "antitheists" rather than atheists, saw such a supreme person in heaven as the great enemy of man's coming of age. This was the God they must "kill" if man was not to continue dispossessed and kept in strings. Few Christians have been able to understand the vehemence of their revolt because for them he has not been the tyrant they portrayed, who impoverishes, enslaves and annihilates man.[86]

It is no wonder that Robinson's theological program in its entirety resembles that of Nietzsche. For them both, the clash of religious cultures, namely the antithesis caught between scientific western culture and the magical culture of the Bible, has been inevitable. Traditional Christianity promotes its slave morality and annihilates human will. It prevents people from living a mature, independent life. Such a conviction results in a completely inversive adaptation of Christian tradition.

Robinson's aims are similar to those of the new gospels' authors. Jesus' image must be reconstructed, as well. According to Robinson, he was neither a supernatural magician nor a God, but an exemplary person with high morals. In this early phase ethics was still considered a justifiable and understandable element. But the church is no longer entitled to preach about the incarnation. Naturalism has taken over. Its

---

85. Robinson, *Honest to God*, 40–41.
86. Ibid., 41.

theses must be made the theses of the church. "Once the 'dogma' of his deity has been put out of the way, the humanist picture of Jesus is noticeably sympathetic, especially when compared with the sharpness of its 'antitheism.'"[87]

The reductive changing of Jesus' person and character results in problems that the authors of Jesus-novels must grapple with. What can one do and how far can one go without making Jesus insignificant? Robinson expresses his concern that this may lead to a faded or lame view of Jesus. If Jesus is considered merely as an average Jewish man from Galilee he is no longer interesting. This is why Robinson himself seeks for a kind of Zarathustra. His messiah is some kind of *Übermensch*. "According to this view, the divine is simply the human raised to the power of 'x.'"[88] Jesus' divinity is humanity at its highest potential. In many respects Robinson prepared the ground for deconstructive fictionalisations of Jesus even though his messiah is still an exemplary, strong individual. Factual poststructural elements entered death-of-God theology only later in the course of history.

In the United States Thomas Altizer developed death-of-God theology in a radical direction. "Nietzsche's proclamation of the death of God shattered the transcendence of Being." For him there is just one route to choose. According to Altizer, Christian thinking is to be directed solely by Nietzsche's guidelines. "Nietzsche was, of course, a prophetic thinker, which means that his thought reflected the deepest reality of his time, and of our time as well; for to exist in our time is to exist in what Sartre calls a 'hole in Being,' a 'hole' created by the death of God."[89]

In the beginning of his *The Gospel of Christian Atheism* Altizer quotes Nietzsche's *Antichrist*. In section 18 of *The Antichrist* God is reprimanded for having degenerated into a contradiction of life itself. Being God means, for Nietzsche and Altizer, enmity towards both nature and the will to live.[90] Only the death of God can liberate humanity from the

87. Ibid., 68.
88. Ibid.
89. Altizer, *Radical Theology*, 98; cf. *Gospel of Christian Atheism*, 22.
90. "The Christian conception of God—God as god of the sick, God as a spider, God as spirit—is one of the most corrupt conceptions of the divine ever attained on earth. It may even represent the low-water mark in the descending development of divine types. God degenerated into the *contradiction* of life, instead of being its transfiguration and eternal Yes! God as the declaration of war against life, against nature, against the will to live!" Section 18 in the *Antichrist*, cited in Altizer, *Gospel*, 21–22.

Attacking Biblical Theism

oppression under which Christianity has subjected it. The basis for this, according to Altizer, lies especially in the critique against metaphysics that has changed the thinking of the western world.[91]

Altizer writes like the authors of the Jesus-novels investigated in this study, even though he does not write fiction. In his adaptation there is but one "real" Christian, and he dies on the cross. Since his death the Christian message has been corrupted, it is "*ill* tidings, a *dysangel.*" What Christianity has traditionally called the gospel is, for Altizer, actually "the opposite of that which Jesus lived."[92] In this respect his theology is a suitable parallel to the novels. In fiction the authors just turn a similar conviction into a narrative.

There are also detailed analogies with the Jesus-novels. Most of the investigated novels treat the supernatural in the Gospel story in an ambiguous way. Their Jesus does heal some of the sick and often even the fate of Lazarus is discussed. Jesus' resurrection does not always fit in the time span of the story and so is not commented upon, but Fredriksson and even Mailer maintain it as part of their narrative.[93] Simultaneously, however, Jesus' humanity is emphasised so much that many canonical miracle stories are given a naturalist interpretation. For instance Mailer's Jesus in not certain whether he himself has really calmed the waves on the sea of Galilee, and Saramago lets Lazarus lay in his grave in peace.[94] The authors tend to give in to *Entmythologisierung* but their play with the source story sometimes prevents this.

In *Deconstruction and Theology* (1982) Altizer joins Derrida in claiming that "the sign and divinity" have the same place of birth. The age of the sign is the age of the church. If one is to assume that the justification of the "transcendental signified," the Derridean *logos*, has depended on a Christian concept of God, the concept of God is then inevitably dependent on a sign.[95] In his writings Altizer combines Derrida's thoughts with his previous death-of-God theology. Hence, as

---

91. Altizer, *Radical Theology*, 98: "No longer is there a metaphysical hierarchy or order which can give meaning or value to existing beings (*Seiendes*); as Heidegger points out, now there is no *Sein* of *Seiendes*."

92. Ibid., 100. Nietzsche, *Antichrist*, § 39.

93. In feminist novels this is expected since in the narrative, it is the resurrected Jesus who teaches Mary Magdalene after Easter. The story would be inconsistent without letting Jesus rise from the grave.

94. Mailer, *Gospel*, 93; Saramago, *Gospel*, 328.

95. See Raschke, Preface, viii.

an "atheist" theologian, Altizer has gradually grown into poststructuralist atheism. This kind of move resembles Saramago's treatment of the Gospel narrative.

> Once we recognize that radical Christianity is inseparable from an attack upon God, then we should be prepared to face the possibility that even Nietzsche was a radical Christian.[96]

This is probably the situation in which the investigated Jesus-novels also find themselves. They still work with the Bible but their inversion of the original narrative approaches the frontiers of pure atheism. Saramago may be regarded as an intentional atheist in this sense, but many other novels probably wish to represent a "radical Christianity" similar to the one about which Altizer speaks. And this feature, once again, unites these novels with Nietzsche.

Deconstructionist theology found its most brilliant representative in Mark C. Taylor, who added certain new elements to the death-of-God tradition. After quoting Nietzsche in a lengthy citation he states that the death of God "is not a tragedy passively suffered by hapless and helpless servants but an event enacted and embraced by rebellious and self-confident human beings." Therefore, for Taylor, the death of God is the only option the church has left.[97]

As a second-generation writer, Taylor made a distinction between the earlier "modern" form of the death of God and the current postmodern version of nihilism (1984). The modern tradition had its shortcomings, and Taylor wished to avoid them in his a/theology. An ideal deconstructionist, for Taylor, is a nomad who has no origin or purpose in life. "By negating 'negative excentricity,' this affirmation of centerlessness opens the possibility of exorbitant erring."[98] This is where Taylor needs Nietzsche again. His Zarathustra is an everyman, an Anti-Christ who has a new concept of grace. Once more, he is like the Jesus-figure in Saramago's *Gospel*. Salvation in this postmodern world is found in carnival and comedy. God is dead, and human beings are open to ever changing meanings.

> When becoming no longer needs to be validated by reference to past or future but can be valued at every moment, one has broken

---

96. Altizer, *Gospel*, 25.
97. Taylor, *Erring*, 19–20.
98. Ibid., 156–57.

(with) the law. Such transgression does not breed guilt and sin. In this case, lawlessness proves to be inseparable from grace – grace that arrives only when God and self are dead and history is over. The lawless land of erring, which is forever beyond good and evil, is the liminal world of Dionysus, the Anti-Christ, who calls every wandering mark to carnival, comedy, and carnality.[99]

Taylor's messianic program suggests new standards for the postmodern figure of Jesus. His carnivalism "neither ends nor cures." In this a/theology, Dionysus, Anti-Christ, and the Crucified are one and the same. So the theology of deconstruction means profanation. "The 'epidemic play of perversity' subverts the opposition between the sacred and profane."[100]

Similarities between recent Jesus-novels and the death-of-God movement are striking. It seems apparent that there has been a post-Christian metanarrative growing gradually during the twentieth century. It is a new narrative based on discontinuity and contradiction. Traditional Christian conceptions of what it means to be human have been abandoned and even condemned as unhealthy. This is the hermeneutical background affecting the adaptation and appropriation conducted in the investigated Jesus-novels. In the Nietzschean tradition God has been a problem for a century and finally, in these novels, the divine Being has become merely a symbol for a life-denying attitude.

Both for Saramago and Mailer the canonical God is an empty concept. Feminist writers themselves usually are content with a somewhat more concealed language but even for them the Bible's patriarchal God is a violent misogynist. Mailer in his almost-Manichean dualism makes God struggle with equal powers in the universe. The post-Holocaust culture both for Mailer and his Jesus is a frightening reality where nobody can be certain where all will end. There is only one escape. Since his Jesus still tells the story as the risen Christ, Mailer may be guarding a secret hope but, nevertheless, is suffused with doubt.

Saramago, in turn, retires into his pessimism and exchanges the biblical roles of God and the Devil. There is no real struggle between these heavenly powers. The God of history is omnipotent and makes both Jesus and the Devil his servants in order to submit the whole world

---

99. Ibid., 157–58.

100. Ibid., 169. Taylor's carnivalism reinstates Nietzsche's Dionysian orgy, the "overflowing" feeling of energy. Nietzsche, *Twilight of the Idols*, 119.

to his control. Whatever Saramago's own convictions, his narrative represents atheist reasoning. Therefore, these novels represent their own time more than they probably would wish to. Even when writing about the New Testament and showing interest in Christian tradition, they in fact proclaim the death of the Christian God.

7

Reinjecting Mystery into Religion

IN SPITE OF ALL the antagonism towards metaphysics in the Nietzschean poststructuralist tradition, there has always appeared a paradoxical interest in mysticism. This feature is common both to philosophy and theology, and recent Jesus-novels reflect this discussion. Side by side with rationalistic naturalism and the critique against theism, in the cultural history of the West, there have coexisted different ways of mystical contemplation. Something similar can be detected in the investigated novels. In several Jesus-novels, Gnostic religion with its heavenly wisdom is presented as the true cradle of Christianity and even as the heir to Jesus' original teaching. Gnostic writings are perfect for that kind of reinterpretation for many reasons. Their topic is separated from history, working merely on the hierarchical levels of spiritual growth. They claim to be the original or most authentic Christianity, and they oppose the canonical, apostolic Church. Furthermore, the re-enchantment of the secularised world, a well-known aim of postmodern thinking, puts an ideological pressure on the present intellectual community that affects the reception of Christian thought. Since this very Nietzschean interpretation of culture opposed the cold, materialist, mechanical world-view of modernity, some of its supporters aim at new spirituality in a post-Christian world.

1. MARY MAGDALENE AND HEAVENLY KNOWLEDGE

Considering the question theoretically, who could best be elected as a key figure between Jesus and a rebellious Christian group opposing the great apostles? One should find a person who was close to Jesus, but who was not completely under the command of his disciples. There should be a special relationship between this figure and the Saviour. In both Gnostic writings and several Jesus-novels such a person is Mary Magdalene. Mary is perfect for this role because there is no doubt that she is close to Jesus. She has followed him for a long time and even watches him die on Golgotha. The literary speculations of a sexual relationship between them can be bypassed without damage to the essential story. In terms of heavenly knowledge, the relation between Mary and Jesus is essentially spiritual. For the development of the idea it is sufficient that Mary is Jesus' follower. She did not have a Jewish theological education. Nor can she have been, in real history, the pupil of a rabbi. Furthermore, as a woman, she was not allowed to call a synagogue meeting in the Jewish community. Therefore, everything this woman says later in the context of any narrative, must come from Jesus directly—if the author wishes to create such a connection.

There is one more important factor. Prototypical rewriting has a sound point of departure. Even the canonical Gospels show Mary Magdalene as the first person to meet Jesus after his resurrection. The event in the garden outside the empty tomb is suitable for transmitting heavenly knowledge. Jesus has already tasted death and seen the heavenly realms. He must have new visions and an altered message that he can transmit to Mary. If the cosmic history of the world has actually changed in the realisation of the eschatological resurrection of the dead, Jesus' new message must necessarily differ from the teaching the male disciples have received earlier.

The Gnostic writings and Jesus-novels approach Jesus from similar perspectives. The novels imitate Gnostic gospels in many respects and so can be assessed similarly too. In fact there is an interesting hermeneutical principle at work in the Gnostic gospels that makes its way into the novels. The innovative doctrines of Gnostic theologians needed to be anchored in canonical writings. They were justified only if they had somehow originated in the life of the historical Jesus. This hermeneutical strategy can be found in recent Jesus-novels as well. An intentional reinterpretation of the Jesus narrative seems to be plausible only when it can be rooted in certain words or events in the original story. So it is important to focus on Mary instead of just introducing revolutionary doctrines even on their own merit.

The Magdalene's character is actually used in two different ways in the novels. Probably the most important of these is making Gnosticism a feminist religion that favors women and their hierarchy. Mary herself becomes a leader of the community or at least her feminist message becomes the ideology of the congregation. The second feature centers on Mary as a transmitter of heavenly wisdom. This change leads to a new spirituality and a different religious experience.

Concerning the first aim mentioned above, Roberts makes Mary Magdalene a leader of the church. Mary's voice must be heard in the community or Jesus' original message will vanish.

> We sat in our circle in silence, with bowed heads, each one of us, I am sure, filled with perplexity and sorrow and inwardly calling out for relief. My heart ached, and I felt very anxious. Arrogant and proud and scornful as I knew myself capable of being, in this matter of reporting the Lord's words I knew myself to be simply telling the truth. If the other disciples chose not to believe me, then the Lord's message would be lost. How, then, could we fulfil our mission as disciples? The Lord was snatched from us by a violent and unjust death before he had been able to complete his teaching, and I believed that my vision of him was intended to help us grasp the fullness of what he offered us, but I was doubtful, suddenly, that we would be able to achieve this if the most respected in our little group persisted in denying the validity of my words.[1]

Roberts constructs a feminist religion especially with the help of intertextual change. The tone suggests Gnostic writings as the source, evidently the Nag Hammadi texts and its later commentaries. In this sense, Roberts's book resembles a historiography, since the author builds up a new understanding of history by making deliberate choices on what material should be used. Selective use of original sources provides for an interpretation of history that contradicts that of male dominated historicism. What is at stake, though, is a subtext existing merely inside the novel itself. The original Nag Hammadi texts are much more complex, as was seen earlier.[2]

Fredriksson connects Mary's figure with a new Gnostic church but does not make her its leader. Long after the death of Jesus, Mary attends a Christian meeting lead by women. She is astonished to hear the preacher refer to her own name when speaking about Jesus' heavenly wisdom.

---

1. Roberts, *Wild Girl*, 114.

2. "In this way the narrative of *The Wild Girl* mirrors historiography: the process by which history is divided into neat events; the process of deciding which events make history and which do not." White, "Wild Girl."

Many elements in the teaching of the group resemble the convictions of Mary, as well. The first of these is equality: "No definite hierarchy is allowed."[3] Mary then hears a female preacher speak to the congregation:

> "We who have renounced the demiurge know that the power the naive worship as Creator and Almighty is nothing but an image," she began. "The true God is not King and Lord. It is not he who makes the laws, demanding revenge and leading us into bloody wars." She kept moving all the time she was preaching, her arms speaking in great gestures, her feet moving as if in a dance. Then she stood still for a moment. "Gnosis is to acquire insight into the true source, namely the depths in everything that is. All those who have learned to know this source have learned to know themselves."[4]

In Fredriksson's narrative Mary Magdalene discovers that a Gnostic community has transmitted stories about her and even her teachings. "We know that after his crucifixion Christ appeared to certain disciples in visions. First and foremost to Mary Magdalene. At a troubled meeting in Jerusalem, she told them what he had said to her."[5] The basic starting point has been taken from Gnostic tradition. Mary's exceptional status is based on her close relationship to the resurrected Jesus. Links to the canonical tradition stop here, though.

Prototypical rewriting in these passages exploits Nag Hammadi texts, and the description of the Magdalene group is more Gnostic than other passages that try to justify the *sacred feminine* through the Gnostic gospels. Here we have, for instance, a rare mention of the Demiurge whose creation is to be renounced. Souls are imprisoned in flesh, in the evilness that is matter, and true wisdom will be found in heavenly gnosis. This wisdom reveals that souls must be released from their prison, just as Jesus' soul was released in his spiritual resurrection.[6]

In spite of the fact that Mary has had nothing to do with the birth of the feminist congregation—a point that may reflect ancient reality at least insofar as it recognises that Gnosticism evolved outside main-

---

3. Fredriksson, *According to Mary*, 156.
4. Ibid.
5. Ibid., 156–57.
6. Roberts never speaks about the Demiurge. Even though there is some dualism in her description of creation, it produces masculine and feminine and, therefore, these two must be held equal. Roberts, *Wild Girl*, 78. "In the beginning, there was a unity" (123).

stream Christianity—she notices that the community's teachings follow her own words: "Mary could only occasionally take in the way the woman on the podium repeated word for word what she had once said."[7] Jesus' message as transmitted by Mary had begun to live a life of its own.

This is the general method by which feminist novels, with the help of Gnostic writings, confirm Mary's extraordinary status. The most important of these writings is the *Gospel of Mary*. Authors exploit two central features from this work, Jesus' love of Mary Magdalene and the unknown words of the risen Lord.

> Peter said to Mary, "Sister, we know that the Savior loved you more than the rest of women. Tell us the words of the Savior which you remember—which you know (but) we do not nor have we heard them."[8]

The tension between the male apostles and Mary Magdalene recurs in the novels. Peter in particular, who is her opponent in the Gnostic *Gospel of Mary*, becomes a prominent figure. Peter's suspicions even emphasise Mary's role. "Did he really speak privately with a woman (and) not openly to us? Are we to turn about and all listen to her? Did he prefer her to us?"[9] Such antagonism towards male apostles supports women's partaking in church leadership. These passages clearly contest Christian patriarchy as represented by Peter and other dominating figures in the canonical Gospels.

Roberts and Fredriksson also resuscitate Jesus and Mary's special relationship and alleged love affair in their novels. This, however, is based on a reader-oriented interpretation of the Gnostic writings. Mary is Jesus' "companion" in the Gnostic gospels, but they are not lovers. Mary's role is emphasised merely by the fact that she had been entrusted with the secret message that led to illumination.[10] The new reading stems from a partial passage in the *Gospel of Philip* about kissing: "And the companion of the [savior is] Mary Magdalene. [But Christ loved] her more than [all] the disciples [and used to] kiss her [often] on her [mouth]."[11] Originally the corrupt manuscript does not have the word for mouth but this fea-

---

7. Fredriksson, *According to Mary*, 157.

8. *Gospel of Mary* 10:1–6.

9. Ibid., 17:18–22. Peter's hostility towards Mary Magdalene is a common feature in Gnostic writings. See, e.g., *Gospel of Thomas*, logion 114.

10. See for instance the *Gospel of Philip* 63:32.

11. Ibid., 63:32–36.

ture can be inferred from other passages. In Gnostic writings kissing is an important feature but it has no erotic connotations. A kiss symbolises the transmission of secret wisdom. Therefore the Gnostics can say that they "give birth" to new members by kissing: "For it is by a kiss that the perfect conceive and give birth. For this reason we also kiss one another. We receive conception from the grace which is in each other."[12] In another text Jesus trusts his secret message to his brother James in a similar way: "And he kissed my mouth. He took hold of me, saying, 'My beloved! Behold, I shall reveal to you those (things) that (neither) [the] heavens nor their archons have known.'"[13]

Gnosticism, or at least those groups that produced the extant manuscripts, forbade women any special role in their communities. Women could become followers of the secret tradition but that was no novelty vis-à-vis Christianity. Gnostic soteriology despised sexuality and was not particularly interested in the roles of the sexes. There is one interesting passage concerning this issue, though. At the end of the *Gospel of Thomas* the male is made the model of true faith.

> Jesus said, "I myself shall lead her in order to make her male, so that she too may become a living spirit resembling you males. For every woman who will make herself male will enter the Kingdom of Heaven."[14]

This logion is quoted in an altered form in Fredriksson's novel:

> "Even more important should be that Jesus himself did not regard women as lower beings. Peter, do you remember what he once preached? "
> "You mean when he said men should be like women and women like men?' said Peter reluctantly." [15]

The intertextual strategy of the passage is somewhat confused. Separate expressions have been taken from Gnostic texts and planted in a new context in order to expand the traditional understanding of the canonical Gospels. The revised quotation does not serve as a direct link to Gnostic writings, though. Instead, it aims at an intertextual development

---

12. Ibid., 59:1–6.

13. *Second Apocalypse of James*, logion 56. The origin of the tradition of the holy kiss as a greeting derives from the early church. See, e.g., 1 Cor 16:20; Rom 16:16. It has also had long lasting influence in different churches.

14. *Gospel of Thomas*, logion 114.

15. Fredriksson, *According to Mary*, 152.

changing the religious convictions of the original text. In many Gnostic writings there was an androgynous ideal, and sexuality was neglected in theology. Therefore, the idea of becoming male must have been more of a metaphorical expression. Gnosticism was interested in spiritual illumination where sexuality was seen mainly as a hindrance.

In the novels, all this has gone. Such changes show that Fredriksson's prototypical rewriting intends to depict an altered version of Gnosticism. In the inversion, Gnosticism appears as a feminist religion with an egalitarian programme. When Jesus and Mary's sexual relationship and "kissing" are added, the wisdom of the new direction of Christianity is no longer very heavenly. Instead, its earthly tones often play down the beliefs of the original Gnostic spirituality.[16]

Mary Magdalene is also a transmitter of heavenly knowledge, which was the second theme mentioned above. Jesus-novels offer much detail about her role. One of the most visible features in the Magdalene's new spirituality is the introduction of a goddess. God is not to be depicted merely as a heavenly Man. Instead, the holy Trinity has its feminine part, so Roberts and Fredriksson describe the heavenly Being with feminine properties. Here they follow the Gnostic Nag Hammadi texts verbatim since the latter substitute a heavenly Mother for the Holy Spirit. "We have lost the knowledge of the Mother," states Roberts's Mary Magdalene. "We do not fully know God if we drive out this name of God."[17]

In the Gnostic *Apocryphon of John* the disciple John has a vision of a revised heavenly Trinity: "there was a [likeness] with multiple forms." The three forms he sees are explained in the vision as the heavenly figure speaks: "I [am the Father], I am the Mother, I am the Son." (II.1.2, 9–14.) In Gnostic theology, the dogmatic Trinity was understood in terms of a heavenly family. In this scheme the biblical concept of the Holy Spirit became a feminine person.

> [The first power], the glory, Barbelo, the perfect glory in the aeons, the glory of the revelation, she glorified the virginal Spirit and praised him, because thanks to him she had come forth. This is the first thought, his image; she became the womb of everything for she is prior to them all, the Mother-Father, the

---

16. Fredriksson's inversion corresponds to Pagel's feminist reading of Gnostic writings according to which several texts "use the figure of Mary Magdalene to suggest that women's activity challenged the leaders of the orthodox community, who regarded Peter as their spokesman." Pagels, *Gnostic Gospels*, 64.

17. Roberts, *Wild Girl*, 111.

first man, the holy Spirit, the thrice-male, the thrice-powerful, the thrice-named androgynous one, and the eternal aeon among the invisible ones, and the first to come forth.[18]

References to a heavenly Mother suit the ideology of feminist Jesus-novels well. Despite the fact that, in Gnostic theology, they mainly denote the androgynous spirituality of the sect, a novel does not need to select all extant features for their story. Hence Roberts lets Jesus remark: "the light of the Father married to the darkness of the Mother." According to *The Wild Girl* there are two (or even three) divinities in heaven, and this is why human beings must find their masculine part and feminine part within themselves. "Mary has reminded us of this, and I bless her for it."[19]

The Mother-Father idea is further discussed in Roberts's *The Wild Girl* by quoting from a mysterious text called *The Thunder, Perfect Mind*. In this passage, however, the original idea of a feminine deity is adapted in the description of Mary. In Roberts's text, Mary Magdalene sings a song together with Jesus' mother Mary, and the hymn describes the female part within oneself.

> – I am the whore, sang the mother of the Lord: and the holy one.
> – I am the virgin, I sang: and I am the mother.
> – I am the midwife, she sang: and she who is sterile.
> – I am the honoured one, I sang: and she who is scorned.
> – I am she whose wedding is great, she sang: and I have not taken a husband.
> – I am the bride, I sang: and I am the bridegroom.[20]

---

18. *Apocryphon of John* 2.1.4, 36—5, 11.

19. Roberts, *Wild Girl*, 63.

20. Ibid., 64. This passage is also quoted in the Introduction of Pagel's *Gnostic Gospels*, xvii. In Roberts's text the original has been only slightly altered; cf. *The Thunder, Perfect Mind* 6.13, 16-26:

For I am the first and the last.
I am the honored one and the scorned one.
I am the whore and the holy one.
I am the wife and the virgin.
I am <the mother> and the daughter.
I am the members of my mother.
I am the barren one and many are her sons.
I am she whose wedding is great,
and I have not taken a husband.
I am the midwife and she who does not bear.

The original Nag Hammadi text is a rare passage describing a revelation given by some kind of female deity. The text itself is constructed of antitheses or paradoxes that apparently reach beyond conventional descriptions of heavenly beings. The text in *The Thunder, Perfect Mind* goes as follows:

> I am the bride and the bridegroom,
> and it is my husband who begot me.
> I am the mother of my father
> and the sister of my husband,
> and he is my offspring.
> I am the slave of him who prepared me.
> I am the ruler of my offspring.[21]

In her inversive reading Roberts has turned the Nag Hammadi hymn's meaning into its opposite. By exploiting individual expressions she has changed the traditional roles of Mary Magdalene and Mary the mother of Jesus. Mary Magdalene the whore becomes a virgin and Mary the eternal Virgin becomes a harlot. When one finds her or even his true female part within, all concepts of humanity and morality will be transformed. This clearly continues Jesus' abovementioned teaching where he gives several definitions of evil. These descriptions no longer have anything to do with moral values. "Evil is indeed powerful, but it is a gesture of loneliness and desolation. It is hatred, which means a place of exile, of coldness and stiffness." Moral oppositions are changed into personal feelings. A similar transformation takes place in the women's hymn above.

Furthermore, as we saw in chapter 1, these Jesus-novels tend to emphasise bodily existence and corporeal reality. Gnostic faith is said to maintain the pure unity of body and soul and oppose the alienation of these two under the oppression of the Old Testament God. This view also contradicts the orthodox patriarchal asceticism according to which the "flesh" usually produces only sinful lust. Fredriksson even argues for such unity by reinterpreting a Gnostic story about the heavenly journey of the soul. If the soul cannot recognise the body during this lifetime, it has been following a false spirituality.[22]

The identification of the text is difficult since it presents no distinctively Gnostic themes. See *Nag Hammadi Library*, 271.

21. *The Thunder, Perfect Mind* 6.13, 28—14, 1.

22. "The body says, 'I did not see you.' And the soul replies, 'I saw you. But you neither saw nor recognized me.'" Fredriksson, *According to Mary*, 5.

There may be a link to poststructuralist hermeneutics here, as immediate experience of this world and phenomena become the only reality in this world governed by illegitimate discourses. When meaning is dissolved in wordplay, and concepts of God vanish in the polytheistic plurality of religions, one's own body is something one cannot or at least should not question. Roberts and Fredriksson argue on this level. They write beyond good and evil where desire is a gateway to the divine. This is probably also the reason why sexuality becomes a central theme when describing Jesus and his new message. Both Roberts and Fredriksson make Mary Magdalene Jesus' teacher who introduces the Saviour-to-be to the world of sensuality.

The new Gnostic subtext constructed in the novel on the basis of Nag Hammadi texts could, thus, in *The Wild Girl*, "too easily be represented as an alternative feminist version of Christianity," as White notes in her criticism.[23] In the prototypical rewriting, the ancient hostility towards the material world of the demiurge must step aside while the new Christianity, based on an erotic corporeality, emerges. Such reformulations have not come simply out of the blue, though. The connection between Roberts's and Fredriksson's novels on the one hand and Pagels's earlier monograph on Gnosticism on the other has turned out to be surprisingly close. The authors hardly ever quote any other passage in the Nag Hammadi texts or other Gnostic writings than those printed in Pagels's book. And vice versa, all the important passages quoted in that book have been taken into these novels.[24] This offers a likely explanation for their similarity in approaches. Pagels, in her feminist reading of Gnostic writings, never presents a thorough analysis of the cosmology, soteriology, Christology, or anthropology in Nag Hammadi texts or the Valentinian passages. She ignores the dualistic worldview typical of most of the texts.[25] The problem of the evil Old Testament God is not treated properly in Pagels's book and, therefore, her soteriological views remain

23. White, "Wild Girl."

24. These passages comprise, for instance, *Gospel of Mary* 10:1–6; *Gospel of Thomas*, logion 114; *Gospel of Philip* 63:32–36; *Apocryphon of John* 2.1.4, 36—5, 11; *The Thunder, Perfect Mind* 6.13, 16–26; *Hypostasis of the Archons* 94.21–95.7; and *Trimorphic Protennoia* 45.2–1.

25. Furthermore, one must remember that Pagels wrote her monograph in an early phase of Gnostic studies. Not all Nag Hammadi texts are now considered Gnostic, but many different groups are represented in that library. See Robinson's Introduction in *Nag Hammadi Library*, 3–10.

pale. Moreover, this is probably the reason why Gnostic anthropology is not given proper attention. According to Gnostic dualism, the soul is imprisoned in the corrupt body and the aim of the whole process of gaining heavenly knowledge, gnosis, is liberation from bodily existence.

To summarise, feminist Jesus-novels construct a kind of proto-feminist Gnostic Christianity both by selecting a particular subtext and by revising the ideas of Nag Hammadi texts completely. Intertextual analysis shows that, in the novels, the original source text is not the basis for the fictional rewriting of history. Instead, the religion formulated by Roberts and Fredriksson often contradicts ancient Gnosticism. Both the new soteriology and the new anthropology oppose original Gnostic beliefs.

2. JESUS AS AN EXAMPLE OF A NEW EXPERIENCE OF THE DIVINE

In many Jesus-novels Jesus too teaches Gnostic wisdom. Mary Magdalene is the transmitter of the new message but Jesus himself is the source of heavenly gnosis. In this respect it is not Mary alone who is responsible for the renewed gospel. The revised "historical" Jesus is made an opponent of his followers. He may have had male disciples but they did not learn much. Instead, they attempt to confuse Jesus' original teaching and turn Christianity into a dogmatic system. Hence, in these novels, Jesus is set against his followers and made a proponent of Gnostic mysticism.

These novels' revised Jesus-figure propounds a Gnostic soteriology even though the new message appears in a psychologised form. According to this salvific message redemption is in finding one's innermost hidden nature. The Gnostics proclaimed that this divine spark was imprisoned in flesh. Jesus-novels give their own interpretation of this. For instance Roberts makes her Jesus define the evil in terms of Gnostic dualism. "It is the absence of the fullness of God in you." This statement is reminiscent of Pagels's conclusion in her monograph:

> Whoever comes to experience his own nature—human nature—as itself the "source of all things," the primary reality, will receive enlightenment. Realizing the essential Self, the divine within, the gnostic laughed in joy at being released from external constraints to celebrate his identification with the divine being.[26]

---

26. Fredriksson, *According to Mary*, 63; Pagels, *Gnostic Gospels*, 144.

In Gnostic soteriology salvation has nothing to do with sin nor penitence and repentance. Instead, it is a matter of proper knowledge, gnosis. Therefore, in many writings, one is told to find one's true nature. In the *Gospel of Thomas* there are passages where Jesus' canonical words have been adapted to a Gnostic anthropology.

> Rather, the Kingdom is inside of you, and it is outside of you. When you come to know yourselves, then you will be known, and you will realize that you are the sons of the living Father. But if you will not know yourselves, then you dwell in poverty, and it is you who are that poverty.[27]

Having an uncertain identity is thus the psychological basis from which Gnostic soteriology grows. Salvation cannot be separated from individualisation and mental growth. "Light the lamp within you," writes the *Teachings of Silvanus*.[28] Furthermore, however, there remains a close unity between mental growth and divinisation. True gnosis, according both to the novels and Gnostic writings, leads to the finding of one's divine nature. Many novels share this orientation with the Nag Hammadi texts.

Roberts's Jesus proclaims the divinisation of human beings in a proper Gnostic way: "You can see the Spirit and become Spirit. You can see me, the Christ, and become Christ. You can see God, and become God."[29] Similarly, Berlinghof's Mirjam in her euphoria after heavenly sex with Jesus concludes: "We are the Universe." Her divine experience climaxes in pantheistic proclamation: "God is the All, and we are God!"[30] Even though the latter passage is probably meant to be a poetic hyperbole or a metaphorical expression concerning the summit of experience, there is a tendency in feminist Jesus-novels to dissolve the line between human and divine. These passages refer apparently to the *Gospel of Philip*.

> But you saw something of that place and you became those things. You saw the Spirit, you became spirit. You saw Christ, you became Christ. You saw [the Father, you] shall become Father.[31]

---

27. *Gospel of Thomas* 32.19—33.5.
28. *Teachings of Silvanus* 106.14.
29. Roberts, *Wild Girl*, 59.
30. Berlinghof, *Mirjam*, 382: "Gott ist das Ganze, und wir sind Gott!"
31. *Gospel of Philip* 61.27–31.

Pagels notes that, according to Gnostic spirituality, he who achieves gnosis also participates in divinity. He "becomes what he sees."[32] The feminist Jesus-novels in particular adopt this view in their story. In Fredriksson's novel this "doctrine," which it no doubt is, becomes the basis for Jesus' message. As a feminine element, inner experience is a trustworthy source for truth. Truth, paradoxically, is not clear to all people but to be found merely on a subjective basis. Therefore, all concepts must be defined anew. What is really real in this world is what is true for me in my inner reality. Hence, one's inner self also becomes the place, according to Fredriksson, where God can address human beings.

> "Man's real nature, the innermost core, is of God. From there speaks what I call the voice of God."
> "To everyone?"
> "Yes. But they have isolated themselves, and don't listen."[33]

Such claims are theological by nature and also reveal the belief structure in Fredriksson's feminist gospel. These ideas are no longer dependent on Gnostic writings or stories of Osiris. For Fredriksson the innermost core of human beings is of God. It is unspoiled and pure. Salvation in life means finding one's inner nature, real nature. And its opposite is to live untrue to oneself. This is what Fredriksson's Jesus calls evil. It is in the sin that people do not listen to their heart: "Mary, I had no inkling man was so evil."[34] If early Nietzschean criticism opposed traditional Christianity as life-denying, the new version opposes it for being inner-life-denying.[35]

This is also Jesus' new insight in Berlinghof's novel, where he abandons his patriarchal devotion to God the Father. Inner conviction and personal experience have revealed to him that "there is no longer any difference between us Jews and heathen people." This prototypical rewriting, starting from the apostle Paul's missiology concerning the salvation of "heathen people," ends up by denying Old Testament religion and the canonical Jesus' proclamation of the Father. As long as Jesus has believed in the Father, his love has been half-hearted. Sincere faith encourages

---

32. Pagels, *Gnostic Gospels*, 134.
33. Fredriksson, *According to Mary*, 141.
34. Ibid.
35. In this respect these novels do not differ at all from New Age literature popular in the 1990s. The most enthusiastic example of this line of thought among Jesus-novels is Longfellow's *The Secret Magdalene*.

one to keep looking into one's own heart and to find there an immediate experience of the divine.[36]

Furthermore, such theological convictions affect one's soteriological views. It is interesting that precisely these themes about inner truth become the principles directing the intertextual rendering of the New Testament message. This can easily be seen in many programmatic statements about the Christian message. When Fredriksson makes Mary answer Paul about the "most important" feature of Jesus' teaching she psychologises traditional catechesis:

> Reconciliation and forgiveness, what we talked about yesterday. You have to start with yourself, admit your fear and your selfishness. Regret what has happened and forgive yourself. When you can do that, you have no need to blame others.[37]

Confession, in this text, is no longer a matter of confessing sins in front of the Creator and righteous Judge, as it is in the canonical Gospels. Instead, it is a moment of self-consciousness and a realisation of one's situation in this world. It is awareness about one's feelings, such as fear, when facing the threatening conditions of life. Hence there is no absolution for sins, either. One is just supposed to forgive oneself. Furthermore, this new confession becomes the source of Christian love and compassion. These virtues are no longer the fruit of Jesus' sacrificial reconciliation but fruit of one's finding his or her true self.

In these novels, Jesus as Mary's secret teacher and a proclaimer of heavenly wisdom reveals the true nature of religion. Christianity is not a religion of sin and salvation. Instead, it is a meditative technique for releasing the divine soul from the bondage of this world's evil God. Based on their intertextual rewriting, these Jesus-novels, especially Roberts's and Fredriksson's, end up with a Gnostic polarisation. Since the canonical teaching of the male apostles is false and distorts Jesus' original message, the idea of the biblical God who is at the centre of the apostles' proclamation must also be false. The apostolic church that clings to its doctrines champions an evil God who has no knowledge of redemptive gnosis.

---

36. Berlinghof, *Mirjam*, 377, 383, 392.
37. Fredriksson, *According to Mary*, 136.

3. INTERPRETATION OF SIGNS AND CODES

Gnostic knowledge is secret knowledge. This is the basic point of departure for the whole train of thought in an esoteric movement. Salvation is dependent on inside information that is controlled by a small group of experts. Only gradually will the spiritual elite reveal redemptive knowledge to novices that proceed through the different stages in their practice. Such control is a sign of unconditional authority and sectarian exclusiveness. The exclusivity of Gnostic spiritual groups was the opposite of the apostolic church's open work and its widely known message.

Another important feature in Gnostic knowledge is that the divine message is given through signs and symbols. The logic behind this belief is simple. Our extant world as a creation of an evil god conceals heavenly truth from our eyes. Therefore one can find divine revelation only through hints that have been left in this world. The scenario is similar to fictional novels. There is an Author behind all "texts" who is detectable by human beings. The omnipotent writer organises his world so as to orient readers in the direction he wishes. One can see this strategy already in the *Gospel of Philip*: "Truth did not come into the world naked, but it came in types and images. One will not receive truth in any other way."[38]

These signs are not usually found in the canonical scriptures of any religion, and particularly not in the Bible. In Gnosticism, however, several canonical Jesus-stories and statements have been preserved and adapted to service the esoteric movement. Nevertheless, most signs are from elsewhere. Therefore, one can find hidden meanings in common things and small details. This strategy is exploited mainly in *The Da Vinci Code*, where the whole story is dependent on the explanation of signs. Some details in Leonardo's paintings, for example, are considered more informative than the whole New Testament.

> The Grail story is everywhere, but it is hidden. When the Church outlawed speaking of the shunned Mary Magdalene, her story and importance had to be passed on through more discreet channels... channels that supported metaphor and symbolism.[39]

According to the eccentric historian Teabing in Brown's *The Da Vinci Code*, the Christian God is just such an omnipotent Author be-

---

38. *Gospel of Philip* 67.9–12.
39. Brown, *Da Vinci Code*, 348.

hind the whole of Western cultural history. Building on his implied Jesus-story, Brown makes many artists and architects mediums for the revelation of a secret: that of Jesus' family and later descendants. Since Jesus and Mary Magdalene had had a child, God himself had wanted to preserve the knowledge of this legacy in cultural tradition. Therefore, several servants of God had left the marks of Jesus' dynasty in public masterpieces. Decoding these signs will lead any sincere seeker of truth to the threshold of a Gnostic religion of the sacred feminine.[40]

There are several different ways to read *The Da Vinci Code*, though. Public opinion has naturally promoted the view that the book critiques traditional Christianity as many of the other investigated novels do. The narrative structure of the work, however, may also be interpreted from another angle entirely. This book does not necessarily play with or oppose the church's message. *The Da Vinci Code* can rather be understood as an attempt to destroy any strains in Western thought that oppose the church. There are several indications in the story that support such a conclusion.

Brown's narrative is filled with seeming inconsistencies, and this can be interpreted as an intentional feature in the work. But as we analyse what the major characters really do, simplistic public opinion must be reconsidered. The story itself is rather complex. There is a group of Catholic elders (men) who wish to assassinate the members of some secret Priory as well as the alleged descendants of Jesus and Mary. They are commanded by a mysterious "Teacher" who also gives directions to an albino assassin. At the end of the narrative the plot is revealed. The key character is the one playing the role of the "mad professor," Sir Leigh Teabing. He is a keen friend of the heroine and the hero, but the final struggles reveal that he has been the Teacher all the time.[41]

Simultaneously, however, the same character has appeared to be a historian who has dedicated his whole career to searching for the Holy Grail. Teabing has devoted his life to the descendants of Mary Magdalene. He has been convinced that Jesus' relatives could change history and make our world a better place. Why, then, would this Teabing want to kill the descendants of Mary Magdalene? In the story, Sir Leigh is re-

---

40. Ibid., 311–13.
41. Ibid., 532–33.

sponsible for several murders of both Jesus' alleged relatives and their loyal guardians.[42]

The real villain in this messy tale with bloody murders, which are naturally needed in any detective story, is the Catholic Church. The roles of Teabing and the Church are confused if not transposed. It is actually the Church that attempts to assassinate the members of the Priory and the descendants of Jesus through the hand of one poor creature, the sadomasochist monk Silas. The real contradiction, according to the novel, can thus be found between the lies of the Church and the truthful humanism of the historian. The Catholic Church has oppressed the Western world with its dogma for centuries. At the same time, Jesus' real descendants have been hiding and keeping the revolutionary truth about God and human beings secret.

All this reasoning, however, takes place only in the mind of Sir Leigh, an apparent lunatic who is not certain even of his own aims. For him, the Church is just an artificial construction filled with power struggles that express the religion's violence and meaningless asceticism. It has been a centre for the patriarchal domination of society. So Brown writes like other authors of the Jesus-novels investigated in this study. He just transfers the ideas to the present world and builds his narrative on an implied Jesus-story, which resembles that of Roberts and even Saramago.[43]

> "Three centuries after the crucifixion of Jesus Christ, Christ's followers had multiplied exponentially. Christians and pagans began warring, and the conflict grew to such proportions that it threatened to rend Rome in two. Constantine decided something had to be done. In 325 AD, he decided to unify Rome under a single religion. Christianity." Sophie was surprised. "Why would a pagan emperor choose *Christianity* as the official religion?" Teabing chuckled. "Constantine was a very good businessman. He could see that Christianity was on the rise, and he simply

---

42. Ibid., 322–24.

43. This is precisely why Teabing represents the Nietzschean attitude towards traditional Christianity in the novel, but his views are shared by the hero Langdon, as well. "'The Grail,' Langdon said, 'is symbolic of the lost goddess. When Christianity came along, the old pagan religions did not die easily. Legends of chivalric quests for the lost Grail were in fact stories of forbidden quests to find the lost sacred feminine. Knights who claimed to be "searching for the chalice" were speaking in code as a way to protect themselves from a Church that had subjugated women, banished the Goddess, burned nonbelievers and forbidden the pagan reverence for the sacred feminine.'" Ibid., 322.

backed the winning horse. Historians still marvel at the brilliance with which Constantine converted the sun-worshipping pagans to Christianity. By fusing pagan symbols, dates and rituals into the growing Christian tradition, he created a kind of hybrid religion that was acceptable to both parties."[44]

In this respect Teabing is a mystic. His primary aim is to bring the real descendant of Mary and Jesus into the public. He wants to present "new wisdom," Sophie Neveu, to the world. This is how sacred feminine can be revealed so that the gentle nature of the original religion will prevail.

Based on the narrative, one should clearly think of Teabing as exploiting some members of the Church, especially certain fallen angels of the Opus Dei organisation, in order to oppose the Church itself. When doing this he is willing to sacrifice the lives even of the descendants of Jesus—not to mention the lives of all the harmless scholars and nuns that are being slaughtered during the race. So Sir Leigh is helping the Catholic Church to destroy the Priory that he himself wants to protect. And all this is done in the name of a greater humanism than the one that the Church offers. Such a narratological analysis changes the popular understanding of *The Da Vinci Code*. The figure of Sir Leigh Teabing is so negative and contradictory that one cannot sympathise with him. Therefore, it is actually this violent historian who is being rejected in the story. The book becomes a sharp critique of many of the recent enemies of the Christian gospel.

Hence, *The Da Vinci Code* is not just another book railing against the Church or against traditional Christianity. The narrative as it is, is rather a parody of a secular humanism that attempts to destroy the core of Christian tradition. *The Da Vinci Code* is a deconstruction of post-Christian Western thinking whose friendly face is merely a mask for violence, deception, and murder. And more important still, the story can be read as criticism of revived New Age Gnosticism with its sacred feminine and *hieros gamos* games.[45] The narrative as a whole mocks the whole tradition of populistic Holy Grail literature. This is why *The*

---

44. Ibid., 313–14.

45. I admit that this interpretation may not be the whole truth about the novel's intention since it seems plausible that, in the end, Sophie Neveu turns out to be Jesus' descendant. The story itself, however, justifies also this kind of conclusion. Seen in this light, Brown's novel bears the marks of an apology.

Da Vinci Code becomes also a severe criticism of recent feminist Jesus-novels proclaiming a new Gnosticism in Jesus' name.

4. BETWEEN GNOSTICISM AND NEGATIVE THEOLOGY

One might wonder how it is possible that, in the literary atmosphere where Nietzschean nihilism has made Schopenhauerian materialism a norm of modern worldviews, there has also been room for the emergence of a new mysticism. This development is not at all paradoxical. One might state that in a post-Enlightenment situation, where the mandate of religion has been transferred from the area of reason and science to the area of feeling and experience, it is only natural that religion will be defined in terms of mysticism.

This kind of transformation has been detected in several instances of theological thinking throughout the centuries. In the context of neo-Kantian mechanical positivism in nineteenth-century Germany, religion was defined as personal experience (*Erlebnis*) and its contents were filled with a priori epistemology, and this belief was then applied to our knowledge about God. There was still a way to reach the realm of the divine even though the result could no longer be completely explicated by traditional verbal expressions and explorations. Also in Rudolf Bultmann's rationalistic history-of-religions interpretations in the 1920s and early 1930s, the reduction of myths, *Entmythologisierung*, was accompanied by apophatic existentialism. For Bultmann, there were no words for faith. Religion is an existential experience. Every time this experience is put into words, it loses its original silent nature and is perverted into doctrines. It becomes part of history, dependent on cultural concepts and prevailing myths.[46]

An experience of the divine was essential for these existentialists exploiting Heidegger's *Angst* and *Sorge* in their hermeneutics. In a theoretical sense it was the experience of God that needed to be made the core of theology. Everything concerning history or texts had become uncertain and relative. Therefore inner experience was made the point of contact between human beings and divine revelation. But there was more to this, still. On the basis of Heidegger's phenomenological existentialism, personal feelings became essential elements of Christian

---

46. For Bultmann's views, see his article in Bartsch, *Kerygma and Myth*, 1–44; and also Kümmel, *Investigation*, 400–403; Berger, *Exegese und Philosophie*, 134–36.

theology. With such an emphasis, one can then see parallel features between existentialism and Nag Hammadi Gnosticism.

These themes drifted into postmodern poststructuralism through many channels. Derrida was influenced by Heidegger, and Nietzschean death-of-God theologians admired both of them. A critique against the materialist aspect of modernism has always been in the heart of postmodernism. According to Zygmunt Bauman, modernity brought with it the secular. Therefore, "postmodernity can be seen as restoring to the world what modernity, presumptuously, had taken away; as a *re-enchantment* of the world that modernity tried to *dis-enchant*."[47]

Both poststructuralist ideology and the postmodern tradition in general proclaim the death of the sign. Many writers also speak about the erasure of the transcendental signified, the permanent meaning that gives speech its substantial content. For Derrida, the biblical God with his creation is the ground for the meaning of a sign. Therefore, the death of the sign means the death of God, too.[48] For many writers, however, this does not mean the complete rejection of the transcendent. Even some phenomenologists maintain the idea of metaphysics despite their philosophical stance. For these writers, as well as for the death-of-God theologians, God is present in his absence. Meaning is to be encountered without signs. To accomplish this these authors quote from the medieval mystic tradition of negative theology.

Generally defined, negative theology holds that the nature of the Divine is ineffable. Theology itself, though, can be expressed verbally but God cannot be described in detail. In Christian tradition, some descriptions of God based on revelation may be allowed but the essence of the divine Being remains a mystery. According to medieval Catholic negative theology, the Via Negativa, religious experience is primarily an abstract experience, and it can be approached and explicated only through a negation. Hence, negative theology is also called apophatic theology, a theology that cannot be put into words.[49]

Poststructuralist negative theology, once again, is Nietzschean, which should not come as too much of a surprise. The dialectics of negation that Thomas Altizer promoted already in the 1970s is an inheritance from Nietzsche. According to Altizer, the "eternal recurrence"

---

47. Bauman, *Intimations of Postmodernity*, x. Italics original.

48. Derrida's views were treated above; see chapter 6.4.

49. See for instance the article by Schmidt, "Eckhart," 304–5.

that Nietzsche presented in *The Twilight of the Idols* and in *Thus Spoke Zarathustra* was a pattern that left room for atheistic mysticism by playing with death and new birth.[50] "Only when God is dead can Being begin in every Now. Eternal Recurrence is neither a cosmology nor a metaphysical idea: it is Nietzsche's symbol of the deepest affirmation of existence."[51] "Authentic" theology, a term borrowed from Heidegger, (a theology directing itself at Being, not individual beings with measurable properties) must resist metaphysics, but only to a point. Altizer constructs Nietzschean *nihil*/ism where nothingness, the emptiness of the transcendent, is symbolised by the self-annihilation of God.

> Rather, an authentic language speaking about the death of God must inevitably be speaking about the death of God himself. The radical Christian proclaims that God has actually died in Christ, that this death is both a historical and a cosmic event, and, as such, it is a final and irrevocable event, which cannot be reversed by a subsequent religious or cosmic movement.[52]

Since the God-sign has been rejected, the concept of the divine has no content in any traditional sense. In the death-of-God theology this does not lead to the rejection of God, though. In Altizer's hermeneutics, the divine will be known on the basis of its absence. "While that presence can now only be actually known or experienced as absence, it is a full presence nonetheless, and is so if only by virtue of the fact that it is actually experienced and known."[53]

In Altizer's atheist theology the path from the death of God to ineffable mysticism is a Nietzschean development. Hence this brand of mysticism belongs to the Nietzschean tradition even though Nietzsche himself is not a clear example of such a turn. Nietzsche's philosophy of religion had some general concept of the divine, but he rejected metaphysics completely. His followers turn to mysticism, though, and this is why it is legitimate to place such a view in the Nietzschean tradition. Altizer states: "Once we recognize that radical Christianity is insepa-

---

50. See especially Nietzsche, *Twilight of the Idols*, 120.
51. Altizer, *Radical Theology*, 99.
52. Altizer, *Gospel*, 103.

53. Altizer, *Deconstruction and Theology*, 171. "Now grace is everywhere because it is nowhere, nowhere that is where it is only itself, or where it can be known and named as the grace of God" (174).

rable from an attack upon God, then we should be prepared to face the possibility that even Nietzsche was a radical Christian."[54]

There are several features that recent Jesus-novels share with Altizer. Neither believes that the historical Jesus is relevant nor even that the canonical Gospels contain trustworthy historical material. Altizer states: "No radical Christian believes in the possibility of returning to either the word or the person of the original Jesus of Nazareth."[55] This is precisely the conviction according to which the Jesus-novels have been written, although the latter show merely little more than a literary motivation for this tendency.

In the shadow of Nietzsche, both history and Christian doctrine die with God. New readings and new interpretations occupy the space of religious experience. This produces a programme of negative theology where God is dead and theology silent. This does not lead to total nihilism though, but to mysticism. Therefore, these writers refer eagerly to the prominent fathers of the Catholic apophatic spirituality, such as Meister Eckhart. For instance, Don Cupitt first adapts Derrida's ideas to Christian theology and then moves to mysticism. "Art is no way to immortality, for it comes into being only by the acceptance of delay and deferral, Derrida's *différance* which is both Death and God."[56] For Cupitt, the postmodern critique of Western tradition is on a right track: "the vacancy at the Centre of all things and the vacancy at the centre of the self coincide." Artists as well as theologians are doomed to remain in *nothingness*.

In his *Mysticism after Modernity* (1998) Cupitt then attempts to solve the problem his views create in the construction of new theological views. By referring to Eckhart he ends up in mysticism, which reaches beyond words:

> [W]e must indeed take leave of any God who is describable in human language, because the true God, The Godhead (*deitas*), is *différance*, the non-word, non-concept, non-thing prior to language that makes all meaning possible. The Negative Theology/ *Différance* God would then be universal, ineffable, transcendental condition of everything—but not itself "a being" at all.[57]

---

54. Altizer, *Gospel*, 25.
55. Ibid.
56. Cupitt, *Long-Legged Fly*, 145–46.
57. Cupitt, *Mysticism after Modernity*, 96. Cf. Moore, *Poststructuralism*, 39: "I have

Cupitt's existentialist mysticism is identical with Fredriksson's feminist view in that it values religious experience only when it is meaningful for his own experience of life. "So God is simply the Fountain (in my own terminology), the self-outpouring play of pure secondariness (or contingency, or 'life') that continually produces me and my world from moment to moment."[58] This is also a point of contact with Gnostic soteriology. The Gnostic Divinity in several Nag Hammadi writings is merely a heavenly principle or impersonal power. Only the evil Old Testament God is a person with properties. Roberts and Fredriksson actually renounce the Old Testament God when disdaining Jewish descriptions of God and his precepts. This is probably also the reason why their own Divinity escapes definitions and can be detected behind almost any religious sign meaning god, be it Gnostic or that of Greek mystery religions. The only place where God can be met, according to these novels, is in the person of the worshiper her- or himself.

In deconstructionist feminism, Jantzen took the new Gnosticism to its limit. As the title of her *Becoming Divine* proclaims, the sins of those who have been oppressed by male domination are negligible. When the feminine interpretation of divinity prevails, humanity will be more conscious of the evil things in this world. In the name of the new religion, *ecclesia* can begin to fight the corruption of patriarchy. This, quite expectedly, will stand on the shoulders of postmodern moralising well known from the writings of the Parisian poststructuralists. In Jantzen's feminist utopia, pantheist theology finally distills merely into a combat against patriarchy, i.e., against the world of men as such. This results in an ontological postmodernism where dualism between men and women is re-established. Jantzen is optimistic, though. She suggests the "becoming divine" of human beings. Where Christianity and the Bible failed, feminist pantheism will succeed. Jantzen's good "Christian" is truly an *Übermensch* quite in the manner Nietzsche described. He/she is Zarathustra whose divinity is beyond good and evil. Salvation in this new religion means liberation from Christian faith as we know it.[59]

Although the motivation is different, Roberts too proclaims the divinisation of human beings. Salvation, for her Jesus, means "becoming

---

argued that Derrida has written repeatedly, even incessantly, on *différance*, and that this writing has always had an intimate relationship to negative theology."

58. Cupitt, *Mysticism after Modernity*, 99.
59. Jantzen, *Becoming Divine*, 13.

light" itself.[60] Other authors also play with the Gnostic idea of becoming divine. Thus, even though Jantzen's version of deconstructionist feminism may sound rather extreme, it does have certain parallels in feminist Jesus-novels. Furthermore, Jantzen's utopia is no longer just a language game where the meaning of a sign does not touch reality. Instead, she presents a postmodern metanarrative which introduces a new class struggle and aims at a revolutionary rejection of patriarchal subordination. At the end of feminist novels such as Roberts's, Fredriksson's, and Berlinghof's, the only sin that people need to exorcise is male domination. Its corruption has spoiled the Christian church and holds it imprisoned in a circle of violence. This is approximately what Jantzen claims even though her rhetoric is more severe than that of the novels.

In such a setting, Christian theology becomes an epistemology of darkness, as Winquist says. "We must deliberately choose to go into the night of our experience to be hearers of the unsaid word."[61] For him, language can never reach beyond its limits. In poststructuralist theory language remains caught in the general code of the linguistic system. Therefore explicated theology becomes a language game, a discourse that has no counter points in reality. "Theology can be thought of as an experience, but it is an experience of itself internal to language."[62] According to Winquist, religions attempt to put into words the "epiphanies of darkness" human beings meet when facing the ultimate questions of life. This leads to the polytheism favoured also by Roberts and Fredriksson.

> When theology talks about God, the Brahman, ultimate reality, or Holy Nothingness instead of talking about talking about God, the exigencies of the unrestricted desire to know force the question to the gap between immediate experience and meaning into awareness. *Theology's god is always a god of the gaps.*[63]

Therefore, the statement, found in several Jesus-novels, that God is a fountain of life inside each person's heart does actually coincide with

---

60. Roberts, *Wild Girl*, 59.

61. Winquist, *Epiphanies of Darkness*, 41.

62. Ibid., 83. I use the word "theory" here despite the fact that in this context it is a contradiction in terms. Poststructuralists hate theory since even the concept fights against their view on transcendental meaning. Their only problem is that they consistently construct theories that are applied in particular issues—a problem that is well recognised in philosophy of science.

63. Ibid., 99.

poststructuralist mysticism in the death-of-God movement. It becomes an expression of negative theology, and attempts to find traces of the divine among the fallible and errant signs of extant religions. Also the dissolving of the traditional Christian concept of God, or at least the speculation on the polytheistic view by paralleling the Christian God with other gods, is related to the death of the sign, the God-sign. For instance, Fredriksson, like Winquist, claims that the different ancient Middle Eastern gods are all quite similar.

It is only logical that there are no doctrines in the new mysticism that some of the Jesus-novels reflect. Since the true nature of God in this apophatic tradition cannot be put into words, God must always remain a mystery. Therefore, according to the novels, any expression of personal belief in the context of any religion must be considered as genuine as any other. The authors admit no restrictions in describing the ineffable. This also justifies the contrast with the religion of the male apostles. The male version of Christianity is dismissed because the apostles break the rule. They demand strict definitions and orthodox dogmas. This is why there is, in the novels, an irreconcilable conflict between Mary Magdalene's church and the apostolic church.

One important change since the days of Meister Eckhart and his colleagues takes place in the apophatic tradition, though. These medieval theologians still read the Bible and believed that it was divine revelation. Their mysticism is in accordance with the message of the Bible and is located in the meditative context of ecclesial liturgy.[64] Poststructuralist philosophers see a discontinuity here. For them, there is no revelation. All words about God are just useless signs that remain imprisoned in the system of language. Their apophatic theology becomes epistemological scepticism. Jesus-novels such as Fredriksson's *According to Mary* and Roberts's *The Wild Girl* base their mysticism precisely on such a poststructuralist interpretation. Therefore, their new mysticism that blossoms in Mary Magdalene's polytheist theology is related with Altizer's atheist radicalism and Winquist's epiphanies of darkness.

The new mysticism of many of the investigated novels is Nietzschean in the sense that the apophatic death-of-God a/theology builds on Nietzschean premises. An author can surely write a Jesus-novel without reading any of the books written by Nietzsche, Altizer, Cupitt, or Winquist. The purpose of this analysis is not to claim that

64. Schmidt, "Eckehart," 304–5.

there is direct influence between such monographs and the Jesus-novels. The main purpose of the comparison is to show that, in the same period, similar descriptions concerning the death of meaning have appeared. They all reject biblical doctrine and replace it with a new mysticism where different conceptions of God merge into one. Religious experience is directed towards one's own heart, the innermost feelings. It is a matter of opinion whether this is an expression of genuine tolerance or narcissistic subjectivism.

Thus the new gospel writers' recourse to third-century Gnosticism is to be expected. Gnostic writings represent almost everything a critical author could wish for: they rely partly on the New Testament, they stand in sharp opposition to the canonical Gospels, and they transfer divine salvation from history to personal experience and secret wisdom. Gnostic wisdom is not apophatic, not without words, though. In this respect it is not just mysticism on the level of pure experience. Instead, it has been written down. It has produced both a cosmological view and a tension between the evil Creator and the spiritual Divinity. It is based on strict doctrines. Pure mysticism, however, is not what these Jesus-novels even require. Instead, they are quite content with the possibility of using words, concepts, doctrines, ideologies, and worldviews. A true apophatic tradition would have been an irritating nuisance for them. The canonical Jesus needs a foil. There must be a real alternative for him, one that is also verbally explicated. This is probably why Gnosticism is a perfect basis for a reinterpretation of the canonical tradition.

8

Iconoclastic Intertextualism

Reading the controversial Jesus-novels of the 1980s and 1990s may be a confusing experience. The stories resemble those of the New Testament but the images they create through intertextual comparisons are often dark and desperate. These ideas do not usually appear explicitly in the narrative as it is but, instead, they form the basis for its literary strategy. Because of this, they can be a bit deceptive initially. A thematic treatment of such strategies will conclude this analysis on recent Jesus-novels.

1. READING HISTORY BACKWARDS

On the basis of a preliminary reading, the Jesus-novels by Saramago, Mailer, Roberts, and Fredriksson sound philanthrophic and idealistic. One could even consider them contemplative and philosophical. Their criticism is hidden, as it is in Nietzsche's *Thus Spoke Zarathustra*. In these novels, Jesus appears to be a nice chap attempting to cope with the practical questions of how to live a Jewish life. Admittedly, he is no orthodox Jew. He is more like an icon of the social awareness of left-wing humanism, or an ideologue of postmodern Judaism, rather than a practitioner of profoundly religious beliefs. So during the narrative, this Galilean treats questions concerning God and salvation as a postmodern ideologue.

But in the novels' intertextual reality things are different. Behind the inversive adaptations there is an implied interpretation of the original gospel story. According to these emancipated authors at the turn of the millennium, original Christianity represents a patriarchal and violent slave morality. The New Testament with its theistic claims supports a false view of divinity. Furthermore, its casuistic view of life has deprived divinity of its proper mystery. And since the story portrays the deification of Jesus it has separated him from ordinary people, that is, if we collect all the different features in the novels together and force them into one imaginative ideological pattern. There are, thus, influential literary strategies working in these writings, and they have several recognisable features.

One effective form of adaptation and a strategy for rewriting the gospel narrative is that of writing later history into the story itself.[1] There are several different possibilities for reading later history back in Jesus-novels. The combative, negative, rhetorical discourses already bring current ideologies into the ancient gospel story. For many writers, Christianity represents a pitiable discourse that suppresses maturity and independence. This results in a new interpretation of Jesus as the saviour of the marginalised, or of Jesus as a proto-feminist. Some scholars call this "actualisation" but this term apparently works better in German or Spanish than English.[2]

The method of rewriting in these novels is most similar to feminist interpretive appropriation where women are written into history anew. For instance, Roberts, Berlinghof, and Fredriksson construct a patriarchal Christianity that prevents women from expressing their religious convictions in their own manner, just in order to tear it down. Feminist ideology is contrasted with the early church and old statutes are overturned. When Christianity is on trial, it turns out be a system that oppresses women and supports a male dominated community. Therefore women must be written into the history of the church, and this usually done by making Mary Magdalene, one of the early leaders of the community. She represents the alleged Gnostic branch of Christian tradition and preserves what is supposed to be Jesus' original and genuine teaching.[3]

---

1. Cf. Wesseling, *Writing History*, 164–65.

2. In this way Peña: "El aspecto de *actualización*, por otro lado, viene especialmente señalado por la posición del narrador, quien continuamente se refiere a ideas, reflexiones y comentarios que cronológicamente son muy posteriores a los hechos que se narran." [The aspect of *actualisation,* on the other hand, is especially notable for the position of the narrator who continuously refers to ideas, reflections and comments that are chronologically much later than the events of which he narrates.] Peña, *José Saramago o la intertextualidad inversa*, 28. According to Peña, mythical aspects are useful in referring to realities that reflect contemporary society.

3. See the discussion in chapter 4.4. Anderson remarks that this is a wide phenomenon in recent feminist literature: "Like Rosamund Meridew's, the quest of many

In the same way, then, other novels make deliberately anachronistic moves and bring elements from later church history into the narrative. This most often devolves into iconoclasm where the biblical God and Christian doctrines are attacked. One can detect the Nietzschean spirit here through the condemnation of Christian doctrines as dangerous for or even destructive of human beings. In fierce opposition to the church's own self-understanding, church history is regarded as proof of the ontological corruptness of Christianity. Doctrinal faith is essentially violent and evil. It destroys humankind whenever it can, and it binds Christians to habits and regulations that deny and oppress their maturity and independence.

For instance, Saramago alludes to Voltaire's disciples who easily detect that, in God's world, "purity can only be maintained so long as there are innocent creatures to sacrifice in this world."[4] Such an enlightened reading of sacrificial religion exposes the dark core of Christian faith and biblical teaching. Similarly, others such as Freud, Jung, Groddeck, and Lacan can be consulted when describing the mental capacities of the young Jesus, who, according to Saramago's novel, "may not be exactly a genius or luminary," but, nevertheless, is a persistent seeker of new insights.[5]

Such a use of persons more or less of the present age is, however, not yet a new reading of history. The method becomes clearer when real history is brought into the narrative. Saramago does this especially when he treats the theme of suffering in relation to Jesus' death. Saramago's Jesus asks God what will happen after his death since God has revealed that Jesus' death is part of a larger plan of usurping other gods' places. "I'm waiting. . . . For You to tell me how much death and suffering Your victory over other gods will cost, how much suffering and death will be

---

recent feminist historians has been to recover women's submerged or unrealized past." Anderson, "History," 130. She recognises, however, that there are theoretical problems involved in this: "One of the paradoxes that we face is that even as poststructuralist theory frees us from paradigms which underwrite the (masculine) subject, it catches us back in theoretical toils in which we can also lose ourselves and thus renews our need to reach beyond texts into the materiality of our lives" (135).

4. Saramago, *Gospel*, 67.

5. Ibid., 146. Krysinski remarks that Saramago, as a representative of the Enlightenment ("En homme des Lumières, matérialiste, communiste, sceptique et ironiste de surcroît"), reconstructs a history where you have all the reason to doubt. Krysinski, "Observations," 407.

needed to justify the battles men will fight in Your name and mine." In his answer God states that "the assembly I mentioned will be founded, but in order to be truly solid, its foundations will be dug out in flesh, and the bases made from the cement of abnegation, tears, suffering, torment, every conceivable form of death known or as yet unrevealed."[6] The church's violent history will prove that the God of the Bible is a violent God who—as Camus along with numerous atheists would put it—is either unwilling or incapable of preventing such course of history.[7]

Next come the crusades and the Inquisition. In these phases of history thousands of heretics, infidels, and adherents to other religions will be massacred. Saramago's God attacks Lutherans and Calvinists, Molinists and Judaisers. The Inquisition is a "necessary evil" needed so that God can proceed with his plans.[8] Traditional oppositions are reversed in Saramago's deconstruction. What was previously considered the work of church's enemies is now God's own work. There must, of course, be a rationale for this. According to a rather conventional deistic speculation based on natural religion, the world as such must be completely under the guidance of the omnipotent God. If there are problems in God's world, he can be held responsible for them. By using this traditional problem of theodicy Saramago identifies even the violence against the church as God's work. The church's own horrors, the Crusades and the Inquisition, further this view. The church's mistakes are described as a deterministic history where God produces evil in the conventional pattern: if human beings sin, God is to be held responsible.

Such an approach resembles poststructuralist deconstruction, which is based on polarising principles. These "binary oppositions," namely conceptions of good and evil, God and Devil, justice and injustice, are turned into their opposites.[9] In early poststructuralist theory, the idea was that opposites in a "binary opposition" gradually turn out to be identical. Jesus-novels do not stop here. God not only looks like the Devil, he becomes evil. In the spirit of this exchange then, divine features are actually transferred onto human beings, or even onto the Devil.

---

6. Saramago, *Gospel*, 290.

7. This is the passage where Saramago introduces his long list of the church's martyrs; see chapter 5.1.

8. Saramago, *Gospel*, 291–92.

9. Kaufman assumes that binary oppositions function as an organising principle for the whole narrative. Kaufman, "Evangelical Truths," 454.

All sinful characteristics, as mentioned, are laid on God. Therefore, the intertextual strategy in many of these novels is not precisely deconstructive but inversive. This is a Nietzschean strategy based on the conviction that Christianity is a slavish religion.[10]

Saramago's God is dead. He is dead in the way of Nietzsche's God: "We have killed him." Were anyone to prove the existence of the biblical God, Saramago, like his nihilist predecessor, would be even less willing to confess him. There is no rescue and return from the Galilean lake where the boat became a floating courthouse, and where the heteronymic divinities stood accused, no escape and no justification for a later devout worship in the church.[11] Therefore, as Teresa Cristina Cerdeira has noted, Saramago's novel is sacrilegious because it does not invent a different story in order to illuminate the difficult problems of pain and the fate of humankind. It is sacrilegious because he presents the very same history and the same characters and unflinchingly condemns them.[12]

In Mailer's *Gospel According to the Son* there are some short passages where history is read backwards. These descriptions, however, are much more conventional than Saramago's statements. On one occasion Mailer comments on Jesus' saying: "Render to Caesar the things that are Caesar's. And to God the things that belong to God." The Jesus of the story wonders whether God has decided to allow churches "to grow in the swamps of pride and Mammon." "While many a church would survive in evil lands by giving homage to Caesar, I was not here to build churches but to bring sinners to salvation."[13]

The question in Mailer's example is vaguely similar to that of Saramago's criticism. It is the question about power and authority, which Tunström too often treats. But Mailer, like Tunström, remains on a safe level. They do criticise the possibility of the church becoming just an-

---

10. As Emery noted, Saramago's Devil appears as Prometheus who combats God in the name of liberty. Emery, "Pasteur," 81; see chapter 2.2.

11. Bloom assumed that only a fool would claim such a thing (see chapter 6.3; Bloom, "One with the Beard," 155). This, however, is not the case. Saramago's Nietzschean intention proves that he is not playing with words. What would be left of the novel should one hold the idea of a bloodthirsty God as just a fabulous joke? Saramago's magical realism is realism, real reality where people die and are buried. He keeps looking for those who are guilty of violence. In the end the author, or at least the narrator, becomes one with the cosmic prosecutor of this new gospel.

12. Cerdeira da Silva, "Saramago," 251.

13. Mailer, *Gospel*, 159.

other ruler attempting to acquire as much power as it can and serve Mammon. Their answer is conventional enough, though. It is rooted in Jesus' original canonical message, which should be able to prevent the church from falling. This lags far behind Saramago's fierce attack and inversive interpretation.[14]

In his prototypical rewriting, Mailer does apply a strategy that openly reads history backwards. As we saw already in his construction of the subtext, Mailer presents Jesus as a deeply divided personality. Jesus does not know where his words come from and what the power with which he is invested is. Two different men struggle inside him. Thus, Mailer's Jesus is simultaneously both the canonical figure and his agnostic reader. In the novel, Mailer's modern scepticism is disguised as theological doceticism. Jesus in Mailer's new story is simply on a journey where everything ends well. Therefore, the narrator's status is steadfast. While Mailer's risen Jesus appears as the divine narrator, he is also the omniscient narrator, privy to every detail of history. The person Mailer describes, the Jesus-character of the story, is alive only in the Christian story. Hence, Mailer's description of Jesus is dependent on a Nietzschean dichotomy between slave morality and modern scepticism. The risen Jesus must write his story anew, but when he does, his character turns into a rationalist agnostic who cannot accept any Christian doctrines or any of his original teachings—despite all the lengthy quotations found in the subtext.

Furthermore, in the post-Holocaust world, one would expect at least some of the authors to comment on Christianity's historical attitude towards the Jews. Postmodern moralism has often warned against the ancient, anti-Semitic accusation of Jews as the murderers of Jesus. This theme appears solely in Fredriksson's novel, and even there its treatment is somewhat vague. In the end of the story Leonidas, Mary Magdalene's benefactor, speculates on the reasons for Jesus' execution and transfers the responsibility to the Roman authorities. "Do you think a Roman governor would let himself be influenced by a screaming mob? Jesus was condemned as an agitator after a Roman trial and sentenced to crucifixion, a punishment only the Romans use."[15] This short statement

---

14. Ibid., 159–60; cf. Tunström, *Ökenbrevet*, 196.

15. Fredriksson, *According to Mary*, 148–49. The statement in itself is not in accordance with historical evidence. In Jerusalem, for instance, the Jewish Hasmonean ruler Alexander Jannaeus crucified hundreds of Pharisees and so destroyed political opposition a few generations before Jesus' time. Saldarini, "Pharisees," 292.

implies, at the very least, that the traditional picture of Jews as persecutors of Jesus was wrong. Such a presentation is rare in contemporary Jesus-novels, though. Even Mailer, who himself comes from a Jewish background, does not refer to this subject.

Instead, my analysis shows that the novels discussed adopt somewhat surprisingly anti-Judaist views. Both the Jewish way of conducting life and the traditional Jewish concept of God are considered erroneous in these books. These views are probably not intentional in every novel but, even in the feminist novels, which want to portray the best of positive humanism, these views sneak in under the radar. Hence, we can detect one more method of reading history backwards in these stories. Instead of defending Judaism against the church's later accusations, these contrast-novels adopt anti-Judaist attitudes and describe Judaism as a slavish religion. This reversal exposes the vast influence Nietzsche has had on the whole of enlightened criticism on Christianity. It also raises the question of ethical reading, which will be dealt with below.[16]

Such examples expose the technique by which Christian history is anachronistically written into these latter-day gospels. The events of history become the means for an inversion of the Christian narrative. The revision itself is made, as Ben-Porat has suggested, as prototypical rewriting. Original Gospel material serves as the basis for the intertextual change and the measuring stick for faithful representations: "the fidelity of the rewriting to its origin at the points of diversion."[17] This can call to one's awareness, for instance, the relocation of Jesus' words into a new context so that the original meaning is modified if not changed into its opposite. When the whole narrative or train of thought is reversed, the elements of the original biblical story are usually still present just drastically altered. This happens when the Good Shepherd becomes Pastor/the Devil in Saramago's story. The Old Testament Messiah of the prophets turns into the new messenger that Hades has sent into this world. Even the Devil would convert to the Judeo-Christian tradition if God would just cancel his horrifying plans.

Kort has noted that postmodern moralism and "postmodernist discourses," as he calls them, tend to devalue the language of place and space and consider events as processes.[18] In this respect, these Jesus-novels are

16. See chapter 8.3.
17. Ben-Porat, "Prototypical Rewriting," 99.
18. Kort, "Religion," 581–82.

not purely postmodern since they go even further. Prototypical rewriting does separate moral issues from history but, simultaneously, it rewrites history. In contemporary Jesus-novels, place and space become the locus where critical moralism becomes flesh and when later history is written into the gospel story. Rehabilitated persons and rejected groups are rewritten directly into history. Hence, in Jesus-novels, processes are made part of history in deliberate chosen place and space.

Furthermore, these authors use prototypical rewriting as a justification for the reversal of traditional doctrinal hierarchies. Subversive imitation results in new readings of the canonical Bible. The present meaning of the Scriptures is something quite other than the descriptive content of the texts. All this justifies the hypothesis of the present analysis and the search for Nietzschean themes. The themes themselves are not merely Nietzsche's themes or ideas, but Nietzsch*ean*. In contrast-novels, any attack upon a patriarchal power structure or any claim about Christianity as a negation of life betrays the assumption that the Nietzschean description of biblical slave morality is accurate. Moreover, the authors' habit of justifying their claims with later Christian history proves that they still cling to a positivist "modern"—that is, historicist—view of the past, where the omniscient narrator knows both history and truth. In this respect, the authors create a story that cannot be doubted. Such attitude is a reminiscent of the Nietzschean choice: we decide! The authors' reasoning seems solid and their accusations valid, but only in a positivist setting where truth claims are certain and language reflects reality. This creates a tension between the very point of departure on the one hand, which in most cases is based on poststructuralist subjectivity and textual relativism, and hard-boiled historicism on the other hand, which appeals to history "as it really happened."[19] The existence of such a difficulty proves that these novels are not that far from the rationalist Jesus-novels investigated by Ziolkowski.

---

19. It is only natural that these novels reflect the great philosophical debates between positivism and poststructuralism, or empiricism and phenomenology. They belong to the cultural tradition where the epistemological search for truth has been a battlefield for very different approaches. Justification, on the one hand, has constantly been a matter of empiricism at least in some pragmatic form. Interpretation, on the other, has been a matter of treating phenomena. Proponents of the latter have not been able to justify their statements without some sort of empirical proof, and proponents of the former have long ago admitted that all data leaves room for interpretation. Ideological Jesus-novels do wish to play with interpretations but they still need to justify some of their literary inventions with ideas that derive from straightforward historicism.

Most of the investigated novels bring us to a court of law where God is on trial. Authors read history backwards and real events prove that the God of the Bible, even if only a mere fabrication with a terrible history of influence, is guilty of "creating" a violent culture. The gospel has not merely been about to Judaise the Western world but, rather, it has succeeded. The Christian world has been the world of inquisitions, mass murders, intrigues, patriarchy, exploitation and chauvinism. In this respect these novels conduct and complete Nietzsche's program of eradicating Christian tradition from our culture. The authors write against the metanarratives that form the basis of the vast Catholic-Protestant tradition.

2. THE REVERSAL OF ROLES

In recent Jesus-novels, authors happily play with traditional biblical roles but this is not done for fun. Despite the playfulness, the reversal is often quite serious, and this duality supports my hypothesis that such intertextual strategy is crucial for the ideological intention of the work. One of this study's interesting discoveries is that these novels come close to the original Nietzschean conviction that Jesus' character in the canonical Gospels is a literary creation.[20] And since we are dealing merely with a literary figure, it can be freely altered or changed on the basis of religious criticism challenging the standard Christian view. Jesus-novels written in the era of early twentieth-century historicism still attempted to detect a historically justifiable and scientifically solid picture of the founder of Christianity. In these revisions Jesus was made a model of altruist love or social responsibility. In the new situation the approach has changed. Recent Jesus-novels are picking a fight.

In contrast-novels the literary Jesus-figure found in the canonical Gospels is replaced by new constructions. The Christian story is replaced by a new story in which the human ways of interpreting religion have changed. The inversive adaptation is made to conflict with the original story. The definition of the contradiction is Nietzschean indeed. Both Christian moral values and religious beliefs are turned inside out. This approach is based on discontinuity, if not a clash of ideologies.

---

20. This was also the view of nineteenth century Protestant biblical scholarship, as we have noted earlier. Scholars assumed that there is a crucial difference between the Jesus of history and the invented, religious picture of the Jesus in the Gospels. See chapter 2.1.

To produce these inversions, the authors often employ the similar primary strategy of changing the main characters' traditional roles. Contrast-novels present provocative settings where not only the nature and integrity of subordinate characters are changed but also Jesus' traditional status is shaken. When Jesus' and Judas' roles are thus adapted, Judas becomes an upright man who is prepared to follow his understanding of justice to the bitter end. Integrity is attributed to Judas while Jesus, in turn, becomes a timid and hesitant person who wavers even before his own calling and mission. Judas may not be completely a man of God, but he is honest. Thus, Judas becomes a prototype of a post-Christian Western humanist whose ethical views surpass those of Jesus.[21]

Judas as a character and person is even well suited to the role of an agnostic since in the original story he denies Jesus and abandons his eschatological vision. This may be why Mailer's and Saramago's messages closely resemble both the ideas of death-of-God theology and aggressive atheism. Following in Nietzsche's footsteps, these ideologies proclaim that Christian values are harmful to human beings, and are a contradiction of life, as Nietzsche himself put it. Modern humanism, in turn, is held to be a mature way of life that recognises its responsibilities and duties in a democratic way. In atheist philosophy, liberal theology, and these conflict-novels, all good, humane beliefs and features previously attributed to Christianity are now attributed to humanism. The reversal is complete.[22]

Saramago takes this reversal to the limit. When the roles of God and the Devil are transposed, Christian religion as such is condemned. The Judeo-Christian God becomes what Nietzsche called the "angry Jehovah." The God of the *Anti-Christ* is a despot whose person and work should be considered a "crime against life" itself.[23] But again in Saramago's reversal one does not encounter mere deconstruction. The reversal of roles means making God evil. The God of the Bible starts to look like the Gnostic Demiurge, the hostile God of the Old Testament. Hence, the opposition is the same as it was over a 1500 years ago in Egyptian Gnosticism. Saramago's God of light, however, is no longer a

---

21. See chapter 3.1. above.

22. This view will further develop into the rewriting of biblical myths, and this ultimate form of inversive adaptation will be discussed below in section 4.

23. Nietzsche, *Gay Science*, § 137; *Anti-Christ*, § 47.

mystic power but the light of the Enlightenment, which becomes the opposite of the canonical divine Being.[24]

One might assume that feminist novels would never subscribe to such an opposition or dualism but it is obvious that Roberts and Fredriksson do accept the Gnostic view of divinity. The latter even accepts the Demiurge as the God of the Old Testament and has her characters challenge it. Their basic view about God then is anti-Judaist and implies that the God of the Old Testament represents the contradiction of love and justice. Mailer, in turn, is somewhat cautious about this issue, but he too has inverted the roles of God and the Devil to a certain degree. In his story God learns from the Devil—just as Jesus had when spending time with the Devil in the wilderness. After Easter God adopts the Devil's strategy of speaking. He begins to "preach the defeat as a victory." According to the novel, this move is a fraud. God is just attempting to salvage what he can after his original plan has been ruined.[25] This is Mailer's riff on the reversal of roles.

As noted before, the figure of Mary Magdalene is contrasted with several characters in the canonical Gospels. She is naturally a contradiction of the canonical Magdalene, who in reality had almost no role at all in the original story. She was just a silent follower of Jesus. In the Bible, she is a woman who has experienced a miracle, but she is not a harlot with a long history of working in a whorehouse, as she is for instance in Fredriksson's novel. In several contrast-novels, Mary Magdalene becomes almost a goddess of free sexuality. As Jesus' mistress she teaches the wonders of creation to this ignorant and insignificant ascetic figure who appears to have no knowledge whatsoever of God's real world.[26]

Furthermore, Mary's figure in the novels is contrasted with the biblical character of Jesus. As the founder of the Gnostic sect, a true line of Jesus' heritage, she becomes the source of salvation. She is contrasted with male apostles who, according to Roberts and Fredriksson, cannot teach the proper message of the kingdom. Men in these novels pervert Christianity and make it a dogmatic system of doctrines. They confine Christians to a slavish religion, which prevents them from finding true

---

24. For Pires-O'Brien this leads to the conclusion "that Christianity is simply the anathema of Jesus's life, a damned assembly, even though it was engendered by 'God.'" Pires-O'Brien, "Novel View," 187.

25. Mailer, *According to the Son*, 241.

26. See chapter 4.1 above.

joy in their life. Both Roberts and Fredriksson make Jesus the source of true Gnostic religiosity, which allows different ways of expressing one's inner experience.

Therefore, in feminist novels, Jesus starts to acquire feminine features if not the Magdalene's particular properties. The reversal works in two directions. Jesus teaches gnosis, which is understood as feminine knowledge, a kind of heavenly *sofia*-wisdom, which is sensitive and dedicated to unity and tolerance. Judaism, Christianity, the religion of Isis, and Indian religions will eventually turn out to be identical, and real wisdom recognises this already now. The essence of a universal religion, for this Jesus, is everywhere the same. Jesus the feminist represents everything that opposes male dogmatism. In the philosophy of religion, such belief is defined as monism, so such a description implicates theology. Feminist Jesus-novels oppose the Christian dualism that proclaims the contradiction between sin and grace.[27]

In the inversive adaptation of recent Jesus-novels Mary Magdalene is also, at least to some extent, contrasted with Jesus' mother Mary. The Magdalene acquires features that the mother Mary has in Christian tradition. She is close to Jesus and takes care of his needs. Her character is filled out with many new features: she becomes a gentle and faithful woman who eventually is the founding pillar of Christianity. In Roberts's novel she even composes hymns, which the church can sing later. Thus she inherits the role of the woman who presents her Magnificat for the Christian community.

When assessing these two stratagems, the anachronistic reading of later history back into the gospels and the characters' role reversals in comparison to the canonical stories, one gets the distinct impression that for the authors Jesus is but a symbol for a contemporary man. He is post-Christian, and his enlightened education makes him question Judeo-Christian tradition and the Mosaic Law. He is not usually even engaged by any remarkable ideology, unless feminism or Western humanism can be so described. He appears to have less purpose in his doings than the novels' authors. In many respects, the Jesus-figures of Mailer and Saramago are quite shallow and narrow-minded. His metanarratives have died. Since he no longer believes in the "Law and the Prophets" he has no eschatology and no real message for salvation, and so he begins to resemble previous rationalist Jesus-figures. In many

---

27. See especially Fredriksson, *According to Mary*, 151–54; and chapter 4.3.

cases his primary purpose appears to be the breaking of the conservative Jewish community's taboos.

3. JESUS BEYOND GOOD AND EVIL: AN ETHICAL READING

In many of the investigated novels Jesus moves beyond good and evil, at least as far as the traditional Christian view on ethics is considered. He opposes the Mosaic Law, the Old Testament. In this new estimation, as also emphasised by his legacy in Mary Magdalene's memoires, Jewish precepts are only restrictive commands that have no justifiable purpose in everyday life. According to the appropriation of the feminist novels, these precepts are furthermore assumed to be patriarchal and to be maintaining male dominion in Church. A summary of recent Jesus-novels could state that God's law is the opposite of love. The Jesus-figure of the novels attacks this oppressive law and proclaims a new version of a loving message.

The novels' treatment of particular ethical subjects is somewhat ambivalent, though, as in Nietzsche's writings. Sexuality is a clear example of where the new Jesus-figure often explores frontiers his canonical predecessor never broached. While Mary Magdalene often becomes Jesus' mistress, they never establish a clearly defined and committed relationship, to say nothing of marriage. Only in Roberts's and Brown's novels so Jesus and Mary have a child. The new Jesus-figure, or at least Mary Magdalene following his command, rails against the biblical view on sexual morals. On other issues, however, the fictive Jesus still stands behind conservative values. He is honest and avoids violence. He supports the poor and heals the sick. However, he never adopts the "hard and frightening" values Nietzsche suggested in his *Herrenmoral*. Therefore, it is not easy to know exactly what these novels mean when they oppose the Mosaic commandments. These authors claim the will to power and contest only (post)modern sins: patriarchy and chauvinism.

This is also what connects these novels with postmodern moralism. Each novel presents the reader with a *perfect moralist*, be it the narrator, as in Saramago's work, or the author, as in Mailer's *Gospel*.[28] In Fredriksson's novel the perfect moralist is one of the characters, predict-

---

28. Saramago's narrator is difficult to identify. He could even be the Devil who appears to know everything and is as well informed about events as the narrator (or even the author). The risen Jesus himself is Mailer's narrator and, therefore, one must conclude that the perfect moralist in this novel is simply the author.

ably Mary Magdalene. She is responsible for the most ethical discernment in the narrative, and Roberts's Mary is in a similar position. These books are morality novels because their perfect moralists know the distinction between right and wrong perfectly.[29] The aim of these stories is almost without exception to make things right. The sins of Christianity, or even the "sins of Scripture," as Spong once put it, must be dealt with. In a Nietzschean setting the perfect moralist performs his or her task and criticises Christian ethics and the church's morality.[30]

As the investigated novels appear to be ethical readings of the Bible, how should one attempt an ethical reading of the novels themselves?[31] How should one assess Jesus-novels that contradict Christian ethics with post-Christian humanism? The extolling of traitors and the straightforward acceptance of the lifestyle of the masses are features that need to be addressed, especially because the novels justify their inversions via ethical reasoning. God becoming a symbol for evil and his law becoming a list of selfish demands are intertextual changes that possess ideological content. Even though some of these cases were unintentional, their occurrence must be subjected to ethical assessment.

In the novels, the enlightened culture of the West opposes the stagnation of Jewish/Christian religion that clings to its commandments, slavish attitude, and negative view of humankind. This is precisely what Saramago, Roberts, and Mailer are doing. Both the intertextual changes they have made and the utopia they propose reveal a split that can no longer be reconciled. Instead of defending the weak, or supporting those discriminated against, the authors' Christianity rejects the rejected and oppresses the oppressed. The followers of Jesus have not really been able to help the marginalised, or to promote feminism. Tunström searches after higher morals, and Mailer's Judas criticises Jesus for forgetting the poor. Roberts makes Jesus represent the opposite of biblical chastity, and

---

29. Even Saramago belongs to these moralists; see Klobucka, "Introduction," xix.

30. There is an interesting parallel for these novels in nineteenth-century Swedish literature where Strindberg, Hansson, and Heidenstam have openly adopted Nietzsche's ideas. In his analysis Harold Borland mentions their interest especially in Nietzsche's "militant individualism," but also that his hatred of Christianity has had its consequences. Borland, *Nietzsche's Influence*, 133–36.

31. For the distinction between ethical *reading* and ethical *readings* see the Introduction above.

Fredriksson depicts him as a defender of free sexuality. Christianity has reached its finale.[32]

In good Nietzschean style, anything negative within humanity is considered the result of religion as such. This interpretation rests on a claim that the dualism between good and evil, as well as the idea of salvation through a Jewish Messiah, to say nothing of a final battle between God and this world on the day of wrath, are only products of ancient mythical religiosity. Since the Bible, and in this case especially the original Jesus-story, demonises natural desires and perverts our understanding of humanity and human beings, it must be opposed. False metaphysics ruins all genuine life. Hence the ancient myths of the Bible needed to be altered and written anew. Saramago's Jesus, for instance, learns a spirit of refusal from the Devil and becomes a rebel who finally joins Satan in his campaign against God's planned history of violence. He also joins Nietzsche's followers who "admit to a *joy* in saying No."[33]

Therefore also the greatest metanarrative, that of the cosmic battle between God and Satan, is transformed in the novels. Since some of them focus on the Devil, making him Jesus' teacher or the twin brother of God, a reference to Faust is thus also proper. Saramago makes the Devil attempt to save the world from the bloody hands of the violent God. Now neither Jesus nor the church are justified in their missions. The traditional polarities on which he had based his message were only binary oppositions that must now be dissolved. The Devil is not to be blamed for the horrors of this world. Life must be interpreted according to natural causes, and if God is to be taken into account, he will inevitably be written into the role of a cruel divine Being.

This is still theology of a sort, despite the nihilistic downplay of traditional theological themes. It can be called negative theology, at least in the sense the death-of-God writers used the term. In these novels we meet an ideology that resembles that of Altizer, writing his *Gospel of Christian Atheism* and proclaiming that religion in a modern sense can

---

32. Kaufman describes Saramago's Jesus. "He is defeated because he fails to perform a truly revolutionary act: to overturn the patriarchal structure itself." Kaufman, "Evangelical Truths," 457.

33. Frier, "Outline," 376: "The spirit of refusal to accept the inevitability of what exists and the notion of the ongoing perfectibility of God's creation, in a sense the spirit which always says 'no,' is as essential to successful human existence as are the qualities more traditionally associated with goodness . . ." Cf. Nietzsche, *Beyond Good and Evil*, § 210.

begin anew only after the previous versions have been destroyed. The biblical God, the heavenly person who guides all humankind and all history, is not to be accepted as the centre of enlightened faith.[34] Taylor called it the "epidemic play of perversity" that "subverts the opposition between the sacred and profane." This is common secularised theology where a/theology confesses only immanent values.[35]

Traditional theologians, however, would probably say that these authors misrepresent the ideas of the New Testament and Christian doctrine. They make straw men that are easy to fight and to overcome. In a theological sense this is apparently true, at least for certain issues. Christian faith is famous enough for the concepts of mercy and forgiveness. A transition to depicting faith as fear or oppression is not consistent unless something essential is changed on the level of basic beliefs. The crucial contradiction arises only when, in the ideology of the new reading, there is nothing left to forgive. The concept of mercy may be turned inside out, but this cannot be done in terms of Christian theology but only by distorting its premises and its purposes.

The question about the nature of the novels' morality is not easy, though. In practice, the authors adopt rather conservative Christian morals when writing about different ethical subjects, at least apart from the details on which their polarisations are constructed. In these passages the Jesus of the novels seldom differs from the canonical Jesus the friend of sinners or Jesus the one who emphasises with the despised. Mailer's Jesus keeps performing miracles and helping the disabled. Tunström's Jesus is actually quite sympathetic, and Fredriksson's Nazarene is a delicate preacher. Even in Saramago's novel the main theme of speculating on the Bethlehem massacre reveals that salvation history can be deconstructed on ethical grounds. Joseph did not do his duty and prevent the killing even though he clearly had a chance to do so.[36] Similarly, Mailer makes Jesus, in spite of his friendly nature, betray the poor. If Camus already rejected God in the name of morality, these novelists follow in his footsteps.

This is the reason why authors have had to rely on a reduced subtext in order to build an effective contradiction between the canonical Gospels and the new narrative. It is not easy to work with the canonical

---

34. For negative theology, see chapter 7.4.
35. Taylor, *Erring*, 169.
36. Saramago, *Gospel*, 81.

Gospels since they do not provide enough material for an effective contradiction. Excluding sexuality, relevant subjects are few. In the novels, the line between good and evil remains in its traditional place. Violence is wrong and deprivation is deprivation. Moses' stone tablets are not broken after all. In practice it is not so easy to be revolutionary when renewing the Jesus-character since, as some scholars have said previously, the original story as such is not that poor.[37]

In certain respects, then, these authors have been inventing their own enemies. When writing their narratives, they accidentally identify themselves with their alleged opponent, the canonical Jesus-figure. This was Nietzsche's problem as well, since both in essays and in *Zarathustra* he arrived at ethics that were quite conservative. In his novel the great nihilist speaks about love and even about an altruistic state of mind. Love makes the world go round. Authors of the Jesus-novels are in danger of inadvertently running parallel with the original text and of their Jesus being compared with the canonical Jesus. They are compelled to compete with Jesus, and thus they corner themselves into needing to be better saviours than the Nazarene. This, one must acknowledge, may prove difficult.[38]

Because genuine opposition on moral issues is actually rare, the attitudes towards Judaism rise above other problems. It is evident that in most of the investigated novels Judaism is depicted in negative terms. Jewish doctrines are held to be irrational, Jewish morality as a part of the abovementioned restrictive law is considered inhuman, and the Jewish conception of God horrible. The Old Testament God especially in Saramago's novel is a monster. But even in the tolerant feminist novels Jewish precepts are considered poisonous. The original Jesus in the canonical Gospels is not free from this sickness since "he was a Jew," as Nietzsche said. Intertextual polarisation in these contrast-novels sets up an opposition between the original Jewish Jesus and the new European humanist Jesus.[39]

---

37. In the Finnish discussion, this remark has been made by Envall, *Pitkä marssi*, 44–45.

38. Nietzsche's ideas were treated in detail in the Introduction above.

39. There has been a straightforward rehabilitation of Nietzsche taking place among philosophers towards the end of the twentieth century, as Plotnitsky points out: "In contrast to our views of Nietzsche even a few decades ago, the subject of Hebraism in Nietzsche no longer appears unorthodox. This change results from massive rethinking of his work during recent decades, which included a sustained exploration of connec-

This kind of approach is unavoidably anti-Judaist. Despite all the post-Holocaust remorse the literary community may have concerning Judaism—not the least of which is Mailer's own agony about it, ironically—these novels are not tolerant. To paraphrase Saramago's Pastor: they have not learned a thing. They forbid Jewish faith a place in Western society. One finds no traces of the new attitude towards Judaism that is so prevalent in biblical studies and scholarly investigations of the historical Jesus.[40] The novels go beyond presenting just an ideological rival to Judaism. They call their opponent dangerous. The novels hold that Jewish beliefs and habits are unhealthy for any one following them. According to the inversive adaptation of biblical passages, the original religion represents slave morality and, therefore, it must now be fought against by means of poetry. This is quite open in Saramago's *Gospel*, where God is made to look like the Devil and his world is made to look like a slaughterhouse, but one can detect similar features in Mailer's novel. In feminist novels, the presence of these issues may be partly unintentional but, nevertheless, they are very clear in passages where Jesus' teaching is presented in opposition to Old Testament law and standard Jewish beliefs are contrasted with the novels' Gnostic ideology.[41]

The basic question of ethical reading goes as follows: Is it proper for the novels to adopt Nietzschean principles that elsewhere create ideological problems? We face the problem posed by Camus that was discussed in previous chapters. Camus had stated that we must become

---

tions between Nietzsche and Hebraism, his uncompromising critique of anti-Semitism, and related issues." Plotnitsky, "Zarahustra's Ladders," 200–201. I see this merely as secondary rationalisation for the poststructuralist movement. Nothing can mitigate Nietzsche's furious rejection of the so-called Jewish slave morality in all of his works from *The Gay Science* to *The Anti-Christ*.

40. Such a view is thus confirmed when compared with postwar theology, where attitudes changed and scholars deliberately aimed at a rehabilitation both of Judaism and Jewish studies, as noted in chapter 2.3.

41. The famous Jewish writer Hans Jonas reminds us that, for Jews, the Holocaust was about dehumanisation: "Dehumanization by utter degradation and deprivation preceded their dying, no glimmer of dignity was left to the freights bound for the final solution, hardly a trace of it was found in the surviving skeleton specters of the liberated camps. And yet, paradox of paradoxes: it *was* the ancient people of the 'covenant,' no longer believed in by those involved, killers and victims alike, but nevertheless just this and no other people, under which the fiction of race had been chosen for this wholesale annihilation—the most monstrous inversion of election into curse, which defied all possible endowment with meaning." Jonas, *Mortality and Morality*, 133. Jesus-novels have not been able to free themselves of such an attitude.

"the advocates for the defence of Nietzsche," even thought he knew well that this has its dangers. In developing the rebellion, he then admits: "In a certain sense, rebellion, with Nietzsche, ends again in the exaltation of evil."[42] Reaching beyond good and evil inevitably leads beyond loving one's neighbor. It is not possible to reject Christian ethics without abandoning its precepts.

When assessing the rejection of slave morality there are at least two questions that need to be dealt with. Firstly, what is the new standard, and secondly, how far are the authors ready to go in their search for the new human independence? The first can be answered rather easily. It is to be found unequivocally in the idealist formulations of European Enlightenment humanism. Ever since the French Revolution's arrogant attacks against the Christian church, individual freedom and moral independence have been the abstract ideas that have been contrasted with Christian tradition. Nietzsche had little to contribute to this when writing within his own polarisations. The philosophy of religion's classical problem here is that these new values are highly abstract and hard to apply practically.

How far did Nietzsche himself go? Already in the short analysis of Nietzsche's ideas in the Introduction we noted that his rebellion was somewhat irrational. For instance, in his *Zarathustra* Nietzsche actually had recourse to the Christian conception of love and even ended up championing an altruistic code of conduct. In a sense then, the very contradiction between *Sklavenmoral* and *Herrenmoral* is fictive, based on an imagined feeling that any speech about sin sounds restrictive to independent humanists and exposes religious power structures.

In reality, in real moral issues that is, it is difficult to find authors who would suggest violence or fraud as proper ethical norms to be followed. This is a common difficulty in atheist discourse as well. Only a few proponents of natural religion argue that violence may be good for the evolution of humankind in the long run. Other atheists soon silence these voices, though. In the investigated Jesus-novels, even lying is usually held to be immoral, and the authors often speak of truth and justice.[43]

---

42. Camus, *Rebel*, 66.

43. For the discussion of recent atheists, see Beattie, *New Atheists*, esp. 76–79. John Gray belongs to the few who support violent naturalism; Gray, *Straw Dogs*, 110–12. Onfray, in turn, speaks of the need of atheist atheism, which is no longer trapped in Christian concepts. Onfray, *Atheist Manifesto*, 214–19.

The problem of ethical reading is not off the hook, though. As long as these novels apply inversive adaptations in a Nietzschean spirit it is justified to ask how far they are willing to go. One must not forget that Nietzsche's original polarisation resulted in "hard and frightening" values. He was ready to twist the knife despite the pain—at least in his philosophical ponderings. And many were to appear who followed his Master morality, creating an ideology that fostered what we now consider the darkest pages of Western history. What is the ethical responsibility of these authors in the present post-Holocaust situation?[44]

The final result of applying an ethical reading to these contrast-novels reveals that they cannot be read as neutral, impartial acts of the imagination. They cannot be seen merely as offering inspiring and entertaining new insights into our Christian tradition. They do not merely play with deconstructive ideas where any thesis calls for an antithesis or any writing asks for a rewriting. Instead, they fall into the Nietzschean tradition where the opposition to an alleged slave morality implies a potential exaltation of evil, a possibility of supporting murder and violence. This has to be said on a very theoretical level. On a practical level, then, this means that any author must carefully assess his or her writing process and be critical of his or her choices concerning values and contradictions.

4. REWRITING ANCIENT MYTHS

In their inversive adaptation, the Jesus-novels investigated in this study suggest a fierce reassessment of the Gospels. They go farther than to criticise biblical texts for their supernaturalism or for their old-fashioned advice for daily life, as the enlightened novels of the nineteenth century did. These novels also propose new ideologies and new ways of understanding the nature of religion. In most cases the stories can really be called utopias, written in the spirit of Thomas More but working along the lines of quite another tradition—one that claims to be superior to the New Testament.

---

44. The only way to find some reason for Saramago's and Mailer's treatment of theodicy seems to be by locating these authors in the post-Holocaust tradition where they simply forbid theodicy to exist. Instead, God is put into a Manichean struggle with the Devil, or these two are made to be twins. For such a view in Holocaust literature, see Pinnock, *Beyond Theodicy*, 135–38. This view, however, makes the abovementioned denigration of Judaism look even more repulsive.

This, once again, is clearly a Nietzschean feature in this literature. Contrasting this "ethical" utopia with a Christian ethical community is an expression of *Herrenmoral* reaching beyond good and evil in the sense that the Bible has defined them. This comparison stems from their claim that neither the Bible, nor Jesus, nor the religion of his disciples has been able to fulfil the expectations they have laid concerning a good life. This criticism plays on a paradox within Christianity, on an assumed tension between the Sermon on the Mount and the life of the church during two millennia. Or, from a Nietzschean perspective, it is a paradox inside the reading community itself, a contradiction between the values of the present day and contemporary Christianity.[45]

The approach of many novels is nihilist because, in their adaptation of religious ideas, they no longer accept a theological interpretation of human existence. Appropriation turns into deconstruction. For instance, Saramago and Mailer wrote their Jesus-stories in terms of materialistic ideology. Theirs is a gospel deprived of divine revelation and God's salvation history, which naturally are the preconditions of the original story. In this sense, for these writers, the original canonical Bible is flat, a one-dimensional storehouse of religious statements. Their reading no longer has religious expectations in a traditional sense. Sin and salvation are no longer on the agenda. Instead, the agenda is rather written in terms of the post-Christian world. It embodies the "Faustian soul" of the West, which contests the world of alleged stagnation represented both by Judaism and Christianity.

Furthermore, these novels often fall into theological speculation concerning traditional subjects and doctrines such as soteriology or pneumatology. In other words they comment on the premises of salvation, or on the function of the Holy Spirit, without any carefully considered opinion. For instance, for Mailer the power of the Holy Spirit working in Jesus' deeds is akin to a yin-yang stream of power common in Buddhist alternative medical theory and treatment.[46]

Focusing only on theological matters, however, would lead our analysis astray. These novels do not primarily aim at doctrinal theologi-

---

45. Detweiler has noted that it is typical of postmodern fiction to long for a better world, and he calls it the eschatological feature of such literature. Detweiler, "Theological Trends," 234. The same feature can be seen in Jesus-novels, but it should be understood in terms of their nature as morality novels.

46. Mailer, *Gospel*, 87.

cal disputations. Their assessment is not a matter of deciding between the dogmas of rivaling denominations. We are facing neither a reformation nor a purification of the temple. These authors are rewriting ancient myths. They openly reject a theological approach in their adaptation. Therefore, they are not only adopting material, but also exploiting, consuming, reversing, and even perverting the original stories for their own purposes. Instead of a reformation, this is the end of religion.

In practice, the object of inversive rewriting is easy to define. These novels contest all the particular stories of the biblical metanarrative. One does not need to make a deep inquiry to detect the nature of the contradiction. These Jesus-novels attack, one by one: the myth of creation, the myth of the fall, the myth of Christian morality, and the myth of the nuclear family. They attack the first by questioning God's omnipotence in many ways. Almost each and every one of them rewrite the myth of the fall. In Nietzschean terms they contest the sinfulness of human beings. Concerning the foundation of ethics, the novels dissolve the myth of Christian morality. They follow the path beyond good and evil but seldom end up in nihilism as their predecessors did. And they also appear to contest the myth of the nuclear family by attacking the biblical view of familial Christian sexual morals and by reforming the relation between women and men.

As regards Christology, these novels contest the myth of the incarnation. Most authors describe Jesus as a normal Jewish man with no superhuman qualities apart from certain charismatic phenomena. In agreement with such a point of departure they also deny the myth of sacrificial atonement. Jesus did not die for our sins. According to the novels, he died at best a meaningless death in a violent world—or at worst as a victim of God's devious plans. Considered from the perspective of the Bible's grand metanarrative, these novels finally rewrite the whole myth of salvation.

But how are the myths actually rewritten? This is the crucial question and its answer will open the dynamics of the novels' intertextual strategy. Jesus-novel ideology is hardly ever contrasted directly with the canonical New Testament. Instead, it is contrasted with a hypothesis, a Nietzschean reading of the New Testament that opposes oppressive religion. These authors choose their enemies, and the "omnipotent author" defines their convictions. They actually become "omnipotent *theologians*" who can both create a religion and subvert it. The myth that is rewritten, thus, is not actually the myth of orthodox Christian faith but, instead, the myth of *Sklavenmoral*. The countering point in this case is an interpretation of Christian faith constructed through the subtext that represents the original Gospels inside the new narrative. This is the myth imagined by Saramago and Roberts, who depict Jesus as a free spirit, opposing the Mosaic commandments and living according to his natural desires. What is contested is slavish religion, not canonical Christianity or the Jesus of the Sermon on the Mount.

Furthermore, there are subjects that relate more directly to the canonical writings. In spite of certain developments in the role of women in the early church, the world of the Bible is undeniably patriarchal. The apostles are men and the structure of early congregations repeats the patterns of the Jewish synagogue. Some changes have occurred, though. Even in New Testament times, women attended church meetings and were no longer behind curtains. They were also allowed to take part in prayers and to utter prophesies in the congregation (cf. 1 Cor 11). Nevertheless, they lived in a male world. When feminist Jesus-novels confront the primacy of male apostles and rewrite the myth of patriarchy, they seek after a utopia of feminist culture.[47]

Despite the amount of potential material in the Bible, feminist Jesus-novels do not always oppose extant New Testament writings. Sometimes their criticism is also directed against a construction. In their reconstruction, feminist authors not only anticipate a world where equality prevails but anticipate a world, or a church, where the destructive dominion of men will be defeated and feminine values will redeem people (namely women) from slavery. In such aggressive attack against the Christian myth, focus is once again on a myth of misogynistic violence. Writers such as Roberts and Fredriksson no longer speculate merely on issues concerning equality. Instead, they adopt a version of Nietzschean antagonism, polarising different views and excluding the opinion they dislike. For instance Mary Magdalene in Fredriksson's new gospel drifts into a conflict with the apostle Paul and later attempts to replace his religion with a women's version of Christianity.

Violence has been on the agenda in most of the investigated themes. Jesus-novels appear to contest the violent nature of Christian faith. This conviction belongs to the Nietzschean tradition and can be

---

47. For the role of women in New Testament times see for instance Witherington, "Women," 957–61.

counted among its most prominent features. According to this view, Christian faith is injurious and even noxious to human beings. It is the myth of violent religion. This view is actually based on a poststructuralist inversion of the original religion. Canonical Christianity has always been considered a religion of mercy and forgiveness. Jesus is the Good Shepherd who desires for even the basest among sinners to turn to him. The myth of violent religion is only a construction and, as such, it is a perfect target for the authors.

Finally, one of the most essential polarisations attacks the concept of God. It is an adaptation that is quite expected when an inversive rewriting treats the basic conceptions of biblical doctrine. Rewriting the story about God means obviously a recasting of the very God acting in the New Testament. Here again though it is an interpreted construction of God that is under attack. There are assuredly features included from canonical Scriptures. Mailer speaks of a God who demands monotheism. For Fredriksson this is a God who makes a distinction between the Chosen People and other peoples. In such cases the novels intentionally reject the "myth," that is the doctrinal concept of God found directly in the canonical Gospels.

The main objection, however, is directed against a constructed myth. This appears in the analysis of Saramago's *Gospel*, which attacks the biblical God by focusing on a constructed myth of the divine Despot. For Saramago, God is not merely Moses' Lord with his Ten Commandments and his monotheistic religion. As we saw in the analysis, Saramago's God is an evil God. He is a monster. God is to be rejected because he is violent and dangerous. Saramago's God is something like the Demiurge, the evil Divinity of the material world that the Gnostics felt impelled to resist. Such polarisation, even though ancient by birth, now follows the Faustian consciousness of the *Anti-Christ*. It results in denying the authority of the divine Being presented by the Bible.

Saramago's approach is paralleled somewhat surprisingly both with certain writings of theologians and with those of convinced atheists. In the Western history of ideas such views are quite well represented in the twentieth century. In the death-of-God movement, Spong speaks of the horrible God of the Bible. Also in the sphere of Christianity, the new *Übermench* must raise himself against the biblical concept of God.

> The angry deity who judges human life from some heavenly throne might make us feel safe, but this deity always shrinks life,

or that is what guilt, fear and righteousness do. That is a god-image that must be broken; but when it is, the traditional way we have told the Jesus story will surely die with it.[48]

In the post-Anglican tradition of Robinson, Spong's mentor, this proudly Nietzschean death-of-God theology seeks to destroy the traditional concept of God, which, Spong claims, adores a sadistic God.[49] However, such views are to be more expected in standard atheistic works, such as that of Albert Camus, treated already above, or the desperate characters in Dostoyevsky's *The Brothers Karamazov*. In these atheistic convictions, the dualistic problem of Gnostic thinking, as well as that of several other religions adopting a polarisation between good and evil divinities, has been solved. Divinity is not to be split. If this kind of world has a God, he must be evil. In a paradoxical way, such a statement implies a biblical belief in creation, since it would no longer be valid in a polytheistic context. Theistic creationism, however, is probably not the proper context for this kind of reasoning. Instead, it depends on monistic naturalism, which profoundly influences atheistic speculation in the Western world.[50]

Similarly, some of the investigated novels adopt atheist rhetorics in their treatment of the Divinity. The God of the biblical story is to be rejected, because he is an evil Being who promotes guilt and fear. But these novelists share a paradoxical point of departure. God is to be made responsible since he is the creator of all things. In spite of being a creator, however, he is not God the almighty. Such a view creates problems for the concept of God in general. How does one describe a creator whose work is unacceptable? Is he an incompetent construction worker or an unskilled building engineer? There are different answers to these silent questions in the Jesus-novels. The first of these is Saramago's suggestion that the concept of God deconstructs itself. These problems and paradoxes reveal that there actually never was a God. There are merely stories that dissolve under the judgment of history. Mailer suggests that

---

48. Spong, *Sins of Scripture*, 174.

49. Ibid., 172.

50. In the Finnish context a convinced atheist, professor V. T. Aaltonen, in the 1950s, argued against the goodness of God on these premises. Since then it has been a standard subject in Finnish discussions both among atheists and among death-of-God theologians. The reference is made to Aaltonen, *Miksi en ole kristitty*, 90.

there may be a Jewish God, but he is not the only one. And Fredriksson arrives at polytheism.

There are also claims that confront and contradict traditional doctrines of the church, and especially Christology. It is only natural that, in a rewritten gospel, it is precisely the person of Jesus that is demythologised. Some of the investigated novels parallel the discussions of the so-called radical theology or rationalistic theology of the twentieth century. Their criticism is directed against the myth of God-incarnate. This was also the aim, for instance, of the *Entmythologisierung* project of existentialist theology. By deifying Christ, the church separated him from ordinary people. This is rectified in the rewriting when Jesus is presented as a Jewish man living under the same conditions as all those around him.[51]

In Fredriksson's *According to Mary* there is a discussion between Leonidas, Mary, and the apostle Paul, where such demythologising is brought into biblical history. It needs closer examination. The passage starts with Leonidas's speculation.

> "I realize there is bound to be lively myth making around Jesus. But sometimes it seems to be taking on distasteful expressions, like the virgin birth."
> "I never speak of it," said Paul. "But I know the legend flourishes in many circles."[52]

In concluding, it is possible to note that many of the recent Jesus-novels are not content with rewriting the biblical Jesus-story as it stands in the original texts. They are not simply contrasting their revised Jesus with the extant writings of the New Testament. Rather, the hero of the story, be it the revised Jesus figure, Judas, or Mary Magdalene, or someone else, opposes a religious world that no longer resembles that of the Bible. The attack is directed against the myths of slave morality, misogynistic violence, or the divine Despot. There is, thus, an evident Nietzschean undercurrent in the intertextual rewriting of the novels.

In all cultures myths have an important role in the development of the culture's self-understanding. Sanders writes:

> A culture's mythology is its body of traditional narratives. Mythical literature depends upon, incites even, perpetual acts

---

51. See especially the collection John Hicks edited, *The Myth of God Incarnate*.
52. Fredriksson, *According to Mary*, 149.

of reinterpretation in new contexts, a process that embodies the very idea of appropriation.[53]

The investigated Jesus-novels, however, do not use the Bible as a source for meaningful myths. The stories of the New Testament are not held in high regard like the stories of Ovid or the legends concerning the characters of Greek Pantheon, which have been used countless times in Western literature. There is no "perpetual reinterpretation" where the point of departure would still have significance for new meaning. Instead, Jesus-novels in the twentieth century aim at demythologising based on Nietzschean antagonism. This means that New Testament message is seen as a cultural threat that has started to defile the Western world and is about the destroy humane conduct completely. One could even say that, in these novels, there is a postcolonial need to challenge and oppose the sources that provide the original myths. One could not imagine a clearer example of Nietzschean spirit in reinterpretation and adaptation.

This, of course, does not mean that the novels do not discuss the original New Testament or the person of Jesus. Quite the contrary. This is merely a notion concerning the method of writing. Many of the investigated novels reveal nihilist intentions in their treatment of the Gospels, and their aim is to reverse the structures of the Christian religion these texts represent. This reversal is made in the tradition of *The Anti-Christ*, by making the defendant so repulsive and oppressive that readers will instantly judge in favor of the author.

The problem of describing Jesus or reinterpreting his message is a difficult one, though. In Saramago's novel a reader encounters an oscillating narration where an almost perfect knowledge of the Scriptures and a deep theological insight are contrasted with overwhelming reductionism. Starting with the title of the work we are facing a *gospel* (O Evangelho), which speaks about Jesus. All the biblical characters are present and the story itself proceeds from virgin birth and Bethlehem to Jerusalem and Calvary. In spite of all this, at the end of the story, the reader knows practically nothing about this new Jesus. He has no special message and he has done almost nothing during the journey. The focus has constantly been on the Pastor, Mary Magdalene, and God. The Jesus-figure follows other characters' agendas and comments on issues presented to him by other people.

53. Sanders, *Adaptation and Appropriation*, 63.

Earlier we noted that the nature of the subtext reveals the distance between the source text and hypertext. In Mailer's and Fredriksson's novels the distance is remarkably wider than in traditional Jesus-novels that content themselves with imaginative paraphrasing. Saramago, however, provides a new story that becomes almost the opposite of the canonical Gospels, despite the fact that he uses several New Testament passages and creates a subtext in his novel. His subtext is in fact distorted. It contains few direct quotations, and when they are used, their changed context turns their meaning into something completely new. Mailer too, one has to admit, uses this method, and in some passages his solutions resemble those of Saramago.

One is entitled to ask whether Saramago's gospel is a book on Jesus at all. Or is the truncated Jesus-figure in this novel just a symbol for mankind, a prototype for ordinary people who attempt to find a way to live under the oppressive powers of society? Many scholars have called Saramago's book as well as all the other novels an interpretation of the New Testament. On the basis of the present analysis, it is apparent that such convictions can be questioned. An interpretation should, first of all, describe the object that will be interpreted. Furthermore, an interpretation should be constructive: it should have a result and it should define the new features that are to replace previous ideas. In a Jesus-novel, thus, an interpretation should describe the features and message of the new Jesus. Saramago fails to present this kind of reinterpretation, and Mailer's thinking remains deficient or inadequate on this question. Feminist novels succeed somewhat better since the new Jesus, despite his general humanist orientation, represents feminism quite openly.

Hence, it is easy to understand why most of these novels reject a theological interpretation of human existence. Heaven has been forced onto earth and the authors are interested only in humanity. A new point of departure has replaced theological interpretation. If Christian faith, or a (post)modern Jesus-movement, is to be accepted among the readers, its values must be defined in terms of present reality. Many novels are quite specific about this. If there used to be a tension between the Revelation, i.e., the Bible as God's message, and the values of the fallen world, this contradiction is now invalid. The church no longer has a prophetic mission to bring an alternative to the sinful world, as both the Jesus of the original narrative as well as his disciples proclaimed.

The opposition must be dissolved and the Bible rewritten on the readers' terms.[54]

There is some kind of bizarre apologetics in these novels, in spite of all their antagonism.[55] They still write on the New Testament. They still seek a Nazarene with whom they could identify themselves. Thus readers witness a phenomenon that Sanders calls "fidelity-in-betrayal."[56] These novels do not aim at pure blasphemy, as one might suppose when reading about reckless Saviours and evil Gods. This, however, is no longer orthodox Christian theology. Rather, it is a Faustian reversal where the whole culture including the Bible is woven into a new fabric—whether traditional Christianity accepts it or not. There may thus be found some answers to the essential question of why authors still write on Jesus even though they no longer believe in him as Christ. Novelists are under his spell, as was Nietzsche all his life until the writing of *The Anti-Christ*. Jesus' figure stands in the middle of European culture, and one feels need to write about him, even if it means turning him into a Zarathustra.

---

54. "The semiotic key to Saramago's Jesus is reversal, a reversal of godly rhetoric into human wisdom; this is not a blunt reversal, but one that is based on irony, understatement and implication." Fokkema, "Art of Rewriting," 397.

55. According to Ziolkowski, even a critical rewriting shows keen interest in the original work: "it is still the greatest story ever told, or at least the most familiar one." Ziolkowski, *Fictional Transfigurations*, 232. Langenhorst, in turn, thinks that daring new interpretations attempt to challenge traditional theology. Langenhorst, "Rediscovery," 97.

56. Sanders, *Adaptation and Appropriation*, 51; referring to Steven Connor's original idea. They state that rewriting never amounts to a simple denial of the original text, even though it compromises its cultural authority.

Conclusion: Nietzschean Themes in Contrast-Novels

Late twentieth-century Jesus-novels are filled with evil gods and reckless saviours. The purpose of this investigation was to test a hypothesis concerning the nature of the adaptation and aims of the intertextual change made in several recent Jesus-novels. Quite unlike earlier Jesus-novels written in the beginning of the twentieth century, investigated mainly by Theodore Ziolkowski, these novels propose an inversive revision that aims at a deliberate contradiction with the original source text, namely the New Testament. The intertextual strategy is based on contrast. The reader witnesses authors attack biblical beliefs and attempt to dissolve Christian doctrines.

In the intertextual process of adaptation and appropriation, authors create a new gospel or Jesus-novel that gives a completely different picture of Jesus' life than the one found in the New Testament. Jesus-novels' intertextual method is what Ziva Ben-Porat has called prototypical rewriting and what Francisco Peña Fernández investigates as inversive intertextuality. Authors usually transfer their material into a new context in order to change the meaning and make canonical words serve their own designs. Such adaptation aims at a recognisable rendition. For the literary effect to function, the original text must still be recognisable. Simultaneously the main intention is to rework it so that the original meaning is turned into its opposite.

The investigation of the relationship between the selected Jesus-novels and their three different kinds of source texts has shown that the basic motivation for an interpretive appropriation derives from Nietzsche's ideology. Nietzschean values are criteria for the adaptation and rewriting. This can be seen already in the overall attitude that relies on an opposition towards slavish Christianity. Such a "clash of ideologies" is characteristic for all of the main novels in this investigation and most of the other Jesus-novels from the end of the twentieth century and the beginning of the present century.

Is it justified to interpret such novels as ideological writings? During the analysis we have discussed different aspects of this methodological problem. Late twentieth-century Jesus-novels are not just fiction that plays with religious ideas. The point of departure, namely taking the New Testament as a source text, makes the difference. Every novel is an adaptation of the canonical Gospels, and each author makes a statement on Christian faith. The intertextual relationship cannot be overlooked or rejected in the interpretation of the novels' motivation for inversive appropriation. Should some imaginary right-wing capitalist write an adaptation of Karl Marx's *Capital* where he proves Marx actually the inventor of free market economy, nobody would read the novel without presupposing an intertextual relationship. In the case of the Bible the issue is even clearer. If there is an essential change in the story and, furthermore, if the adaptation is inversive, there must be a reason. Our analysis has detected several Nietzschean themes that motivate the authors' presentations.

Starting with perspectives on the historical Jesus, Nietzsche's influence is evident. For him, the biblical Jesus is an almost entirely literary figure and as such a forgery. The investigated Jesus-novels also distinguish between the Jesus of history and the Christ of the Christian confession. This, however, concerns only the general picture because these novels go much further in particular issues than previous Jesus-novels.

Furthermore, in many of the investigated novels Jesus is no longer a Jewish preacher with a Jewish identity. He does not follow Moses, and he does not even worship Yahweh, the God of Israel. And why should he, as God in these novels is not the source of love? A Nietzschean contradiction governs the authors' interpretations. By making the canonical Jesus' message of love the opposite of human freedom the authors deliberately reject the biblical teaching of genuine love. The Old Testament Law, the Torah that the canonical Jesus appears to preach, represents slavish religion. Therefore, the intertextual inversion drives at only one conclusion: the Jesus of the New Testament was wrong. God's word has nothing to do with love.

The new Jesus in most of the investigated novels contests the Mosaic Law, despises orthodox Judaism, abandons Jewish customs, and even goes up against Old Testament monotheism. These features create a tension in the new interpretation. The novels intentionally transfer Jesus out of Judaism. Due to the contradiction itself, Jewish faith appears in a negative light. The move is Nietzschean by nature: Christianity has attempted to Judaise the Western world, and this process must be stopped. Such a hostile appropriation does not depend on open anti-Semitism but it is on the verge of attacking Jewish worship. One is entitled to ask why this kind of change has been made. It is likely that this reveals an irrational or unconscious element of the novels. It is difficult to think that these anti-Judaist antitheses would be intentional or ideological.

These details prove that the investigated Jesus-novels cannot be interpreted merely as literary experiments playing with the idea of incarnation and asking how human can the Son of God get if he is treated just as a Galilean man. This kind of discussion followed Kazantzakis's Jesus-novel where he described Jesus' temptation to live an ordinary life, but now the setting is different. In recent novels there is no positive image of Jesus. Authors rather ask: how reckless can Jesus get? They experiment with what Jesus would look like if he were a contemporary Nietzschean, post-Christian person.

How is it possible, then, that novels that apparently wish to promote humane values end up with unfashionable anti-Judaist prejudices? The only explanation for these attitudes is that European culture still carries unconscious anti-Judaist attitudes beneath the surface covered by sentiments of equality and tolerance. The novels' interpretations are strongly supported by the pervasive Nietzschean belief that the whole Jewish religion with its horrible view of God is a life-denying ideology. Therefore, these authors no longer accept the canonical Jesus with his conservative views. He has given in to the oppressive concept of God that his tradition has taught him. A new figure must be constructed in his stead. So, against all the logical expectations one might have, and despite the evident post-Holocaust consciousness present in the novels, they actually present an arrogant and ironical refutation of Jewish beliefs and Old Testament faith. Jesus is made into the complete opposite of and antithesis to Judaism.

The investigated Jesus-novels usually put Jesus through a process of supposed humanisation, as Ilan Stavans and Douwe Fokkema have suggested. The newly constructed Jesus usually trusts his inner feelings and aims at expressing his individuality. The contribution of the present study is in the more detailed identification of such adaptation and rewriting. Jesus practices free sex and supports non-marital sexual relationships. Some scholars might say that he embodies the carnivalisation of religious beliefs. The new Jesus appears as a herald of freedom and conducts his mission by attacking Jewish taboos and also, anachronistically, taboos to come during the course of Christian history.

Nietzschean criticism repeatedly challenges Christian faith by claiming it is nothing but slavish morality. A similar opposition becomes one of the main signs betraying the relationship between the novels and their ideological foundation. For the investigated novels, Christian ethics is life-denying. One of the literary strategies showing this attitude is the rehabilitation of the alleged victims of Christianity's oppressive fundamentalism. Judas becomes an upright man devoted to social renewal. Jesus, in turn, appears as the opposite: a man who gives in to selfish principles.

The feminist novels, despite their somewhat different point of departure, also adopt a strictly Nietzschean approach in their rewriting of the Christian gospel. For instance, Roberts and Fredriksson identify doctrines with Mosaic Law and thus make them a Jewish phenomenon. This is how the dogmatic male interpretation of Christianity, opposed in the novels, becomes a token of the Judaisation of Jesus' religion. In the adaptations, apostles represent canonical Christianity, and Mary Magdalene and Jesus represent the new Dionysian faith.

As could be expected, canonical Christianity is usually depicted as a rigid ideology that considers sex dirty. In the novels, adaptation turns into appropriation when Jesus becomes the Magdalene's lover. Some feminist novels describe him almost as a gigolo who has nothing to do with Jewish moral values. As the authors' main purpose in this case is to support feminist values, they create a story where traditional oppressive conceptions are reversed. As these novels depend on second-wave feminist ideology, their basic motivation is a new understanding of sexual experience. Mary and Jesus' relationship in these novels signals women's particular way of experiencing the divine. This is how sexuality is freed from patriarchal hierarchies and power structures. Mary and Jesus' intercourse symbolises a sacred marriage where the divine is not imprisoned in doctrines.

The main problem with this kind of interpretation, however, is that the novels fail to achieve. Instead, many novels themselves legitimise traditional roles and even male oppression by making women into sexual objects. This tension is not resolved by the attempt to invert the whole concept of prostitution because then the authors cannot prevent women's exploitation on the basis of the new moral values.

The novels' treatment of moral issues confirms the above picture. Due to Nietzschean influence these novels confront an alleged biblical slave morality. From Saramago's *Gospel* to Tunström's *Ökenbrev* and the feminist novels, the picture remains the same. Authors brand dogmatic Judaism and early Jewish Christianity as violent and slavish religions. Quite in contrast with the recent cultural renewal of appreciation of Judaism, these novels adopt anti-Judaist attitudes.

After reading feminist Jesus-novels it is easy to see that early German feminism learned much from Nietzsche. Elisabeth Schüssler Fiorenza's attack on patriarchal Christianity is based on discontinuity and negative rhetoric. The main theses of this tradition question the Bible's androcentric language and men's domination in the church. For feminist writers, both philosophers and theologians, this further explains the progressive patriarchalisation of the church. Jesus-novels rewrite all this from the perspective of women's experience.

Traditional biblical hierarchies are turned inside out in the investigated novels, especially by making Mary Magdalene more important than the canonical Jesus. In the new narratives Jesus and Mary have a close relationship and usually they are also lovers. Mary learns from Jesus, and she also becomes the main messenger for Jesus' original although secret message. This Jesus-figure no longer resembles the Jesus of the canonical Gospels, though. He is a hypothetical construction viewed through a Gnostic lens, despite the fact that his religious teaching differs from the convictions found in ancient Gnostic gospels. In this way Jesus' and Mary's roles are in fact reversed.

Another example of Nietzschean influence is the treatment of sacrificial soteriology. For Nietzsche, this idea represented the essential pagan nature of Christianity as a religion. For Saramago, for example, this tradition confirms the assumption that Christianity is a violent ideology. Many Jesus-novels play with the bloody images temple worship provides and exploit readers' repulsion toward the killing of innocent animals for religious purposes. This interpretation can be easily transferred to the treatment of Christ's death on the cross. It was Nietzsche who stopped painting pictures of the Crucified, and this is what most of the investigated novels do as well.

The main motivation for such an adaptation appears to be anthropological, though. The idea of sacrifice is to be rejected because it depends on the biblical or even Jewish concept of sin. Here we finally find the core of Nietzsche's critique against Christian *faith*. Traditional Christianity is to be considered slavish because it oppresses normal healthy people under the psychological feeling of guilt. Because sin is merely a "Jewish invention," modern people cannot base their interpretation of human existence in its terms. Most novels abandon the whole concept even though. Paradoxically, they simultaneously assume that there is some kind of sickness or absurdity in the world that contaminates innocent humanism.

Such an approach sees Christianity just as a form of sadomasochist domination. Oppression, also according to the novels, is typical of religion as such and especially of Christian faith. In fact, many novels claim that polytheistic religions are more tolerant than the violent monotheist tradition. Like the liberal theology movement, many of these novels have the new Jesus or Mary Magdalene liberate humanity from the hierarchic patriarchy of canonical Christianity.

As the novels reject the Christian dogma of atonement they proclaim that perfectly good and innocent citizens must not be accused of leading immoral lives. This view is part of the *Herrenmoral* that prevails in this tradition even though the authors may not be aware of it. Such an appropriation is based on atheist rhetoric, and it is repeatedly used in contemporary atheist attacks on religion. It is one of the conclusions of the present analysis, and probably not a novelty for many readers, that most of these novelists adopt atheist ideas and nihilist discourse in their narrative. In this respect they fit in perfectly with the post-Christian Western society that has based its culture on secularism for centuries.

These adaptations necessarily depend on the severe crisis in metaphysics that took place in the twentieth century. This is clearly the reason why many authors implicitly proclaim the death of God. These novels are no longer theistic in the traditional sense of the word. The inspiration for rewriting the New Testament is encouraged by the Nietzschean zeal for rebellion against the metaphysical. In this respect these books belong to the network of negative theology that has flourished in the post-Holocaust reality of Western thinking, theological as well as philosophical.

In Mailer's *Gospel*, death-of-God ideology appears in the form of a Manichean uncertainty, if one is to exploit the more general definition of Mailer's ideology given by Brian McDonald and Jeffrey Partridge. Human life is only a struggle between impersonal powers that draw people in opposite directions. Mailer can no longer rely on a monotheistic solution for the absurdity of life because the reality of the Holocaust has deprived us of simple answers. His theodicy has no other kind of aim. Mailer resembles Camus in his metaphysical rebellion where there is little hope for those living under the hard conditions of this world.

Saramago takes the reasoning further and questions the very goodness of God, even though his point of departure is the same. The horrible events of history, as well as the examples taken from the Holy Scriptures themselves, prove that any God conducting this kind of operation must be evil. In this respect, Saramago's narrative is based on the same premise as aggressive atheism: if there is an omnipotent God—and Saramago's God is the sovereign controller of history—he cannot be good. This is Saramago's main motivation for using his brilliant idea of heteronyms. By exploiting a literary invention familiar from many of his other novels he has been able to perfectly create a critical view of Christianity in terms of his own personal conviction.

Taking these conclusions into account, Mailer can be assessed as more biblically faithful than the other writers. His semi-Manichean conviction about the combat between good and evil forces makes him ultimately a Jewish author, even though no one would call him a traditionalist. Saramago assesses the difficulties and evil in the world like a feisty atheist. He is not able to explain evil, and he does not really even attempt to. He is content with claiming that Christianity cannot fight it. Therefore, Saramago remains in a materialistic ambivalence. There is killing and oppression in this evolutionary process we are going through, but there is no remedy for it.

This makes his programme Nietzschean in a very profound sense. Christianity must be fought because it offers vain hope and groundless mercy to this terrible world that struggles against the powers of natural selection. The real solution must be different. Only some kind of existentialist rebellion can provide people with a new consciousness that will help them overcome the problems of corruption. The Nietzschean answer emphasises human dignity and individual will to power. This, however, will not produce any proper ethical theory and Saramago, like Camus, probably recognises it. Nietzsche has created the *Übermensch* and once he has been released, who can stop him?

Authors do play with the problem of theodicy, and this makes their novels ideological. One of the difficulties here is that they are not philosophers. Saramago's and Mailer's treatments of the problem remain on a relatively simplistic level. They locate the problem of evil in the context of a deterministic worldview. In these novels God is responsible for suffering because he is the deterministic creator of this world. Such a view is fitting for the novels because God is described as an author of a cosmic script and human beings are depicted as mere actors. This view, in the novels, collides with the idea of individual freedom. However, their critique is possible only if the world is not deterministic. But to state such a premise destroys the primary accusation about God's guilt. This philosophical incoherence is why these novels are not to be read as philosophy of religion but merely as fiction.

Such a conclusion does not mean that, in contrast with everything that was said above, these Jesus-novels were not atheistic after all. These stories in their present form deliberately attack theism. They agree completely with the works of Albert Camus, as well as with those of many death-of-God theologians. Saramago, in particular, and in many respects Mailer, belong to the wide post-Christian secularist movement where Thomas Altizer, Don Cupitt, and John Spong have suggested a special "atheist" Christianity, making even Nietzsche himself a radical Christian. Jesus, in these novels, can easily be explained as one more radical Christian himself, following the ideas that Nietzsche later refined into nihilism.

The result of analysing Nietzschean themes in recent Jesus-literature is inevitable. Even if none of these authors would ever have read a single book by Nietzsche, they all follow his hermeneutical dichotomy and reflect his ideological motivations in their writing. In the Western literary tradition there is a pantextual flow that appears to affect authors writing about Jesus and the New Testament. Nietzschean ideology has become a cultural narrative that infiltrates the novelistic reading of the New Testament. Therefore, it is not too much to state that these novels as hypertexts embody a real crusade against Judeo-Christian "slavish" religion.

Such dependence on nihilist tradition produces problems for both the consistency and message of the novels. Even though these books are not deliberately and thoroughly poststructuralist or postmodern they nevertheless suffer from the essential problem of the nihilist's ethical paradox. The death-of-God movement and its literary sympathisers face a difficult choice: what constitutes a person's identity? Saramago and Mailer develop their stories to the point where both God's and Jesus' identities vanish. God looks like the Devil, and Jesus reverts to being a deprived child without a mission in life. Postmodern speculation drifted into a blind alley over this same issue because its theorists gradually became convinced that the person dies with the death of meaning. There is no basis for true speech about being human. Throughout history, the only justification for the transcendental signified had been divine authority, but when its time had come, all proof for certainty disappeared. With the death of God, poststructuralist theory minimises the value of human identity.

This is the very same tension Nietzsche faced in his philosophy. How could he defend an even higher humanity and a Superman after the death of meaning and the death of God? The answer for him, and apparently for the writers of recent Jesus-novels as well, is nihilist irrationalism. Ideology is a matter of taste, not of reasoning, despite all the rational arguments exploited to bolster the arguments. This, furthermore, is the reason why these books, like numerous other works of poststructuralist philosophers, are morality novels.

Secularisation, for this tradition, is not merely a process of the degeneration of religious rites and customs. It is more. It is the fulfilment of Kantian eschatology in a Nietzschean context. The decline of the church is considered inevitable. The New Testament must be written anew. Christianity must be made responsible for its deeds. But unlike Kant, postmodern authors and the authors of the investigated Jesus-novels are convinced that religion cannot be replaced simply by an ethical community. It can only be replaced by *Herrenmoral*: by new ethical standards that challenge patriarchal hierarchies. The new readings represent emancipation from Christian adherence to slavish religion. This, in a sense, is a search for the "paradise lost" that never existed. Such humanism has attempted to find a place in Western society, but traditional Christianity has been the main obstacle preventing its triumph.

According to the Faustian contradiction presented in the investigated Jesus-novels, the original Christianity supports an inaccurate view of human beings. From Nietzsche onwards, the most perverted doctrine of all is considered to be the concept of sin. Biblical Christianity, and even the biblical Jesus, is considered unacceptable because they represent spiritual violence and religious oppression. From the perspective of the new ideology, which includes Roberts, Saramago, and Fredriksson, the canonical source text is inhuman. If there was any transgression in this world, it was to be found in the original story. According to the Nietzschean accusations in these novels, Christianity is the only sin or evil one needs to be delivered from.

In this respect one may even say that some of these Jesus-novels aim at a unique cultural purification where the exploitative Christian dogma and the horrible history of the church are washed away. This secular reconciliation entails the abandonment of both the violent sacrificial gospel and *Sklavenmoral*, which corrupt human freedom. To accomplish this, the authors choose the New Testament as their subject. It also explains the intertextual changes they make in the story. Through this redemption human beings will create the secular utopia of a post-Christian society.

Therefore, these authors rewrite ancient myths. These myths are not simply the myths of the incarnation or creation or the fall, though. Instead, they oppose the myths they have themselves constructed. Recent Jesus-novels rewrite the myths of slave morality, patriarchal oppression, and violent religion. The naive *Entmythologisierung* of rationalism tackling the supernatural has turned into a postmodern struggle against slavish Christianity. These novels demythologise ideas that have been constructed through the lens of postmodern moralism inside the poststructuralist movement, and this alone identifies these novels—at least from this perspective—as postmodern. Nietzschean inheritance is vast and influential in Western culture.

Furthermore, we must remember that the basic purpose of the investigated Jesus-novels depends completely on their intertextual relation to the canonical New Testament. These stories are rewritten gospels. Meaning in these narratives depends on adaptations that are constructed as polarised and inversive readings of biblical events. Their paradise is a utopia about Faustian freedom beyond good and evil where Christian values, signs, and symbols have been transformed, inverted, or abandoned. In their iconoclastic zeal these novels contrast their revised gospel with the evil God of the allegedly slavish Christianity, and replace them with the reckless Saviours of the new narratives. All this, being fiction, is not intentional blasphemy as such. However, these stories can be heard in such a way since any denigration of delicate religious beliefs may be experienced as blasphemous.

When writing on the New Testament, these authors, despite their apparent moral convictions and humane ethics, depend on Nietzschean views and attitudes in their intertextual revision of the canonical Gospels. Probably against the beliefs of the authors themselves, their stories betray both anti-Judaist arrogance and attack Christianity as a slavish religion.

The intertextual process involving three different kinds of source texts is dynamic, and the authors make the New Testament responsible for the faults in the church's history. Their intention cannot help being ideological since the revised gospel is written within the sphere of a Nietzschean critique of religion. These novels suit Western cultural history well, and they parallel both poststructuralist philosophy and death-of-God theology. Therefore it is precisely their ideological background that explains the motivation for their inversive adaptation and antagonistic intertextual strategy.

Bibliography

SOURCES

Atwood, Margaret. *Alias Grace*. London: Bloomsbury, 1996.
Berlinghof, Regina. *Mirjam: Maria Magdalena und Jesus*. Eschborn: Klotz, 2004.
Brown, Dan. *The Da Vinci Code*. London: Corgi, 2004.
Bulgakov, Mihail. *The Master and Margarita*. Glasgow: Fontana/Collins, 1974.
Caldwell, Taylor, and Jess Stearn. *I, Judas*. London: New English Library, 1984.
Camus, Albert. *Le mythe de Sisyphe*. Paris: Gallimard, 1942.
———. *The Myth of Sisyphus*. Translated by J. O'Brien. Harmondsworth: Penguin, 1979.
———. *L'étranger*. Paris: Gallimard, [1942] 1957.
———. *L'Homme révolté*. Paris: Gallimard, 1947.
———. *The Rebel*. Translated by A. Bower. Harmondsworth: Penguin, 1978.
———. *La peste*. Paris: Gallimard, 1947.
———. *La chute*. Paris: Gallimard, 1956.
———. *The Fall*. Translated by Justin O'Brien. New York: Vintage, 1991.
Crace, Jim. *Quarantine*. New York: Picador, 1998.
Douglas, Lloyd C. *The Robe*. Boston: Houghton Mifflin, 1947.
———. *The Big Fisherman*. Boston: Houghton, Mifflin, 1948.
Dostoevskij, Fedor. *The Brothers Karamazov*. Translated by C. Garnett. Chicago: Encyclopedia Britannica, 1952.
Dowling, Levi H. *The Aquarian Gospel of Jesus the Christ: The Philosophic and Practical Basis of the Religion of the Aquarian Age of the World*. Transcribed from the Akashic Records by Levi. London: Fowler, 1974.
Fredriksson, Marianne. *Enligt Maria Magdalena*. Stockholm: Wahlsröm & Widstrand, 1997.
———. *According to Mary*. London: Orion House, 2002.
Goethe, Johann Wolfgang von. *Faust*. Translated by P. Wayne. Harmondsworth: Penguin, 1981.
Graves, Robert. *King Jesus*. New York: Minerva, s.a.
Jens, Walter. *Der Fall Judas*. Stuttgart: Kreuz, [1975] 1989.
Kazantzakis, Niko. *The Last Temptation of Christ*. Translated by Peter A. Brien. New York: Simon and Schuster, 1960.
Lawrence, D. H. *The Man Who Died*. London: Heinemann, 1935.
Lonfellow, Ki. *The Secret Magdalene*. New York: Three Rivers, 2005.
Mailer, Norman. *The Gospel According to the Son*. London: Little, Brown, 1998.
Moore, Christopher. *Lamb: The Gospel According to Biff, Christ's Childhood Pal*. New York: Harper, 2004.

Mishnah. *A New Translation*. Translated by J. Neusner. New Haven, CT: Yale University Press, 1988.
Papini, Giovanni. *Storia di Cristo*. Firenze: Vallecchi, 1921.
Park, Paul. *The Gospel of Corax*. London: Harvest, 1996.
Renan, Ernest. *Vie de Jésus*. Paris: Calmann Lévy, 1947.
Rice, Anne. *Christ the Lord: Out of Egypt*. New York: Ballantine, 2006.
Ricci, Nino. *Testament*. Boston: Houghton Mifflin, 2003.
Rinser, Luise. *Mirjam*. Frankfurt: Fischer, 1983.
Roberts, Michè[<grave>]le. *The Wild Girl*. London: Methuen, 1984.
Saramago, José. *O Evangelho segundo Jesus Cristo: Romance*. Lisboa: Caminho, 1997.
———. *The Gospel According to Jesus Christ*. Translated by Giovanni Pontiero. London: Harvill, 1993.
Sirola, Harri. *Jeesus Enkelinpoika Nasaretilainen*. Jyväskylä: Gummerus, 2001.
Stead, Christian K. *My Name Was Judas*. London: Vintage, 2007.
Tunström, Göran. *Ökenbrevet*. Stockholm: Bonniers, 1978.
———. "The Letter from the Wilderness." Translated by Eivor Martinus. *Swedish Book Review* 1 (1996) 11–19.
Vaaskivi, Tatu. *Pyhä Kevät: Elämäkerrallisen esipuheen kirjoittanut Elina Vaara-Vaaskivi*. Porvoo, Helsinki: Werner Södustïom, 1943.
Wallace, Lewis. *Ben-Hur: A Tale of the Christ*. New York: Harper, 1880.
Waltari, Mika. *Valtakunnan salaisuus: Markus Mezentius Manilianuksen yksitoista kirjettä keväästä 30 jKr*. Porvoo, Helsinki: Werner Södustïom, 1961.

GENERAL BIBLIOGRAPHY

Aaltonen, V. Toivo. *Miksi en ole kristitty*. Toinen, uusittu painos. Helsinki: Kansankulttuuri, 1952.
Abercrombie, N., S. Hill, and B. S. Turner, editors. *The Penguin Dictionary of Sociology*. London: Allen Lane, 1984.
Allen, Brooke. "The Gospel of Norman." *New Criterion* 15.10 (1997) 77.
Allen, Graham. *Intertextuality*. The New Critical Idiom. New York: Routledge, 2000.
Altizer, Thomas J. J. *The Gospel of Christian Atheism*. Philadelphia: Westminster, 1966.
———. "History as Apocalypse." In *Deconstruction and Theology*, edited by Thomas J. J. Altizer et al., 147–77. New York: Crossroad, 1982.
———. *Total Presence: The Language of Jesus and The Language of Today*. New York: Seabury, 1980.
Altizer, Thomas J. J., and William Hamilton. *Radical Theology and the Death of God*. Indianapolis: Bobbs-Merrill, 1966.
Anderson, Gary A. "Sacrifice and sacrificial offerings: Old Testament." In *Anchor Bible Dictionary* 5:870–86.
Anderson, Linda. "The Re-Imagining of History in Contemporary Women's Fiction." In *Plotting Change: Contemporary Women's Fiction*, edited by Linda Anderson, 129–41. Stratford-Upon-Avon Studies, 2nd series. Melbourne: Edward Arnold, 1990.
Anderson, Pamela. "Myth, Mimesis and Multiple Identities: Feminist Tools for Transforming Theology." *Literature & Theology* 10 (1996) 112–30.
Bakhtin, Mikhail. *Problems of Dostoevsky's Poetics*. Translated by C. Emerson. Theory and History of Literature 8. Manchester: Manchester University Press, 1984.

Barthes, Roland. "From Work to Text." In *Textual Strategies: Perspectives in Post-Structuralist Criticism*, edited by J. V. Harari, 73–81. Ithaca, NY: Cornell University Press, 1979.

Bauman, Zygmunt. *Intimations of Postmodernity*. London: Routledge. 1992.

Beattie, Tina. *The New Atheists: The Twilight of Reason & the War on Religion*. New York: Maryknoll, 2007.

Ben-Porat, Ziva. "Saramago's Gospel and the Poetics of Prototypical Rewriting." *Journal of Romance Studies* 3 (2003) 93–105.

Benz, Ernst. *Nietzsches Ideen zur Geschichte des Christentums und der Kirche*. Beihefte der Zeitschrift für Religions- und Geistesgeschichte 3. Leiden: Brill, 1956.

Berger, Klaus. *Exegese und Philosophie*. Stuttgarter Bibelstudien 123/124. Stuttgart: Katholischer Bibelwerk, 1986.

Birney, Alice L. *The Literary Lives of Jesus: An International Bibliography of Poetry, Drama, Fiction, and Criticism*. New York: Garland, 1989.

Turner, B. S., editor. *The Blackwell Companion to Social Theory*. Oxford: Blackwell, 1996.

Bloom, Harold. *The Anxiety of Influence: A Theory of Poetry*. Oxford: Oxford University Press, 1975.

———. "The One with the Beard Is God, the Other Is the Devil." In *On Saramago*, edited by Victor J. Mendes, 155–66. Portuguese Literary and Cultural Studies 6. Dartmouth: University of Massachusetts, 2001.

Bloom, Harold, et al. *Deconstruction and Criticism*. New York: Continuum, 1995.

The Book of Saints: A Dictionary of Servants of God Canonized by the Catholic Church. Compiled by the Benedictine Monks of St. Augustine's Abbey. London: Black, 1989.

Borges, Jorge Luis. "Tres versiones de Judas." *Ficciones*, 1944. Online: http://southerncrossreview.org/49/borges-judas-sp.htm (original Spanish) and http://southerncrossreview.org/49/borges-judas-eng.htm (English translation).

Borland, Harold, H. *Nietzsche's Influence on Swedish Literature: With Special Reference to Strindberg, Ola Hansson, Heidenstam and Fröding*. Göteborgs kungl. vetenskaps- och vitterhets-samhälles handlingar A 6.3. Göteborg: Wettergren & Kerbers, 1956.

Bottum, Joseph. "Mailer's Jesus." *First Things*, August/September 1997, 53–56. Online: http://www.firstthings.com/article/2008/09/001-mailers-jesus-33.

Bousset, Wilhelm. *Die Religion des Judentums im späthellenistischen Zeitalter*. 3. verbesserter Auflage. Hrsg. Gressmann. HNT 21. Tübingen: Mohr, 1926,

Brown, D. "HD's *Trilogy*: Modern Gnosticism?" *Literature & Theology* 10 (1996) 351–60.

Bultmann, Rudolf. "New Testament Mythology." In *Kerygma and Myth: A Theological Debate*, edited by Hans W. Bartsch, 1–44. Translated by R. H. Fuller. The Cloister Library. New York: Harper, 1961.

Calinescu, Matei. *Five Faces of Modernity: Modernism, Avant-Garde, Decadence, Kitsch, Postmodernism*. Durham, NC: Duke University Press, 1987.

Cerdeira da Silva, Teresa Cristina. "José Saramago." In *O Avesso do Bordado Ensaios de literature*, 197–252. Estudos de literature Portuguesa. Lisboa: Caminho, 2000.

Charlesworth, James H. "The Dead Sea Scrolls and the Historical Jesus." In *Jesus and the Dead Sea Scrolls*, edited by James H. Charlesworth, 1–74. Anchor Bible Reference Library. New York: Doubleday, 1992.

Chatman, Seymour. *Story and Discourse. Narrative Structure in Fiction and Film*. Ithaca, NY: Cornell University Press, 1978.

Cockerill, Gareth Lee. "Judas." In *Anchor Bible Dictionary* 3:1090–91.

Crook, Zeba. "Fictionalizing Jesus: Story and History in Two Recent Jesus Novels." *Journal for the Study of the Historical Jesus* 5.1 (2007) 33–55.
Crossan, John D. *The Historical Jesus: The Life of a Mediterranean Jewish Peasant.* San Francisco: HarperSanFrancisco, 1991.
Cuddon, John A. *Dictionary of Literary Terms and Literary Theory.* Revised by C. E. Preston. Oxford: Blackwell, 1998.
Cupitt, Don. *Crisis of Moral Authority. The Dethronement of Christianity.* London: Lutterworth, 1972.
———. *A Long-Legged Fly: A Theology of Language and Desire.* London: SCM, 1987.
———. *Mysticism after Modernity.* Oxford: Blackwell, 1998.
———. *The New Christian Ethics.* London: SCM, 1988.
———. *Taking Leave of God.* London: SCM, 1980.
De Man, Paul. *Allegories of Reading: Figural Language in Rousseau, Nietzsche, Rilke, and Proust.* New Haven, CT: Yale University Press, 1979.
Dennett, Daniel C. *Breaking the Spell: Religion as a Natural Phenomenon.* London: Penguin, 2006.
Derrida, Jacques. *Of Grammatology.* Corrected ed. Baltimore: Johns Hopkins University Press, 1997.
———. *Margins of Philosophy.* Translated by Alan Bass. Brighton: Harvester, 1982.
———. *Speech and Phenomena, and Other Essays on Husserl's Theory of Signs.* Translated by D. B. Allison. Evanston, IL: Northwestern University Press, 1973.
———*Writing and Difference.* Translated by Alan Bass. London: Routledge and Kegan Paul, 1981.
Detweiler, Robert. "Theological Trends of Postmodern Fiction." *Journal of the American Academy of Religion* 44 (1976) 225–37.
Diethe, Carol. *Historical Dictionary of Nietzscheanism.* 2nd ed. Historical Dictionaries of Religions, Philosophies, and Movements 75. Toronto: Scarecrow, 2007.
Diski, Jenny. "Your Own Personal Judas." *The Guardian*, 18 November 18 2006. Online: http://www.guardian.co.uk/books/2006/nov/18/featuresreviews.guardianreview27/print.
Drabble, Margaret, editor. *The Oxford Companion to English Literature.* 5th ed. Oxford: Oxford University Press, 1985.
Eisenmann, Robert. Maccabees, Zadokites, Christians, and Qumran: A New Hypothesis of Qumran Origins. Studia post-Biblica 34. Leiden: Brill, 1983.
Emery, Bernard. "Pasteur, ou le Diable berger, dans *L'Évangile selon Jésus Christ* de José Saramago." *Iris: Les Cahiers du Gerf* 25 (2003) 67–88.
Envall, Markku. *Nasaretin miehen pitkä marssi: Esseitä Jeesus-aiheesta kirjallisuudessa.* Helsinki: Werner Södustïom, 1985.
Eskola, Timo. *Uuden testamentin hermeneutiikka: Tulkintateorian perusteita.* Helsinki: Yliopistopaino, 1996.
Evans, Craig, A. *Mark 8:27—16:20.* Word Biblical Commentary 34b. Nashville: T. Nelson, 2001.
Fleischer, Margot. "Nietzsche, Friedrich (1844–1900)." *Theologische Realenzyklopädie,* hrsg. Gerhard Müller, TRE (1994) 506–24.
Flusser, David, in collaboration with R. S. Notley. *Jesus.* Jerusalem: Magnes, 1998.
Fokkema, Douwe. "The Art of Rewriting the Gospel." In *Colóquio-Letras. José Saramago: O ano de 1998,* edited by Maria Filipe Ramos Rosa, 395–402. Lisboa: Fundação Calouste Gulbenkian, 1999.

Foucault, Michel. *The Archaeology of Knowledge*. Translated by A. M. Sheridan Smith. London: Routledge, 1995.
Frier, David. "José Saramago's *O Evangelho Segundo Jesus Christo:* Outline of a Newer Testament." *Modern Language Review* 100.2 (2005) 367–82.
Frye, Northrop. *The Great Code: The Bible and Literature*. New York: Harvest, 1982.
Fulkerson, Mary McClintock. "Changing the Subject: Feminist Theology and Discourse." *Literature & Theology* 10 (1996) 131–47.
Gelernter, David. "One Gospel Too Many." *National Review* 49.14 (1997) 55–56.
Genette, Gérard. *Palimpsestes: La littérature au second degré*. Paris: Èditions du Seuil, 1982.
Gilman, Sander L., et al. *Friedrich Nietzsche on Rhetoric and Language*. Oxford: Oxford University Press, 1989.
Gilman, Sander L. Nietzschean Parody: An Introduction to Reading Nietzsche. 2nd ed. Aurora: Davies Group, 2001.
Gordon, Mary. "Jesus Christ, Superstar." *The Nation*, 23 June 1997, 27–29.
Gray, John. *Straw Dogs: Thoughts on Humans and Other Animals*. New York: Farrar, Straus, & Giroux, 2007.
Gray, Paul. "Using the Lord's Name." *Time* 149.17 (1997) 77.
Grylls, David. "My Life as Jesus' Friend." *The Sunday Times*, 19 November 2006. Online: http://entertainment.timesonline.co.uk/tol/arts_and_entertainment/books/article636481.ece.
Haapala, Arto. "Fiktio ja todellisuus." *Kanava* 4 (1986) 222–25.
Häkkinen, Sakari. *Kenen poika sinä olet?: Isättömän Jeesuksen perhearvot*. Helsinki: LK-kirjat, 2003.
Hallikainen, Tiina. "'Se oli näin, se ei ollut näin, kaikki on niin kuin sanomme sen olleen': Postmoderni uudelleenkirjoitus historian ja fiktion suhteiden problematisoijana José Saramagon romaanissa *Jeesuksen Kristuksen evankeliumi*." MA thesis, University of Turku, 19 October 2009. Online: http://www.doria.fi/bitstream/handle/10024/47625/gradu2009hallikainen.pdf?sequence=1.
Harnack, Adolf von. *Das Wesen des Christentums*. Gütersloher Taschenbucher Siebenstern 227, 2nd ed. Gütersloh: Gütersloher Verlagshaus Mohn, 1985.
Hartman, Geoffrey H. "Preface." In *Deconstruction and Criticism*, edited by Harold Bloom et al., vii–ix. New York: Continuum, 1995.
Haskins, Susan. *Mary Magdalen: Myth and Metaphor*. London: HarperCollins, 1993.
Hengel, Martin. *The Zealots: Investigations into the Jewish Freedom Movement in the Period from Herod I until 70 A.D.* Translated by D. Smith. Edinburgh: T. & T. Clark, 1989.
Henn, David. "History and the Fantastic in José Saramago's Fiction." In *A Companion to Magical Realism*, edited by S. M. Hart and Wen-Chin Ouyang, 103–13. Woodbridge: Tamesis, 2005.
Hennecke, Edgar. *New Testament Apocrypha I–II*. Edited by Wilhelm Schneemelcher. English translation by R. McL. Wilson. Philadelphia: Westminster, 1963.
Hicks, John. *The Myth of God Incarnate*. London: SCM, 1978.
Hogue, Bev. "Naming the Bones: Bodies of Knowledge in Contemporary Fiction." *Modern Fiction Studies* 52 (2006) 121–42.
Hutcheon, Linda. "Incredulity Toward Metanarrative: Negotiating Postmodernism and Feminisms." *Labrys: Études féministes* 1–2 (July/December 2002). Online: http://vsites.unb.br/ih/his/gefem/labrys1_2/linda2.html.
———. *A Poetics of Postmodernism: History, Theory, Fiction*. London: Routledge, 1988.

———. *A Theory of Adaptation*. London: Routledge, 2006.
Ihonen, Markku. *Museovaatteista historian valepukuun: T. Vaaskivi ja suomalaisen historiallisen romaanin murros 1930-1940-luvulla*. Suomalaisen Kirjallisuuden Seuran Toimituksia 573. Helsinki: Suomalaisen Kirjallisuuden Seura, 1992.
Irenaeus. *Against Heresies*. In *Ante-Nicene Fathers*, edited by A. Roberts and J. Donaldson 1:309–460. Peabody, MA: Hendrickson, 1994.
Irigaray, Luce. *Ethics of Sexual Difference*. Translated by C. Burke and G. C. Gill. London: Athlone, 1993.
Janzen, Grace M. *Becoming Divine: Towards a Feminist Philosophy of Religion*. Indianapolis: Indiana University Press, 1999.
Jenny, Laurent. "The Strategy of Form." In *French Literary Theory Today: A Reader*, edited by Tzvetan Todorov, 34–63. Cambridge: Cambridge University Press, 1982.
Johnston, George Sim. "The Revised Nonstandard Version." *Wall Street Journal* (Eastern ed.), 18 April 1997, 16.
Jonas, Hans. *Mortality and Morality: A Search for the Good after Auschwitz*. Edited by Lawrence Vogel. Northwestern University Studies in Phenomenology and Existential Philosophy. Evanston, IL: Northwestern University Press, 1996.
Josephus. *The Jewish War*. Books I–III. With an English Translation by H. St. J. Thackeray. Loeb Classical Library 203. Cambridge, MA: Harvard University Press, 1989.
Kant, Immanuel. *Religion within the Boundaries of Mere Reason, And Other Writings*. Translated by A. W. Wood and G. di Giovanni. Cambridge: Cambridge University Press, 1998.
Kasser, Rodolphe et al. *The Gospel of Judas: From Codex Tchacos*. Washington, DC: National Geographic, 2006.
Kaufman, Helena. "Evangelical Truths: José Saramago on the Life of Christ." *Revista Hispánica Moderna* 47.2 (1994) 449–58.
Kelley, Shawn. *Racializing Jesus: Race, Ideology, and the Formation of Modern Biblical Scholarship*. Biblical Limits. London: Routledge, 2002.
Kelly, John N.D. *Early Christian Creeds*. 3rd ed. Harlow: Longman, 1991.
Kettunen, Keijo. "Tehty menneisyys. Historiallisen romaanin genrestä." In *Teksti ja konteksti*, edited by J. Anttila, 107–21. Kirjallisuudentutkijain seuran vuosikirja 40. Pieksämäki: Suomalaisen Kirjallisuuden Seura, 1986.
Kierkegaard, Soren. *Fear and Trembling: Dialectical Lyric by Johannes de Silentio*. Translated by A. Hannay. London: Penguin, 1985.
Klein, Dietrich. *Hermann Samuel Reimarus (1694-1768): Das theologische Werk*. Beiträge zur historischen Theologie 145. Tübingen: Mohr/Siebeck, 2009.
Klobucka, Anna. "Introduction: Saramago's World." In *On Saramago*, edited by Victor J. Mendes, xi–xxii. Portuguese Literary and Cultural Studies 6. Dartmouth: University of Massachusetts, 2001.
Kort, Wesley A. *Narrative Elements and Religious Meanings*. Philadelphia: Fortress, 1975.
———. "'Religion and Literature' in Postmodernist Contexts." *Journal of the American Academy of Religion* 58 (1990) 575–88.
Koskenniemi, Erkki. *Old Testament Miracle-Workers in Early Judaism*. WUNT 206, 2nd ser. Tübingen: Mohr/Siebeck, 2005.
Kraft, H. "Marcion." In *Die Religion in Geschichte und Gegenwart: Handwörterbuch für Theologie und Religionswissenschaft*, 3rd ed., edited by Kurt Galling, 4:740–42. Tübingen: Mohr/Siebeck, 1960.
Kristeva, Julia. *Revolution in Poetic Language*. New York: Columbia University Press, 1984.

Krysinski, Wladimir. "Le Romanesque et le Sacré: Observations sur 'L'Évangile Selon Jésus-Christ.'" In *Colóquio-Letras. José Saramago: O ano de 1998*, edited by Maria Filipe Ramos Rosa, 403–11. Lisboa: Fundação Calouste Gulbenkian, 1999.

Kümmel, Werner G. *The New Testament: The History of the Investigation of Its Problems*. London: SCM, 1978.

Langenhorst, Georg. "The Rediscovery of Jesus as a Literary Figure." *Literature & Theology* 9 (1995) 85–98.

Lottman, Herbert R. *Camus: A Biography*. London: Pan Books (Picador), 1981.

Lüdemann, Gerd. *Der Grosse Betrug: Und was Jesus wirklich sagte und tat*. Lüneburg: zu Klampen, 1998.

Lyotard, Jean-François. *The Postmodern Condition: A Report on Knowledge*. Translated by G. Benninton and B. Massumi. Theory and History of Literature 10. Manchester: Manchester University Press, 1987.

MacRae, G. W., and R. McL.Wilson. "The Gospel of Mary (BG 8502, 1)." Introduced and translated by G.W. MacRae and R.McL. Wilson. In *The Nag Hammadi Library*, edited by James M. Robinson, 471–74. 3rd ed. San Francisco: Harper & Row, 1988.

Mailer, Norman. "The White Negro." (Fall, 1957.) Reprinted in *Dissent*, 20 June 2007. Online: http://dissentmagazine.org/online.php?id=26.

Manley, Will. "From Goth to God." *Booklist* 105.5 (2008) 7.

Martínez, Florentino García. *The Dead Sea Scrolls Translated*. The Qumran Texts in English. Translated by W. Watson. Leiden: Brill, 1994.

Martins, Adriana Alves de Paula. "José Saramago's Historical Fiction." In *On Saramago*, edited by Victor J. Mendes, 49–72. Portuguese Literary and Cultural Studies 6. Dartmouth: University of Massachusetts, 2001.

McDonald, Brian. "Post-Holocaust Theodicy, American Imperialism, and the 'Very Jewish Jesus' of Norman Mailer's '*The Gospel According to the Son*.'" *Journal of Modern Literature* 30.1 (2006) 78–90.

McHale, Brian. *Postmodernist Fiction*. London: Routledge, 2001.

Michalson, Gordon E., Jr. *Kant and the Problem of God*. Oxford: Blackwell, 1999.

Miller, Ryan. "The Gospel According to Grace: Gnostic Heresy as Narrative Strategy in Margaret Atwood's *Alias Grace*." *Literature & Theology* 16 (2002) 172–87.

Moore, Stephen D. *Poststructuralism and the New Testament: Derrida and Foucault at the Foot of the Cross*. Minneapolis: Fortress, 1994.

Nietzsche, Friedrich. *Beyond Good and Evil*. A new translation by Marion Faber. Oxford World's Classics. Oxford: Oxford University Press, 2008.

———. *The Gay Science*. With a Prelude in Rhymes and an Appendix of Songs. Translated with commentary by Walter Kaufmann. New York: Vintage, 1974.

———. *Human, All Too Human: A Book for Free Spirits*. Translated by R. J. Hollingdale. Cambridge Texts in the History of Philosophy. Cambridge: Cambridge University Press, 1996.

———. *On the Genealogy of Morals*. Translated by Walter Kaufmann and R. J. Hollingdale. New York: Vintage, 1967.

———. *Thus Spoke Zarathustra*. A new translation by Graham Parkes. Oxford World's Classics. Oxford: Oxford University Press, 2008.

———. *Twilight of the Idols: and, The Anti-Christ*. Translated by R. J. Hollingdale. London: Penguin, 2003.

———. *Unmodern Observations*. Edited by W. Arrowsmith. New Haven, CT: Yale University Press, 1990.

———. *The Will to Power*. Translated by Walter Kaufmann and R. J. Hollingdale. New York: Vintage, 1968.
O'Brien, Conor C. *Camus*. Suom. L. Krohn. Helsinki: Tammi, 1970.
Onfray, Michel. *Atheist Manifesto. The Case Against Christianity, Judaism, and Islam*. New York: Arcade, 2007.
Onimus, Jean. *Albert Camus and Christianity*. Translated by E. Parker. Dublin: Gill and Macmillan, 1970.
Orr, Mary. *Intertextuality: Debates and Contexts*. Cambridge, UK: Polity, 2003.
Ostriker, Alicia S. *Feminist Revision and the Bible*. Bucknell Lectures in Literary Theory 7. Cambridge, MA: Blackwell, 1993.
Pagels, Elaine. *The Gnostic Gospels*. New York: Vintage, 1979.
Pál, Ferenc. "Saramago and the Traditions of the European Novel." *Studia Slavica Academiae Scientiarum Hungaricae* 52 (2007) 327–34.
Partridge, Jeffrey F.L. "*The Gospel According to the Son* and Christian Belief." *Journal of Modern Literature* 30.1 (2006) 64–77.
Passoja, A. "Merten urhojen jälkeläiset. Silmäyksiä 1900-luvun portugalilaiseen kirjallisuuteen." In *Kirjaimia kiikarissa. Näkymiä eurooppalaiseen kirjallisuuteen*, edited by M. Ihonen and H. Koivula, 99–143. Tampere: Tampereen yliopistopaino, 2001.
Pelikan, Jaroslav. *Jesus Through the Centuries: His Place in the History of Culture*. New Haven, CT: Yale University Press, 1985.
Peña Fernández, Francisco. *José Saramago o la intertextualidad inversa: Transformación de la tradición apócrifa en O Evangelho segundo Jesus Cristo*.' Ilu. Revista de Ciencias de las Religiones 14. Madrid: Publicationes Universidad Complutense, 2006.
Perls, Frederick S. *Gestalt Therapy Verbatim*. Edited by J. O. Stevens. New York: Bantom, 1974.
Phelan, James. *Living to Tell about It: Rhetoric and Ethics of Character Narration*. Ithaca, NY: Cornell University Press, 2005.
Pinnock, Sarah K. *Beyond Theodicy: Jewish and Christian Continental Thinkers Respond to the Holocaust*. SUNY Series. New York: State University of New York Press, 2002.
Pires-O'Brien, Joaquina. "A Novel View of the Gospels." *Contemporary Review* 274 (1999) 187.
Plotnitsky, Arkady. "Zarahustra's Ladders: Hebraism, Hellenism, and Practical Philosophy in Nietzsche." *Poetics Today* 19.2 (1998) 199–219.
Price, Reynolds. "Mailer, Mark, Luke and John." *New York Times Book Review*, 4 May 1997, 9.
Pyper, Hugh S. "Modern Gospels of Judas: Canon and Betrayal." *Literature & Theology* 15 (2001) 111–22.
Rabinowitz, Peter J. *Before Reading. Narrative Conventions and the Politics of Interpretation*. Ithaca, NY: Cornell University Press, 1987.
Raschke, Carl A. *The Alchemy of the Word: Language and the End of Theology*. AAR Studies in Religion 20. Missoula, MT: Scholars, 1979.
———. "The Deconstruction of God." In *Deconstruction and Theology*, edited by Thomas J. J. Altizer et al., 1–33. New York: Crossroad, 1982.
———. "Preface." In *Deconstruction and Theology*, edited by Thomas J. J. Altizer et al., vii–ix. New York: Crossroad, 1982.
Richmond, S. D. "Deconstruction." In *The Oxford Companion to Philosophy*, edited by T. Honderich, 180–81. Oxford: Oxford University Press, 1995.

Riikonen, Hannu K. *Die Antike im historischen Roman des 19. Jahrhunderts. Eine literatur- und kulturgeschichtliche Untersuchung.* Commentationes Humanarum Litterarum 59. Helsinki: Societas Scientiarum Fennica, 1978.
Robinson, John A. T. *Honest to God.* London: SCM, 1963.
Robinson, James M. *The Nag Hammadi Library.* 3rd ed. San Francisco: Harper and Row, 1988.
Rosenbaum, Ron. "Mailer Was the Rage." *The New York Observer*, 21 January 2007. Online: http://bookrags.com/news/mailer-was-the-rage-moc/.
Rosenberg, Alfred. *Der Mythus des zwanzigsten Jahrhunderts: Eine Wertung der seelisch-geistigen Gestaltenkämpfe unserer Zeit.* Munich: Hoheneichen, 1935.
Rowland, Susan. "The Body's Sacred: Romance and Sacrifice in Religious and Jungian Narratives." *Literature & Theology* 10 (1996) 160–70.
Ruether, Rosemary R. *Sexism and God-Talk: Toward a Feminist Theology.* Boston: Beacon, 1993.
Ruokanen, Miikka. *Hermeneutica moderna: Teologinen hermeneutiikka historiallis-kriittisen raamatuntutkimuksen aikakaudella.* Helsinki: Gaudeamus, 1987.
Saari, H. "Mielikuvitusta vai historiaa—historiallisen romaanin suhteesta todellisuuteen ja historiantutkimukseen." *Historiallinen Aikakauskirja* 3 (1989) 217–24.
Saldarini, Anthony J. "Pharisees." In *Anchor Bible Dictionary* 5:289–303.
Sanders, E. P. *Paul and Palestinian Judaism.* Philadelphia: Fortress, 1977.
Sanders, Julie. *Adaptation and Appropriation.* The New Critical Idiom. London: Routledge, 2006.
Saramago, José. Review of *O Evangelho segundo Jesus Cristo*, by Richard A. Preto-Rodas. *World Literature Today* 66.4 (1992) 697.
Sarles, Harvey. *Nietzsche's Prophecy: The Crisis in Meaning.* New York: Humanity, 2001.
Schlechta, K. "Nietzsche." In *Die Religion in Geschichte und Gegenwart: Handwörterbuch für Theologie und Religionswissenschaf,* edited by Kurt Galling, 4:1475–79. 3rd rev. ed. Tübingen: Mohr/Siebeck, 1960.
Schmidt, M. A. "Eckehart." In *Die Religion in Geschichte und Gegenwart: Handwörterbuch für Theologie und Religionswissenschaft,* edited by Kurt Galling, 2:304–5. 3rd rev. ed. Tübingen: Mohr/Siebeck, 1958.
Schürer, Emil. *The History of the Jewish People in the Age of Jesus Christ (175 B.C.–A.D. 135).* 3 vols. Revised and edited by G. Vermes, F. Millar, and M. Black. Edinburgh: T. & T. Clark, 1987.
Schüssler Fiorenza, Elisabeth. *In Memory of Her: A Feminist Theological Reconstruction of Christian Origins.* New York: Crossroad, 1989.
Schweitzer, Albert. *The Quest of the Historical Jesus: A Critical Study of Its Progress from Reimarus to Wrede.* Edited by F.C. Burkitt. Baltimore: Johns Hopkins University Press, 1998.
Selden, Raman, Peter Widdowson, and Peter Brooker. *A Reader's Guide to Contemporary Literary Theory.* 4th ed. New York: Prentice Hall/Harvester Wheatsheaf, 1997.
Shaw, Harry E. *The Forms of Historical Fiction: Sir Walter Scott and His Successors.* Ithaca, NY: Cornell University Press, 1985.
———. "The Historical Novel." In *Encyclopedia of Literature and Criticism*, edited by M. Coyle et al., 531–43. London: Routledge, 1991.
Spong, John S. *The Sins of Scripture: Exposing the Bible's Texts of Hate to Reveal the God of Love.* San Francisco: HarperSanFrancisco, 2005.

Sprintzen, David. *Camus: A Critical Examination*. Philadelphia: Temple University Press, 1988.

Stavans, Ilan. "A Fisher of Men." *The Nation*, 16 May 1994, 675–76.

Stegemann, Hartmut. *The Library of Qumran: On the Essenes, Qumran, John the Baptist, and Jesus*. Grand Rapids: Eerdmans; Leiden: Brill, 1998.

Steigmann-Gall, Richard. *The Holy Reich: Nazi Conceptions of Christianity, 1919–1945*. Cambridge: Cambridge University Press, 2003.

Strong, Tracy B. *Friedrich Nietzsche and the Politics of Transfigurations*. Expanded Edition. Berkeley: University of California Press, 1988.

Svenskt Litteraturlexikon. Edited by L. Vinge. 2nd ed. Lund: Gleerup, 1970.

Talbert, Charles H. *Reimarus: Fragments*. Translated by R. S. Fraser. Philadelphia: Fortress, 1970.

Taylor, Mark C. *Erring: A Postmodern A/Theology*. Chicago: University of Chicago Press, 1984.

VanderKam, James C. *The Dead Sea Scrolls Today*. Grand Rapids: Eerdmans, 1994.

Vanhoozer, Kevin, editor. *The Cambridge Companion to Postmodern Theology*. Cambridge: Cambridge University Press, 2003.

Vermes, Geza. *Jesus and the World of Judaism*. London: SCM, 1983.

———. Jesus the Jew: A Historian's Reading of the Gospels. London: Fontana/Collins, 1977.

Vettenniemi, Erkki. "Jeesus-marssi jatkuu. Otteita uudesta Kristus-kirjallisuudesta." *Parnasso* 2 (1998) 213–17.

Ward, Graham. "Deconstructive Theology." In *The Cambridge Companion to Postmodern Theology*, edited by Kevin Vanhoozer, 76–91. Cambridge: Cambridge University Press, 2003.

———. "Postmodern Theology." In *The Modern Theologians*, edited by D. Ford, 585–601. Oxford: Blackwell, 1997.

Wesseling, Elisabeth. *Writing History as a Prophet: Postmodernist Innovations of the Historical Novel*. Utrecht Publications in General and Comparative Literature 26. Amsterdam: John Benjamins, 1991.

Whiston, William. *The Works of Josephus: Complete and Unabridged*. New updated ed. Peabody, MA: Hendrickson, 1987.

White, Rosemary. "Miche[<grave accent>]le Roberts: *The Wild Girl*." *The Literary Encyclopedia*, 20 February 2004. Online: http://litencyc.com/php/sworks.php?rec=true&UID=10197.

———. "Permeable Borders, Possible Worlds: History and Identity in the Novels of Michèle Roberts." *Studies in the Literary Imagination* 36.2 (2003) 71–90.

Wilson, Andrew N. "Jesus Wept: Norman Mailer Takes on Christ." *Slate*, 30 April 30 1997. Online: http://www.slate.com/?id=2979.

Winquist, Charles E. *Epiphanies of Darkness: Deconstruction in Theology*. Philadelphia: Fortress, 1986.

Witherington, Ben, III. "Women. New Testament." In *Anchor Bible Dictionary* 6:957–61.

Wolpers, Th. "Motif and Theme as Structural Content Units and 'Concrete Universals.'" In *The Return of Thematic Criticism*, edited by W. Sollors, 80–91. Harvard English Studies 18. Cambridge, MA: Harvard University Press, 1993.

Wood, James. "He Is Finished." *The New Republic* 216.19 (1997) 30–35.

---. "Jesus, Would You Stop Exaggerating." *The Telegraph*, 26 November 2006. Online: http://www.telegraph.co.uk/culture/books/3656783/Jesus-would-you-stop-exaggerating.html.

Wright, N. Thomas. *Jesus and the Victory of God*. Christian Origins and the Question of God 2. Minneapolis: Fortress, 1996.

Zima, Peter V. *Deconstruction and Critical Theory*. London: Continuum, 2002.

---. *The Philosophy of Modern Literary Theory*. London: Athlone, 1999.

Ziolkowski, Theodore. *Fictional Transfigurations of Jesus*. Princeton, NJ: Princeton University Press, 1978.

Žižek, Slavoj. *The Puppet and the Dwarf: The Perverse Core of Christianity*. Cambridge, MA: MIT Press, 2003.

www.ingramcontent.com/pod-product-compliance
Lightning Source LLC
Chambersburg PA
CBHW070012010526
44117CB00011B/1535